REVELATION VISUALIZED

NEVER BEFORE so crystal clear and current an explanation of the last book of the Bible!

™

VERSE BY VERSE   King James Version

P9-AOS-121

Each verse includes

COMMENTARY
by Dr. Gary G. Cohen
(a born-again Jew)

and

BACKGROUND
by Salem Kirban
(a born-again Arab)

© 1971, 1973, 1979, 1981 by Salem Kirban

Library of Congress Catalog Card No. 78–146–684

ISBN 0-89957-616-8

Published by Future Events Publications, an imprint of AMG Publishers, P. O. Box 22000, Chattanooga, TN 37422.

FUTURE EVENTS PUBLICATIONS

Printed in the United States of America
02 01 00 99 98 97 –Q– 17 16 15 14 13 12

CHRIST	ANTICHRIST
Christ came from **Above.** John 6:38.	**Antichrist** ascends from **The Pit.** Revelation 11:7.
Christ came in His **Father's** name. John 5:43.	Antichrist comes in his **Own** name. John 5:43.
Christ **Humbled** Himself. Phil. 2:8	Antichrist **Exalts** himself. 2 Thessalonians 2:4.
Christ **Despised.** Isaiah 53:3; Luke 23:18.	Antichrist **Admired.** Rev. 13:3, 4.
Christ **Exalted.** Philippians 2:9.	Antichrist **Cast Down to Hell.** Isaiah 14:14, 15; Rev. 19:20.
Christ to do His **Father's** will. John 6:38.	Antichrist to do His **Own** will. Daniel 11:36.
Christ came to **Save.** Luke 19:10.	Antichrist comes to **Destroy.** Daniel 8:24.
Christ is the **Good Shepherd.** John 10:4-15.	Antichrist, the **Idol** (evil) Shepherd. Zechariah 11:16, 17.
Christ is the **"True Vine."** John 15:1.	Antichrist, the **"Vine of the Earth."** Revelation 14:18.
Christ is the **"Truth."** John 14:6.	Antichrist is the **"Lie"** 2 Thessalonians 2:11.
Christ, the **"Holy One."** Mark 1:24.	Antichrist is the **"Lawless One."** 2 Thessalonians 2:8, A.S.V.
Christ is the **"Man of Sorrows."** Isaiah 53:3.	Antichrist is the **"Man of Sin."** 2 Thessalonians 2:3.
Christ is the **"Son of God."** Luke 1:35.	Antichrist is the **"Son of Perdition."** 2 Thessalonians 2:3.
Christ, **"The Mystery of Godliness,"** is **God** manifest in the flesh. 1 Timothy 3:16.	Antichrist, **"The Mystery of Iniquity,"** will be **Satan** manifest in the flesh. 2 Thessalonians 2:7.

PROMISES OF GOD IN BLUE

4 And God shall wipe away all tears from their eyes; and there shall be no more death, neither sorrow, nor crying, neither shall there be any more pain: for the former things are passed away.

JUDGMENTS OF GOD IN RED

14 And death and hell were cast into the lake of fire. This is the second death.

15 And whosoever was not found written in the book of life was cast into the lake of fire.

Every page has a RED ARROW pointing to the TIME PERIOD these particular verses relate to.

PAST	PRESENT	RAPTURE	FIRST 3 1/2 / LAST 3 1/2 TRIBULATION	ARMA-GEDDON	MIL-LENNIUM	NEW HEAVENS & EARTH

When the RED ARROW points to the vertical line this indicates that these par-

FIRST 3 1/2 / LAST 3 1/2 TRIBULATION	ARMA-GEDDON

ticular verses relate to an occurrence *between* or *connecting* two TIME PERIODS. A typical example is Revelation 16:16-18.

When the RED ARROW points to the beginning (or the end) of a TIME PERIOD block this indicates that these

MIL-LENNIUM

particular verses relate to an event that occurs at the *beginning* (or near the end) of this TIME PERIOD. See Revelation 14:2-3 and 15:1.

DEDICATION

By
Dr. Gary G. Cohen

TO

Steven Reed Cohen

by
Salem Kirban

TO

My dear wife, Mary,
whose love and devotion is beyond all measure.

ACKNOWLEDGMENTS

To Dr. Gary G. Cohen, President, Clearwater Christian College, Clearwater, Florida, who not only wrote the Commentary section but checked the final manuscript and supplied Scripture references.

To Bob Krauss, Edston Detrich and Dick Miller, artists who skillfully created the artwork throughout **Revelation Visualized.**

ABOUT THE AUTHORS

Because of the Grace of God, **Dr. Gary G. Cohen,** a JEW, and **Salem Kirban,** an ARAB, were able to combine their efforts in the writing of **Revelation Visualized.** While the Middle East conflict has pitted Arab against Jew how thrilling to know that *". . . ye are all one in Christ Jesus."* (Galatians 3:28).

Gary G. Cohen, Th.D.
President
Clearwater Christian College
Clearwater, Florida

After receiving his B.S. degree from Temple University and the B.D. and S.T.M. degrees from Faith Seminary, he was granted his doctorate in Theology in 1966 from Grace Theological Seminary, Winona Lake, Indiana. He is the author of **The Horsemen Are Coming, Understanding Revelation,** and **Weep Not For Me** (Moody Press). He is married and has 3 children.

Salem Kirban
President
Salem Kirban, Inc.

Salem Kirban is a graduate of Girard College and received his Bachelor of Science at Temple University in Philadelphia. He majored in journalism. He has traveled extensively and has been around the world three times. He is the author of over 37 books which include **Guide To Survival, 666/1000, The Rise Of Antichrist** and **Satan's Angels Exposed.** He is married and has 5 children.

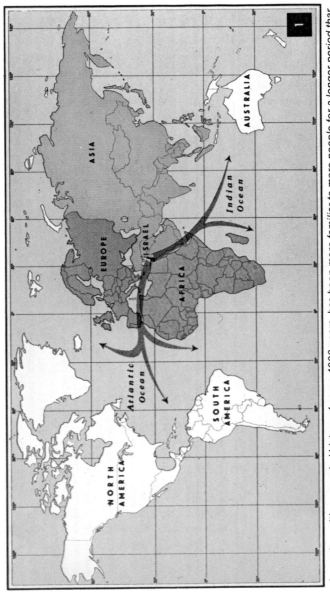

Jerusalem with a recorded history of some 4000 years, has been more familiar to more people for a longer period than any other place on earth. This map shows the centrality of its location in respect to the nations of the world.

THE HOLY LAND

Look at the photograph below. It is an aerial view of the Holy Land taken from outer space.

It may seem hard to believe that this small area has had so great significance in the past and will have even greater impact in the future.

Here is where the great powers of the ancient world clashed. Here is where great powers of the modern world are clashing. And here is where all the great powers of the world *will* clash. And here is where fiery judgment will come when the KING returns (Revelation 19:11-16).

But let's pause for a moment to look intently at the faces of the Holy Land on the following pages.

Then search your own heart. What are *you* doing to reach them for Christ?

GOD'S PROMISES TO THE ARABS
by Salem Kirban

The heritage of the Arab peoples begins with Abram (who became Abraham) about 2000 B.C. Genesis 16 records this event.

Sarai, Abram's wife, was 75 years old at this time and was barren. Abram was 85 years old. In Genesis 16:2, Sarai said to Abram:

Behold now, the Lord hath restrained me from bearing: I pray thee, go in unto my maid; it may be that I may obtain children by her.

So Sarai selected Hagar, her maid. Hagar was an Egyptian who had served Abram for ten years in the land of Canaan.

Abram listened to Sarai's suggestion and followed her plan. He accepted Hagar. She conceived.

Although Sarai's conduct in offering Abram her handmaid as a secondary wife was wrong and sinful Sarai was acting in full accord with the customs of her day. In her day marriage contracts stated that it was the responsibility of the wife to bear children. If she did not do so, she was obligated to provide a handmaid. This Sarai did.

When Hagar realized she was going to have a child by Abram she had contempt for Sarai. Sarai dealt hard with her (Genesis 16:6). Because of this Hagar fled into the wilderness.

GOD'S PROMISE

It was then the angel of the Lord appeared to Hagar and made a promise to the Arab people. The angel first directed Hagar to return to her mistress, Sarai, and then the Angel of the LORD said:

I WILL MULTIPLY THY SEED EXCEEDINGLY, THAT IT SHALL NOT BE NUMBERED FOR MULTITUDE (Genesis 16:10).

Genesis 16:11 is a most interesting verse, too. For here we find that Hagar's son by Abram is the first person whom God named *before* his birth.

...the angel of the Lord said unto her (Hagar), Behold, thou art with child, and shalt bear a son, and shalt call his name ISHMAEL; because the Lord hath heard thy affliction.

Ishmael means, "God hears."

The angel of the Lord makes a further promise to Hagar in Genesis 16:12.

...he (Ishmael) will be a wild man; his hand will be against every man, and every man's hand against him; and he shall dwell in the presence of all his brethren.

Here in verses 10 and 12 we see FIVE PROMISES:

1. Hagar's seed (the Arab peoples) would be multiplied to the point where it could not be counted.
2. ...*will be a wild man* refers to the fact that the Arab peoples will be free and roving, and is certainly not meant as an insult. For 4000 years now God has enabled Arab nations to keep their independence as both a lasting monument of His providential care and a fulfillment of His promise.
3. ...*his hand will be against every man*.... This foretells the sin of the Arab people engaging in wars and uprisings.
4. ...*and everyman's hand against him*.... This is the punishment that Arab nations have experienced and will experience in this world.
5. ...*and he shall dwell in the presence of all his brethren.*

ABRAHAM'S CONCERN FOR ISHMAEL

Thirteen years after the birth of Ishmael, Isaac is born to Sarah. Actually Sarah laughed when God revealed that she would give birth...for she was now 90 and Abraham, 100.

It is interesting to note that even after God had promised him a son through Sarah, Abraham's concern for Ishmael was so great he said to God:

...Oh, that Ishmael might live before thee! (Genesis 17:18)

Abraham loved Ishmael and was concerned lest by the birth of Isaac, Ishmael might be abandoned and forsaken.

But God promised Abraham that Ishmael (the Arab peoples) would not be forgotten. In fact *to some degree* their promises parallel those given to the Jew. Let's look at these promises.—

Here they are as revealed in Genesis 17:20:

1. *...I have blessed him (Ishmael), and will make him fruitful, and will multiply him exceedingly....*
2. *...twelve princes shall he beget....*
3. *...I will make him a great nation.*

God assured Abraham that Ishmael would be the father of a great people—although the specific line of the covenant promise would be realized in a son of Sarah to be named Isaac.

Although Ishmael's descendants do not form the line of promise, the blessings of the covenant are available to them. And Ishmael is encouraged to hope for a share in the Messianic blessing.

PROMISE IN THE WILDERNESS

When Ishmael was about 15 years old he was playfully teasing Isaac. This was the spark that aroused Sarah's anger and she demanded of Abraham that he expel Hagar and Ishmael from the household (Genesis 21:9-11).

Abraham rose up early in the morning, took bread and a goat-skin filled with water and gave it to Hagar.

Hagar left with Ishmael and wandered in the wilderness of Beersheba (about 50 miles south of Jerusalem in the desert).

Soon the water supply was exhausted. Carefully she laid Ishmael beneath the shrubs to protect him from the burning sun as he lay dying of thirst.

Then Hagar said: ...*Let me not see the death of the child....*

And she wept!

And God answered...again reaffirming to Hagar His promise to the Arab peoples:

> *Arise, lift up the lad, and hold him in thine hand; for I will make him a great nation.* (Genesis 21:18)

This must have been a touching scene. Hagar, apparently alone, unwanted, dying in the desert with her only son. BUT GOD! How important it is for the Arab peoples to remember this covenant of blessing which came when humanly speaking all hope was gone!

ISHMAEL'S HERITAGE

Ishmael grew up and became famous as an archer. He married an Egyptian wife.

He became the father of 12 sons and a daughter whom Esau took for his wife.

He died at the age of 137.

The 12 sons are described in Genesis 25:12-15. Three of the 12 sons (see verse 14) are Mishma, Dumah, and Massa. These names mean *hear, keep silence* and *bear.* These appear in the same order in James 1:19 which tells us:

> ...*let every man be swift to hear (mishma), slow to speak (dumah), slow to wrath (massa).*

This may well be a good admonition for us, the Arabs of today!

PROMISES FULFILLED

Today these 12 sons of Ishmael could possibly be considered the people of Lebanon, Syria, Yemen, Jordan, Egypt, Saudi-Arabia, Sudan, Libya, Algeria, Tunisia, Morocco and Iraq.

These Arab countries have two-thirds of the world's proven oil resources. The Arabs control *three million square miles of territory!*

God has certainly fulfilled His promises made over 4000 years ago to Abraham and Hagar. The Arab people are blessed. They have multiplied exceedingly. They and their lands are fruitful.

And just as God has made these promises to be fulfilled...His promise that the Arab's ...*hand will be against every man...and everyman's hand against him...*is also being fulfilled (Genesis 16:12).

PROMISES TO COME

There will come a time when travel between Israel and the Arab nations will be unhindered by barriers of any kind. No need for passports. No trade restrictions.

One must remember that in Scriptures Egypt was often looked upon as a *place of escape.*

Abraham went to Egypt to escape the famine.

The sons of Jacob went to Egypt to purchase food.

Jeremiah went to Egypt at the time of the Captivity.

Joseph and Mary took Jesus to Egypt to escape Herod.

And in this context it is interesting to read the following verses regarding Israel's relation to Egypt:

And the Lord shall bring you into Egypt again with ships, by the way about which I said to you, You shall never see it again; and there you shall be sold to your enemies for bondmen and bondwomen, and no man shall buy you (Deuteronomy 28:68 Amplified).

They sacrifice flesh for the sacrifices of mine offerings, and eat it, but the Lord accepteth them not; now will he remember their iniquity, and (judge) their sins; they shall return to Egypt. For Israel has forgotten his Maker...(Hosea 8:13,14).

But Egypt will not always be a *place of escape.* There are indications in Scripture that Antichrist will come in and possess the treasures of Egypt.

We now see on the world scene Egypt making plans to merge with other Arab nations. This could be the beginning of a combined powerful bloc headed by one leader. Before Egypt finally comes to Christ...she will be humbled.

But the promises God gives to the Arab nations during the Millennial reign of Christ are her crowning glory. Let's read what these promises are in Isaiah 19:19-25...for THE LORD SHALL YET BLESS EGYPT.

In that day there will be an altar to the Lord in the midst of the land of Egypt, and a pillar to the Lord at its border.

And it shall be for a sign and for a witness to the Lord of hosts in the land of Egypt; for they will cry to the Lord because of oppressors, and He will send them a savior, even a mighty one, and he shall deliver them.

And the Lord will make Himself known to Egypt, and the Egyptians will know (have knowledge of, be acquainted with, give heed to and cherish) the Lord in that day and will worship with sacrifice of animal and vegetable offerings; they will vow a vow to the Lord and perform it.

And the Lord shall smite Egypt, smiting and healing it, and they will return to the Lord, and He will listen to their entreaties and heal them.

In that day shall there be a highway out of Egypt to Assyria (area of Iraq and Syria), and the Assyrian will come into Egypt, and the

Egyptian into Assyria, and the Egyptians will worship the Lord with the Assyrians.

In that day Israel shall be the third with Egypt and with Assyria (in a Messianic league), a blessing in the midst of the earth,

Whom the Lord of hosts has blessed, saying, Blessed be Egypt My people, and Assyria the work of My hands, and Israel My heritage.

(Isaiah 19:19-25 Amplified Bible)

ARABS MAY CLAIM ETERNAL LIFE

The Arabs must come to realize that Genesis 15:18 and Jeremiah 23:7,8 along with other Scripture references promise Palestine to Israel (from the river of Egypt to the river Euphrates...some 180,000 square miles).

And while Israel is the inheritor of this hallowed area called The Promised Land...she also has been and will be the inheritor of many trials and tribulations that Arab nations will not be subjected to.

The real tribulations for the people of Israel are again beginning. (For a detailed explanation of this read GUIDE TO SURVIVAL by Salem Kirban).

Yet the Arab people may claim ALL THE PROMISES OF GOD....the promise of eternal life by accepting Christ as Saviour and Lord (Romans 10:9-13), the promise of a Heavenly home (John 14:2,3), and reigning forever with our Lord in the Heavenly City New Jerusalem (2 Peter 3:13,14; Revelation 21:2ff).

That if thou shalt confess with thy mouth the Lord Jesus, and shalt believe in thine heart that God hath raised Him from, the dead, thou shalt be saved.

For with the heart man believeth unto righteousness; and with the mouth confession is made unto salvation.

For the scripture saith, Whosoever believeth on Him shall not be ashamed.

For there is no difference between the Jew and the Greek: for the same Lord over all is rich unto all that call upon Him.

For whosoever shall call upon the name of the Lord shall be saved.

(Romans 10:9-13)

As Arabs...all these PROMISES are ours if we but believe. But to Israel belongs the promise of Palestine. And this will yet be fulfilled to those end-time Jews who will accept Christ as Saviour and Lord.

With such an overflowing abundance of promises to the Arabs, our hearts should be filled with everlasting joy and thankfulness!

An artist's conception of how the Rapture may occur. Some in your family may be left behind!

GOD'S PROMISES TO ISRAEL
by Gary G. Cohen

THE PROMISES TO ABRAHAM
The heritage of the Children of Israel begins with Abraham. Indeed, Genesis 17:7-8 declares,

> And I will establish my covenant between me and thee and thy seed after thee in their generations for an everlasting covenant, to be a God unto thee, and to thy seed after thee. And I will give unto thee, and to thy seed after thee, the land wherein thou art a stranger, all the land of Canaan, for an everlasting possession; and I will be their God.

Thus did God pick a man, Abram, out of the corrupt and idolatrous world of antiquity and God, by grace, promised to bless this man who believed on Him—and He promised to bless Abraham's seed. This promise, or covenant, was an *everlasting* promise. God was (1) to be the God of the people descending from Abraham, and (2) these people, Israel, were to receive the land of Canaan as their everlasting property.

Also to Abraham came the wonderful *good news* (gospel),

> And in thy seed shall all the nations of the earth be blessed... (Genesis 22:18).

This promise, as the Apostle Paul clearly explains in Galatians 3:6-9, was an early announcement of the Gospel message. The seed of Abraham was to be the Messiah, the Christ, and through Him the nations, the believing gentiles, would be blessed with forgiveness for their sins.

Thus the children of Abraham, Israel, were to (1) have Jehovah as their God and the God of their children; (2) they were to inherit the land of Palestine forever; and (3) they were to be the nation out of which the Messiah was to come. These are the basic promises to Israel, to the Jews, and out of these have flown the various other countless promises which were later given to them through the subsequent centuries.

THE LINE OF THE COVENANT
The covenant, or agreement, which God gave to Abraham concerned his seed after him. The line of this covenant, however, was restricted by God according to His sovereign pleasure (Romans 9:6-16). The covenantal line of promise thus went through Isaac, not Ishmael, and then through Jacob, and not Essau. Thus the primary promises made unto Abraham were inherited by the children of Israel whose fathers are Abraham, Isaac, and Jacob—rather than by the Moabites and Ammonites (relatives to Abraham by Lot) or by the Arabs (sons of Ishmael) or by the Edomites (sons of Essau). The Ishmaelites, true, received promises of their own—but it was Israel who became the "chosen people."

14

DISOBEDIENCE SCATTERED ISRAEL

John the Baptist, when he came proclaiming the coming of the Messiah, attempted to teach to Israel the lesson that only by faith in God could one inherit the blessings promised to Israel through the covenant which God made with Abraham. He declared,

> Bring forth therefore fruits meet for repentance: And think not to say within yourselves, We have Abraham to our father...(Matthew 12:8-9).

In other words, John was declaring that the pharisees before him should not think that they would *automatically* have a place in the Kingdom of God just because they were Jews, the children of Abraham. No, they had to repent of their sins and trust in the Messiah who in this case was about to be revealed. Otherwise they too, as so many of their fore-fathers, would cut themselves off from the covenant blessings by their sin and unbelief. And...generally speaking, the nation did not heed the message of John and they were evicted by God from *their promised land.*

This is precisely what Moses had prophesied would happen.

Moses warned,

> But it will come to pass, if thou wilt not harken unto the voice of the LORD thy God...the LORD shall cause thee to be smitten before thine enemies...and (thou) shalt be removed into all the kingdoms of the earth...(Deuteronomy 28:15, 25, 63-67).

So God permitted the northern half of the nation, Israel, to be taken off of *the promised land* and scattered in 721 B.C. The southern half of the nation was taken off of *the promised land* and scattered into Babylon in 606, 597, and 586 B.C. Then again later the Romans in 70 A.D. drove the Jews out of *the promised land* after the majority of that nation rejected in unbelief the Messiah of Israel and of all nations, Christ. Again too, in 132 A.D., Hadrian, the Roman Emperor, once more banished the Jews from *the promised land.* Thus we see that because of sin they have been for a time unable to receive the promises of the convenant to Abraham.

GOD WILL YET RESTORE ISRAEL

The Apostle Paul in Romans chapters 9-11, the three which deal with Israel, explains that God is not yet done with Israel! He likens Israel to an Olive Tree whose roots are Abraham. He says that because of unbelief they, the Jews, have been broken as dead branches off of the Tree of God's Covenant to Abraham. And...the Gentiles who have trusted in Jesus have been grafted in to Abraham's tree. The Gentiles who have trusted in Jesus, then, have become by faith the "children of Abraham" (Galatians 3:26-29). Paul, then warns the Gentiles if they too should turn to unbelief then God can and will graft the Jewish branches back into Abraham's tree. Then he announces that indeed the JEWS WILL YET AGAIN IN THE FUTURE COME TO BELIEVE IN GOD AND THEY WILL BE REESTABLISHED INTO THE TREE OF ABRAHAM.

THEY WILL YET AS A NATION INHERIT THE PROMISES...AND THE LAND. Thus Paul writes prophetically,

> And they (the Jews) also, if they abide not still in unbelief, shall be graffed in: for God is able to graff them in again.

> For if thou (the Gentile believers) wert cut out of the olive tree which is wild by nature, and wert graffed contrary to nature into a good olive tree (Abraham): how much more shall these, which be the natural *branches,* be graffed into their own olive tree?

> For I would not, brethren, that ye should be ignorant of this mystery, lest ye should be wise in your own conceits; that blindness in part is happened to Israel, until the fulness of the Gentiles be come in.

> And so all Israel shall be saved: as it is written, There shall come out of Zion the Deliverer, and shall turn away ungodliness from Jacob: (Romans 11:23-26)

Thus Paul by revelation looks forward to that future day when "All Israel shall be saved" (Romans 11:26). God will again be their God and the God of their children. Then...they will also be eligible to receive the Land of Palestine, according to the promise, as "an everlasting possession" (Genesis 17:7-8) and indeed this will come to pass.

GOD WILL SAVE ISRAEL OUT OF TRIBULATION

We do not know the future; but God does. God has declared in His word many many prophecies concerning Israel and the end-times. God will yet deliver them from some future massive Northern (Russian) Invasion (Ezekiel 38:1-39:16). They will yet go into the Tribulation Period and this will indeed be a time of unparalleled Satanically led persecution against the Jew (Daniel 12:1; Matthew 24:20,21). Jeremiah 30:7 calls this end-time era "The time of Jacob's trouble," but he adds, "but he shall be saved out of it." Revelation chapter 12 also describes this period as a time of persecution against Israel led by Satan! So great will be this trouble that Zechariah 13:7-8 indicates that two-thirds of them will be tragically killed...but God will deliver by His power the elect one-third. Zechariah 12:9 and 14:2 speaks of this time when armies from "all nations" shall come "against Jerusalem to battle." This is at Armageddon at the end of the seven year Tribulation Period. Just when everything seems again lost to Israel, Zechariah tells us that Jesus Christ Himself shall come in power and glory to rescue the Jews. At this time Israel will at last be ready with joy to receive the Saviour. The Prophet writes of this:

> And it shall come to pass in that day, *that* I will seek to destroy all the nations that come against Jerusalem.

> And I will pour upon the house of David, and upon the inhabitants of Jerusalem, the spirit of grace and of supplications: and they shall look upon me whom they have pierced, and they shall mourn for him, as one mourneth for *his* only *son,* and shall be in bitterness for him, as one that is in bitterness for *his* firstborn.

In that day shall there be a great mourning in Jerusalem, as the mourning of Hadadrimmon in the valley of Megiddon.

(Zechariah 12:9-11)

Then shall the Lord go forth, and fight against those nations, as when he fought in the day of battle.

And his feet shall stand in that day upon the mount of Olives, which *is* before Jerusalem on the east, and the mount of Olives shall cleave in the midst thereof toward the east and toward the west, *and there shall be* a very great valley; and half of the mountain shall remove toward the north, and half of it toward the south.

(Zechariah 14:3-4)

ISRAEL SHALL TRUST IN CHRIST
AND BE CLEANSED FROM SIN

In that day there shall be a fountain opened to the house of David and to the inhabitants of Jerusalem for sin and for uncleanness.

And it shall come to pass in that day, saith the Lord of hosts, *that* I will cut off the names of the idols out of the land, and they shall no more be remembered: and also I will cause the prophets and the unclean spirit to pass out of the land.   (Zechariah 13:1-2).

JERUSALEM SHALL BECOME THE CAPITAL
OF THE EARTH IN THE KINGDOM AGE

And it shall come to pass, *that* every one that is left of all the nations which came against Jerusalem shall even go up from year to year to worship the King, the Lord of hosts, and to keep the feast of tabernacles.

And it shall be, *that* whoso will not come up of *all* the families of the earth unto Jerusalem to worship the King, the Lord of hosts, even upon them shall be no rain.

And if the family of Egypt go not up, and come not, that *have* no *rain;* there shall be the plague, wherewith the Lord will smite the nations that come not up to keep the feast of tabernacles.

This shall be the punishment of Egypt, and the punishment of all nations that come not up to keep the feast of tabernacles.

In that day shall there be upon the bells of the horses, HOLINESS UNTO THE LORD; and the pots in the Lord's house shall be like the bowls before the altar.

Yea, every pot in Jerusalem and in Judah shall be holiness unto the Lord of hosts; and all they that sacrifice shall come and take of them, and seethe therein: and in that day there shall be no more the Canaanite in the house of the Lord of hosts.   (Zechariah 14:16-21).

CHRIST SHALL SIT ON DAVID'S THRONE AND ISRAEL SHALL BE REGATHERED INTO THEIR PROMISED LAND FOREVER

Behold, the days come, saith the Lord, that I will raise unto David a righteous Branch, and a King shall reign and prosper, and shall execute judgment and justice in the earth.

In his days Judah shall be saved, and Israel shall dwell safely: and this *is* his name whereby he shall be called, THE LORD OUR RIGHTEOUSNESS.

Therefore, behold, the days come, saith the Lord, that they shall no more say, The Lord liveth, which brought up the children of Israel out of the land of Egypt;

But, The Lord liveth, which brought up and which led the seed of the house of Israel out of the north country, and from all countries whither I had driven them; and they shall dwell in their own land.

(Jeremiah 23:5-8).

MARVELOUS PROMISES

What marvelous promises to Israel! And...now as the Gentile nations the world over are in general forsaking the historic Christian Faith...at this same time God is beginning to regather Israel to Palestine.

Israel rejects the Saviour:

Israel driven off of the Land; and the Gentiles are grafted in as the children of Abraham by faith (Romans 11:15-36).

The Gentiles reject the Saviour:

Israel begins to be restored to the Land; and the time approaches when Israel shall again be grafted back into the Olive Tree of Abraham by faith (Romans 11:15-36).

Through it all, however, the best promise of all—the promise of eternal life—is extended to any individual who will trust Christ as his or her sin bearer, be that person a Jew, an Arab, a Gentile, or be that person of any skin color. For God's Word declares,

For there is no difference between the Jew and the Greek: for the same Lord over all is rich unto all that call upon Him. For whosoever shall call upon the Lord shall be saved (Romans 10:12-13).

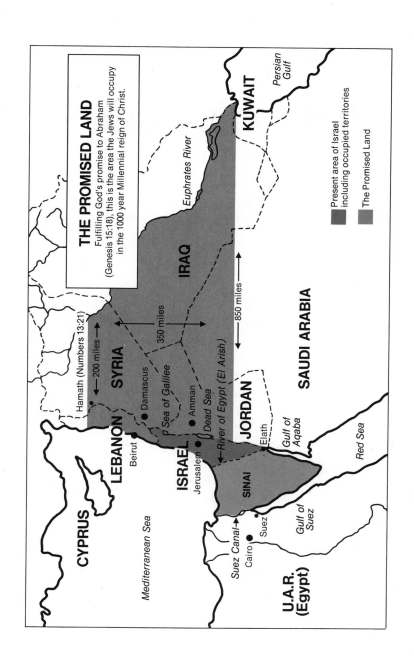

THE PROMISED LAND

Fulfilling God's promise to Abraham (Genesis 15:18), this is the area the Jews will occupy in the 1000 year Millennial reign of Christ.

■ Present area of Israel including occupied territories

■ The Promised Land

CYPRUS

Mediterranean Sea

LEBANON

Beirut

ISRAEL

Jerusalem

SINAI

Suez Canal→

Suez

Cairo

Gulf of Suez

U.A.R. (Egypt)

Red Sea

Gulf of Aqaba

Elath

JORDAN

SAUDI ARABIA

River of Egypt (El Arish)

Dead Sea

Amman

Sea of Galilee

Damascus

SYRIA

Hamath (Numbers 13:21)

200 miles

350 miles

850 miles

IRAQ

Euphrates River

KUWAIT

Persian Gulf

19

OUTLINE of the
BOOK of REVELATION

The basic outline of the book is supplied for us by the divine originator in 1:19. Here the Revelation vision is divided into three parts:

PART 1. "THE THINGS WHICH THOU HAST SEEN"

CHRIST   Chapter 1. The vision of the risen and glorified Christ, the Lord of the Church.

PART II. "THE THINGS WHICH ARE"

CHURCHES   Chapters 2-3. The letters to the 7 churches in Asia.

PART III. "THE THINGS WHICH SHALL BE HEREAFTER"

HEAVEN   Chapters 4-5. The scene in heaven before the seven year Tribulation period begins.

SEALS   Chapter 6. The Tribulation begins as the seal judgments are released upon those left on earth.

SAVED   Chapter 7. A parenthetical chapter showing that (a) Jews, and (b) members of every nation and tribe will be saved during the Tribulation.

TRUMPETS   Chapters 8-9. The trumpet judgments fall upon the earth.

ANGEL	Chapter 10. The angel gives John a book.
TWO WITNESSES	Chapter 11. Two Witnesses will speak for God on earth; the 7th Trumpet judgment falls upon the earth.
ISRAEL	Chapter 12. The Antichrist persecutes Israel and all who turn to Christ.
ANTICHRIST	Chapter 13. Antichrist rises to world power.
GRAPES	Chapter 14. The 144,000 of chapter 7 are seen safe with Christ; Antichrists armies marching to Armageddon appear as grapes ripe for crushing.
BOWLS	Chapters 15- 16. The Bowl of Wrath judgments are poured out upon an earth following the Antichrist (Bowls — "vials" in the King James).
BABYLON	Chapters 17-18. The Satanic "Babylon" of the end-time is destroyed at last. Chapter 17 — the Babylon Harlot world church; and 18 — the Babylon commercial empire of Antichrist.
ARMAGEDDON	Chapter 19. The time for the Marriage of the Lamb (Christ) to the bride (the true church) has come; Christ with His armies comes to earth to destroy the forces of Antichrist now gathered in Palestine at Armageddon. The 7 years are now over.
KINGDOM	Chapter 20. Christ establishes the 1000 year Kingdom of peace prophecied in Isaiah 11; the unsaved dead of all the ages are judged before the Great White Throne and cast into the Lake of Fire.
NEW EARTH	Chapters 21-22. The New Heavens and Earth are formed, the New Jerusalem descends to earth, and the redeemed are with Christ in joy for all remaining eternity.

An easily memorized outline of the entire book would be as follows:*

THE REVELATION OF CHRIST AS THE LORD OF THE CHURCHES (Chapters 1-3)

THE REVELATION OF CHRIST AS THE LION OVER THE NATIONS (Chapters 4-20)

THE REVELATION OF CHRIST AS THE LAMB AMONG THE REDEEMED (Chapters 21-22)

*Dr. Herman A. Hoyt, Grace Theological Seminary, Winona Lake, 1965.

How is Revelation to be Interpreted?

THAT IS,
DO the Major Events of Revelation in Chapters 6 to 19 Show:

NO PAST EVENTS already fulfilled in the history of the Roman Empire of the first century with Nero being the Antichrist? This is called the *Preterite (Past) Approach* to the Book of Revelation.

NO EVENTS OF THIS PRESENT AGE such as the early persecutions, the barbarian invasions, the Dark Ages, the French Revolution, Russian Revolution, WWI, WWII, and the Vietnam War? This is called the *Historical Approach.*

NO NO EVENTS AT ALL, rather general visions which teach of no future specific events, but which assert over and over merely the lesson that eventually God will win over Satan in every sphere of life. This is the *Topical or Cyclical Approach,* so called because the God over Satan lesson is repeated in cycles of chapters.

NO NO EVENTS AT ALL, the book being merely a long allegory or picture story with hidden themes of philosophy and love disguised under the external less important words of the book. This is the *Allegorical-Mystical Approach.*

NO ONLY HUMAN GUESSES of what would happen to Nero, Rome and the new religion as time went on? This is the *Liberal or Modernistic Approach.*

YES EVENTS STILL IN THE FUTURE which will occur in the 7 year coming Tribulation Period called Daniels' 70th Week (Dan. 9:27).
• The Rapture will occur, the Antichrist will be revealed and he will become a world leader, God will pour out judgments upon the earth which will culminate in the destruction of Antichrist's armies at Armageddon at the Revelation of Christ (Rev. 19:11-20:2) at the end of the seven years (Joel 3; Zech. 12 to 14; Isaiah 63; Matthew 24 to 25). This is the *Futuristic Approach.*

Here are some of the reasons why the
FUTURISTIC APPROACH
to Revelation is correct:

1. The Beast of Revelation 11-19 is the same as Daniel's fourth beast (Dan. 7) which is that *yet future* final kingdom which is destroyed just prior to the establishment of the Kingdom of Heaven.

2. The five time specifications of the Book of Revelation (11:2, 11:3; 12:6,14; 13:5) upon study harmonize perfectly with the time specifications and events which surround the yet future seven year period known as Daniel's seventieth week (Dan. 9:27; 8:25; 12:7).

3. The **FUTURISTIC** approach to the Apocalypse is the only one *(contra* —Liberal; Allegorical; Preterit; Historical; & Topical) which harmonizes Daniel (9:24, 26-27; 7:19-27: 8:23-25); Matthew (24 and 25—esp. 24:15-23, 29-31); 2 Thess. (2:1-12); Jer. 30:4-10; Rom. 11:25-26; Jn. 5:23; Zech. 12:9-14; 8:23; Jer. 23:5-8; *et cetera* into one unified eschatological program.

4. The **FUTURISTIC** approach is the only one that accomplishes the purpose enunciated in Rev. 1:1, "to show unto his servants things which must shortly come to pass."
(The *Liberal* approach denies this ability; the *Allegorical* allegorizes away the things revealed; the *Preterit* relegates that which is to be future to the past; the *Historical* approach presents items so veiled that they cannot be identified even after they are completed; and the *Topical* sees only general trends rather than future "things.")

5. The **FUTURISTIC** approach does not resort to unwarranted allegorization of the symbolical as well as literal details of the Apocalypse as the Historical and Topical views do.

6. The **FUTURISTIC** view yields a premillennial coming of Christ; while the Topical view with its cyclic pattern placing Rev. 20 before Rev. 19 logically leads to amillennialism.

Historical Outline

Background for the Book of Revelation

HERE ARE THE KEY DATES OF
OLD TESTAMENT HISTORY (All dates B.C.)

Before Abraham (Genesis 1-11) .... Dates uncertain
Abraham .... (Copper Age Begins) 2000
Moses .... (Egypt) .... (some say 1200) 1400
David .... (Philistines) ..... (Iron Age Begins) 1000
Division of the Kingdom (into Israel, N.; and Judah, S.) 931
Fall of Israel to Assyria (Northern 10 Tribes scattered) 721
70 Year Babylonian Captivity of Judah begins 606
Jerusalem and the Temple Destroyed........................ 586
Persia Conquers Babylon: Babylonian Captivity Ends 535
Alexander the Great Conquers Persia & Begins
    the Greek Period...336-313
Antiochus IV, the Greek King of Syria, Desecrates 2d Temple....168
Temple Recaptured and Rededicated to God (Jn. 10:22; Hannukah)
    by Judas Maccabee 165
Palestine Falls to Pompey and Roman Rule.................... 63
Herod the Great Dies After Massacring the Innocents in Bethlehem 4

Red Underlining denotes the dominant nation of the Biblical period.

THE REVELATION
OF JESUS CHRIST

INTRODUCTION

- **TITLE**   The title given by the King James Version is, "The Revelation of Saint John the Divine." This title is not an ill one for John, who was a *believer* (a "saint"), did write this work. John was also a *theologian* and the Old English label for such a one was "divine." No one should think— and the King James translators never thought it—that John was in any sense himself divine (part of the deity).

The best and proper title for this wonderful book, however, is its Biblical one taken from 1:1, "The Revelation of Jesus Christ." In the Greek the initial word "The" does not occur, thus the exact title would be, "A Revelation of Jesus Christ." And this is precisely what this book is; it is a showing forth of Jesus Christ as Lord of Lords and King of Kings who is coming forth in the end times to rescue His people, to judge the wicked, and to subjugate at last the earth to the will of God.

Another title for this book is, "Apocalypse." This is the anglicized spelling of the first word of this book as it is found in the original Greek. This word means, "A Revelation." The Greek word *apocalypse (apokalupsis)* comes from *apo,* meaning "from," and *kalupto,* meaning "to conceal." Thus "Apocalpse" signifies literally a removing of the veil "from" that which was previously "concealed." Hence it is a "Revelation;" and thusly this book shows forth things previously hidden. Many of its visions, however, are in substance identical to those in Daniel, Isaiah, Joel, etc., only now additional details are added. The Old Testament in many cases is truly the dictionary which explains the Apocalypse.

- **AUTHOR AND DATE**   That the Apocalypse was written by the Apostle John (Rev. 1:1,4,9) at about 95-96 A.D. is firmly substantiated by the testimony of Irenaeus (c. 170 A.D.). Irenaeus was the pupil of Polycarp who in turn sat at the feet of John himself, and his words constitute extremely strong evidence. Irenaeus wrote, "John also, the Lord's disciple, . . . says in the Apocalypse and then he quotes 1:12-16; 5:6; 19:11-17 almost word for word. He later quotes from 17:12-14, and from nearly every chapter in the Book of Revelation. He declares the Apocalypse was seen by John "towards the end of Domitian's reign," 81-96 A.D. (Irenaeus, *Against Heresies,* IV, xx; V, xxvi, xx.)

The testimony of the early church fathers confirms Irenaeus' words, as do the words of the Book of Revelation itself. Such scholars as Alford, Thiessen, Lenski, Barnes, Milligan, Orr, Moffatt, Zahn, and Hoyt hold this view. Modernists who advocate that it was written in the second century do so primarily because they cannot believe that Jesus Christ could really give such a vision; thus they seek for a later purely human author who merely used the name of John.

Explanation of Terms

Abomination of Desolation

A desecration of the temple by Antichrist. His final attempt to force the Jews to worship him (Daniel 9:27; Matthew 24:15; 2 Thessalonians 2:3-4.)

Antichrist

A name taken from I and II John. In Daniel he is referred to as the little horn and the vile person; In II Thessalonians as the Son of Perdition; and in Revelation as the Beast out of the sea.

Satan so completely possesses this man as to amount almost to an incarnation. Scriptures appear to indicate that he, as Judas Iscariot, will become indwelt by Satan.

Antichrist will oppose Christ, the saints, and the Jews. He will be first hailed as a Man of Peace and given unlimited power by the European countries, the United States and Israel. At his rise, Antichrist will be only a man, but with satanic power. His sudden, sensational rise as the saviour of a world threatened by destruction will mark the beginning of the Time of the End.

His later attempt to annihilate the Jews will bring about his defeat at Jerusalem by the return of Christ. All prophecy up to the return of Christ will be fulfilled in his day.

Apocalypse

Apocalypse comes from the identical Greek word, *apokalipsis,* which is *apo,* "from" and *kaplipsis,* "that which is hidden." Hence it means "Revelation," and it is so used as the first word in the book of the same name, that is, in the Book of *Revelation,* also called, The *Apocalypse* (Revelation 1:1).

Born Again

When Nicodemus, a ruler of the Jews, asked how he could enter Heaven, Jesus answered, "'...Except a man be born again, he cannot see the kingdom of God" (John 3:3).

The condition of this new birth is faith in Christ crucified (See John 3:14, 15 and Galatians 3:24).

Through the new birth (being born again) the believer becomes a partaker of the divine nature and of the life of Christ Himself (Galatians 2:20).

The term "born again" and "saved" are used synonymously.

For further light on this, read the definition for SAVED and also THE SAINTS.

Catholic

From the Greek *katholikos,* meaning "general, universal, everywhere." This word appears no where in the Greek New Testament except as a title before the book of James in Eusebius' Bible (4th century). Here it reads, "Epistles Catholic," and denotes the NT letters addressed not to any one church or person, but to *all Christians universally*. In the early church this term denoted the *generally held orthodox trinitarian faith as distinguished from the heresies and cults which had arisen*. The "Modern Catholic Church" is well dated from Gregory I, the Great, who as Bishop of Rome in 590 A.D. advanced many of the dogmas which are now incorporated into present day Roman Catholicism—e.g., purgatory, etc. Protestantism did not really start with Luther in 1517, but at 1517 under Luther's impetus there was an attempt to return to the Apostolic faith of the New Testament. Protestantism was thus a return to the original historic Christian faith.

Covenant

Covenant is the word for a binding agreement, a treaty, or a pact made with a solemn oath. God in His grace has made certain covenants with mankind. In Genesis 9:8-17 God makes a covenant with man not to destroy the world again by a flood. The rainbow is given as the token of this covenant. In Genesis 17:1-14 God makes a covenant with Abraham to bless him and his seed and to give them Canaan (Palestine). Circumcision was given as the sign of this covenant. The Law given to Moses at Sinai was God's covenant with Israel (Exodus 24:7-8), and the Ark which held the two tablets of the Law was called the Ark of the Covenant (Numbers 10:33). God promised in Jeremiah 31:34 to make a New Covenant with Israel someday. Christ's death inaugurated this New Covenant (Testament) sealed with His blood (I Corinthians 11:25).

Day of the Lord

Day of the Lord, DAY OF GOD, DAY OF RETRIBUTION are kindred expressions which denote time periods in which God will be supreme, destroy and judge the wicked, and reward them for their wickedness. Paul in I Thessalonians 5:2 speaks of the Day of the Lord as the coming 7 year awful Tribulation period when God, before the Millennium begins, will pour out His wrath on a world which is following the Antichrist. Peter in II Peter 3:10 uses this same expression referring to the final destruction of the earth prior to the formation of the new earth. Jeremiah 46:10, however, uses the expression "the Day of the Lord God of Hosts" to refer to God's destroying Pharaoh Necho's army which took place in 605 B.C.

Diaspora

Gk. diaspora, "that which has been scattered; dispersion." This refers to the Jews who were scattered over Europe and Asia by Assyria (721 B.C.), Babylon (606-535 B.C.), and Rome (70 A.D.). These lost their tribal lands but not their Israelite identity (Jn. 7:35). The term can also refer to scattered Christians (Jas. 1:1; 1 Pet. 1:1). Someday the "diaspora" shall be ended (Jer. 23:7-8).

Eschatology

Eschatology is from the Greek words *eschatos*, "last," and

logos, "word; knowledge," hence it refers to Knowledge of the Last Things—the study of the prophecies which tell of the future consumation of this world.

The False Prophet

Antichrist will be the political ruler who will work the works of Satan. *The False Prophet* will be the religious ruler who will undergird the work of the *Antichrist.* Both get their power from Satan.

The False Prophet never will attempt to promote himself. He will never become an object of worship. He will do the work of a prophet in that he directs attention away from himself to one whom he says has the right to be worshipped (the Antichrist).

The False Prophet will imitate many miracles of God. He will cause fire to come down from heaven imitating the miracles of Elijah in order to convince the nation Israel that he (The False Prophet) is the Elijah whom Malachi promised was yet to come! Having achieved this deception the False Prophet will declare that since this miracle (bringing fire from heaven) shows that he is Elijah . . . then, therefore, the Antichrist is truly Christ and should be worshipped.

He will also build a statue, and through some satanic or technological miracle cause this statue (image) to talk and somehow come to life. When the people see this miracle they will fall down and worship the Antichrist believing him to be Christ (Revelation 13:11-18).

Heaven

Heaven refers in the Scripture to (a) the far off starry heavens, Genesis 1:1; (b) the atmospheric heavens in which the birds fly, Jeremiah 4:25; and to (c) the place wherein God specially manifests His presence, Matthew 6:9. This Third Heaven is where the redeemed have an eternal place prepared for them (2 Corinthians 5:1; John 14:2). Before Christ's resurrection it was sometimes called "Abraham's Bosom" or "Paradise" (Luke 16:22; 23:43). In the New Testament it is especially marked by the fact that there the believer is alive and "present with the Lord" (2 Corinthians 5:8). In the future, after the millennium and after sin is forever done away with, God will make a "New Heaven and a New Earth" (Revelation 21:1). Upon this New Earth the heavenly New Jerusalem will descend wherein (i.e., on the New Earth and in this New city) the redeemed will dwell throughout all eternity with Christ (Revelation 21 and 22).

Hellenization

From the Greek, *Hellen,* meaning "a Greek." Thus this term denotes the movement to spread Greek language and culture to the rest of the world. This desire received its impetus from the conquests of Alexander the Great (336 - 313 B.C.) and from this time onward it spread. The Pharisees opposed the hellenistically-minded Herodians and Saducees on this. They hated that which was Greek, but Herod adored it.

Immortality

Immortality is the state of living forever. The Bible indeed makes it clear that human souls are immortal. Man's sin has brought to man spiritual death (separation from God) as well as physical death (separation of the soul from the body); but Christ's substitutionary death on the cross has made forgiveness and true immortality (union forever with God) possible to those who will repent and trust Him. Both those who now die in Christ (believers) and the Old Testament saints have everlasting life; they are conscious today, they are in joy and peace present with Christ awaiting their resurrection bodies (John 11:25-26; Matthew 22:31-32; Luke 16:19-31; 2 Corinthians 5:8; 1 Corinthians 15:35-58). These are immortal in the true sense of the word! Those, however, who die in unbelief are now in hell, the unseen world, awaiting consciously their resurrection, final judgment, and final fate of being sent to dwell in the "Lake of Fire" forever and ever. Here they are not annihilated, for their souls remain alive (Mark 9:48; Revelation 20:10). Hence these "lost souls" are in this sense also immortal. But, since the Lake of Fire involves eternal separation from God, they are spiritually *eternally dead!* Hence the Lake of Fire is rightly given the awful title of "The Second Death" (Revelation 20:10-15)! Thus only the redeemed, the saved, have true immortality—for these are *both* eternally conscious (as are the lost) and eternally with God (which the lost are not).

Last Days

Our reference to the Last Days means the *days immediately* prior to the "Rapture" of the saints and the ushering in of the Tribulation Period of 7 years.

Mark of the Beast

During the second half of the seven year Tribulation Period the Antichrist (who previously was setting himself up as a Man of Peace) will suddenly move against the Jews and all those who have accepted Christ as Saviour during the first 3½ years of this period. In Revelation 13:16,7 we read that". . . he (False Prophet) causeth all, both small and great, rich and poor, free and bond, to receive some mark in their right hand, or in their foreheads: And that no man might buy or sell, save he that had the mark . . ."

Therefore those who refuse to submit to the authority of this system by having this mark (The Mark of the Beast), face either starving to death slowly, or being slain by the representatives of the government, who will treat as traitors all who refuse to accept this identifying mark.

Millennium

Millennium is from the Latin, *mille,* "thousand," and *annum,* "year." It thus refers to the prophesied coming 1000 year period when Christ shall reign on the earth with a rod of iron (Revelation 20:4; 12:5; etc.). Satan shall be bound at this time and a period of earthly peace shall prevail (Revelation 20:1-10). In the Old Testament this period is described as the period of the Kingdom of Heaven (Daniel 2:44; 7:13-14). Isaiah 11 is the key O.T. passage which tells of the peace and righteousness of this time. Israel shall be restored and converted, and it shall have an honored place in this Millennial Kingdom (Zechariah 8:20-23; Acts 1:6).

Pre-Millennialism

Pre-Millennialism (*pre,* "before," the *mille annum,* "1000 year") advocates that the Second Coming of Christ will occur *before* the *millennium.* In fact, it believes that the 1000 year Kingdom Age of the earth (the *Millennium)* cannot be started until Christ, the King, comes again personally and visibly. Matthew 25:21-34 indeed shows that the Second Coming of Christ is the event which does inaugurate this 1000 year reign of Christ (Revelation 19:11-20:6).

Post-Millennialism

Post-Millennialism *(post,* "after, the *mille annum,* "1000 year") advocates that the Second Coming of Christ will be *after* the Church has led the world into conversion and 1000 years of earthly bliss. This opinion, once popular when it seemed as if the missionary message was going to bring the whole world to Christ, has today been largely abandoned. It is now clear that until Christ comes there will be no 1000 year millennial peace.

Amillennialism

Amillennialism comes from the Greco-Latin, *a,* "no," and *mille-annum,* "thousand year." Thus those who hold to this school of thought say that there will be No *Future* Millennial reign of Christ on the Earth. They say that the prophecies of the millennial kingdom are *not* literal; but rather that they refer figuratively to the happy state of the Church *today.* They understand Satan to be bound *today* "so that he should deceive the nations no more" (Revelation 20:3). (When one compares however, the state of the nations and the church today with Revelation 20:3 it is difficult to defend the amillennial notion that Satan is today bound "so that he should deceive the nations no more").

Mystery

Mystery *(musterion* in the Greek) is a term used in the New Testament which can only be truly understood in the light of its Greco-Roman usage in the ancient world. There it referred to a secret known only to the *initiated* members of a secret or exclusive group—for example, the "mystery religions" of the time were those with secret oaths, rites, laws, and books. Hence in the New Testament a "mystery" is a truth, plan, or program of God which has been either kept secret in prior ages or which, though hinted at in the Old Testament, is yet too profound for the human mind to fully grasp. To the disciples and believers, the initiated, these are revealed (Matthew 13:11; Luke 8:10; Romans 11:25; I Corinthians 4:1; Ephesians 5:32; 6:19; Colossians 1:26).

Pre-, Mid-, Post-Tribulationist

Pre-, Mid-, Post-Tribulationist is a person who is of the persuasion that the Rapture of the Church (1 Thessalonians 4:13-18) is respectively before (Pre), in the midst of (Mid), or after (Post) the Prophecised Tribulation Period—the final 7 year period when Antichrist rises and reigns (Daniel 9:27; Matthew 24:15; 21; etc.). Pretribulationists believe that since the Church is said to have been delivered from the "wrath to come" (I Thess. 1:9-10; 5:9; Romans 5:9), it, the Church, therefore must be raptured before the Tribulation Period which is the great day of God's wrath (Revelation 6:17). See Genesis 19:22!

Rapture

This refers to the time, prior to the start of the 7 year Tribulation Period, when believing Christians (both dead and alive) will "in the twinkling of an eye" rise up to meet Christ in the air.

". . . if we believe that Jesus died and rose again, even so them also which sleep in Jesus will God bring with Him. For this we say unto you by the word of the Lord, that we which are alive and remain unto the coming of the Lord shall not precede them which are asleep.

For the Lord himself shall descend from Heaven with a shout . . . and the dead in Christ shall rise first: Then we which are alive and remain shall be *caught up* (RAPTURED) together with them in the clouds, to meet the Lord in the air: and so shall we ever be with the Lord" (I Thessalonians 4:14-17).

The Saints

Those who accept Christ (in their heart) as both personal Saviour and Lord.

"Verily, verily, I say unto you, He that heareth my word, and believeth on Him that sent me, hath everlasting life, and shall not come into condemnation; but is passed from death unto life" (John 5:24).

"For the wages of sin is death but the gift of God is eternal life through Jesus Christ our Lord" (Romans 6:23).

"For by grace are ye saved through faith and that not of yourselves: it is the gift of God: Not of works, lest any man should boast" (Ephesians 2:8, 9).

"All honor to God, the God and Father of our Lord Jesus Christ for it is His boundless mercy that has given us the privilege of being born again, so that we are now members of God's own family. Now we live in the hope of eternal life because Christ rose again from the dead. And God has reserved for His children the priceless gift of eternal life; it is kept in heaven for you, pure and undefiled, beyond the reach of change and decay" (I Peter 1:3, 4 Living New Testament).

Through the quoting of these Scripture verses God's Word

defines (a) how you can be a saint, (b) the rich promises that will be yours when you accept Christ as your personal Saviour, and (c) your eternal rewards in heaven.

Saved

The term "saved" and "born-again" are used interchangeably. One who has accepted Christ as His personal Saviour is *born again* into the family of God and is *saved* from an eternity in Hell and is assured of an eternity with Christ in Heaven.

In Acts 16:30, 31 we read:

"... What must I do to be saved? And they (Paul and Silas) said, Believe on the Lord Jesus Christ, and thou shalt be saved ..."

And the well known verses in John 3:16, 17 tell us:

"For God so loved the world that He gave His only begotten Son, that whosoever believeth in Him should not perish, but have everlasting life.

For God sent not His Son into the world to condemn the world but that the world through Him might be saved."

For further light on this, read the definition on THE SAINTS.

Second Coming of Christ

This is one of the most prominent doctrines in the Bible. In the New Testament alone it is referred to over 300 times. His First Coming was over 1900 years ago when He came on earth to save man from sin. The Second Coming is an event starting at the Rapture and comprehending four phases: *First,* at the Rapture Christ takes the believers out of this world to be with Him (I Thessalonians 4). *Second,* Christ pours out His judgments on the world during the 7 year Tribulation Period. *Third,* Christ at the end of the 7 year Tribulation destroys the Antichrist and his wicked followers (Revelation 19). *Fourth,* Christ sets up His millennial Kingdom prophesied so often in the Old Testament.

Theocracy

Theocracy from the Greek *Theos,* "God," and *cracy* "rule." Hence, this term denotes a rule or kingdom where God Himself is both the acknowledged supreme leader and the actual supreme leader. This was the case of Old Testament Israel. There the religious laws were as binding as the civil laws—and indeed there was no real distinction between the two. God was worshipped by the state as well as by the individual. God ruled in actuality by His Law being the law of the land, and by His revealing His will to the nation through the High Priest and through His prophets. The millennium shall be a world-theocracy, and since the Only True God is righteous, holy, good, kind, and loving the Millennium shall be the earth's Golden Age.

Tribulation

In our reference to the Tribulation Period we mean that period of phenomenal world trial and suffering that occurs during the seven-year reign of Antichrist (Daniel 9:27). Daniel 12:1 tells us, "...there shall be a time of trouble, such as never was since there was a nation."

It is at this time that the Jews (and those who accept Christ as Saviour during this seven-year period) will be severely persecuted through imprisonment, torture and death (Jeremiah 30:7; Revelation 12). The final 3½ years of this period will be characterized, in Christ's words, by "great tribulation, such as has not occurred since the beginning of the world" (Matthew 24:21).

Photograph shows Salem Kirban, Background author of Revelation Visualized, interviewing refugees. This was at Shuneh, an Arab refugee camp 50 miles from Amman, Jordan. Photo was taken shortly after 6-Day War. These refugees had fled from Jericho and Bethlehem.

CHAPTER 1

The Revelation of Jesus Christ, which God gave unto him, to shew unto his servants things which must shortly come to pass; and he sent and signified *it* by his angel unto his servant John:

Isa. 46:9-10
Dan. 9:22-23

2 Who bare record of the word of God, and of the testimony of Jesus Christ, and of all things that he saw.

2 Pet. 1:16-21
1 John 1:1-3

3 Blessed is he that readeth, and they that hear the words of this prophecy, and keep those things which are written therein for the time *is* at hand.

Commentary

PRELUDE (1:1-8)
AND
THE VISION OF THE RISEN AND GLORIFIED CHRIST,
THE LORD OF THE CHURCH. (1:9-20)

Here we receive the announcement of the vision, are informed of its purpose and of its human receiver, and are told of the blessings which are pledged to all who read and hear its words.

1. The purpose of this Revelation is to show God's servants the events which will climax this age. In God's everlasting vision these things are spoken of as that "which must shortly come to pass"..."the time is at hand." Thus God enjoins us to have an attitude of expectancy.

2. John "bare record" of these things which he heard and saw. If as the modernists suggest, the name John was just used to cover up this book's clever forgery, what blasphemy we would have here. But no, Jesus showed it, and John saw it and wrote it down without error through divine inspiration for our benefit.

3. Here we learn of the blessedness of the reader (singular) and of the hearers (plural). The early church did not have a Bible for each person; one person read while all others listened. All would be blessed we are promised. And what a blessing this book is, despite the multitude of divergent opinions concerning its details, for in this book the final triumph of God over sin and Satan is unmistakeably revealed; and in it the final safety of every believer is assured. Halleluia!

Location of Isle of Patmos and Seven Churches in Asia.

Background

To many the book of Revelation is most confusing. To the non-Christian it appears to be unbelievable, strange and filled with fairy-tale-like frightening events. They read this book but without understanding. And Jesus Christ, himself spoke of such a confusion when he said in Luke 8:10,

> ...Unto you [His followers] it is given to know the mysteries of the kingdom of God: but to others [non-believers] in parables; that seeing they might not see, and hearing they might not understand.

Because the book of Revelation was written in about A.D. 95 some took the phrase in Revelation 1:1 "...things which must shortly come to pass..." to mean these events would occur within a few years after John was inspired of God to write this book. However 2 Peter 3:8 tells us that "...one day is with the Lord as a thousand years, and thousand years as one day." Only in this current day does it appear that the prophecies of Revelation are finally becoming fully ripe for fulfillment. God's next event is the Rapture.

PAST	PRESENT	RAPTURE	FIRST 3 1/2	LAST 3 1/2	ARMA-GEDDON	MIL-LENNIUM	NEW HEAVENS & EARTH
			TRIBULATION				

(v. 1,2)   (v.3)

4 John to the seven churches which are in Asia: Grace *be* unto you, and peace, from him which is, and which was, and which is to come; and from the seven Spirits which are before his throne;

5 And from Jesus Christ, *who* is the faithful witness, *and* the first begotten of the dead, and the prince of the kings of the earth. Unto him that loved us, and washed us from our sins in his own blood.

6 And hath made us kings and priests unto God and his Father; to him *be* glory and dominion for ever and ever. Amen.

Rev. 1:18; 3:14

Heb. 10:22

Eph. 1:3
Heb. 4:14-16

Commentary

4. John addresses his letter to the seven churches which were in the Roman province of Asia. This area was governed by a Proconsul and is hence sometimes called, Proconsuler Asia. This is our present Western third of Turkey.

"Seven churches" or assemblies (not "buildings") and "seven spirits"— Just as the seven days of the Genesis creation account included the entire creative action of God and even the subsequent rest, so the sevens of this book represent the entirety of the subject at hand. Thus the seven churches represent all the churches, and the seven spirits portray the omnipresent Spirit of God. So too, the 7 seals, 7 trumpets, 7 bowls, and 7 thunders, described later, all represent the total span of these judgments.

There were more churches than 7 in Asia; at Colosse and at Hierapolis there existed congregations (Hence Paul's epistle To the Colossians). These seven, however, represent all.

5. Christ's attributes and coming are now lauded in a Prelude Hymn, vss. 5-8. See how this verse sings of His trustworthiness, His power over death, His lordship over earthly potentates, and His saviorhood in washing away our sins by His dying at Calvary.

6. We who have trusted in Christ are today kings and priests. We are kings in that as Christ's servants we are under bondage to no man; we are priests in that we ourselves can come directly to God in prayer because of Christ's finished work—we need no other human priests.

See and meditate upon the cry of adoration towards God with which this verse closes.

How refreshing to sit atop a hill at Three Hills, Alberta, Canada and view God's handiwork unmarred by concrete highways and towering buildings. But far greater beauty awaits us as we look for that blessed hope, and the glorious appearing of the great God and our Saviour Jesus Christ (Titus 2:13).

Background

Many Christians are not fully aware of the royalty of their inheritance. We tend to look with awe at those in high office such as Presidents and Kings. We see their privileged position and all the benefits they derive from this elevation.

But Christ has made every Christian a king and a priest. He has given us royalty. And our destiny is a royal destiny.

In the Old Testament only the priest had the right of access to God. When a male Jew entered the Temple, he could pass through the Court of the Gentiles, the Court of the Women, the Court of the Israelites— but there he must stop; into the Court of the Priests he could not go.

By our new birth in Christ we now have royal blood and can come directly and boldly unto the throne of Grace (Hebrews 4:16). In John's day Roman citizenship was for the privileged few. John was not a citizen. But he rejoiced in the fact that in Christ he now had a celestial citizenship.

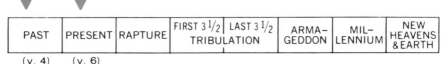

PAST	PRESENT	RAPTURE	FIRST 3½ TRIBULATION	LAST 3½	ARMA-GEDDON	MIL-LENNIUM	NEW HEAVENS & EARTH
(v. 4)	(v. 6)						

7 Behold, he cometh with clouds; and every eye shall see him, and they also which pierced him: and all kindreds of the earth shall wail because of him. Even so, Amen.

8 I am Alpha and Omega, the beginning and the ending, saith the Lord, which is, and which was, and which is to come, the Almighty.

Dan. 7:13-14
Matt. 24:29-31, 25:31
Zech. 12:8-14

Rev. 22:13; 21:6
Isa. 44:6; 45:5-6

Definition:
KINDREDS All the nations of the earth (Greek: phule, tribe, nation).

Commentary

7 John here sings of Christ's coming in the clouds with power and glory at the end of the 7 year Tribulation Period (Daniel's 70th week. Daniel 9:27).

The Lord Himself had earlier spoken of this in Matthew 24:29, 30; 25:31. At this time He will slay the armies of Antichrist gathered in Palestine at Armageddon (Revelation 19:11-20:2). Thus here the Prelude at the beginning of the Revelation flashes out with one of the mighty themes of the book: Behold, He comes in the clouds (Daniel 7:13, 14)!

The wailing here is that of the remnant of Israel and the gentiles who have turned to Christ during the Tribulation Period. These cry because they and their kindred have for so long turned their backs on their Saviour. As they see the One who suffered so for their sins they break into a weeping as they behold His wounds on their behalf (See Zechariah 12:10).

8 Here is the self-proclamation by Christ that He is the Alpha and Omega! If there is any doubt here as to whether these verses apply to the Father or Son, in 22:13 they are shown unmistakably to apply to the Son!

Since Alpha and Omega were the first and last letters of the Greek alphabet here the announcement is that Christ is the very start and the very conclusion of every matter. This could only be said of God! This verse alone proves the deity of Christ. He is the eternal was, is, and shall be, the Almighty. What a prelude!

Background

Until a few years ago ministers and laymen alike wondered how it would be possible for "every eye" to see the Lord Jesus Christ as He came through the clouds.

From a human standpoint this seemed an impossibility. But with the space age this has become more clear. On Sunday, July 24, 1969 people from all over the world watched Neil Armstrong as he took his first step on the moon. Through orbiting satellites that bounced back to earth radio and TV signals "every eye" was able to see the exact same occurrence simultaneously.

PAST	PRESENT	RAPTURE	FIRST 3½ LAST 3½ TRIBULATION	ARMA-GEDDON	MIL-LENNIUM	NEW HEAVENS & EARTH

9 I John, who also am your brother, and companion in tribulation, and in the kingdom and patience of Jesus Christ, was in the isle that is called Patmos, for the word of God, and for the testimony of Jesus Christ.

Acts 14:22

Commentary

9. In verses 9-10 we learn of the circumstances of the Apostle when the Revelation vision was given to him. His spiritual location is that he is the brother of believers everywhere. He is as human as we are. Thus 2 Peter 1:21 tells us that it was through *men* "moved by the Holy Ghost" that prophecy came.

The Apostle, even he, is our "companion" (Gk *sugkoinonos,* "partner" in business) in tribulation. All believers will have tribulation in this life, Acts 14:22; yet John was not in that still future period which we call, *Daniel's 70th week of years* (Dan. 9:27), which is *The Tribulation Period.* In Matt. 24:21 Jesus speaks of the latter 3 1/2 years of this future period and labels it as a time of "Great Tribulation"—hence it has been so named.

Because of faithfulness to God the apostle, who lived his twilight years in the Ephesus area, was banished to the island of Patmos by the anti-Christian Roman emperor Domitian (reigned 81-96 A.D.). Irenaeus, who wrote at about 170 A.D., declared that John saw his vision "towards the end of Domitian's reign" (*Against Heresies,* V:xxx). Patmos is an isle which runs N. to S. and is 8 miles long; it is located in the Aegean Sea 25 miles due S. of the W. edge of Samos.

What good could come out of this banishment?

Air view of the Isle of Patmos.

Background

Imagine yourself banished in exile on a lonely island about 50 miles from the nearest town. And Patmos was no paradise island! Then possibly wearing chains, being poorly fed and clothed and made to sleep on the bare ground. This is the life John faced as he took refuge on Patmos.

And yet persecuted by Rome's attempt to shut off his witness for the Lord, John found triumph in tragedy.

For as a virtual prisoner on Patmos, away from the activities of the world, God used him as a witness to reveal things to come.

You will recall some of Paul's greatest epistles came while he was a prisoner in Caesarea and in Rome. Perhaps now Romans 8:28 becomes clearer to us as Christians.

It was the Emperor Domitian who banished John to Patmos. Domititian rebuilt the empire's shrines of Jupiter, Juno and Minerva in Rome. He spent an equivalent of $22 MILLION dollars on its gold-plated doors and gilded roof alone! And yet in the midst of this idolatrous world, John was an unflinching witness for Christ.

▼

PAST	PRESENT	RAPTURE	FIRST 3 1/2 LAST 3 1/2 TRIBULATION	ARMA– GEDDON	MIL– LENNIUM	NEW HEAVENS & EARTH
			FIRST 3 1/2 | LAST 3 1/2			

Revelation 1

10 I was in the Spirit on the Lord's day, and heard behind me a great voice, as of a trumpet,

11 Saying, I am Alpha and Omega, the first and the last: and, What thou seest, write in a book, and send *it* unto the seven churches which are in Asia; unto Eph-e-sus, and unto Smyrna, and unto Per-ga-mos, and unto Thy-a-ti-ra, and unto Sardis, and unto Philadelphia, and unto La-od-i-ce-a.

Dan. 9:3,20,21ff

Exod. 17:14; Deut. 17:18

Commentary

10. The meaning of this verse has occasioned great debate in evangelical circles. Was John "in the spirit on the Lord's day"—meaning (a) that he was in prayer on the day of worship, the first day of the week, the day the Lord rose; or (b) that he was in the realm of the Holy Spirit, in the mystical prophecy world, on the "Day of the Lord," that is, in the end-time Tribulation Period? Good men differ on this. The Greek does not give us the answer as the adjective "Lord's" in "Lord's day" is *kuriakos* ("pertaining to the Lord") and it is used only this once in the entire Greek New Testament. When the verse is studied in context, in light of its place before his heavenly ascent in 4:1, it seems that John received the vision while in the Spirit in prayer on the day of worship, the Lord's Day (See Dan. 9:20-21ff).

The voice of the omnipotent deity sounded to John's ears in majesty like a trumpet.

11. "Saying, What thou seest ...," is how the ancient Greek manuscripts read. "I am Alpha and Omega, the first and the last, and" crept into the 10th century manuscript named "Porfirianus," The missing words do appear, however, in the combination of 1:8; 1:17; 21:6; 22:13, so no one need be dismayed.

"Write in a book"—A *scroll* was the ancient form of the book, as the bound book with pages as we know it—called a *codex*—was not invented until about the beginning of the 3rd century.

Let us note that God—the One responsible for the (a) revelation, (b) inspiration, (c) preservation, and (d) interpretation of Scripture—commands John to put the matter in written form.

Tischendorf's greatest find, the Codex Sinaiticus was bought by the British Museum from Russia in 1933 for about $500,000. Written in Greek about the 4th century A.D. this ancient bible text in brown ink, on 326½ leaves was found in Monastery of St. Catherine on Mt. Sinai.

Background

Papyrus was too brittle to be folded, and so it was rolled to form a scroll. Sometimes a scroll was 40 yards in length. The more durable animal parchment scroll, however, was mainly a possession of the wealthy.

The first Christians were not wealthy and could not afford costly parchment scrolls. Their only means of writing the Christian message was on any strips of papyrus which they could obtain. These strips were then sewn together and formed a scroll. The Greek word for scroll is *biblos,* "book," and hence "Bible." Thus the directive by God to "write in a book" His revelation. The "book" of pages which we are familiar with today—called a "codex"—did not come into use until the 2d century A.D. at the earliest.

Here at Patmos, some 40 miles off the coast of Asia Minor (which is now Turkey) John, inspired of God, wrote.

Skeptics, who fail to understand God's miracle powers to create this world and the universe, try to find mechanical explanations for everything. Many feel man has made a great stride in landing on the moon... yet when we compare man's scientific achievements with God's handiwork, man's advances are very small.

PAST	PRESENT	RAPTURE	FIRST 3½ TRIBULATION	LAST 3½	ARMA–GEDDON	MIL–LENNIUM	NEW HEAVENS & EARTH

Revelation 1

12 And I turned to see the voice that spake with me. And being turned, I saw seven golden candlesticks;

13 And in the midst of the seven candlesticks *one* like unto the Son of man, clothed with a garment down to the foot, and girt about the paps with a golden girdle.

Exod. 25:31-40;
Zech. 4:1-6

Dan. 7:13-14; 3:25
Dan. 7:9
Eph. 6:14; Isa. 11:5

Definition:
Messiah—the Hebrew word meaning the oiled or Anointed One. The anointing with olive oil of the king, priest, and prophet symbolized God's Spirit being upon that one (See Zech. 4). The Spirit was to dwell in fulness on the prophesied Anointed One. "Christ," from the Greek Christos, "oiled, anointed," is the anglicized Greek word which perfectly translates the Hebrew "Messiah."

Commentary

12-13. The candlestick, or better "lampstand," of the Old Testament Tabernacle was called the "Menorah" (Hebrew). It too had *seven* branches, or rather, one main and six side branches (Exod. 25:31). The olive oil that burned its *seven* lights represented the Spirit of God's omnipresence and His giving light to the world (Zech. 4:1-6). It well typified Christ, filled with the Spirit, the Light of the World (John 8:12).

Here Jesus is seen in the midst of the seven candlesticks (or better: "lampstands"). These seven are not connected into one large multi-branched lampstand as in the ancient Tabernacle, they are rather seven separate ones; and Jesus is seen standing in the midst of them. They surround Him. Soon, in 1:20 and 2:1, we shall learn more about these.

The title, "Son of Man," means "a genuine man," but it also was one of the Old Testament's names for the Messiah. This usage comes from Dan. 7:13-14—which is one of the most striking passages in all of the Old Testament. Thus, Jesus, who is a real man and who is also the Messiah who is to be served forever by all people (Dan. 7:13-14), is seen here by John in the midst of the lampstands. John now sees Him, not as the lowly babe of Bethlehem, but as the risen and glorified King of Kings.

"Garment down to the foot"—the dress of a majestic ruler; "clothed about the chest with a golden sash"—this symbolizes His absolute righteousness (Isa. 11:5; Eph. 6:14).

Background

It is interesting to note that nowhere in the Bible is there a description of the face of Christ. We do, however, have the promise of 1 John 3:2 which tells us:

> ...we know that, when He shall appear,
> we shall be like Him, for we shall see
> Him as He is.

Scriptures in many places describe the attire Jesus wore. And these verses depict him in His royal attire.

In David's day such kingly robes were made of fine linen (1 Chronicles 15:27). The kings of Israel and Judah were always decked in richly colored robes of scarlet or purple.

Jesus wore a seamless coat "woven from the top throughout" (John 19:23). The scarlet robe in which soldiers derisively attired Jesus (Matthew 27:28) was a military cloak worn over armor by officers.

PAST	PRESENT	RAPTURE	FIRST 3 1/2 LAST 3 1/2 TRIBULATION		ARMA–GEDDON	MIL–LENNIUM	NEW HEAVENS & EARTH

Revelation 1

14 His head and *his* hairs *were* white like wool, as white as snow; and his eyes *were* as a flame of fire;

Dan. 7:9
Rev. 2:18

15 And his feet like unto fine brass, as if they burned in a furnace; and his voice as the sound of many waters.

16 And he had in his right hand seven stars: and out of his mouth went a sharp twoedged sword; and his countenance *was* as the sun shineth in his strength.

Rev. 3:1
Heb. 4:12; Rev. 19:15

Definition:
Revelation—*This word is sometimes used to speak of Christ's coming in glory at the end of the 7 year Tribulation (See 2 Thess. 1:6-7).*

Commentary

14. Here the pure white head and hair matches exactly the scene of Dan. 7:9. There it represents the everlasting antiquity of God the Father, and here it can symbolize only this same thing with reference to the Son. He too is eternal; He too is God.

His flaming eyes show His supernatural ability to see everything. He sees what is going on upon the earth at all times; He sees into the heart of every man—He is omniscient. How fearful is this portent of judgment to the one who has yet not asked Christ in repentance to wash away his sins (Rom. 10:9,13).

15. His feet seem to be clad in brass boots, still glistening white hot from the furnace. This symbolizes the fierce judgment which is about to fall upon the ungodly from the feet of the Son of Man. In Dan. 7:7 the third beast, the Grecian empire, stamped in judgment and in destruction with its feet. Christ will stamp in judgment all through the seven year Tribulation and especially at Armageddon at its close, Rev. 6:16-17; 14:19; 16:1; 19:15-21.

16. Seven stars in His right hand—We shall soon see this explained for us in verse 20.

The twoedged sword out of His mouth—In Rev. 19:15 we are told that this is the Word of God whereby Christ smites the wicked nations at His Revelation from heaven at the end of the Tribulation. Christ speaks and it is done; thus His word of judgment is like a sharp swift-cutting sword. At this time Christ comes like the *shining sun* in power and glory.

Farmers plow as the sun sets to take advantage of the relative coolness of late afternoon (110°)!
This scene in the Holy Land reminds us of the outpouring of the Fourth Vial when the sun scorches all men with its fire (Revelation 16:8-9).

Background

The phrase in verse 16, "...His countenance was as the sun shineth in His strength" is perhaps difficult to understand.

Many will remember the eclipse of the sun and moon in March, 1970 and the many warnings given in newspapers, radio and television not to look directly at this occurrence. Yet some did and as a result were blinded.

Our sun is 109 times the diameter of the earth. Of all the heavenly bodies, the sun is the most important to us here on earth. The temperature on the surface of the sun is about 11,000° Fahrenheit. It takes this light about 8 1/3 minutes to reach the earth....some 93 million miles away. Yet even from this distance all of us have experienced the warmth and brilliance of the sun. But its brightness is still so intense, we cannot look at it.

Saul, who became Paul, was blinded by the countenance of God. The disciples were likewise overcome at the Mount of Transfiguration. And 2 Thessalonians 2:8 reveals to us that Antichrist will be destroyed by "the brightness of His coming." What POWER!

▼

PAST	PRESENT	RAPTURE	FIRST 3 1/2 TRIBULATION	LAST 3 1/2	ARMA– GEDDON	MIL– LENNIUM	NEW HEAVENS & EARTH

17 And when I saw him, I fell at his feet as dead. And he laid his right hand upon me, saying unto me, Fear not; I am the first and the last:

18 *I am* he that liveth. and was dead: and, behold, I am alive for evermore, Amen; and have the keys of hell and of death.

Lk. 5:8

Matt. 16:18,19
Rev. 6:8

Definition:

Omniscent—*From the Latin* (omnis—*all;* scientia—*knowledge, hence "science"). This is an attribute of God wherein He knows and comprehends all things and all minds which were, are, and ever shall be. He knows all things which might have been (Matt. 11:21, 23). He knows the future because He works all things according to the counsel of His own will (Eph. 1:11)—i.e., according to His plan.*

Hell—*The Greek word here is* hades (ha *or* a, *"not;"* ides *"seen") and it refers to the "unseen" world to which the dead go. The Christian usage of the word carries with it none of the Greek mythology concerning the underground River Styx, etc. Hades, or hell, represents the present place of the spirits of the unsaved dead. The righteous dead before Christ were spoken of as being in "Abraham's Bosom" and in "paradise," but now they are described as being "with Christ" in heaven "which is far better" (Lk. 16:23; 23:43; 2 Cor. 5:6-8; Phil. 1:23).*

Commentary

17. John, a sinful mortal, finding himself before manifest deity, collapses in fear and awe. See Peter's reaction in Lk. 5:8. How different is Christ's response to a man prostrate before Him from that of the angel in 19:10. The angel was concerned that God only be bowed to, but Christ does not speak of this—He is deity and prostration before Him is no sin.

18. This verse can be of great comfort to all who have lost Christian loved ones. Christ Himself experienced death. Through the resurrection He merged the victor over death; and now as Lord He has the authority over death and hell. "Keys" represent *authority*. Christ controls all who enter and all who leave death and hell. Let us, therefore, who bury loved ones in Christ, not despair knowing that our Saviour has the keys. Death cannot keep them when the one holding the keys has promised that they shall yet live (John 11:25-26; Rom. 8:31,38).

PAST	PRESENT	RAPTURE	FIRST 3½ TRIBULATION	LAST 3½	ARMA-GEDDON	MIL-LENNIUM	NEW HEAVENS & EARTH

19. Write the things which thou hast seen, and the things which are, and the things which shall be hereafter;
20. The mystery of the seven stars which thou sawest in my right hand, and the seven golden candlesticks. The seven stars are the angels of the seven churches: and the seven candlesticks which thou sawest are the seven churches.

Mt. 13:11, 35

Commentary

19. Here is the divine outline of the book (Discussed earlier in the Introduction).

20. The Greek word *musterion,* "mystery," has its roots in the Greek Mystery Cults. The *mysteries,* or secrets of the cult, were known to its initiated members, but not to those on the outside. So here, the Lord reveals to us secrets which now only we Christians know. Those on the outside neither know nor comprehend these things.

The solutions to two of the mysteries are here supplied. Here is a key to understanding this book of signs (1:1 "to show"). Items seen in the vision will often represent things, people, events, and places which pertain to the spiritual struggle of the ages; this book is one vast parable or allegory. Here lampstands stand for churches and stars are not really stars, but angels.

This verse teaches the grand truth that Christ ever stands in the midst of His congregations (the lampstands) where He can quickly see all, help all, or judge. He is always concerned and nearby. What a fitting precursor this sight is to prepare John and us for the letters to the churches which will follow.

Christ controls the angels of each church—He holds them in His right hand. The Greek word *anggelos* means "messenger," and either a human messenger (the one who carries the letter to each church *or* its pastor) or a divinely appointed spirit (an angel) could be meant. Commentators differ. I am inclined toward the latter view, i.e., that Christ intimately controls the appointed spirit, the angel, who ministers to each congregation (Hebrews 1:14).

PAST	PRESENT	RAPTURE	FIRST 3½ LAST 3½ TRIBULATION		ARMA– GEDDON	MIL– LENNIUM	NEW HEAVENS &EARTH

THE LETTERS TO THE
SEVEN CHURCHES IN ASIA (CHAPTERS 2-3)

INTRODUCTION TO THE LETTERS

The congregations to whom these letters are addressed were *historical* churches which actually existed in Asia at the time John wrote (about 95-96 A.D.). These seven, as the number seven in this book indicates, were *typical* of the strengths, problems, and weaknesses of not only all of the early churches, but also of churches today.

"...the one thing upon which there seems to be general agreement is that 'seven' here speaks of a totality of characteristics. In the seven churches we have both every kind of church and every kind of member, which not only existed on earth in John's generation but also will exist throughout all ecclesiastical history. In other words, we have in the seven selected local churches a composite picture of *all* local churches on earth at any particular time." Alva J. McClain *(The Greatness of the Kingdom,* Zondervan, pp. 446-47)

As for the major characteristics of the churches, these are as follows:

The Church at Ephesus	—First love lost;
The church at Smyrna	—Persecuted church;
The church at Pergamos	—Faithful church, but tolerates false teachers;
The church at Thyatira	—Church dominated by a powerful false prophet;
The church at Sardis	—Spiritually dying church;
The church at Philadelphia	—Faithful witnessing church;
The church at Laodicea	—Lukewarm church.

The above characteristics of the churches seem to so many to correspond with the epochs of church history that the theory has been suggested that the seven letters of chapters 2-3 are *prophetical.* That is, that in this book of prophecy even in the letters to the churches the Lord has given a veiled prophecy of the course of the age until His return. Since no one could clearly tell, except perhaps at the very close of the age, when the periods had run their course—whether this had been so by A.D. 100 or by A.D. 2000—this theory does not do injury to the promise of the imminent ("any time") return of Christ for His Church. The ages predicted by the various church letters are:

Ephesus	—Apostolic Church	(30- 100 A.D.)
Smyrna	—Persecuted Church	(100- 313 A.D.)
Pergamos	—State Church	(313- 590 A.D.)
Thyatira	—Papal Church	(590-1517 A.D.)
Sardis	—Reformed Church	(1517-1790 A.D.)
Philadelphia	—Missionary Church	(1730-1900 A.D.)
Laodicea	—Apostate Church	(1900- A.D.)

Both learned and unlearned Bible scholars and students debate whether this "Prophetical Theory" is or is not true. This is a book of prophecy and many of the predictions are veiled. Yet many of the Bible's other predictions upon study were found as the years passed to have involved more than their original hearers dreamed (for example, Gen. 3:15). Thus, these seven letters are (a) historical; (b) typical; and (c) very possibly prophetical.

NOTE THE **PATTERN**
USED FOR EACH OF THE LETTERS:

1. Destination—the church to whom the letter is addressed is clearly named.
2. Description—the writer, the Lord Jesus Christ, is described in each letter in a way most *appropriate* to the situation of that church.
3. Commendation—the good qualities and strengths of each congregation is recognized. If the perfect Saviour does this before pointing out faults, we who are ourselves sinful may well take heed to this lesson. Note that the expression "I know thy works" is said to every church.
4. Deficiency—the serious fault or faults of each assembly is brought to their attention. The faults exposed are in each case crucial; they are never petty. Lesson? Only Smyrna, the suffering church, and Philadelphia, the weak church, have no deficiency named. And these, surprisingly enough, are the two locations today—out of the seven—where Christian churches still actually exist.
5. Demand and Remedy—the Lord makes an authoritative command and offers a remedy for each church's problem. Do we likewise always offer a remedy when we expose a fault?
6. Discrimination—"He that hath an ear, let him hear what the Spirit saith to the churches" (2:7; etc.). Here those with spiritual sense are urged to act. Some have not this ear; they will not change.
7. Promise—a promise is held out to each to encourage its reformation. In every case the promise is *appropriate* to the church at hand. Here is another lesson for us. How gracious is the Lord of the churches; how quick to mercy is He.

GEOGRAPHY

The seven cities wherein the seven churches addressed were located formed approximately a circle 100 miles in diameter in the Roman province of Asia (Western Turkey). Sir William Ramsay, the archeological master, said that these seven cities formed the "Great Circle Postal Route" of the province. If one started at Ephesus (at the "7" position on the clock) and traveled clockwise, he would pass through all seven of the cities in their Biblical order by the time he reached Laodicea (at the "5" position). Within this circle Christ walked in Revelation 2:1.

Revelation 2

CHAPTER 2

Unto the angel of the church of Eph-e-
sus write; These things saith he that holdeth the seven stars in his right hand, who
walketh in the midst of the seven golden
candlesticks;

Rev. 1:20
Rev. 1:12,13,20

Commentary

1. Ephesus was the largest city in Asia Minor, and it was the capital of
the province. Paul started the church here and it became the Christian
capital of Asia. Paul's visits to Ephesus are recorded in Acts 18:19-21;
chapter 19; and 20:17-38 (here he speaks to the Ephesian elders who
came to Miletus, 30 miles S. of Ephesus). Paul spent over two years in
Ephesus during his Third Missionary Journey and this is no doubt the
reason for the strong church which grew in this city (c. A.D. 55-57; Acts
19:8,10). He also wrote the two Corinthian epistles while at Ephesus. It
was here, also, that John spent the latter part of his life and from here
wrote his gospel and epistles.

The magnificance of ancient Ephesus can be seen in Acts 19 by the
importance assigned to its religious and political life. Ruins and a small
village now are the only remains.

To this church which has lost its first love (vs. 4) and which is in danger
of losing its life as a church (vs. 5) Christ comes as the sustainer of the
church's life. He holds the star of this church, its angel, in His hand. He
comes to them now as the one "walking in the midst of the seven golden
candlesticks." Thus He is actively *walking* about seeing the true condition of each church and doing whatsoever is necessary to trim their
light. He sees; He is near; He is working!

This knowledge that Christ walks amid His congregations—for these
seven are typical of all—should make all Christians take heart and take
heed.

Greek goddess, Artemis, known to the Romans as Diana. The Artemis of Ephesus was a fertility goddess. She was portrayed as a mature woman with a large number of breasts and various fertility symbols.

Background

One of the Seven Wonders of the World was considered to be in Ephesus. Here stood the largest and most magnificent Temple of Artemis built to the goddess Diana. Artemis was her Greek name; Diana was Roman.

The cult of Diana encouraged much trade. Silversmiths had a prosperous business selling silver shrines and images of Diana (Acts 19:23ff). The image of Artemis (Diana) was one of the most sacred images in the ancient world. It was by no means beautiful. The image depicted her as a lewd goddess having four rows of breasts. Legalized prostitution dominated the city.

Ephesus was considered "The Market of Asia." At one time it was the wealthiest and greatest city in all Asia. Heraclitus, an ancient philosopher, was known as the "weeping philosopher." His explanation of his own tears was that no one could live in Ephesus without weeping at the immorality which he must see on every side.

But sin has its day of judgment and today the place where the temple of Artemis stood is a swamp...the ruins of the temple have sunk into the ground and vanished.

PAST	PRESENT	RAPTURE	FIRST 3 1/2 TRIBULATION	LAST 3 1/2	ARMA-GEDDON	MIL-LENNIUM	NEW HEAVENS & EARTH

Revelation 2

2 I know thy works, and thy labour, and thy patience, and how thou canst not bear them which are evil: and thou hast tried them which say they are apostles, and are not, and hast found them liars:

3 And hast borne, and hast patience, and for my name's sake hast laboured, and hast not fainted.

4 Nevertheless I have *somewhat* against thee, because thou hast left thy first love.

5 Remember therefore from whence thou art fallen, and repent, and do the first works; or else I will come unto thee quickly, and will remove thy candlestick out of his place, except thou repent.

VERSES 2,3,4,5

2 Chron. 19:2; 20:35
Matt. 7:15
Gal. 1:8,9

Matt. 19:29

I Cor. 13:1-3

Commentary

2. Christ who walks among His candlesticks sees how they are burning. He is not a judge who can never be pleased; here He commends the works (accomplishments), labor (toil), and patience of this church. He praises their careful scrutiny of those who claim to be prophets and their rejection of the evil false prophets. Today, so many churches and professed Christians shake hands with and applaud the modernists; but at least at Ephesus Christ could say with approval, "Thou canst not bear them which are evil."

3. This church had suffered for Christ's name; yet it continued on without fainting.

4. "Nevertheless...thou hast left thy first love"—Despite the above good qualities, there existed here a serious wound. The original zeal and love for the Saviour once possessed had now decayed into "church work" and routine. How many Christians and how many assemblies have fallen from their "first love"? The wife no longer enraptured with her husband as on their honeymoon...the church no longer enraptured with her Saviour. No amount of works can make up for this (1 Cor. 13:1-3).

5. Here the command is to repent or to forfeit your life as a church. The flaw is a mortal wound unless repaired immediately. Christ can remove the lampstand of the unprofitable light...and, alas, today the Ephesian church is no more.

PAST	PRESENT	RAPTURE	FIRST 3 1/2 LAST 3 1/2 TRIBULATION		ARMA- GEDDON	MIL- LENNIUM	NEW HEAVENS & EARTH

Revelation 2

6 But this thou hast, that thou hatest the deeds of the Nic-o-la-i-tanes, which I also hate.

7 He that hath an ear, let him hear what the Spirit saith unto the churches; To him that overcometh will I give to eat of the tree of life, which is in the midst of the paradise of God.

Rev. 2:15

Commentary

6. Another commendation comes forward now—lest they be crushed and despair that the Saviour cannot be pleased. They hate the Nicolaitanes. Who were these? Some suggest that these were those who first wished to establish a heirarchy in the church. *Nikao* in the Greek means, "to conquer," and *laos, "people"—hence, conquerors* of the *laity.* Ignatius and Irenaeus, second century church fathers, however, said that these comprised a group who lived immorally.

7. "He that hath an ear"—Full well does the Lord know that all will not truly hear His words of counsel, but those who will hear are urged to do so. "To hear" here means to take to heart and to act.

Here the promise to the overcomer is eternal life. How fitting this is when we consider that the church at Ephesus is in danger of losing its existence (vs. 5). How does one overcome? Rev. 12:11 and Zech. 4:6 give the answer.

What lessons do we learn from this first epistle for our own church and for our own lives? "He that hath an ear let him hear what the Spirit saith unto the churches."

Does this letter not fit the *Apostolic Church era of A.D. 30-100?*

PAST	PRESENT	RAPTURE	FIRST 3½ / LAST 3½ TRIBULATION	ARMA-GEDDON	MIL-LENNIUM	NEW HEAVENS & EARTH

8 And unto the angel of the church in Smyrna write; These things saith the first and the last, which was dead, and is alive; 9 I know thy works, and tribulation, and poverty, but thou art rich and *I know* the blasphemy of them which say they are Jews, and are not, but *are* the synagogue of Satan.

Rev. 2:2
I Cor. 1:26; Mk. 10:25
Rom. 2:28-29
Rom. 10:2

Commentary

8. Some 35 miles N. of Ephesus lies the port city of Smyrna which was known as one of the great cities of the region and as a faithful ally of Rome. During the reign of Tiberius an earthquake devestated the city; yet it survived and rebuilt its buildings in new splendor about its hill, Pagus. The city's coinage bore the inscription, "First in Asia in beauty and size."

Paul may have visited this wealthy city of over 100,000 people when he spent his over two years in nearby Ephesus (Acts 19:8,10). Perhaps he himself started the church here; perhaps not (Acts 19:10)?

To this persecuted church (vs. 10) Christ comes as the Deity who can save them, "the first and the last;" and as the One who has Himself died and conquered death—"which was dead and is alive." To those facing death there could be no more appropriate way for the Saviour to appear.

9. Christ here commends their works and their tribulation for His name's sake. He assures them that they are rich in heavenly rewards although they are financially poor. Since Christ will be the final judge of every man (Matt. 7:21-23; Rom. 14:10-12) His audit of their account is of supreme significance.

Although more Gentiles, disobedient to the teachings of Christ, have harmed the Jews than vice versa, the believers in Smyrna were receiving persecution even from the Jews. The death of Polycarp, A.D. 155, was due in a major part to the demands of the Jews of Smyrna (P. Schaff, *History of the Christian Church,* II, p. 37).

Ismir, the gateway to Bible lands of Turkey. In Bible times Ismir was known as Smyrna. Today it is a thriving port.

Background

Smyrna was the safest of all harbors, and the most convenient. Smyrna was one of the very few planned cities of the world. Most famous of its streets was the "Street of Gold," which began with the Temple of Zeus (supreme deity of ancient Greeks) and ended with the Temple of Cybele (goddess of nature). Smyrna was well known for her loyalty and fidelity. When the soldiers of Rome were suffering from hunger and from cold, the people of Smyrna had stripped off their own clothes to send them to the Roman soldiers in trouble.

The "synagogue of Satan" reminds us of the early persecution inflicted against the Christians by some of the Jews. Such persecution occurred at Antioch (Acts 13:50); at Iconium (Acts 14:2,5); at Lystra (Acts 14:19); at Thessalonica (Acts 17:5).

There was a large Jewish population in wealthy, flourishing Smyrna. Some of them sought to blot out the infant Christian church. Their error, of course, in no way justifies persecution against the Jews or any other people. The Bible's desire is, rather, to weep for their conversion (Romans 10:1).

▼

PAST	PRESENT	RAPTURE	FIRST 3 1/2 LAST 3 1/2 TRIBULATION	ARMA– GEDDON	MIL– LENNIUM	NEW HEAVENS &EARTH

Revelation 2

10 Fear none of those things which thou shalt suffer: behold, the devil shall cast *some* of you into prison, that ye may be tried; and ye shall have tribulation ten days: be thou faithful unto death, and I will give thee a crown of life.

11 He that hath an ear, let him hear what the Spirit saith unto the churches; He that overcometh shall not be hurt of the second death.

Matt. 28:20;
I Cor. 15:50-58
I Cor. 4:2

Rev. 20:11-15

Definition:
Death—*Death in the Bible is separation. Physical death is the separation of the soul from the body. Spiritual death is separation from God. Thus the final separation from God, when the wicked are cast into the Lake of Fire, is called the "Second Death" (Rev. 20:11-15). The penalty for sin is death (Gen. 2:17; Ezek. 18:4); yet Christ has paid this penalty for everyone who will trust in Him (1 Pet. 3:18).*

Commentary

10. When the devil casts some of them into prison, human eyes will only see his followers doing the deeds. It was Satan who was behind Herod earlier trying to slay the Christ child (Rev. 12:4), but men could see only Herod. Satan's servants, ironically enough, may even believe themselves to be serving God and humanity (John 16:2).

The reward for faithfulness unto death is fittingly a "crown of life." Here the word for crown is not *diadema* (as in 12:3; 13:1; 19:12) which refers to the *regal crown* worn by a king; but it is *stephanos* (2:10; 3:11; 4:4,10; 6:2; 9:7; 12:1; 14:14) which is the *victor's crown.* This crown of leaves was awarded to a champion in the games or to a Roman commander who had won a "triumph." Recall here the name of the Church's first martyr—*Stephanos* (Acts 7:59)! The meaningfulness of Christ's promise to Smyrna is further enlarged when we realize that the Hill Pagus with its splendid buildings was called, "The Crown of Smyrna."

11. The overcoming one will have immunity from the "second death" (Rev. 20:11-15). The one way to avoid this second and final death is by receiving Christ as Saviour and thus allowing His death to pay our penalty (Rev. 12:11; Acts 16:31).

No fault is mentioned to this poor but faithful church. And as "Smyrna" means bitter and is related to the aromatic "myrrh;" so too as in the case of myrrh, its fragrance comes from its being crushed.

Does this epistle correspond with the era of the *Persecuted Church of A.D. 100-313?* Could not the "tribulation ten days" (vs. 10) foreshadow the *ten* imperial persecutions that the Church of this epoch passed through at the hands of the Roman emperors?

This donkey is a familiar sight in Jerusalem plodding up a hill over-worked and overburdened...but faithful. How often the Christian suffers trials that seem unbearable...but God!

Background

The Christians of Smyrna were poor and severely persecuted. Poor, because they were plundered and deprived of their right to work. For the most part, they possessed little of this earth's goods.

To add to their misery, some were cast into prison. In the ancient world imprisonment was merely a prelude to death. A man was only a prisoner until he was led out to die.

The famous minister to Smyrna in that day was Polycarp. It was the custom once a year for all to give allegiance to Caesar by saying "Caesar is Lord." This Polycarp refused to do. It was the season for olympian games in Smyrna; the year was about 155 A.D. Suddenly the howling crowds cried for Polycarp. When he entered the arena the proconsul gave him the choice of cursing the name of Christ and making sacrifice to Caesar or death.

Polycarp's reply: "Eighty and six years have I served Him and He has done me no wrong. How can I blaspheme my King who saved me?" And with that Polycarp was burned at the stake by the Romans with the help of Jews who (even though it was their Sabbath...and Sabbath laws prohibited carrying such burdens) helped bring wood for the fire.

PAST	PRESENT	RAPTURE	FIRST 3 1/2 LAST 3 1/2 TRIBULATION	ARMA-GEDDON	MIL-LENNIUM	NEW HEAVENS &EARTH
			FIRST 3 1/2 | LAST 3 1/2			

Revelation 2

12 And to the angel of the church in Per-
ga-mos write; These things saith he
which hath the sharp sword with two
edges;
13 I know thy works, and where thou
dwellest, *even* where Satan's seat *is:* and
thou holdest fast my name, and hast not
denied my faith, even in those days
wherein An-ti-pas *was* my faithful martyr,
who was slain among you, where Satan
dwelleth.
14 But I have a few things against thee,
because thou hast there them that hold
the doctrine of Balaam, who taught Balac
to cast a stumblingblock before the children of Israel, to eat things sacrificed unto
idols, and to commit fornication.

Numb. chs. 22-25

DEFINITION
*Acropolis—from the Greek akron, top; polis, city—hence the high forti-
fied hill-city that was characteristic of nearly every Greek city-state.
The one in Athens is best known.*

Commentary

12-13. Pergamos is inland and 60 miles N. of Smyrna. It was the capital
of Asia before this was moved to Ephesus. Here stood a 200,000
volume library second only to that in Alexandria; and thus it is not
strange that the word *parchment* is derived from the name of this city.
Here among the gods, the deity of medicine, Aesculapius, was honored
("scalpel") often with the sign of a snake (Cp. Numb. 21:8-9). Upon the
city's acropolis stood the Temple of Athena and the great altar to Zeus
which had a base over 100 foot square. These stood 800 foot above the
plain and fittingly could be described as "Satan's Seat" (vs. 13). Others,
however, feel that Pergamos was Satan's seat because here in its three
Imperial Temples the Roman emperor worshipping cult flourished.

14. The doctrine of Balaam (Numb. chs. 22-25) was the encouraging
of Israelites to marry pagan wives; hence here in Pergamos it no doubt
refers to those who teach that it is permissible to mix Christianity and
paganism. The Saviour comes with a sharp sword (vs. 12) to cut these
apart. Any who today further the mixing of believers with the modernists
or -ism cults perpetuate this sin.

"Satan's Throne" in Pergamos may have been this altar to Zeus. A serpent was also used as a symbol of worship.

Background

Pergamos was at the center of the province of Asia and was the place where the state religion was most thoroughly promoted; that is, the worship of emperors.

South of the Athena Temple stood a gigantic altar of Zeus, another of the Seven Wonders of the World. Over 100 feet square and forty feet high, it was the largest and most famous altar in the world. Its appearance was somewhat like a throne; thus possibly "Satan's seat."

Here in Pergamos, with its seat of Satan, a Christian named Antipas died for Christ. Perhaps during Nero's reign (54-68 A.D.)? We know little of Antipas, but God has recorded his name.

And there were those in Pergamos who compromised the Gospel. How often have you heard the cry, "Sure we're Christians but everyone else does it. Do you want us to stick out like a sore thumb...lose our friendships?"

PAST	PRESENT	RAPTURE	FIRST 3½ TRIBULATION	LAST 3½	ARMA– GEDDON	MIL– LENNIUM	NEW HEAVENS & EARTH

Revelation 2

VERSES 15,16,17

15 So hast thou also them that hold the doctrine of the Nic-o-la-i-tanes, which thing I hate.

16 Repent; or else I will come unto thee quickly, and will fight against them with the sword of my mouth.

17 He that hath an ear, let him hear what the Spirit saith unto the churches; To him that overcometh will I give to eat of the hidden manna, and will give him a white stone, and in the stone a new name written, which no man knoweth saving he that receiveth it.

Rev. 2:6

Rev. 19:15; Heb. 4:12

Exod. 16:15;
John 6:31,58
3:12; 13:17; 19:12

Commentary

15. Where one sin is allowed to thrive (Balaamism, vs. 14), a second is not far behind, Nicolaitanism (See 2:6).

16. Christ speaks, and it is done; His word is thus a swift sword of judgment. The command to "repent" *(metanoeo—meta,* "change;" *noeo* referring to the "mind") is an imperative to change one's attitude toward a sin *and* to act from that time on according to this new attitude.

17. Again these words and their divine admonitions are held out for the one who has a heart and willingness to heed them. Both the imperial temples devoted to the emperor and those dedicated to the gods prided themselves in holding "secrets." The health resorts of Pergamos also had its mysteries. Now the Christian was shut out of the temples and their secrets. Yet, however, in Pergamos some evil ones were advocating a permissive mixture. Christ holding the sword of separation (vs. 12) now in this verse, vs. 17, promises to the one who follows Him better secrets than any of the pagan mystery cults are able to offer—hidden manna and a new name. Which will they choose?

The word Pergamos itself seems to be derived from: *pergos,* "tower" and *gamos,* "marriage" (J.B. Smith). This makes us think of the city's "tower" to Athena and Zeus and to its "marriage" of Christianity with paganism. Was not this the ailment of the *State Church of A.D. 313-590* which mixed its Christianity with its now-Christian emperors? It has been said that since Satan could not drive the Church out of the world by persecution during the Smyrna period (A.D. 100-313), he attempted to drive the world into the Church in the Pergamos era (A.D. 313-590).

PAST	PRESENT	RAPTURE	FIRST 3½ / LAST 3½ TRIBULATION		ARMA-GEDDON	MIL-LENNIUM	NEW HEAVENS & EARTH

18 And unto the angel of the church in Thy-a-ti-ra write; These things saith the Son of God, who hath his eyes like unto a flame of fire, and his feet *are* like fine brass;

Rev. 1:14
Rev. 1:15

19 I know thy works, and charity, and service, and faith, and thy patience, and thy works; and the last *to be* more than the first.

Rev. 2:4-5

Commentary

18. Forty miles SE of Pergamos lies Thyatira now occupied by the small village of Akhiser. It is said that it was named by its founder, Seleucus Nicator (a 3d century B.C. ruler of Greek origin), as *Thugatira,* "daughter," upon the news of such a birth to himself and his wife. J. B. Smith, the Greek lexicographer, however, takes it from *thuos,* "sacrifice," and *ateires,* "unweary"—hence, "Unweary of sacrifice."

Thyatira was famous for its commerce and it had a main road passing through it. It is believed that this city had in it more of the trade guilds than did any other city in Asia. Lydia, the seller of purple, was from Thyatira and was most likely the representative of that guild in the city of Philippi (Acts 16:14). The city was known for its cloth production and for its bronze. No evidence has yet been found of an imperial temple here. Did Paul (Acts 19:10) or Lydia (Acts 16:14) start the church in Thyatira??? No one knows.

Christ comes here as the judge who sees with omniscient eyes what is going on in the church of this city, and He comes ready to judge it with His brazen feet. It may be that even here we have allusions which exactly fit this city—the eyes of fire being the color of the famed "turkey-red" Thyatira cloth and the brass (*chalkolibonos,* bronze, brass, or a related metal alloy) boots being one of the city's glorious products.

19. Her latter works, accomplishments, were greater than even her earlier ones. (The Greek construction shows this to be the meaning more clearly than does the English. Gk: "...and the works of you the last-ones more than the first-ones.").

▼

PAST	PRESENT	RAPTURE	FIRST 3 1/2 LAST 3 1/2 TRIBULATION		ARMA– GEDDON	MIL– LENNIUM	NEW HEAVENS & EARTH

Revelation 2

20 Notwithstanding I have a few things against thee, because thou sufferest that woman Jez-e-bel, which calleth herself a prophetess, to teach and to seduce my servants to commit fornication, and to eat things sacrificed unto idols.

VERSE 20

1 Kg. 16:31; chs. 18,19, 21; 2 Kg. 9
Rev. 17:2-6
Rom. 14

Definition

Suffer—*In most cases when this English word is used it means what it usually does to us of the 20th century,* viz., *to experience discomfort and agony. In 1611, however, when the King James Version was translated "to suffer" also meant "to permit, to allow." The word is used in this sense in vs. 20.*

Fornication—porneia *in the Greek, hence our word, "pornography." This word refers to any serious breech of sexual morality, and hence is used also to picture those who forsake the one true God for heathen worship. In 1 Cor. 5:1 the word is used to depict* incest *which is immorality within one's own family—in this case it is* adultery, *one with his "father's wife." In Rev. 17:1 the Great Harlot* (porne) *is guilty of "fornication" (17:2),* porneia, *which here is mass sexual sin and adultery. It here denotes spiritual harlotry. Care should be taken not to limit this word to the* English *meaning which "fornication" has in certain states, namely, sin between the unmarried. Rev. 2:22, compared with 2:20, shows that the Greek word "fornication" encompasses "adultery."*

Commentary

20. Whether the woman "Jezebel" represents an actual woman who was spreading the error, or whether this was some type of movement is not known. The original Jezebel led her husband, Ahab, King of Israel, into Baal worship and murder (1 Kg 16:31 ff). Just as she led Ahab into spiritual fornication, some woman or group was leading this church into a similar sin. "To eat things sacrificed unto idols," would indicate that the church was being led into somehow imbibing some part of the surrounding pagan worship. With all this the Christians here "suffer" her "to teach." Strange? How many born again believers "allow" the modernists "to teach"?

The Altar of Zeus Temple foundation. Pergamos.

Background

The source of trouble in Thyatira was centered around a woman called Jezebel. This woman Jezebel is accused of teaching two things: (1) teaching the Christian people to commit fornication and (2) to eat meat offered to idols.

Often the best meat was that which had been offered to idols. And with the meat, here in Thyatira came the idolatrous customs and ceremonies. Here is where the Jezebel cult came in. It was insisted that there was no harm in accepting the world's customs and the world's ways. In effect it was saying if the standards of the Word of God clashed with business interests, then the standards of God in those instances must be abandoned.

The Jezebel cult would argue that there was no harm in conforming to the outward rituals and ceremonies of this world...that by being sensible in these things, we will win the heathen much more easily.

PAST	PRESENT	RAPTURE	FIRST 3 1/2 LAST 3 1/2 TRIBULATION		ARMA–GEDDON	MIL–LENNIUM	NEW HEAVENS & EARTH

Revelation 2

21 And I gave her space to repent of her fornication; and she repented not.

22 Behold, I will cast her into a bed, and them that commit adultery with her into great tribulation, except they repent of their deeds.

23 And I will kill her children with death; and all the churches shall know that I am he which searcheth the reins and hearts: and I will give unto every one of you according to your works.

24 But unto you I say, and unto the rest in Thy-a-ti-ra, as many as have not this doctrine, and which have not known the depths of Satan, as they speak; I will put upon you none other burden.

25 But that which ye have *already* hold fast till I come.

VERSES 21,22, 23, 24, 25

Lk. 13:6-9

Matt. 24:21
Ezek. 33:11-15

I Cor. 3:13-15

Commentary

21. God gives to even the most wicked an opportunity to repent (Lk. 13:6-9; 2 Pet. 3:9).

22-23. Continuing with the figure of spiritual fornication and adultery, it is here declared that both this false prophetess and those who follow her (those that commit adultery with her) and those produced from this mixture (her children, vs. 23) would all perish. Here we should note that the Alogi claimed that no church existed in Thyatira at the end of the second century.

From God's judgment on those who partake and those who are produced by this Jezebel doctrine all would know that Christ is the One who sees within man and who rewards all as they deserve.

Christ is still speaking; and no one but God could make these claims. He is the divine Son, the second person of the Trinity.

24-25. The Jezebel teaching drinks of the "depths of Satan," and so was of the most serious type of sin.

Does Christ expect perfection? Yes and no! Here He sees the tremendous temptation in this situation and thus says that if the believers can stay out of this sin He will not add to them at this time any new additional duties. He is an understanding Saviour.

The banquet table of the world is tempting often leading Christians to compromise just as in the days of the church of Thyatira.

Background

Oftentimes compromise with the world may occur over what some may term an "insignificant" thing.

One of the greatest problems of the Church at that time was the problem of meat offered to idols. And it was an everyday problem.

When a man made a sacrifice in a Greek temple in Thyatira, very little of the actual meat was burned on the altar. In some instances all that was actually burned was a few hairs cut from the animal.

Then the worshipper, who offered the sacrifice, called his friends, and invited them to the Temple to join him in a banquet.

Could a Christian go to a feast which was held in a heathen temple? Or for that matter, whether in the temple or out, could he eat meat offered to idols? See 1 Corinthians 8.

PAST	PRESENT	RAPTURE	FIRST 3½ LAST 3½ TRIBULATION	ARMA-GEDDON	MIL-LENNIUM	NEW HEAVENS &EARTH

Revelation 2

26 And he that overcometh, and keepeth my works unto the end, to him will I
give power over the nations:

Rev. 12:11

27 And he shall rule them with a rod of
iron; as the vessels of a potter shall they
be broken to shivers: even as I received
of my Father.

*Psa. 2:9; Rev. 12:5;
20:6*

28 And I will give him the morning star.

29 He that hath an ear, let him hear what
the Spirit saith unto the churches.

*Rev. 22:16; 2 Pet. 1:19
cp. 1 Th. 4:13-18*

Definition

Rapture—*The first phase of the Second Coming of Christ. Here Christ
comes FOR His church (1 Thess. 4:13-18). Later, at the end of 7 years
of tribulation (Dan. 9:27; Matt. 24:21) Christ comes WITH His Church at
His Revelation (Rev. 19:11-20:2) in the final phase of the Second
Coming.*

Commentary

26-27. The problem is one of authority and of ruling well. They are
suffering Jezebel to teach; they should not tolerate this and thus they
are not ruling well. Perhaps this Jezebel herself has great power or is
protected by someone either in Roman or Christian influence? In any
case, to the one who overcomes Christ promises the privilege of ruling
in authority with Him over the nations (during the Millennium). What
finer promise could be given to those in Thyatira daily frustrated by
seeing Jezebel "allowed...to teach" among the Christians (vs. 20)?

28-29. The "morning star" is another of those countless allusions
wherein Scripture tells us something in a mystery form but does not
explain it fully. This is one of the reasons that one can read the Bible
again and again without experiencing the boredom characteristic of
rereading other books. Fools fight over such things and dogmatically
assert the correctness of their view when in truth there is insufficient
evidence for super-dogmatism (See Titus 3:9).

The allusion here may well refer to being present at the Rapture (2 Pet.
1:19 compared with 1 Thess. 4:13-18).

Does not Thyatira with its later works surpassing its former (vs. 19) and
with its Jezebel teaching a blending of paganism with Christianity well
depict the *Medieval Papal Church of A.D. 590-1517*? Could her children
be apostate Protestantism?

All that is left of the grandeur of Nebuchadnezar's Palace, 6th. Century, B.C. Man-made castles soon crumble with time. In Christ alone is eternal life (2 Corinthians 5:1-4).

Background

There is a warning here for Christians. A church which is crowded with people and is a dynamo of activity is not automatically a true church. How many churches do you know that are crowded because people come to it to be entertained instead of instructed...to be soothed, instead of challenged.

Too many of today's churches become highly successful Christian clubs rather than a dedicated, humble group desirous of winning others to Christ rather than heaping benefits on self.

The state of the church at Thyatira should direct us to examine our own lives and the direction of the church in which we worship.

▼

PAST	PRESENT	RAPTURE	FIRST 3 1/2	LAST 3 1/2	ARMA-GEDDON	MIL-LENNIUM	NEW HEAVENS & EARTH
			TRIBULATION				

Revelation 3

CHAPTER 3   *VERSE 1*

And unto the angel of the church in Sardis write; These things saith he that hath the seven Spirits of God, and the seven stars; I know thy works, that thou hast a name that thou livest, and art dead.

Rev. 1:4
Rev. 1:20
Heb. 6:1; 9:14; Jas. 2:20

Commentary

1. Thirty-three miles SE of Thyatira stands Sardis with its now partially eroded but once impregnable steep-sided acropolis. Sitting within the Hermus-Gediz fertile river valley and on one of the heights of the Tmolus Range, a commercial route running by, Sardis in antiquity was the portrait of strength, fertility, and wealth. Sardis was the capital of Lydia, whose King Croesus was famed for his riches, and here at this time Aesop told his politically meaningful fables. Sardis fell to King Cyrus and the Persians in 546 B.C. after Croesus lost the Battle of the Halys River. The city was made the capital of the Satrap—a Persian state. Two centuries later in 330 B.C. Alexander conquered it for Greece.

In A.D. 17 an earthquake destroyed the city, but Tiberius the Roman emperor rebuilt the city and cancelled its taxes for five years. Thus began an affinity for Rome which probably lasted until the 11th century when it was captured by the Turks. Destroyed in 1402 A.D. by Tamerlane; only its ruins remain.

Cybele was chief goddess of the city, and two columns of her temple yet stand. Wealth and immorality were its reputation. Melito of Sardis, a 2nd century bishop, wrote an interpretation of the Book of Revelation—probably the first ever written.

This church had "a name," that is, a good reputation, and it appeared to be alive to human eyes; yet God who sees the inner spirit declared it to be dead. To this group the Lord comes as the One having "the seven spirits of God," i.e., as the One possessing the all-seeing all-present Holy Spirit. Thus the Spirit's piercing look saw the inward deadness of this church despite its outward busyness. Christ comes also holding the seven stars (1:20). Thus He reminds them that it is He who yet controls the true ministry of this busy but inwardly dead church. He holds these stars—the church's owner and Lord is not the Pastor, the elders, the congregation; it is Jesus.

PAST	PRESENT	RAPTURE	FIRST 3½ LAST 3½ TRIBULATION		ARMA- GEDDON	MIL- LENNIUM	NEW HEAVENS & EARTH

2 Be watchful, and strengthen the things which remain, that are ready to die: for I have not found thy works perfect before God.

3 Remember therefore how thou has received and heard, and hold fast, and repent. If therefore thou shalt not watch, I will come on thee as a thief, and thou shalt not know what hour I will come upon thee.

Mk. 14:37-38
Gen. 6:9; 17:1

Jer. 18:8
Matt. 24:43-44;
I Thess. 5:2

Commentary

2. Here we see that the words, "Thou...art dead," of verse 1 describe a condition that is essentially and generally true, but that the final death has not yet come. It is as if in verse 1 a physician tells a person bitten by a Cobra, "You are a dead man." and then in verse 2 he adds, "That is, unless you take this anti-venom which I have which can save your life." So here, not all is yet dead—some things remain, but these too are ready to die. Then all will be gone. Certainly this group, as in most of the other churches, has not been "watchful." Thus the Great Physician gives them a correct and honest diagnosis—not a pleasing one—and urges them to take remedial steps.

3. The commands of verses 2 and 3 are significant: watch, strengthen, remember, hold fast, and repent. These are the chemical components of the antidote prescribed. If these *instructions*—for they are commands from the Lord, not merely good advice—are ignored, then sudden judgment will overtake them.

God often waits and pleads with man to repent...He waits...and waits (2 Pet. 3:9)...and then, as the flood in Noah's day, judgment strikes suddenly. Yet even here in Sardis, as long as some life exists, there is still opportunity to avert the judgment (Jer. 18:8).

The coming of Christ to Sardis for judgment is like "a thief" in one respect only; they both come without warning, suddenly, and as a surprise. In this respect, also, the Second Coming of Christ will be like the midnight arrival of a thief. Suddenly He will come at the Rapture for His Church (Matt. 24:43-44) and suddenly will He come upon the unrepentant in the judgments of the Tribulation Period (1 Thess. 5:2).

PAST	PRESENT	RAPTURE	FIRST 3 1/2	LAST 3 1/2	ARMA-GEDDON	MIL-LENNIUM	NEW HEAVENS & EARTH
			TRIBULATION				

4 Thou hast a few names even in Sardis which have not defiled their garments; and they shall walk with me in white: for they are worthy.

5 He that overcometh, the same shall be clothed in white raiment; and I will not blot out his name out of the book of life, but I will confess his name before my Father, and before his angels.

6 He that hath an ear, let him hear what the Spirit saith unto the churches.

Isa. 56:3-7

Rev. 12:11
Matt. 22:11-13;
Rom. 4:5
Rev. 13:8; 22:19
Matt. 10:32; Lk. 12:8

Commentary

4. The deadness in Sardis was at least partially due to some type of defilement. The majority of the church had "defiled" (Gk. *moluno*—to stain, dirty, defile, make impure) their garments—their holiness and testimony had been soiled amid the soil of Sardis. Yet to those who were unstained, Christ pledges, "They shall walk with me [dressed] in white, for they are worthy." Remaining clean now will produce an eternal compensation.

5-6. To the "Overcomer"—who is victorious by faith in the blood of Christ—is the promise that he shall forever be clothed in the white robes of justification from sin (Rev. 12:11; Matt. 22:11-13; Rom. 4:5). This one will be allowed to continue to live; Jesus will confess him before the heavenly throng. Thus amid the defilement of the city, and amid the deadness in the church, when it appears that no one notices the few who still stay true to God, yet here the One who has "the seven spirits of God" (vs. 1)—who is all present—sees and will reward accordingly (Psa. 33:16-22). He will confess us in heaven if we confess Him on earth. *If* we confess the One who deserves all praise, whose name it is wicked to deny; *then* He will confess us as unworthy as we be! Oh the graciousness of the Lord!

What lesson can we learn from this church concerning appearances and reality?

Does not the professing Church in *1517-1790, the Reformed Church,* fit the Sardis picture? Did the Protestant Reformation not seek to "strengthen the things which remain, that are ready to die" out of a Western Catholic Church of works and an Eastern Church which no longer reached the people?

HISTORY REPEATS ITSELF *Russian Foreign Minister Molotov signing non-aggression pact with Germany, August 24, 1939.*

Chancellor Willy Brandt of West Germany and Premier Aleksei N. Kosygin of Soviet Union sign new treaty in Moscow, August 12, 1970.

Background

What a contrast! Here was the Church at Sardis who had a reputation for life...but, indeed, was spiritually dead!

And this once wealthy city was destroyed by an earthquake in A.D. 17. The Roman Emperor donated an equivalent to over $1 million dollars towards rebuilding Sardis. Such recovery came so easily that it again became complacent. Centuries later in 1402 the Turks thoroughly destroyed the city.

Sardis was an excellent example of a church that Paul said, had a form of godliness but denied the power thereof (2 Timothy 3:5).

For the church in Sardis, perhaps its greatest sin was complacency. Throughout the New Testament Christ tells us to WATCH (Romans 13:11, 1 Corinthians 16:13, 1 Peter 5:8).

Today, perhaps as never before in history, dedicated Christians have come under great attack—some forceful...some cunning wiles of the devil (Matthew 26:41). To compromise or be self-sufficient is allowing the "helmet" to fall over the battlements of your testimony...to expose a crack...to let Satan come in...and eventually control and destroy.

PAST	PRESENT	RAPTURE	FIRST 3 1/2 LAST 3 1/2 TRIBULATION	ARMA-GEDDON	MIL-LENNIUM	NEW HEAVENS & EARTH

7 And to the angel of the church in Philadelphia write; These things saith he that is holy, he that is true, he that hath the key of David, he that openeth, and no man shutteth; and shutteth, and no man openeth;

8 I know thy works: behold, I have set before thee an open door, and no man can shut it: for thou hast a little strength, and hast kept my word, and hast not denied my name.

Isa. 9:7; Rev. 1:18

Commentary

7-8. Twenty-five miles SE of Sardis on an 800 foot rise stood Philadelphia. It was situated in the Cogamus Valley and the Roman road which ran tangent to it opened the way from the Aegean-Mediterranean Sea to the upper plateau of Asia in the N. called Phrygia. Philadelphia truly was a "door" amid the mountains.

The city was named for its founder, Attalus II, the Greek King of Pergamum. He lived in the middle of the 2nd century B.C., and because of his loyalty to his brother, Eumenes, he received the title, "Philadelphos" (Gk. *phileo*—love; *adelphos*—brother).

In the period of hellenization this city spread the Greek language and culture until it was destroyed by the earthquake of A.D. 17.

This was the last of the seven to fall to the Turks, and it fell at the close of the 14th century A.D. Today, however, a Christian church once again resides here.

To this city which well understood how a little strength in a narrow valley corridor could hold back a stronger army, Christ comes as the final authority on matters of opening and shutting. If He opens any avenue of opportunity no force can shut it; if He closes the door to any opposition, it cannot enter!

This church has not much strength, but to it He announces that He has already opened for them a door of testimony and success and thus it can be closed by no one. What lesson does this have for us???

That He comes as the One who is holy and true (vs. 7) shows that: (1) His promise to open the door must be true; and (2) that the door must be open for only a holy purpose. His possessing the Key of David means that He has the authority and power (for this is what a key signifies) to sit on the Throne of David as the rightful Messiah-King (Isa. 9:7). He is therefore greater than Pharaoh or Caesar. Hallelujah! See Psa. 33:16-22.

PAST	PRESENT	RAPTURE	FIRST 3½	LAST 3½	ARMA-GEDDON	MIL-LENNIUM	NEW HEAVENS & EARTH
			TRIBULATION				

Revelation 3

9 Behold, I will make them of the syna-gogue of Satan, which say they are Jews, and are not, but do lie; behold, I will make them to come and worship before thy feet, and to know that I have loved thee. 10 Because thou hast kept the word of my patience, I also will keep thee from the hour of temptation, which shall come upon all the world, to try them that dwell upon the earth.

Rev. 2:9
Rom. 2:28-29
Phil. 2:10

Matt. 24:21-22
Dan. 12:1

Commentary

9. Romans 2:28-29 (which see) contains Paul's summation concerning what constitutes a true Jew. A "true Jew" was a true follower of God, according to Paul, and thus those who rejected their messiah were in reality not truly Jews at all!

Christ promises that those Jewish parties who were disturbing the Philadelphians would be humbled, and they would be made to know that it was the Christians at Philadelphia who were the true followers of God. Whether this was to come to pass in the heavenly judgment when every knee bows to Christ (Phil. 2:10) or whether this was to be through some earthly event in Philadelphia we cannot tell.

10. This promise has occasioned much debate among sincere Christians. The issue is whether this verse (1) pledges to the Philadelphia Christians some immunity from an early earthquake or imperial perse-cution; or (2) whether it promises to the Christians alive at the end who are truly saved—Philadelphia type Christians—immunity from the judg-ments of God which will fall during the Tribulation Period. If the latter is true, then here the Bible teaches a *pre-tribulation rapture* (i.e., that the coming of Christ for His Church, called the *"Rapture,"* 1 Thess. 4:13-18, will occur *before* the start of the *Tribulation* Period).

Before answering this question let us note that: (1) the event spoken of is a definite time period—"the hour;" (2) it is a period of trial—"of temp-tation;" (3) it was future from John's day when already Roman imperial persecution had put John in Patmos and when already Peter and Paul had been killed earlier by Nero—"which shall come;" (4) it was to be a world-wide time of trial—"upon all the world;" and (5) the promise is to "keep thee *out of*—Greek *ek*—the hour."

From this, it is the author's opinion that here we have a promise of fu-ture deliverance from the "Great Tribulation" (Matt. 24:15-22ff) which yet faces the world when the wrath of God shall fall upon antichrist and the world that follows him. We do not lie, however, when we add that there are many fine Christian commentators who would not conclude identically on the basis of this verse.

PAST	PRESENT	RAPTURE	FIRST 3 1/2 LAST 3 1/2 TRIBULATION	ARMA-GEDDON	MIL-LENNIUM	NEW HEAVENS & EARTH

Revelation 3

11 Behold, I come quickly: hold that fast which thou hast, that no man take thy crown.

12 Him that overcometh will I make a pillar in the temple of my God, and he shall go no more out: and I will write upon him the name of my God, and the name of the city of my God, *which is* new Jerusalem, which cometh down out of heaven from my God: and *I will write upon him* my new name.

13 He that hath an ear, let him hear what the Spirit saith unto the churches.

VERSES 11,12,13
Rev. 22:20

Rev. 2:10
Rev. 12:11
1 Kg 7:21
Rev. 21:2; Isa. 11:9

Commentary

11. The admonition to "hold...fast...that no man take thy crown" fits this church which only has "a little strength" (vs. 8). This group is admonished to "hold fast" (Gk. *krateo*—grasp, hold, keep, retain) and here the same word is used as in 2:1, "He that *holdeth (krateo)* the seven stars."

God is the ultimate author of all of our strength yet in the Bible there is always the dual presence of God's part and Man's part. Here the weak ones are to "hold fast" and the Mighty One will hold open the door (vs. 7).

12. To the ones with little strength what could be a more encouraging promise than to have their future positions likened to the strong "pillars" before the Temple of God. Everyone in this city was familiar with temple after temple dedicated to the pagan deities, and perhaps some of the travelers had told of the named pillars, Jachin and Boaz (1 Kg 7:21), which stood before the Second Temple of Jerusalem before it was destroyed when the Romans burned the city in A.D. 70.

When Tiberias rebuilt Philadelphia after the earth tremor of A.D. 17 it received its new and second name, "Neocaesarea," i.e., New City of Caesar. How meaningful, then, would it be for these to contemplate the new City of God, New Jerusalem, which was to yet be built out of the sin-ravaged earthly one.

13. Here again all who will listen—you and I if we will—are admonished to harken to what the Spirit is saying to *all of the seven* congregations including, especially, the one at hand.

Does this Philadelphia church not typify the Church of *1730-1900, The Missionary Church?* From 1730-1800 there was the Great Awakening on both sides of the Atlantic with Whitfield and Wesley. Then the 1800's saw a Second Awakening with its Spurgeon's and Moody's. In this century the modern missionary movement broke loose and sent the Gospel to China, India, and Africa. Was this not the age of the open door when the humble church with little strength took the good news to the ends of the earth?

Background

Weddings are a happy time. It is a time which both bride and groom look forward to with great anticipation. They plan for it...and in their minds, live with the dreams of that coming day.

And for the bride, it is a day when she takes on a *new name*...the name of the one she loves.

What a picture here as Christ speaks to the faithful at Philadelphia. He tells them, in effect, that though the road has been filled with danger, with a troubled earth, tremors and fear of death...because they have been faithful..."I will write upon him my new name."

What an inheritance to us as Christians living in today's world...a world which makes it increasingly difficult for the Christian. There is soon coming a day when those that will name the name of Christ will suffer persecution or death. Will the ecology movement and proponents of Earth Day someday blame Christians for the pollution of earth? We are entering an age of great testing!

PAST	PRESENT	RAPTURE	FIRST 3 1/2 LAST 3 1/2 TRIBULATION	ARMA- GEDDON	MIL- LENNIUM	NEW HEAVENS &EARTH

14 And unto the angel of the church of the La-od-i-ce´-ans write; These things saith the Amen, the faithful and true witness, the beginning of the creation of God;

John 1:2, 3

15 I know thy works, that thou art neither cold nor hot: I would thou wert cold or hot.

Matt. 24:12
Psa. 6:1

16 So then because thou art luke warm, and neither cold nor hot, I will spue thee out of my mouth.

Lev: 18:28

Commentary

14. Travelling 45 miles SE from Philadelphia one arrives at Laodicea where several roads come together. This was a fortified city, and it was named for the wife of Antiochus II, the Greek king of Syria who constructed (or reconstructed) the city in the middle of the 3d century B.C. Thus for Queen Laodice was it titled.

Upon being ravaged in A.D. 61 by an earthquake—common in that age in this area—this city restored itself without requiring the aid of Nero, the Caesar. Thus this was a self-sufficient people (vs. 17).

Medicine, production of eye ointment, wool distribution and manufacture, and banking brought fame to Laodicea. Read Vss. 17-18 and see how Christ, the perfect teacher, related His message to these qualities of the city.

To this church Christ comes as the "Amen," (Hebrew: *Aman,* "It-is-true" "It-is-faithful") and as "the Faithful and True Witness." Actually, the "Amen"—as you can see—is the Hebrew way of saying "faithful and true." Thus we end our prayers; and thus Christ comes as the final word of truth. He comes thusly to this group because His testimony (vs. 15) will conflict with their own opinions of themselves (vs. 17). He shows His credentials before He gives His adverse and surprising report.

15-16. His report is that toward the things of God they are neither unconcerned, cold, nor truly concerned, hot. This neutrality toward God is unacceptable; each person and each church must choose (1 Kg 18:21; Josh. 24:15). Thus God will put them out of His presence; their church will not be allowed by God to stand under these circumstances. Indifference is not acceptable on the issues of life; you cannot walk by the cross and be sympathetic with the bleeding Saviour and just keep on whistling as you pass (Heb. 10:28-29). He claims to be the Messiah—Trust in Him or stone Him!

PAST	PRESENT	RAPTURE	FIRST 3 1/2	LAST 3 1/2	ARMA–	MIL–	NEW
			TRIBULATION		GEDDON	LENNIUM	HEAVENS
							&EARTH

17 Because thou sayest, I am rich, and increased with goods, and have need of nothing; and knowest not that thou art wretched, and miserable, and poor, and blind, and naked:

Jer. 9:23

Matt. 6:8; Amos 6:1-7

18 I counsel thee to buy of me gold tried in the fire, that thou mayest be rich; and white raiment, that thou mayest be clothed, and *that* the shame of thy nakedness do not appear; and anoint thine eyes with eyesalve, that thou mayest see.

Rev. 19:14

19 As many as I love, I rebuke and chasten: be zealous therefore, and repent.

Heb. 12:5-13

Definition:
Justification—*is God's declaring that we who have trusted in Him are now righteous in His sight on the basis of Christ's having paid the penalty for our sins by dying on the cross (Rom. 3:20-31).*

Commentary

17. "I am rich, and increased with goods"—This is more literally translated, "I am rich, and I-have-become-rich *(peplouteka)."* Surely Laodicea, the banking and woolen manufacturing center could make this boast, and apparently this was also the attitude of the local congregation. They felt that they needed nothing. Yet these were miserable (they boasted contentment), poor (they claimed to be rich), blind (they made eye-salve for others), and naked (but their woolens covered multitudes)! The greatest boasters and the conceited are often the worst of all (Matt. 7:3)!

18. After His scourging rebuke, Christ the Great Physician does not leave without prescribing a cure (Lesson for us?). Note that this prescription is to be bought "of Me," i.e., from Christ. He not only names the remedy, but He also offers to supply it. "Gold tried"—indicates a metal superior to the glittering money that does not produce spiritual gain. "White raiment" indicates a holiness that must be put on a person. It pictures justification. "Anoint...with eyesalve" commands them to be spiritually anointed, awakened, so that they might see the love which they should have for Christ and the hatred they should have for sin. This would end their lukewarmness.

19. The words of this verse, coming after a strong denunciation and exposure, inspire love, hope, and action.

PAST	PRESENT	RAPTURE	FIRST 3 1/2 LAST 3 1/2 TRIBULATION	ARMA–GEDDON	MIL–LENNIUM	NEW HEAVENS & EARTH

20 Behold, I stand at the door, and knock: if any man hear my voice, and open the door, I will come in to him, and will sup with him, and he with me.

Definition:
Millennium—*From the Latin:* mille, *"1000;"* annum, *"year." This speaks of the prophecied coming Kingdom Age of peace and righteousness (Isa. 11:1-12; Dan. 2:44) which shall precede the Eternal State and which shall last for "1000 years" (Rev. 20:1-6).*

Commentary

20. The promise of this verse applies to "any man" (Greek: *tis*, "any-man;" "any-woman"—it is both masculine and feminine) and hence its offer goes beyond merely those who were at Laodicea at the turn of the 2d century A.D. Christ is standing at the door (He is near to all, Acts 17:27); He is knocking (Greek Present Tense—He now is *continually* knocking—He is thus actively seeking us; He is making the initial overture). Christ's voice is calling—This is heard in the preaching of the Lord's Day, over the air waves, in the printed page, and from Christians's who tell others of the Good News. *Man's part* in salvation involves hearing Christ's voice and opening his heart's door. *God's part* involves the initial call and then upon the opening of the heart in trust, it involves God's entrance and continued abiding fellowship—"I will come in...and sup." The promise is definite; if the door is opened the knocking one will certainly enter. This verse, in an allegory, puts forth the identical truth found in Acts 16:31, "Believe in the Lord Jesus Christ and thou shalt be saved."

Many people believed the preservation of St. Paul's Cathedral, London, during the fire bombing raids of 1940 was miraculous. This unusual photograph was taken at the height of one night's bombing. Note the Cathedral engulfed by smoke but undamaged!

Background

Laodicea was also proud of its clothing trade...but Christ says that Laodicea was spiritually naked.

In fact Christ speaks of the "shame of thy nakedness."

Even the water supply in Laodicea was an indication of their spiritual condition. The water was brought by a six-mile aqueduct from the south. The water either came from hot springs and was cooled to lukewarm or came from a cooler source and warmed up in the aqueduct on the way.

In St. Paul's Cathedral in London is a famous painting by Holman Hunt called "The Light of the World." It is a picture of a run-down cottage with thistles and grass grown up to the height of the window. The hinges on the door are rusty. And there stands the Lord, a lantern in one hand, knocking at the door. A man, looking at the painting, told the artist, "You made a mistake, you didn't put a handle on the door."

The artist replied, "No, not a mistake. The handle is on the inside. We must open the door."

What about you? Have you opened the door?

PAST	PRESENT	RAPTURE	FIRST 3 1/2	LAST 3 1/2	ARMA-GEDDON	MIL-LENNIUM	NEW HEAVENS & EARTH
			TRIBULATION				

21 To him that overcometh will I grant to sit with me in my throne, even as I also overcame, and am set down with my Father in his throne.
22 He that hath an ear, let him hear what the Spirit saith unto the churches.

Isa. 55:1-3
Rev. 12:11
Eph. 1:3;
Rev. 20:6; 4:4
Psa. 110:1

Commentary

21-22. To the one who overcomes by walking by faith (Gal. 3:3), Christ promises that he will be privileged to sit with Christ upon His throne. Ruling with Christ, beside Him upon the same royal seat, now spiritually, but somehow in a more literal sense in the millennium, is a glorious promise especially to those of Laodicea who face expulsion as a church from Christ's presence. "I will spue thee out" (vs. 16)—"Will I grant to sit with me" (vs. 21)!

With this frightening threat and encouraging promise in our ears, all of us are urged to hear what the Spirit (not John) is saying to all of the churches.

Does this Laodicean condition not portray the condition of much of to-day's end-time professing church, the *APOSTATE CHURCH, 1900-?* It claims to be the best in accomplishing an ecumenical amalgamation of the world's faiths; it brags of its record on the issues of foreign policy and poverty; it is not indifferent cold,to man's needs—but in other ways it is not hot.

In any case, *today* there exists around us Ephesian churches with first love lost, Smyrna churches that are suffering...Philadelphia churches which are faithful, and Laodicean congregations which are neither hot nor cold. Let us harken to what the Spirit has said to each of them.

One of the few remains of the original Ephesus of Bible days is this Magnesia Gate. 1st century A.D.

Background

Ephesus was an ancient city of some 200,000 people at the time John was writing under the inspiration of God at Patmos. Ephesus had heard the Gospel under Tychicus (Ephesians 6:21), Timothy (1 Timothy 1:3), John Mark (1 Peter 5:13), John the Apostle (Revelation 1:11; 2:1) and of course, Paul.

Ephesus was involved in many power struggles and was at one time under the control of Alexander the Great (336-323 B.C.). In 196 B.C. Antiochus of Syria landed at Ephesus but met defeat at the Magnesia gate.

For the Christian these were days of testing, of temptation. How important it is even today to overcome circumstances by faithfulness to God.

PAST	PRESENT	RAPTURE	FIRST 3 1/2	LAST 3 1/2	ARMA-GEDDON	MIL-LENNIUM	NEW HEAVENS & EARTH
			TRIBULATION				

THREE VIEWS ON THE RAPTURE*

These are **NOT** millennial positions but merely three of the views on the exact time of Christ's return within the PRE-MILLENNIAL camp. Correctness on these positions have nothing to do with the salvation of a sinner.

THE RAPTURE POSITIONS	WHAT DOES IT MEAN	WHAT EACH GROUP BELIEVES	WHY MANY BELIEVERS HOLD TO THE PRE-TRIBULATION RAPTURE VIEW
POST TRIBULATION RAPTURE	The Church (believers) will be raptured AFTER THE 7 year Tribulation Period.	The Church will go through the awful Tribulation (Matthew 24:21).	The Church is to be spared God's wrath (Romans 5:9). Since the entire 7 year Tribulation Period is a pouring out of God's wrath (Revelation 6:17), the Rapture must remove the Church before this pouring out occurs. Genesis 19:22 shows this principle. The angel could not begin to destroy Sodom until Lot was safely removed from the area!
MID TRIBULATION RAPTURE	The Church (believers) will be raptured in the midst of the 7 year Tribulation Period.	The Church will be saved only from the last 3½ year "Great Tribulation" (Matthew 24:21).	
PRE TRIBULATION RAPTURE	The Church (believers) will be raptured before the 7 year Tribulation Period starts.	The Church will be saved from the entire 7 year Tribulation (Matthew 24:21).	

On the time of the **RAPTURE**, which is a complex topic, interested readers should refer to:
KEPT FROM THE HOUR, Gerald B. Stanton (Toronto: Evangelical Publishers, 1964);
THINGS TO COME, J. Dwight Pentecost (Grand Rapids, Michigan: Zondervan Publishing Company, 1958);
THE RAPTURE QUESTION, John F. Walvoord (Grand Rapids, Michigan: Zondervan Publishing Company, 1957);
UNDERSTANDING REVELATION, Gary G. Cohen (Clearwater Christian College, Clearwater, Florida 33519).

*RAPTURE: This refers to the time when believing Christians (both dead and alive) will
"in the twinkling of an eye" rise up to meet Christ in the air (I Thessalonians 4:13-18).

THREE HEAVENS

The word *heaven* is used hundreds of times in the Bible. The primary meaning of *heaven* is *"that which is above."* In God's Word *heaven* refers to one of three major realms as noted below.

THE HEAVENS	WHERE IS IT	SOME REFERENCES IN SCRIPTURE
THE ATMOSPHERIC HEAVENS	The atmosphere which surrounds the globe. Our troposphere is a blanket of air around earth. It is no higher than 20 miles above the earth. Most clouds are within 7 miles of the earth.	The Israelites were told that the land they were to possess "is a land of hills and valleys and drinketh water of the rain from heaven" (Deut. 11:11). See also Deut. 11:17, II Chron. 7:13, Isa. 55:9-11, Psalm 147:8, Matthew 24:30, Zach. 2:6.
THE CELESTIAL HEAVENS	This is the sphere in which the sun and moon and stars appear. I Kings 8:27 speaks of the Celestial Heavens when it says, "Behold, the heaven of heavens cannot contain God."	"And God said, Let there be lights in the firmament of the heaven to divide the day from the night..." (Genesis 1:14). "...Look now toward heaven, and tell the stars, if thou be able to number them..." (Genesis 15:5). See also Hebrews 1:10, Psalm 33:6, Isaiah 14:12, Amos 5:26 and Jeremiah 23:24.
THE BELIEVERS HEAVEN (The Abode of God)	This is characterized by holiness because God dwells there. Believers also will dwell in God's heaven because they have been made holy by the grace of God. Jesus assured us of the reality of this place (John 14:2).	"...I dwell in the high and holy place, with him also that is of a contrite and humble spirit..." (Isaiah 57:15). "Look down from heaven, and behold from the habitation of thy holiness and of thy glory..." (Isaiah 63:15). See also Exodus 20:22, Deut. 4:36, Matthew 3:17, Matthew 14:19, Acts 7:55 and John 3:27.

For a fuller treatment of this subject we recommend: THE BIBLICAL DOCTRINE OF HEAVEN, Wilbur M. Smith, Published by MOODY PRESS, Chicago, Illinois

CHAPTER 4

After this I looked, and, behold, a door *was* opened in heaven: and the first voice which I heard *was* as it were of a trumpet talking with me; which said, Come up hither, and I will shew thee things which must be hereafter.	*Rev. 1:10* *Rev. 1:19*

THE REVELATION OF CHRIST AS THE LION OVER THE NATIONS (CHAPTERS 4-20)

CHAPTERS 4-5: THE HEAVENLY THRONE ROOM SCENE BEFORE THE TRIBULATION BEGINS

Daniel 9:27, as well as other verses in Revelation, shows that the coming Tribulation Period which those left upon the earth will face will be seven years in length. Its midpoint will be marked by the Antichrist committing a great evil deed in the rebuilt Temple, this is called the "Abomination of Desolation" (Dan. 9:27; Matt. 24:15ff; 2 Thess. 2:3,4). This will begin the world's worst hour of terror which will last for 3 1/2 years, the latter half of the 7 years, and it will only cease when Christ personally destroys the Antichrist and his armies at Armageddon (Matt. 24:21-31; Joel 3; Isa. 63; Rev. 19:11-20:2). Here now, in chapters 4-5, we are privileged to go into heaven with the Apostle and to see the heavenly sights and ceremonies which take place as a Prelude to the Tribulation (which begins in 6:1). God is about to re-possess His universe.

1. The trumpet-like voice which spoke to John at first in 1:10 was clearly, as we saw from the rest of chapter 1, Christ. Here the trumpet-like voice may again be Christ.

John is now called into heaven to see the "things which must be hereafter" (4:1). Thus we now come to the third section of the book in terms of the outline given to us in 1:19 (which see). The identity between the words of 4:1 and those of the third section of 1:19 are unmistakeable; we now enter the realm of the future.

The words here in 4:1, "Come up hither" and the mention of a "voice" and a "trumpet," because of their similarity with the description of the Rapture found in 1 Thess. 4:13-18, have occasioned a debate. Some feel that the similarity warrants the conclusion that John here in 4:1 is a type of the Church which is caught up to be with Christ before the start of the Tribulation Period. Other interpreters feel that the similarities are only superficial. What do you think (Compare 1 Thess. 4:13-18 with Rev. 4:1)??? [See comments on vss. 2-3 and 4]

PAST	PRESENT	RAPTURE	FIRST 3 1/2	LAST 3 1/2	ARMA-GEDDON	MIL-LENNIUM	NEW HEAVENS & EARTH
			TRIBULATION				

Revelation 4

2 And immediately I was in the spirit;
and, behold, a throne was set in heaven,
and *one* sat on the throne.
3 And he that sat was to look upon like a
jasper and a sardine stone: and *there was*
a rainbow round about the throne, in sight
like unto an emerald.

Rev. 20:11-15;
Dan. 7:13-14

Commentary

2-3. John is now in the realm of the spirit. He beholds a throne either "sitting" or "being set" (the Greek allows both) in heaven. The One upon the throne is glorious and it can be none other than God before whom all prostrate themselves. From 5:6-7 wherein it is clearly Christ who takes the book from the One on the throne, it would appear that here the Father is seen as the One upon the throne.

This is the "Throne of Adjudication" (Newell); it is the royal celestial headquarters of deity for the judgment of the Tribulation now about to fall upon the earth. *God's wrath* is about to be poured out in fury upon a rebellious world (6:16-17; 14:19; 16:1).

The rainbow around the throne tells us in a sign that there shall be MERCY IN THE MIDST OF JUDGMENT during this Tribulation Period. This is the significance of the bow, Gen. 9:8-17. Revelation chapter 7 will soon show us that indeed multitudes shall turn to Christ during this judgment era. There is, by contrast, no bow around the Great White Throne of 20:11-15 for before that throne's holiness the unrepentant will without exception be cast into the Lake of Fire.

Since *1 Thess. 5:9 promises that* God's wrath *will not fall upon us who are the believers of this age;* and since *in the past God was careful to remove his children from the area of the falling of heavenly judgment (Gen. 19:22!—Lot);* and since *the Tribulation described in Revelation chapters 6-19 is a period of God's wrath falling upon all the world (6:16-17; 14:19; 16:1);* it therefore *appears that Christ will catch us up to be with Him in the Rapture (1 Thess. 4:13-18) before the Tribulation begins.*

▼

PAST	PRESENT	RAPTURE	FIRST 3 1/2 / LAST 3 1/2 TRIBULATION		ARMA-GEDDON	MIL-LENNIUM	NEW HEAVENS & EARTH

Revelation 4

4 And round about the throne *were* four
and twenty seats: and upon the seats I
saw four and twenty elders sitting, clothed in white raiment; and they had on their
heads crowns of gold.

Rev. 21:12-14
Acts 20:17
Rev. 2:10; 3:11

5 And out of the throne proceeded lightnings and thunderings and voices: and
there were seven lamps of fire burning
before the throne, which are the seven
Spirits of God.

Rev. 3:1; Acts 2:33

Commentary

4. Who are these? "Elders" are not only the leaders of the congregation, but they are its *representatives*. These elders represent some
group. Their number, 24, leads me to conclude that these represent the
redeemed of both the Old Testament and New Testament dispensa-
tions; 12 for the tribes of Israel and 12 for the Apostles. Rev. 21:12-14
seems to confirm this interpretation. They, furthermore, are "sitting"
(they are in heaven resting from their earthly labors); they are clothed
in "white raiment" (justified from their sins by a garment of righteousness provided by God); and they are wearing "crowns of gold" *(stephanos*—victor's crowns of leaves; hence these are in a glorified and rewarded state having been crowned as OVERCOMERS through Christ's
blood in the struggle upon earth; Rev. 12:11).

Thus here we see represented by the 24 elders the redeemed in glory.
That much seems clear. Then I personally would add the suggestion that
these are the Raptured Saints of both the Old and New Testament
epochs who with Christ in heaven now await here in this scene the in-
auguration of the Tribulation Period.

5. We must now ask what do these lightnings and thunders signify?
They occur in 4:5; 6:12; 8:5; 10:3-4; 11:13; 11:19; and 16:18-21. As
these phenomena are examined it is apparent that the "lightnings and
voices and thunders" symbolize God's presence *coming nigh* for judgment. Thus they are seen at the giving of the Law at Sinai (Exod.
19:16ff). Earthquakes and hail have this same significance here in the
Apocalypse but they also bring with them great physical violence and
disaster (Rev. 11:13;16: 18-21).

Thus judgment and wrath are about to fall; and the seven lamps before
the throne portray the all-present all-knowing all-holy Holy Spirit who
witnesses against the sin of the world and to the righteousness of the
wrath about to be unloosed.

One of the first nuclear explosions here conveys some of the awesome destruction that is now possible by man.

Background

If you ever had the opportunity to witness an atomic or hydrogen bomb explosion...you would notice two things. First, the deadly quietness as the time for devastating destruction drew near. Second, as the nuclear explosion occurred the initial response would seem insignificant. But slowly it would build into a deafening, terrifying, catastrophic cloud of fire and death.

The lightening and thunderings in these verses seem to indicate the foretelling of ominous judgment ahead...the so called "lull before the storm."

Man's chief sources of power are (1) men and animals, (2) water, (3) wind, (4) steam, (5) internal combustion engines, (6) electricity, and (7) atomic energy.

But on this occasion, man will witness power he could never before imagine...God's power!

PAST	PRESENT	RAPTURE	FIRST 3 1/2	LAST 3 1/2	ARMA-GEDDON	MIL-LENNIUM	NEW HEAVENS & EARTH
			TRIBULATION				

Revelation 4

6 And before the throne *there was* a sea of glass like unto crystal: and in the midst of the throne, and round about the throne, *were* four beasts full of eyes before and behind.

Ezek. 1:5-10ff.

7 And the first beast *was* like a lion, and the second beast like a calf, and the third beast had a face as a man, and the fourth beast *was* like a flying eagle.

Ezek. 1:10

Definition:

Transcendence—*the quality of being above and beyond the normal bounds. God has the dual attributes of being both transcendent (above, beyond, and possessing superior powers to His creation and creatures) and* immanent *(He is here, and near us all). The latter word should not be confused with* imminent *which means, "overhanging, about to happen,"—thus the Second Coming of Christ for His Church, the Rapture, is* imminent (Matt. 24:42-44).

Commentary

6-7. "Sea of glass like unto crystal"—Here John speaks in *the language of appearance.* This is how it appeared to John's eyes and he describes it in terms of that which he has experienced. He is not necessarily affirming that this "sea" *(thalassa)* is a liquid sea with ocean waves, nor is he declaring that the "glass" is a silicaoxide compound as we know glass. He is rather telling us that this is how the surface before the throne looked, and we can be sure that could we see the same sight we would affirm the accuracy of his description. This usage of the language of appearance must be realized, for it will be used in the Revelation more and more as we go onward.

Around this throne the Apostle sees "four beasts;" they have many eyes. Here the word "beast" is *zoon* in the Greek (compare our word, "zoo") and it means "living creature" or "animal." This is a different word from that used in 13:1 which is also translated "beast." There, in 13:1 the Antichrist and his system is referred to as the "beast," and the Greek word is *therion,* "vicious-wild-beast."

These living creatures are proclaimers of God's glory and they seem to represent His government over the *four* corners of the earth. The creatures are: a *lion* (majesty, authority, and power); a *young bull* (strength; the word for this animal is *moschos,* and it means young bull, ox, or cow—it is a general word); a *man* (intelligence; moral choice and responsibility); and a *flying eagle* (majesty, swiftness, and transcendence).

This sight is much like that of Ezekiel 1:5-10ff, especially *Ezek. 1:10,* but yet there does seem to be some differences between the two visions.

Background

It should be interesting for the reader to note that in John's day glass was usually dull and semi-opaque. Thus glass that would be as clear as crystal was then as precious as gold...for it was rare.

Glass was first made in Egypt 2500 years before Christ. Mirrors were made of polished bronze by the Hebrews (Exodus 38:8). The only direct reference to glass found in the Old Testament is in the book of Job, Job 28:17, where gold and crystal are compared with wisdom.

Remember the verse in 1 Corinthians 13:12

> For now we are looking in a mirror that gives
> only a dim (blurred) reflection...
> (Amplified New Testament)

Glass in those days, not silver-backed, gave back only a dim reflection. Thus, John's comment of a "...sea of glass like unto crystal..." must have made a great impression on the mind.

Just as...we have seen fuzzy photos of the moon...then suddenly our astronauts land on the moon and bring back, sharp, clear photos. What a contrast!

PAST	PRESENT	RAPTURE	FIRST 3 1/2 TRIBULATION	LAST 3 1/2	ARMA– GEDDON	MIL– LENNIUM	NEW HEAVENS & EARTH

8 And the four beasts had each of them six wings about *him;* and *they were* full of eyes within: and they rest not day and night, saying, Holy, holy, holy, Lord God Almighty, which was, and is, and is to come.

Isa. 6:2

Isa. 6:3

Commentary

8. Here we see essentially the same vision as that of *Isaiah 6:2-3*. This, however, should surprise no one. The primer of New Testament prophecy is the Old Testament. Just as one cannot fully understand the Gospels and Epistles of the NT without a knowledge of the OT, so this is even more true in the realm of prophecy. The vision of Revelation in case after case adds to the details of basically identical visions already given in Ezekiel, Isaiah, Daniel, and Joel, etc. We shall come across this again and again. Even Genesis will supply us with many a key as will the Psalms (For example: Rev. 12:1 and 12:9 will be illumined by Genesis and Rev. 12:5 by a Psalm).

Here the creatures give us the triad of "HOLY HOLY HOLY" as they ceaselessly glorify God. Rev. 4:8 and Isa. 6:3 shows that other statements of praise to God are added in their continual adoration. It is difficult to accept any other explanation for the fact that both Rev. 4:8 and Isa. 6:3 cite the continual usage of the word "Holy" in groups of three, except that here one "holy" is given for each of the three co-eternal co-equal persons of the single Godhead. Here, as in the baptismal formula of Matt. 28:19, I do not think that God is leading us astray. God is a TRI-UNITY (a trinity) and these creatures proclaim it so.

Are these creatures only visionary—or do they actually exist in heaven where God's presence is manifest? I think the latter; they exist and are there. It is not strange that the God who has created an infinitude of animal types—witness the number of insect species that exists—would also create many spiritual beings: angels, archangels, seraphim, cherubim, etc.

Note how well the declaration of God's holiness fits this Prelude to the Tribulation judgments when God's wrath falls upon unrepentant sinners. Note also, that the creatures do not shout, "Wise, wise, wise," as their primary accolade—although they could. God in His infinite wisdom and majesty, to the praise of His everlasting glory, seeks to be known to us moral agents as the one who is Holy. Lesson?

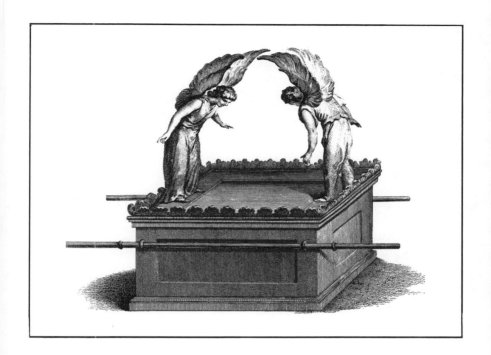

Background

The book of Revelation says three things about the Cherubim. First, their duties have much to do with this world. Second, they have a part in the execution of God's purposes for this world. Third, they are instruments of grace used of God.

It has been said the Cherubim are living emblems of God's protecting care.

The Cherubim have played several roles throughout the Bible. Their first was at the Garden of Eden. Here the cherubim with a flaming sword were placed to protect the tree of life, after Adam and Eve were expelled (Genesis 3:24).

The curtains of the tabernacle were embroidered with cherubim (Exodus 26:1). God directed Moses to place two cherubim of beaten gold on the mercy seat above the ark, where God would commune with Moses in the tabernacle (Exodus 25:18-22, 37:7-9).

A modern-day comparison might be the President of the United States and his ambassadors. While the President runs the nation, his ambassadors carry out his wishes in each foreign country.

PAST	PRESENT	RAPTURE	FIRST 3 1/2 LAST 3 1/2 TRIBULATION	ARMA-GEDDON	MIL-LENNIUM	NEW HEAVENS &EARTH

9 And when those beasts give glory and honour and thanks to him that sat on the throne, who liveth for ever and ever,

10 The four and twenty elders fall down before him that sat on the throne, and worship him that liveth for ever and ever, and cast their crowns before the throne, saying,

11 Thou art worthy, O Lord, to receive glory and honour and power: for thou has created all things, and for thy pleasure they are and were created.

Dan. 7:13-14

Eph. 1:11

Commentary

9-11. Surely there is a lesson here for us when we see the four living creatures giving "glory and honor and thanks" to God. So too the 24 elders adore and praise God and cast their victory-wreath-crowns *(stephanos)* before the throne. Note the attributes of God which are here magnified:

- "Who liveth for ever and ever" (His eternal being and duration);

- "Thou art worthy..." (His worthiness to receive worship, glory, and honor; and His worthiness to receive "power" [*dunamis*—"power" from which root we get *"dynam*ite"]);

- "Thou hast created all things" (He is the CREATOR OF ALL THINGS—despite what evolutionists claim);

- "And for thy pleasure they are and were created" (God is the God of Purpose, Eph. 1:11. Literally translated the final words of Rev. 4:11 read, "And on account of the will of you they were and they have been created." The word for "will" is *thelema*. It means "will, desire" as in its usage in Matt. 6:10; it does not mean "pleasure" in the sense of "whim," "amusement," or "recreation."

Oh what a glorious sight! Oh how we should praise our God!

AN INTERESTING SUGGESTION

You might wish to consider and discuss the following interpretation of Rev. 4:7. It is said that the four faces represent the characteristics of Christ as they are made known to us in the *four* Gospels. *Matthew* wrote primarily for the *Jews* as his multitude of OT quotations show. His gospel sees Christ as the LION of Judah (Rev. 5:5), the King of Israel. *Mark* was written by John Mark who accompanied Peter to Rome (Papias). He writes for the *Romans* who were interested in seeing the perfect servant, such as is the OX. *Luke,* a Greek, wrote in the best style of Greek for *Greeks.* These were interested in the perfect MAN. *John* wrote later, at the end of the century, and he writes especially for *Christians.* His gospel shows the deity of Christ and is thus portrayed by the high FLYING EAGLE soaring above.

Background

One day our daughter, Dawn, outstretched on our lawn, studied for a long time the wonders of the lowly dandelion.

Its brilliant yellow-gold fascinated her. It was a real treasure. That night she proudly presented it to us as her gift. How happy she was to give this to us. This was her crown.

As Christians there are five crowns which we can share:

       1. A Crown of Life (James 1:12)
       2. A Crown of Righteousness (2 Timothy 4:8)
       3. A Crown of Glory (1 Peter 5:4)
       4. A Crown for Soul Winners (1 Thessalonians 2:19)
       5. A Crown for Martyrs (Revelation 2:10)

Yet, so overjoyed will we be in the heavenly Kingdom that we will cast our crowns at His pierced feet.

Imagine the joy that will be ours, eternally, in the Day that Never Ends!

PAST	PRESENT	RAPTURE	FIRST 3 1/2 LAST 3 1/2 TRIBULATION	ARMA-GEDDON	MIL-LENNIUM	NEW HEAVENS & EARTH

Revelation 5

CHAPTER 5

And I saw in the right hand of him that sat on the throne a book written within and on the backside, sealed with seven seals.
2 And I saw a strong angel proclaiming with a loud voice, Who is worthy to open the book, and to loose the seals thereof?
3 And no man in heaven, nor in earth, neither under the earth, was able to open the book, neither to look thereon.
4 And I wept much, because no man was found worthy to open and to read the book, neither to look thereon.

Dan. 7:9-10

Dan. 12:4;
Psa. 24:3-5

Isa. 53:6; Rom. 3:23;
Isa. 63:3

Commentary

1. The final three verses of the previous chapter showed us that the one upon this throne is He who lives forever, the Creator. Since 5:6-7 show Jesus receiving the Seven Sealed Book from the One on the throne, the One on the throne must be God the Father who is both at once specially manifest here in heaven and yet present everywhere.

John beholds in the Father's right hand a book *(biblion,* a "Scroll"). While in awe he informs us that both sides of the scroll is written upon—thus it is a full book, and hence the judgments and woes pronounced by this scroll are full and known in detail before they occur.

The seven seals will be seen in detail beginning at 6:1. A seal was a device—often made with wax and having an imprint pushed upon it—which forbade the unauthorized from opening. Once broken, a seal was impossible to repair without leaving tell-tale traces; thus here we are certain that this book with its woes for the earth has never yet been opened. It was certainly not opened prior to the crucifixion as vs. 9 shows; and its contents (chapters 6-19) do not mesh with these past 2000 years of church history. The opening is set for the start of the Tribulation Period! The fact that there are seven seals shows that the entire matter—here Tribulation judgments for the ungodly upon earth—will be completely dispatched by these seven seals.

2-4. No one was worthy (*axios*—here "morally fit" or "fit" by other qualifications). Since the opening of this book brings speedy judgment to the rebelous earthlings (6:1ff), the question of opening the book was basically the question, "Who is worthy to cast the strenuous plagues contained in the book upon the earth *to reclaim the planet for God?*"—for this is precisely what the judgments of the book do. The answer: No man! Why? Answer: Romans 3:23. So too John 8:7. Why were the unfallen holy angels not worthy??? John weeps much. Why?

PAST	PRESENT	RAPTURE	FIRST 3 1/2 LAST 3 1/2 TRIBULATION		ARMA–GEDDON	MIL–LENNIUM	NEW HEAVENS & EARTH

Revelation 5

5 And one of the elders saith unto me, Weep not: behold, the Lion of the tribe of Judah, the Root of David, hath prevailed to open the book, and to loose the seven seals thereof.

Gen. 49:8-12; Isa. 9:7; 11:1

Definition:
Shiloh—In Genesis 49:10 this word refers to the Messiah who shall take the scepter, the symbol of the right to govern, from Judah. David, Solomon, Rehoboam, etc. were actually kings from this line of Judah and Jesus Himself was of this tribal lineage (Mt. 1:3, 6). The word Shiloh comes from the Hebrew Sh-l-oh (Sh, "whom;" l, "to;" oh, "him") and thus Gen. 49:10 teaches that the scepter shall not depart from Judah until Shiloh ("the one to whom it belongs") comes.

Commentary

5. "The Lion of the Tribe of Judah"—The ancient symbol for this tribe was a lion. In fact, in the Six Day War of June 6-11, 1967 the Old City of Jerusalem was taken by the Israelis by means of an attack at the *Lion's* Gate. Originally this thrust was to be made at the Dung Gate, but the cry of the soldiers was, "Judah first" (Jud. 20:18), and hence the Judah-Lion Gate became the objective.

Judah was the Lion because of Jacob's prophecy of Genesis 49:9-10; and from these verses even the famed Rabbi Kimchi acknowledged that the Messiah was to come from Judah. The Messiah was to sit on David's Throne and He was to be of the Davidic royal line, the line of the kings of Judah, the Southern Kingdom. By Jeremiah's time the royal line of David was almost destroyed and the Davidic kings of his day were among the worst sinners of the kingdom—and thus did the Babylonian Captivity come (606-535 B.C.). Yet God promised that someday hence *out of the cut down tree* of David's kingly line would a truly righteous king emerge as a *shoot from the roots which still remained* (Isa. 10:33-11:2ff)! This shoot, this sapling, this branch, was the Messiah Jesus, and it is of Him that Revelation 5:5 here speaks as the "Root of David" who has "prevailed."

▼

PAST	PRESENT	RAPTURE	FIRST 3 1/2 LAST 3 1/2 TRIBULATION	ARMA–GEDDON	MIL–LENNIUM	NEW HEAVENS & EARTH

6 And I beheld, and, lo, in the midst of the throne and of the four beasts, and in the midst of the elders, stood a Lamb as it had been slain, having seven horns and seven eyes, which are the seven Spirits of God sent forth into all the earth.

John 1:29, 36;
Exod. 12:3-13

7 And he came and took the book out of the right hand of him that sat upon the throne.

Dan. 7:13-14

Commentary

6-7. As John gazes at the throne having just heard of the Lion of Judah, suddenly he beholds the slain Lamb which now lives. Jesus is thus seen to be both the Lion and the Lamb. At His *first advent* Christ came meekly as the *"Lamb* of God" to die a sacrificial death so that all who trust Him might be saved from the just penalty of their sin (Isa. 53:7; Jn. 1:29, 36). At His *second advent,* however, He will come as a strong *lion* to judge the ungodly (Rev. 19:11ff).

Christ comes as deity with seven horns (complete omnipotent power) and seven eyes (complete omniscient knowledge) to receive this book which some have called, "The Title Deed to the Universe." Only the Father could give it; only the Son could receive it!

Background

This photograph reflects the message of the verses you have just read. The picture taken by the author in Jerusalem shows a street between Gethsemane and the Inner City wall.

The donkey, heavily overloaded, is the burden bearer. So Christ bore our burden of sin at Calvary. In the center of the photograph is the Golden Gate, presently closed. But what a contrast! It is here where many believe the Lord will make his triumphant entry when He returns *with* His saints after the Tribulation...in power and glory (Ezekiel 44:1-3)!

PAST	PRESENT	RAPTURE	FIRST 3 1/2 LAST 3 1/2 TRIBULATION		ARMA- GEDDON	MIL- LENNIUM	NEW HEAVENS & EARTH

8 And when he had taken the book, the four beasts and four *and* twenty elders fell down before the Lamb, having every one of them harps, and golden vials full of odours, which are the prayers of saints.

Psa. 33:2; Rev. 14:2; 15:2

Definition:
Redeem—*The verb "to redeem" used in 5:9, the next verse, is the Greek* agorazo, *"to buy," "to buy at the market." The public market was the* agora. *Thus Christ* bought *us with His blood. Another verb is also translated "redeem,"* lutroo *(1 Pet. 1:18; Lk. 24:21), and this word means, "to loose by paying a ransom price."*

Commentary

8. "Fell down before the Lamb"—Here clearly we have an act of adoration and worship. In 19:10, however, the words of the angel show that only God may be worshipped; hence we must conclude from this that the Lamb who is here rightfully worshipped is God—And the Lamb is clearly Jesus. Thus again this book with its heavenly glimpses exhibits the deity of the Lord Jesus manifest in the celestial spheres.

"...harps and golden vials"—Literally the Greek reads, "Having each a harp and vials golden." The word "vial" could also just as well be translated as "bowl." Thus in this rapturous scene we see these heavenly creatures holding instruments which make music to praise the Lord. From this we ought to observe two things: (1) Those who oppose the using of any and all musical instruments in the church worship service surely err; and (2) the harps here do not by any imagination support that worldly-wise fancy that the redeemed will do nothing throughout all eternity except play harps while sitting on clouds.

It should be noted that the prayers of the saints are not lost, nor do they disappear into the ether vapor. No; they are preserved by God—as is seen here in the vials—until His time for their answering. The 24 Elders having the prayers of the saints further confirms to us that these are the representatives of the redeemed who are with Christ in heaven.

PAST	PRESENT	RAPTURE	FIRST 3 1/2	LAST 3 1/2	ARMA-GEDDON	MIL-LENNIUM	NEW HEAVENS & EARTH
			TRIBULATION				

Young Jewish boy with prayer bands at Wailing Wall.

(Matthew 23:5)

OUTWARD APPEARANCES OF WORSHIP

Beginning around 2 B.C., all male Jews were expected to wear at morning prayers, except on sabbaths and festivals, two **phylacteries.** One was worn on their forehead (frontlet); the other on their left arm. This consisted of small leather cases containing 4 passages of Scripture from the Old Testament: Exodus 13:1-10; 13:11-16; Deuteronomy 6:4-9; 11:13-21.

Many also enlarged the commanded memorial fringes on their robes (Numbers 15:38-39). Outward adornments exist in Israel even today— for example some orthodox Jews wear elaborate fur hats at the Wailing Wall. Thus also many people throughout the world become involved in the trappings of religion, such as lighting candles, saying repetitive prayers, fingering beads...losing sight of the real message of Scripture.

9 And they sung a new song, saying, Thou art worthy to take the book, and to open the seals thereof: for thou wast slain, and hast redeemed us to God by thy blood out of every kindred, and tongue, and people, and nation;

10 And hast made us unto our God kings and priests: and we shall reign on the earth.

11 And I beheld, and I heard the voice of many angels round about the throne and the beasts and the elders: and the number of them was ten thousand times ten thousand, and thousands of thousands;

Rev. 14:3, 4;
  Lev. 25:30, 54.
Rev. 7:9
Isa. 56:7

Commentary

9. The ground of the Lamb's being worthy to take the book, which is the "Repossession Deed of the Universe," is that He died to redeem all of the lost who would but turn in faith to God for salvation. This is why He alone is worthy. The song that sang of these things was not a psalm or hymn that John had ever before heard; it was a "new song."

10. The result of the redemption is that the believer has been taken from his state of utter separation from God and has been cleansed and elevated to a position of *true dominion* (as Adam was originally to enjoy —thus he is a *king)* and to a position of *direct access to God* (as Adam originally had—thus he is a *priest).*

"We shall reign on the earth"—When shall this be? Answer: 20:4 and 21:3, during the Thousand Year Millennial Reign of Christ and in the Eternal State forever after.

11. As the Lamb takes the book all of the heavenly host break into a joyous voice. The time has at last come when the rebellious sinners of the earth are to be judged and their dominion is to be taken away from them. The numbers given show us the staggering multitude of spiritual creatures, the angels, who inhabit heaven. These figures need not be multiplied out and then added (10,000 X 10,000 + 1,000 X 1,000) in order to calculate the exact number of the unfallen angels. They are approximations, but they do represent, no doubt, a number somewhat akin to the true number of the angels. What is this figure?

Seeing the size of the animal population, the human population, and the number of cells...insects...and stars in this universe we need not be surprised to learn that an astoundingly large band of angels exists.

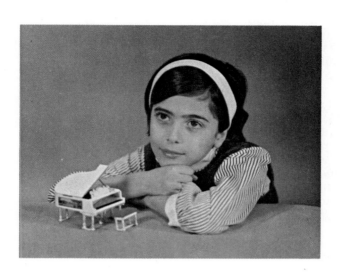

Background

Have you noticed that one of the characteristics of the book of Revelation is that it is the book of new things?

> First, there is the new name (Revelation 2:17).
> Second, there is the new song (5:9; 14:3).
> Third, new heavens and new earth (21:1).
> Fourth, there is the new Jerusalem (3:12; 21:2).
> Fifth, the promise of ALL things new (21:5).

All of us can remember the dreamy anticipation as we waited for some new thing in our life...perhaps a piano, a car, a home. All these quickly vanish away.

And here the Greek is significant...because it has two words for *new*. *Neos* means *new in point of time,* "young," but not necessarily new in point of quality. *Kainos* means *new in point of quality. Kainos* describes a thing which has not only been recently produced but also the like of which has never existed before! All of the verses listed above use the word *kainos.*

Thus when we believe in Jesus Christ He makes us a new *(kainos)* creature—a quality of which *has never existed before* (2 Corinthians 5:17).

▼

PAST	PRESENT	RAPTURE	FIRST 3 1/2 LAST 3 1/2 TRIBULATION	ARMA-GEDDON	MIL-LENNIUM	NEW HEAVENS & EARTH

Revelation 5

12 Saying with a loud voice, Worthy is the Lamb that was slain to receive power, and riches, and wisdom, and strength, and honour, and glory, and blessing.

13 And every creature which is in heaven, and on the earth, and under the earth, and such as are in the sea, and all that are in them, heard I saying, Blessing, and honour, and glory, and power, *be* unto him that sitteth upon the throne, and unto the Lamb for ever and ever.

14 And the four beasts said, Amen. And the four *and* twenty elders fell down and worshipped him that liveth for ever and ever.

Dan. 7:10
Deut. 33:2

Lk. 2:13-14

Rom. 14:11

Commentary

12-14. Here the glorifying of the Lamb spreads in successively outward concentric circles before John's ecstatic eyes and ears. The four Living Creatures, the 24 Elders, the numberless angels, and now all the creatures of the universe all are seen glorifying the Father on the Throne *and* the Lamb. Again Christ must be God for He enjoys equal glory with the Father.

How far are we to press the words, "every creature...in the sea"? Does this teach that at this time every last fish joined in saying the words, "Blessing, and honor ..."? Perhaps the best answer here would be a cautious one lest we *either* force the Bible to teach that which it does not intend to teach *or* we make its words to mean nothing. It seems that somehow in this vision John does see a manifestation of all the universe *visible to him* glorifying God. The heavenly voices do the speaking, most likely, while the presence of the animal kingdom with angelic voices reverberating from even their domains joins in on this anthem.

Note: Do angels sing? Some argue over this almost to the point of violence. The hymns have them often singing. In any case they glorify God, and that is the main thing! Personally, I expect to find them singing in heaven—but we shall see.

We have now completed this heavenly act of our drama, and we must be left in awe as chapters 4 and 5 are contemplated. Glory to God in the highest! Now we shall see the awful judgments from a holy God begin to erupt in their fury upon those left on earth who have stubbornly clutched their sins in rebellion against God and His mercy.

Background

To us the earth looks like a big place. And it's becoming more and more crowded every day. We notice the traffic jams getting worse, problems becoming more complex, and there is the increasing concern about the population explosion.

Yet our astronauts on the ill-fated Apollo 13 were relieved to land safely back on earth.

From their vantage point some 240,000 miles away, circling the moon, this is what the earth looked like. It seemed so small, yet it supports a world population that has grown from about 250 million people at the birth of Christ to nearly 4 billion people *now!*

Understanding this, we can better understand verses 11-14...for in these verses those included are not only on earth but also in heaven.

And all these people with the angels, throughout the whole of the universe, join in a chorus of praise to the Lord!

PAST	PRESENT	RAPTURE	FIRST 3 1/2 LAST 3 1/2 TRIBULATION	ARMA-GEDDON	MIL-LENNIUM	NEW HEAVENS & EARTH

THE TRIBULATION PERIOD (CHAPTERS 6-19)

THE FIRST 3 1/2 YEARS (CHAPTERS 6-11)
Seals; Trumpets; Witnesses.
THE SECOND 3 1/2 YEARS (CHAPTERS 12-19)
Persecution; Antichrist; Bowls: Babylon; and Armageddon.

INTRODUCTION TO CHAPTERS 6-19

When Christ pulls asunder the first seal from off the scroll the judgments of the Tribulation Period begin. Daniel 9:27 describes this final seven year period of history which will start when "The Prince that shall come" (the Antichrist) makes a "covenant" (some sort of peace and protection treaty) "with many" (Israel and others) "for one week" (7 years—the Hebrew reads literally: "for one seven").

Note that something startling happens in the middle of the seven years—"And in the midst of the week (Hebrew: 'seven') he shall cause the sacrifice...to cease...." Thus the period is composed of two halves of 3 1/2 years each with a decisive action in the middle. The time indications in the Book of Revelation (11:2,3; 12:6,14; 13:5) will therefore each speak of one or the other of the 3 1/2 year halves as does Daniel 7:25. *See chart.*

The decisive event of the middle of this period is the Antichrist's entering the rebuilt temple in Palestine and satanically claiming to be the true leader-god of this planet. This is called by Christ "The Abomination of Desolation" (Matt. 24:15) and the Apostle Paul describes it in 2 Thess. 2:3-4 (which see).

After this Abomination of Desolation is committed in the middle of the 7 years the Antichrist begins in full fury a campaign of satanically inspired persecution which is designed to destory both the remnant of Israel and all of the gentiles who reveal themselves to be following Christ. The persecution of this *latter period* is so intense that in Matt. 24:21 Christ labels it as a time of "GREAT TRIBULATION." He further declares that "there should no flesh be saved" (i.e., Antichrist would destroy all who turn to Christ) "except those days shall be shortened" (which they are by Christ's sudden coming at Armageddon 3 1/2 years after the Abomination has been committed. Matt. 24:29-31; 25:31ff; Rev. 19:11ff).

These things have not yet occurred! The Abomination of Desolation described in Dan. 9:27 and written by Daniel in the 6th Century B.C. was still *future* when Christ warned of it in Matt. 24:15. When the Romans tore down Jerusalem in A.D. 70 it was still not committed by the General-in-Command, later Emperor, Titus. Josephus, an eyewitness and Titus' interpreter, has given us a full detailed almost day by day account of the seige and the events after in his lengthy *Wars of the Jews.* He tells of Titus' high regard for the Jewish Temple and for his superstitous fear of it, and he makes it crystal clear that Titus never did anything close to what Paul describes in 2 Thess. 2:3-4, the Abomination of Desolation.

Adolf Hitler in 1934 preparing to address a vast throng promising a world of peace. A greater than Hitler will come on the scene in the Tribulation Period. He will be Antichrist!

Jesus in Matt. 24:15 said that the Abomination—the entrance into the Temple by Antichrist—would be the signal to FLEE from Jerusalem; but the Temple was entered and burned in 70 A.D. only *at the end* of the awful five month seige when flight was impossible as the Romans had been surrounding the city for months! AND BESIDES, Christ promised to appear personally in the clouds "Immediately after the tribulation of those days" (Matt. 24:29ff) and He certainly did not do this when Jerusalem was aflame at 70 A.D.! NO; DESPITE WHAT ANYONE MAY SAY THE ABOMINATION OF DESOLATION AND THE TRIBULATION PERIOD HAS NOT YET COME TO THE EARTH, THEY ARE STILL IN THE PROPHETIC NEAR FUTURE.

Now with the above in mind, let us continue in the Book of Revelation:

THE RAPTURE OCCURS (1 Thess. 4:13-18; 1 Thess. 5-9; Gen. 19-22)!
A PROMINENT RISING DIGNITARY MAKES A SEVEN YEAR PACT WITH ISRAEL AND OTHER NATIONS (Dan. 9:27)!
THE SEVEN YEAR JUDGMENT PERIOD HAS NOW BEGUN AND THE LAMB OPENS THE FIRST SEAL (Rev. 6:1-2)!

THE SEVEN YEAR TRIBULATION PERIOD AND
THE FIVE TIME INDICATIONS OF REVELATION

The Tribulation:

Revelation:

1st Half

Start—Antichrist makes a *seven year* covenant with Israel (Dan. 9:27).

Rev. 11:3—The two witnesses of God prophecy for 42 months (3 1/2 years) until the beast slays them.[1]

1st Half— 3 1/2 years in length (Dan. 9:27).

2nd Half

Middle—Antichrist commits the Abomination of Desolation (Dan. 9:27; Matt. 24:15; 2 Thess. 2:4).

Rev. 13:5—The Beast is given power to continue for 42 months (3 1/2 years).[2]

2nd Half—Antichrist persecutes Israel and the saints (Matt. 24:15-22; Dan. 7:25; Jer. 30: 4-7) 3 1/2 years in length (Dan. 9:27; 7:25).

Rev. 12:6—The woman, Israel, flees from the persecuting Dragon, Satan, for 1,260 days (3 1/2 years).[3]

Rev. 12:14—The woman, Israel, flees from the persecuting Dragon, Satan, for "a time, times, and a half time" (3 1/2 years).[3]

End—Antichrist is destroyed by God who shall set up His kingdom (Dan. 8:25; 7:22, 26-27; Matt. 24:29-31).

Rev. 11:2—The Gentiles shall tread under foot the holy city for 42 months (3 1/2 years)

[1]The Two Witnesses prophesy for 3 1/2 years (Rev. 11:3). This must be placed in the first half of the 7 year week. This is true because at the conclusion of the second half of the week all the foes of God are destroyed and the Kingdom inaugurated, while in contrast to this, here, three days *after* the end of the two witnesses' 3 1/2 year testimony they are still lying dead in the street and God's foes are rejoicing (Rev. 11:7-10).

[2]The era of the Beast's power must go through the persecution period as the ability to persecute inherently demands political power and authority. Revelation 13:5-8 shows that blasphemy against God and persecution against the saints will characterize his activities during this time.

[3]The periods of intense persecution match perfectly.

[4]The treading under foot of the holy city occurs in the second half of the week after the Abomination of Desolation. Until this time Antichrist is keeping his covenant with Israel and not "treading it under foot" (Dan. 9:27).

1st. seal (Antichrist) Chapter *6*
2nd. seal (War) *6*
3rd. seal (Famine) *6*
4th. seal (Death takes ¼ of the earth) *6*
5th. seal (Martyrdom) *6*
6th. seal (Heavenly & earthly disturbances) *6*
7th. seal (Trumpet Judgments) *8*

1st. trumpet (Earth 1/3 smitten) *8*
2nd. trumpet (Sea 1/3 smitten) *8*
3rd. trumpet (Rivers 1/3 smitten) *8*
4th. trumpet (Sun, moon, & stars 1/3 smitten) *8*
5th. trumpet (Locusts torment men for 5 months) *9*
6th. trumpet (200,000,000 horsemen slay 1/3 of men) *9*
7th. trumpet (Heavenly Temple with
           its Bowl Judgments) *11*

Heavenly Temple Opened *11, 15*

1st. bowl (Sores upon worshippers of the Beast) *16*
2nd. bowl (Sea smitten entirely) *16*
3rd. bowl (Rivers smitten) *16*
4th. bowl (Sun scorches men) *16*
5th. bowl (Darkness upon kingdom of the Beast; sores
           give pain) *16*
6th. bowl (Euphrates dried to prepare the way of the
           kings of the East) *16*
7th. bowl (Exceeding great earthquake and hail; Bab-
           ylon remembered for destruction) *16, 18*

ARMAGEDDON *19*

CHAPTER 6

And I saw when the Lamb opened one of the seals, and I heard, as it were the noise of thunder, one of the four beasts saying, Come and see.

2 And I saw, and behold a white horse: and he that sat on him had a bow; and a crown was given unto him: and he went forth conquering, and to conquer.

Matt. 24:5; 7:15
Contra Rev. 19:11ff
Rev. 13:4

CHAPTER 6: THE SEALS

1. Christ tears away the first seal and the seven year Tribulation Period judgments now begin. Is judgment and destruction always unholy as some modern thinkers claim? The answer is that here it is holy and righteous for "one of the four beasts" which constantly proclaim God's holiness (4:8) approvingly invites John to "come" to view these furies unleashed from the divine throne. There is a noise of thunder because, as we are about to see, the thundering judgments of the FOUR HORSE-MEN OF THE APOCALYPSE are approaching.

2. A white horse speaks of peace, righteousness, holiness, and majesty. Yet could this one who rides with horsemen such as War, Famine, and Death-and-Hell, the other three horsemen, be Christ? Is this horseman the same as Christ the Conqueror as He is seen at Armageddon on a white horse in Rev. 19:11ff?

The answer is, "No." Swete well observes:

"... the two riders [that of the first seal (Rev. 6:2) and Christ in Rev. 19:11] have nothing in common beyond the white horse; the details are distinct; contrast e.g., the *diademata polla* ["crowns many"] of xix. 12 with the single *stephanos* ["wreath-crown"] here, and the *hromphaia oxeia* ["sword sharp"] with the *toxon* ["bow"]. A vision of the victorious Christ would be inappropriate at the opening of a series which symbolizes bloodshed, famine, and pestilence." (Henry B. Swete, *The Apocalypse of St. John* (2d ed.; London: Macmillan & Co., Ltd., 1907), p. 86.

The rider holding a bow and crownless, the first horseman, does not fit Christ who *already* has conquered (1:18) and who Himself is distributing crowns (2:10); but it perfectly pictures the Antichrist—a military leader with a "bow" who is now starting his meteoric rise to world power (13:4-8).

Why then the "white" horse? Answer: Matt. 24:5, "Many shall come in my name, saying, I am Christ; and shall deceive many." The rider symbolizes the False Saviour and saviours who will come upon the distraught world with their humanistic schemes of world deliverance.

The FIRST Seal

A RIDER on a WHITE HORSE

PEACE
Antichrist

Background

As the seals are broken, the first judgment that occurs is that Christ allows a man to appear on earth who will pose as a "saviour of the world."

He will be Antichrist. He is carrying a bow...but no arrow. This may indicate in his early years of rule that he will be well-liked because of his dedication to peace.

Already we are seeing a tremendous upsurge for peace in the United States. College students for several years have been most vocal, sometimes destructive, because their voice was not heard. Now, after the deaths of four students at Kent, Ohio in May, 1970, there are indications that war has lost its popularity, even when it appears justified.

Antichrist will eventually become head of the Federated States of Europe, working for peace (2 Thessalonians 2). He will attempt to settle the Arab-Israeli dispute and it appears that he will initially side with Israel (Daniel 9:27).

PAST	PRESENT	RAPTURE	FIRST 3½ TRIBULATION	LAST 3½	ARMA–GEDDON	MIL–LENNIUM	NEW HEAVENS & EARTH

3 And when he had opened the second seal, I heard the second beast say, Come and see.

4 And there went out another horse *that was* red: and *power* was given to him that sat thereon to take peace from the earth, and that they should kill one another: and there was given unto him a great sword.

Zech. 1:8-11;6:1-8
Rev. 17:3,6 (scarlet —blood)

Commentary

3-4. After the false prophets and the Antichrist appear (the White Horse) then the lies and deceptions of these demagogues bear their fruit on the earthly scene. Christ said in Matt. 7:15-20 that teachers should be judged by their fruits, i.e., by their doctrines and the results that these bring. Here the cries of the White Horseman bring on the bloodshed of the second horse—the Red Horse. The color of blood and the sword show that now revolutions and wars are caused *to a hitherto unparalleled scale.* Wars have always existed—before Christ, while Christ lived, after His death and ascension, and to the present day. During the time of the loosing of this Red Horse, however, the bloodshed will be intensified; it will be more widely spread than ever; peace is now taken from the earth!

Why are the first seven judgments *seals?* And why are the first four seals depicted as *running horses* with riders? Answer: The seals portray to us the fact that God's future judgments were ordained in advance but securely held back until God's time of releasing them. Now they are opened for us so that we can see by the eye of faith their devastating effects in advance. To the unbelievers they yet remain fastened until their actual occurrence on the earth. Why the horses? Answer? Horses display rapid motion covering much ground; and horsemen indicate guidance and direction to the horses' strides. Thus the first four seals the horses and riders, tell us that these four judgments of God will *during this period* come rapidly upon the earth and they will overspread the earth swiftly. From the appearance of today's headlines with its false prophets and revolutions, riots, and wars it would appear that the earth is rapidly preparing herself for the racing of the white and red horses.

The SECOND Seal

A RIDER on a RED HORSE

WAR

Background

By mutual consent of all the nations involved, 10 nations will merge into a united force, working for peace under Antichrist (Revelation 17: 12, 13; Daniel 7:24).

However, the Northern Confederacy (Russia) has other plans. The prophet Ezekiel foretold of a day when Russia would plan to go into Israel to gain her wealth. See Ezekiel 38:11,12.

One of the great prizes Russia desires is the vast mineral deposits in the Dead Sea. It is calculated that there is enough potash to provide the needs of the entire world for 2000 years.

Why is potash so valuable?

There are two important reasons:

> 1. Fertilizer. Potash is used in fertilizer. In the end-times with a famine-filled world, potash will represent a life-giving property.
>
> 2. Explosives. Potash is important in the producing of explosives.

It has been estimated that the value of potash, bromine and other chemical salts in the Dead Sea is 1 trillion, 270 billion dollars!

PAST	PRESENT	RAPTURE	FIRST 3½ LAST 3½ TRIBULATION		ARMA-GEDDON	MIL-LENNIUM	NEW HEAVENS &EARTH

Revelation 6

5 And when he had opened the third seal, I heard the third beast say, Come and see. And I beheld, and lo a black horse; and he that sat on him had a pair of balances in his hand.

Zech. 6:2,6

6 And I heard a voice in the midst of the four beasts say, A measure of wheat for a penny, and three measures of barley for a penny; and *see* thou hurt not the oil and the wine.

2 Kg 7:1,16,18

Commentary

5-6. Following the demagogues stirring up the earth and the resultant bloodshed, now comes famine shown as a Black Horse with a rider holding balances. In 2 Kings 7:1, 16, 18 it is seen that the ancient method of selling food was by weighing it on one side of a balance with certain set weights on the opposite side (Prov. 16:11; 11:1). Here the famine is illustrated by the rider having in his hand a pair of balances in order to carefully portion out the scarce quantities of food.

Famine follows warfare because the unsettled conditions (1) do not permit farming in many areas, and (2) they discourage farmers from planting for fear that a year's work will be ruined or stolen in one afternoon by marauding troops or by a confiscating government.

The current population of our globe is 3 1/2 billion, and by 2000 A.D. demographers predict that this figure will double. Malthus, laughed at for years since the inventions of the reaper, the harvester, and the discovery of modern fertilizer, will have the last laugh. We are rapidly approaching the day of this horseman and the spread of birth-control knowledge is not retarding the coming explosion of the biggest bomb of all—the population bomb set to go off at around 2000 A.D. A rising population, hungering, fed on lies and deceptions by false prophets is easily ignited into war and revolution. Then the cry is for a world leader with some earthly solution for the ills of the earth—He will appear; he will be the Antichrist.

What can Christians say as these things appear today to be on the horizon? Answer: Luke 21:28,

"And when these things begin to come to pass, then look up, and lift up your heads; for your redemption draweth nigh."

The THIRD Seal

A RIDER on a BLACK HORSE

FAMINE

Background

We are already seeing the spectre of famine not only in other parts of the world but right in the United States. Right now in the United States over 36 million Americans get some free food!

Already in Brooklyn, New York there is a food products company that sells 30,000 packages of assorted insects a month. Food packages include french fried ants, caterpillars, baby bees and grasshoppers.

In 1950 there were 6 million people on relief. Yet, in spite of the economic growth of this country, in spite of the added luxuries and new inventions...just 18 years later, in 1968, there were 9½ million people on relief! And $9.8 billion was spent in 1968 alone for relief costs.

Abortion laws have been eased. Hospitals are setting up special abortion clinics to speedily handle this operation. It is a simple matter now to arrange for an abortion. Soon the government will be encouraging it. A congressman has already suggested birth *coupons.*

Right now over 10,000 people starve to death every day. In Biafra at one point over 100,000 a month were dying of starvation. It is not difficult, therefore, to picture the relevant closeness of this soon coming judgment.

▼

PAST	PRESENT	RAPTURE	FIRST 3½ TRIBULATION	LAST 3½	ARMA-GEDDON	MIL-LENNIUM	NEW HEAVENS & EARTH

7 And when he had opened the fourth seal, I heard the voice of the fourth beast say, Come and see.

8 And I looked, and behold a pale horse: and his name that sat on him was Death, and Hell followed with him. And Power was given unto them over the fourth part of the earth, to kill with sword, and with hunger, and with death, and with the beasts of the earth.

Rev. 1:18
Rev. 13:5
Rev. 9:15

2 Kg 2:24; Ezek. 34:28

Commentary

7-8. The color of the fourth horse is actually a "pale green" or "yellow-green." The Greek word here is *chloros* which is the root of the modern word *chloro*phyll. This is the horrible hue of sick and dying tissue, and it aptly conveys the image of death.

Death personified rides this mount and fittingly *Hades,* the "unseen world," trails behind to gather up the victims. Their dominion here is specified in detail, literally: *"And there-was-given to-them authority over the fourth of-the earth."* This could mean that a fourth of mankind was slain; yet it may rather mean that death reigned over a region equal to one-quarter of the earth. It speaks *not* of a fourth of mankind; but of a fourth of the "earth" (Greek: *ge*—hence our word *ge*-ology, "earth science"). In either case abundant slaughter reigns. Man refused God and now God unleashes man to devour one another in this first set of judgments.

"With sword, and with hunger, ..."—From this we see that the death of the fourth horseman results largely from the CONTINUING RIDING OF THE FIRST THREE HORSEMEN. The sword was the second, and hunger was the third.

The word for "sword" here *(hromphaia)* in 6:8 is different from the "sword" of the second horseman *(machaira—6:4).* The word here, *hromphaia,* is used also in 1:16; 2:12,16; 19:15,21 and it refers to the barbaric Thracian broad sword. The *machaira* spoken of in 6:4 and 13:10,14 denotes any sword, a Roman short sword, or even a long knife (Mk. 14:43; John 18:10,11; Heb. 4:12). Despite the difference in words it seems evident that the bloodshed of the second seal continues on and that it yields the "sword" death of the fourth seal as its fruit.

Thus these swift FOUR HORSEMEN OF THE APOCALYPSE now continue to ride during the remainder of the Tribulation Period.

The FOURTH Seal

A RIDER on a PALE HORSE

DEATH

Background

Our own generation has seen the wholesale death of Jews as more than 6 MILLION perished under the Nazi regime.

And for the most part, the world stood helplessly by...many in unbelief! It has been said that even many of the Jews as they were being herded into box cars, although warned of their fate, refused to believe that such an event would occur.

And here in the Fourth Seal, following famine, we see one-fourth of the population of the earth destroyed.

If we went on the basis of our present population...this would mean that, in a short span of time, some 750 million people will die.

Whatever the exact figure — or if death *only* reigns over a quarter of the earth's land area — it will be a frightful toll. Today, as never before, one can see how such a catastrophe can easily occur.

PAST	PRESENT	RAPTURE	FIRST 3 1/2 TRIBULATION	LAST 3 1/2	ARMA– GEDDON	MIL– LENNIUM	NEW HEAVENS & EARTH

9 And when he had opened the fifth seal, I saw under the altar the souls of them that were slain for the word of God, and for the testimony which they held:

Rev. 1:9
John 11:25-26

10 And they cried with a loud voice, saying, How long, O Lord, holy and true, dost thou not judge and avenge our blood on them that dwell on the earth?

Rom. 12:19; Isa. 63:4
Gen. 4:10

11 And white robes were given unto every one of them; and it was said unto them, that they should rest yet for a little season, until their fellowservants also and their brethren, that should be killed as they *were,* should be fulfilled.

Eph. 1:11

Commentary

9-11. Following the false Christs, war, famine, and death comes the fifth seal, martyrdom. Amid the turmoil on the world scene the ungodly will grow in hatred against Christ. Instead of deploring sin as the cause of their trouble, their anger will be kindled at those who turn to Christ and who will now no longer cooperate with their humanistic endeavors.

Compare the first five seals with the Olivet Discourse in Matt. 24:4-9...

1st.	Seal	False Christs	False Christs (Matt. 24:5)
2nd.	Seal	War	Wars (24:6-7)
3rd.	Seal	Famine	Famines (24:7)
4th.	Seal	Death	Pestilence (24:7)
5th.	Seal	Martyrdom	Martyrdom (24:9)

Note that in Matt. 24:8 Jesus refers to the *first four* items as "the beginning of sorrows." Thus He segregates these four from those that come later. Likewise Revelation 6 devides the *first four seals* from the others by putting them in their own category of *horsemen.* From this the conclusion would seem to be that, *although* the ills of Matt. 24:4-9 are those which have more or less characterized all history *both* before Christ and after Christ, *nevertheless* here in Matt. 24:4-9 and in the seals of Revelation 6 the beginning of the Tribulation Period is described. Both join in declaring that an early phase of false prophets, war, famine, and death will be soon followed by the making of Christian martyrs. All of this will take place in the first 3 1/2 years of the period, before the Abomination of Desolation is perpetrated and the persecution by Antichrist is unleashed in all of its fury during the second 3 1/2 years (Matt. 24:15,21; Rev. 12 and 13). Revelation 6:11 confirms the fact that more martyrs will come later—in the second 3 1/2 years. Yet, praise be to God, they who have died for Christ still live (6:10)!

The FIFTH Seal

MARTYRED SOULS UNDER ALTAR

PERSECUTION

Background

The spring of 1970 saw a sudden interest in our environment. Even college students became aware that we were polluting our earth. Earth Day (April 22, 1970) was set aside to discuss the issues and the possible solutions.

THE ENVIRONMENTAL HANDBOOK came out of a UNESCO convention and was prepared by FRIENDS OF THE EARTH. It was at this same convention that U Thant praised Lenin as a great humanitarian and defender of liberty!

THE ENVIRONMENTAL HANDBOOK makes among other recommendations the following:

1. Nations must be phased out as quickly as possible.
2. Christianity bears a huge burden of guilt for ecological problems.
3. Experimental living groups should construct their shelters from...church windows.

There is already a growing animosity towards the Bible and Christians. In a coming day those who refuse to accept the Mark of the Beast will be unable to buy food, and will face starvation and possible death.

PAST	PRESENT	RAPTURE	FIRST 3 1/2 LAST 3 1/2 TRIBULATION	ARMA– GEDDON	MIL– LENNIUM	NEW HEAVENS & EARTH

12 And I beheld when he had opened the sixth seal, and, lo, there was a great earthquake; and the sun became black as sackcloth of hair, and the moon became as blood;

13 And the stars of heaven fell unto the earth, even as a fig tree casteth her untimely figs, when she is shaken of a mighty wind.

Exod. 19:18; 20:18

Rev. 8:12
Isa. 34:4

Definitions:

Final fiery cataclysm—*The Bible teaches that someday, after the millennium, God will cause the present earth to be consumed by means of a fiery conflagration (2 Pet. 3-13; Matt. 24:35). The old world will then be replaced by the New Heavens and New Earth. Here the redeemed shall dwell in joy with Christ forever. (2 Pet. 3:13; Rev. 21:1 ff).*

Providential—*Theologically speaking, this word refers to God's holy, just, and wise governing of this world by His use of secondary causes, i.e., by floods, wars, meteors, famines, as well as good happenings. Rom. 8:28. This is in contrast to His governing by miraculous and direct (primary) means.*

Commentary

12-13. At this sixth seal we see heavenly disturbances occur which are so startling that they fittingly show to the world God's displeasure at the slaying of many of His servants during the martyrdom of the fifth seal. Earthquake, blackened sun, red moon, and meteors falling from the sky all spread terror to the heart of man. We must not think of these falling "stars" *(aster)* in terms of our modern limited definition, i.e., as far away gigantic masses of burning gas such as is our sun. The Greek word is far broader and it includes any pinpoint of light up in the sky. Thus meteor showers are signified. In fact, when shooting stars fell for three hours during the evening of November 13, 1833 many thought that the end of the world had come. Perhaps what will occur will be the sudden divinely caused falling of multitudes of pieces of "space junk" which—as remains of satelites shot into the heavens—even now orbit our globe by the thousands! As they fall out of orbit the friction with the atmosphere would light them up as Roman candles driving a population below to the extremes of fright. Recall, John describes what he sees in the language of appearance.

Could falling stars figuratively indicate civil and religious anarchy??? In 1:20; 9:1; and 12:4 (in 12:4 one third of the angels fell with Satan) "stars" do not represent literal heavenly lights but beings. Until the actual fulfillment we must speak cautiously concerning how the details of these wondrous predictions will actually come to pass on the earth.

The SIXTH Seal

CATASTROPHIC CHANGES on EARTH

DESTRUCTION

Background

In these verses (12, 13) we find four catastrophes occurring:

1. EARTHQUAKE
   This is described as a great earthquake, perhaps worldwide.
2. ECLIPSE OF THE SUN
   With the sun becoming black, this possibly could indicate an eclipse.
3. MOON BLOOD-RED
   Some have ventured the thought that hydrogen explosions could so color the atmosphere to make the moon appear blood-red.
4. FALLING STARS (METEORS)
   Imagine the terror when this event occurs.

In recent years we have witnessed many disasters. Here are but a few of them:

TIDAL WAVES	East Pakistan, 1960	10,000 dead
	East Pakistan, 1970	150,000 dead
HURRICANES	East Pakistan, 1965	47,000 dead
EARTHQUAKE	Iran, 1968	11,000 dead
	Peru, 1970	50,000 dead
WORLD WAR 2	1939-45	17 MILLION military dead
		34 MILLION civilian dead

In light of this, one can see we are already living in perilous times.

▼

PAST	PRESENT	RAPTURE	FIRST 3½ LAST 3½ TRIBULATION	ARMA-GEDDON	MIL-LENNIUM	NEW HEAVENS & EARTH

Revelation 6

14 And the heaven departed as a scroll when it is rolled together; and every mountain and island were moved out of their places.

Isa. 34:4

Rev. 16:20

15 And the kings of the earth, and the great men, and the rich men, and the chief captains, and the mighty men, and every bondman, and every free man, hid themselves in the dens and in the rocks of the mountains;

Rom. 3:9-10

16 And said to the mountains and rocks, Fall on us, and hide us from the face of him that sitteth on the throne, and from the wrath of the Lamb:

Rev. 9:6; 20:11

17 For the great day of his wrath is come: and who shall be able to stand?

Exod. 20:19

Commentary

14. The heavens here departing like a scroll must refer to the atmospheric heavens—the clouds—being suddenly rolled away so swiftly and shockingly that men will cry in horror as they stand exposed before an angry God. This verse *cannot* be describing the final fiery cataclysm described in 2 Peter 3:3-13 ("the heavens shall pass away with a great noise...") *because* the earthlings who see these events remain alive after them and many flee to nearby caves and rocks for shelter amid the celestial terrors.

15-17. Modern man marks himself as the king of his destiny and day by day claims to be more and more the master of nature and the elements. Here at God's thunder the sinners quake. Kings and masters as well as the lowest on earth fall in abject dread at these disasters. That inner sense of guilt and sin in all humans, awakened as we shall see in chapter 11 by the testimony of God's end-time witnesses, realizes that, "The great day of His wrath is come." The sinners cringe and know that God's anger is behind these PROVIDENTIAL seal calamities. Soon the Trumpet judgments will sally forth and these will be more severe than the seals; they will be SEMI-PROVIDENTIAL as the supernatural hand is etched even more plainly (chapters 8-9). Then will come the Bowls of Wrath which will be more directly SUPERNATURAL afflictions from the hand of the Almighty (chapters 15-16).

Rebellious man desires to live without God and *God raptures His Church, withdraws His restraints upon sin,* and sinful man brings the curses of the ages upon his own head in this Tribulation Period—lies, wars, famines, and death (2 Thess. 2:7; Rom. 1:24,28; Isa. 5:4-5).

Background

Two more catastrophes are brought to our attention in this Sixth Seal judgment:

1. HEAVENS OPEN
   It is hard for the human mind to fathom this occurrence, and it will be a shock when it occurs.
2. EARTH MOVES
   Imagine living in a day when *every* mountain and *every* island move out of their places!

Scientists are already acknowledging the fact that the earth's crust moves. One encyclopedia published by CBS (Vol. 1, No. 10) devotes a four page article to THE DRIFTING CONTINENTS.

It reports: The Earth consists of a liquid *core* with a radius of about 2,170 miles; a *mantle* (about 1800 miles thick) and a *crust*. The continental crust is on average 20 miles thick. Their theory is that movements in the Earth's mantle is causing continental drifts.

Scientists have recently found that Asia and Africa are splitting apart along a large fault in the center of the Red Sea.

PAST	PRESENT	RAPTURE	FIRST 3 1/2 TRIBULATION	LAST 3 1/2	ARMA– GEDDON	MIL– LENNIUM	NEW HEAVENS & EARTH

CHAPTER 7

And after these things I saw four angels standing on the four corners of the earth, holding the four winds of the earth, that the wind should not blow on the earth, nor on the sea, nor on any tree.

Zech. 6:1,5 ("four")
Rev. 4:6 ("four")

Rev. 8:7-8

Commentary

TWO SAVED MULTITUDES DURING THE TRIBULATION
7:1-8 OUT OF ISRAEL
7:9-17 OUT OF ALL NATIONS

Definition:

Parenthetical vision—*The seals, trumpets, and bowls are unleashed on a wicked world, series after series (Rev. chapters 6; 8-9; 15-16). God, however, often interrupts this chronological progress to give us a parenthesis vision—an aside that explains or reveals other concurrent happenings. Chapters 7, 10-14, 17-18 contain such side glimpses into the times of the Tribulation Period. Chapter 7 shows that many will be saved; 11 shows God's witnesses of the first 3½ years; 12-13 show the forces of evil during the second 3½ years; and 17-18 shows the destruction of the end-time Babylon systems right before Armageddon, chapter 19.*

1. "After these things," Greek: *meta tauta,* is a favorite expression of John who has a keen chronological awareness. It is used often in both Revelation (7:9; 15:5; etc.) and in the Gospel of John (6:1; 7:1; etc.). Here it refers to the next vision which John saw.

After beholding the turmoil of the seal judgments the onlooker will naturally wonder if any shall be saved amid this flood of catastrophes. God now answers that question for us in the two parenthetical visions of this chapter. The first shows that Jews will be turning to Christ at this time; the second vision shows that multitudes out of every nation will also come to Christ during these final days of the age. These two visions are the fulfillment of the "rainbow round about the throne" in 4:3.

Question: Will those unsaved who are left behind at the Rapture yet have opportunity to turn to Christ? Answer: As long as they are alive—until Christ gathers them at the Judgment of the Nations (Matt. 25:31-32ff)—they may turn to Him. If, however, they take the Mark of the Beast, they are irretrievably lost.

Background

"Who has seen the wind? Neither you nor I. But when the trees bow down their heads, The wind is passing by." Perhaps many of us have recited this poem by Christina Georgina Rossetti in our early days of Grammar school?

In some ways the wind is a symbol of fickleness — yet the way it blows is decided by unchanging laws. The sun's heat, the laws of heat transfer, and the shape and rotation of the Earth are the chief causes of the winds. Wind is caused by the uneven heating of the atmosphere (the air around the earth) by the sun.

Near the equator, heated air rises to about 60,000 feet. Yet there are no prevailing winds near the equator and up to about 700 miles on either side of it, because the air rises vertically there instead of moving horizontally across the earth. This calm belt is called the doldrums.

Since scientists believe the winds are caused by *unchanging laws* the miracle by God in this judgment, to us, appears even more remarkable as suddenly there is an awesome silence, a deadly calm.

PAST	PRESENT	RAPTURE	FIRST 3 1/2 LAST 3 1/2 TRIBULATION	ARMA- GEDDON	MIL- LENNIUM	NEW HEAVENS & EARTH

2 And I saw another angel ascending from the east, having the seal of the liv-God: and he cried with a loud voice to the four angels, to whom it was given to hurt the earth and the sea,

3 Saying, Hurt not the earth, neither the sea, nor the trees, till we have sealed the servants of our God in their foreheads.

Rev. 8:7-8

Eph. 1:13;4:30
Rev. 13:16-18

Commentary

2-3. All believers in Christ are sealed with the Holy Spirit when they believe (Eph. 1:13; 4:30). Here for the sake of John's vision and for our edification an angel, seen by John coming from an easterly direction, symbolically carries a visible seal. The actual sealing, however, is done and seen by God; and we never see any physical mark suddenly appear upon the believer's head at conversion. Yet the believer is sealed by God. God's mark of sacred ownership is placed upon the believer, and this seal is the presence of the Holy Spirit indwelling the believer (Eph. 1:13; 4:30). Here in Rev. 7:2 there is apparently also some mark visible to the spirit world placed upon the foreheads.

Verse 3 shows the command given to the four angels who will sound the Trumpet judgments which are about to occur (8:6-13) to refrain from starting their actions until certain ones have been sealed. "Hurt not the earth...sea...trees" refers to those items on earth which will be initially ravaged when the Trumpet afflictions begin (8:7-8). *Thus it would appear that after the initial Seal judgments occur, but before the Trumpets sound, God brings to salvation and marks for preservation the specially elected 144,000 out of Israel described below in vss. 4-8.* (SEE REV. 13:16-18. Significance?)

How are these Israelites saved? Ans.—Probably through the testimony of the Two Witnesses described later in chapter 11. The chaos on earth during the seal afflictions drove them to seek rescue and the Spirit showed them their sin and Christ's remedy.

But hasn't the Spirit departed with the Church in the Rapture? Yes—at least 2 Thess. 2:7 would certainly seem to indicate this—but the Holy Spirit as God still is everywhere *just as He was before He came in that* unique way at Pentecost. It seems that just as He came at Pentecost, He will in like manner leave at the Rapture with all those who have believed up to that moment. He thus can call to faith those alive during the Tribulation just as He could call men and women to faith in the days prior to Pentecost.

▼

PAST	PRESENT	RAPTURE	FIRST 3 1/2 LAST 3 1/2 TRIBULATION		ARMA-GEDDON	MIL-LENNIUM	NEW HEAVENS &EARTH

4 And I heard the number of them which were sealed: *and there were* sealed an hundred *and* forty *and* four thousand of all the tribes of the children of Israel.

Commentary

4. The 144,000 are declared to be out of Israel. Thus they are Jews who will be saved. (Since the Babylonian Captivity, B.C. 606-535, the name "Jew" has been applied to all Israelites both of the tribe of Judah [Jew-dah] and of the other tribes. In the Gospel of John the "Jews" are the political leaders of Judah. Paul, however, reflects the mixing of the names for he calls himself BOTH an Israelite (2 Cor. 11:22; Rom. 11:1) and a Jew (Acts 21:39; 22:3)—although he was clearly of the tribe of Benjamin(Rom. 11:1). He calls Peter a "Jew" though Peter was not from Judea, but from Galilee (Gal. 2:14); and he categorizes all men as either "Jews" or "Gentiles" (Rom. 2:9; 3:9; 9:24).)

PAST	PRESENT	RAPTURE	FIRST 3 1/2	LAST 3 1/2	ARMA-GEDDON	MIL-LENNIUM	NEW HEAVENS & EARTH
			TRIBULATION				

Revelation 7

5 Of the tribe of Judah *were* sealed twelve thousand. Of the tribe of Reuben *were* sealed twelve thousand. Of the tribe of Gad *were* sealed twelve thousand. 6 Of the tribe of A'-ser *were* sealed twelve thousand. Of the tribe of Neph'-ta-li *were* sealed twelve thousand. Of the tribe of Ma-nas'-ses *were* sealed twelve thousand. 7 Of the tribe of Simeon *were* sealed twelve thousand. Of the tribe of Levi were sealed twelve thousand. Of the tribe of Is'-sa-char *were* sealed twelve thousand. 8 Of the tribe of Zab'-u-lon *were* sealed twelve thousand. Of the tribe of Joseph *were* sealed twelve thousand. Of the tribe of Benjamin *were* sealed twelve thousand.

Rev. 21:16

Commentary

5-8. The tribes of Israel—of the Jews—are named. Let us forever abandon all theories that make these to be Britishers, or Anglo-Americans, or Jehovah Witnesses.

God in His sovereign good pleasure has elected to save this number during the early stages of the Tribulation Period, before the Trumpet Judgments fall, so that they can testify for Him to the many Jews and gentiles who are to be persecuted by the Antichrist.

Is 12,000 a literal number? Perhaps yes. Perhaps, however, the rounded number 12,000 represents *the elect found in each tribe* whatever that number turns out to be.

Will these be the only Jews saved during the Tribulation? No. These are saved *during* this period; many more shall be saved at Christ's coming at its *close* (Zech. 12:10; Rom. 11:26).

Note the names of the tribes: (1) originally there were 12; but Joseph's portion was doubled by each of his two sons becoming a tribe—Ephraim and Manasseh, while Levi was scattered among the tribes and not counted. (2) Here Joseph—which would include his son Ephraim—and Manasseh are both counted as is Levi! Dan is omitted. Why? It could not have been a mistake as John would have known these names perfectly. God, however, knows the answer—and for some mysterious purpose "it seemed good in thy sight" (Lk. 10:21) to omit Dan at this point. God, also, is the One who knows who today belongs to each tribe. Thus, we needn't be anxious over the fact that few Jews today are certain of their tribal lineage.

Background

ANGLO-ISRAELISM TEACHES

The 10 Tribes (House of Israel), captured by the Assyrians, migrated westward through Northern Europe, and finally became ancestors of the Saxons who invaded England.

Thus the Anglo-Saxons are the "lost" ten tribes of Israel . . . and heirs to God's promises.

THE BIBLE SAYS

"And I will scatter you among the nations . . ."
". . . to the twelve tribes which are scattered abroad."
Leviticus 26:33; James 1:1

"Behold, the eyes of the Lord God are upon the sinful kingdom, and I will destroy it from off the face of the earth, [except] that I will not utterly destroy the house of Jacob, saith the Lord.

For, lo, I will command, and I will sift the house of Israel among all nations, as [grain] is sifted in a sieve; yet shall not the least [kernel] fall upon the earth."
Amos 9:8,9

The word JEW and the word ISRAEL are often used interchangeably as one. This is especially true after the Assyrian and Babylonian conquests had scattered the Tribes. Ezra records the remnant calling them JEWS (8 times) and ISRAEL (40 times). Nehemiah calls them JEWS (11 times) and ISRAEL (22 times).

The NEW TESTAMENT speaks of Israel and Judah as ONE NATION. The New Testament uses the word JEW (174 times) and ISRAEL (75 times) alternately and often interchangeably. (See Acts 21:39; 22:3; Romans 11:1, 2 Corinthians 11:22; Philippians 3:5.)

Paul says:
". . . I am . . . a Jew of Tarsus . . . " Acts 21:39
". . . I also am an Israelite . . ." Romans 11:1

Paul uses the two terms interchangeably. The British-Israelites claim that this can never be done. Who is correct?

▼

PAST	PRESENT	RAPTURE	FIRST 3 1/2 LAST 3 1/2 TRIBULATION		ARMA– GEDDON	MIL– LENNIUM	NEW HEAVENS & EARTH

HOW THE 12 TRIBES OF ISRAEL ORIGINATED

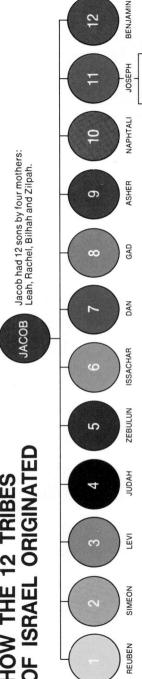

JACOB

Jacob had 12 sons by four mothers: Leah, Rachel, Bilhah and Zilpah.

| 1 REUBEN | 2 SIMEON | 3 LEVI | 4 JUDAH | 5 ZEBULUN | 6 ISSACHAR | 7 DAN | 8 GAD | 9 ASHER | 10 NAPHTALI | 11 JOSEPH | 12 BENJAMIN |

MANASSEH EPHRAIM
2 SONS *

Jacob lived with Joseph in Egypt the last 17 years of his life. Before he died, he placed Joseph's two sons, Manasseh and Ephraim, on the same level as his own sons. See Genesis 48:5, 13-22. Also read the entire 48th Chapter of Genesis.

Now 13, not 12, Tribes came into being since Joseph's Tribe was divided into two Tribes (Manasseh and Ephraim).

HOWEVER, in the distribution of the Land made by Joshua, the Tribe of LEVI had *no share* in the Land (Joshua 13:14), but only cities scattered throughout Israel to dwell in and pasture land for their cattle (Joshua 14:4). Thus God, by dividing Levi among the others, retained the number of land holding tribes at 12, the original number of Jacob's sons.

The LEVITES (Tribe of LEVI) had no inheritance in Israel; the Lord was their inheritance. See Deuteronomy 10:9.

In the MARCHES of the ARMY of Israel The LEVITES performed the priestly functions (Deuteronomy 33:10), marching behind the second echelon of Tribes (Numbers 2:17).

Levites marched with Ark of the Lord

And thus the 12 TRIBES continued as ONE until after the death of Solomon.

*Pharaoh gave Asenath to Joseph as his wife. Asenath was a daughter of Poti-pherah, priest of *On*. *On* is the modern day Heliopolis which is near Cairo, Egypt. Asenath bore Joseph two sons, Manasseh ("causing to forget") and Ephraim ("doubly fruitful") before the famine began. See Genesis 41:45-52.

HOW THE 12 TRIBES SEPARATED

The 12 Tribes were for the most part a united Kingdom under Saul, David and Solomon. When Solomon died a split occurred.

This Division occurred in 931 B.C. and continued until both Kingdoms went into captivity.

NORTHERN KINGDOM ▼ SOUTHERN KINGDOM

1	2	3	4	5	6	7	8	9	10		11	12
REUBEN	SIMEON	ZEBULUN	ISSACHAR	DAN*	GAD	ASHER	NAPHTALI	EPHRAIM	MANASSEH		JUDAH	BENJAMIN

NORTH
HOUSE OF ISRAEL
Made as their King

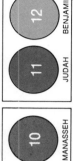

JEROBOAM¹

1 Kings 12:20

SOUTH
HOUSE OF JUDAH
Solomon's son became King

REHOBOAM²

1 Kings 12:1

These catastrophes virtually wiped out tribal distinctions. The tribes are not mentioned by name again except in the book of Psalms and in prophetic portions of Scripture†. While some of the exiles returned to Jerusalem under Ezra and Nehemiah, they never really regained their independence except for a few years under the Macabbees (142 B.C.).

Yet Future:
"The word of the Lord came again unto me, saying, Moreover, thou son of man, take thee one stick, and write upon it, For Judah, and for the children of Israel, his companions; then take another stick, and write upon it, For Joseph, the stick of Ephraim, and for all the house of Israel, his companions; And join them one to another into one stick, and they shall become one in thine hand." (Ezekiel 37:15-17)

1 Jeroboam, of the tribe of Ephraim, founded the Northern Kingdom of Israel when the nation was split following the death of Solomon. Afraid to let his people return to Jerusalem to worship (for fear they would be won back to the House of Judah) he set up centers of worship in Dan and Bethel using the image of the golden calf. He led the people into immoralities of heathenism which eventually led to their destruction.

2 Rehoboam, son of Solomon, was the first ruler of the Southern Kingdom of Judah. Rehoboam raised an army from Judah and Benjamin, but was forbidden by God to attack his brethren, the Northern Tribes, which had seceded from the nation. He then instituted pagan rites and false worship centers and waged a relentless struggle against Jeroboam, King of the Northern Tribes. He was buried in the City of David (part of Jerusalem).

* DAN was originally settled in the southern half of Israel, along the coast. When it was unable to subdue the powerful Anakim, the Tribe migrated to the far north of the nation.

** NEBUCHADNEZZAR began the Babylonian Captivity of the HOUSE OF JUDAH at about 606 B.C. when he took Daniel and others as captives to Babylon. He took more captives again in 597 B.C. Finally when King Zedekiah of the House of Judah revolted against him, Nebuchadnezzar, in 586 B.C., came and destroyed Jerusalem, burned the Temple, and took the rest of the nation to Babylon as captives.

Shalmanser, King of Assyria dispersed the 10 Tribes in 721 B.C.

Nebuchadnezzar, who became King of Babylon, took Jerusalem and burned down the Temple. 586 B.C.**

131

ANGLO-ISRAELISM SAYS

"We want to impress here that Israel and Judah are not two names for the same nation." [1]

HOUSE OF ISRAEL
White Americans and White Englishmen are true Israelites and thus heirs to the promise that go with the Throne of David.

ANGLO-SAXONS 10 TRIBES

HOUSE OF JUDAH
"The House of Judah . . . mongrelized God's Truth so badly, by adding many pagan ideas (for example the immortality of the soul), that a *new-found* religion was born." [2]

JEWS 2 TRIBES

The House of Israel
is not Jewish.

The Jews are the
House of Judah only.

EXCLUSIVE PROMISES of God's prophecy belong to Great Britain and the United States.

BUT Anglo-Israelism neglects:

In the TRIBULATION PERIOD (between the breaking of the Sixth Seal and the Seventh Seal) 144,000 of the children of Israel (12,000 from each of the 12 tribes) will be "sealed." (See Revelation 7:2,3) Revelation 7:4-8 names these 12 tribes including JUDAH.

[1] Thomas: God and My Birthright, page 5
[2] Ambassador College: TOMORROW'S WORLD, Dec. 1969, page 12
[Note: The Throne of David could not possibly belong to the 10 Tribes of the North (supposedly "Britain"), because David himself (and Christ) came from the southern Tribe of Judah.]

THE BIBLE SAYS

". . . I will sift the house of Israel among ALL nations . . ."
(not just into Great Britain) Amos 9:9   About 728 B.C.

"And (you—*all of the tribes)* shall be removed into all the
Kingdoms of the earth." Deuteronomy 28:25. Moses About
1400 B.C. (Thus the 10 tribes, included here, would be scattered
—they would not stay together and wind up in England.)

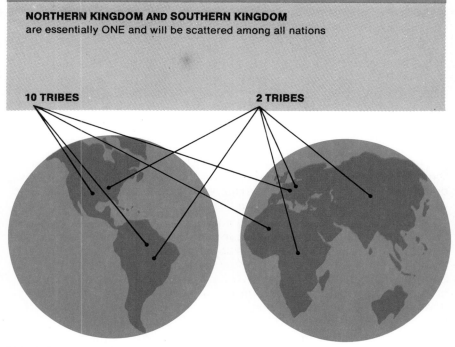

NORTHERN KINGDOM AND SOUTHERN KINGDOM
are essentially ONE and will be scattered among all nations

10 TRIBES   2 TRIBES

INCLUSIVE promises to ALL who profess faith in
Christ Jesus

"For ye are all the sons of God by faith in Christ Jesus.
For as many of you as have been baptized into Christ have
put on Christ. There is neither Jew nor Greek, there is
neither bond nor free, there is neither male nor female;
for ye are all one in Christ Jesus. And if ye be Christ's,
then are ye Abraham's seed, and heirs according
to the promise."   Galations 3:26-29

After the Millennium, with the establishment of the New Heaven
and New Earth,the New Jerusalem will have 12 Gates, each
one bearing the name of one of the tribes of Israel including one
gate named JUDAH.
See Revelation 21:12.

Revelation 7

9 After this I beheld, and, lo, a great
multitude, which no man could number,
of all nations, and kindreds, and people,
and tongues, stood before the throne,
and before the Lamb, clothed with white
robes, and palms in their hands;

Lk.15:22; Mt.22:11ff
John 12:13;1 Kg.6:29

10 And cried with a loud voice, saying,
Salvation to our God which sitteth upon
the throne, and unto the Lamb.

John 1:29

Commentary

9. Now the second parenthetical vision of this chapter begins. Just as
the reader finishes reading in Rev. 7:1-8 that God will save many Jews
during the Tribulation Period, the Sacred Account now reveals that God
will also save a mass out of the gentiles.

These come "out of every nation" and out of "tribes and peoples and
tongues" (Greek), and thus this group is not a Jewish group but a gentile
one from all over the world. It was so large that John despairs of even
trying to assign a number to it. How well this fits our modern era of
burgeoning population. Seven billion on earth by 2000 A.D.! With such
numbers John could see the almost numberless mass of those redeemed during the Tribulation and yet, as the Scriptures show, the
mass of the world will still follow Antichrist (13:8).

The white robes show that they have been washed from their sins—thus
these are people who have turned to Christ for salvation.

10. This verse could be translated as it is in the KJV above or it could
be translated possibly as: "...Salvation is by our God who sits upon the
throne, and by the Lamb." While both of these perfectly fit the Greek,
this latter translation—taking the dative cases as instrumentals*—strikes
me as better fitting the present context.

†The 10 northern tribes were *scattered* in 721 B.C. in fulfillment of the
prophecy of Deuteronomy 28:25, 37. These people were *scattered* eventually into Europe, Asia, Africa, and finally some into the Americas. (They did
not wander off together as a nation into Europe, get LOST, and then finally
still remaining together at about 550 A.D. turn up again in Great Britain as
the British Anglo-Saxons. Such a mythical 1200 year journey—as is ad-
vocated by the British-Israelites—has no support in either Scripture or sec-
ular history.)

* *For students of Greek.*

Golgatha (place of the skull) where Christ was crucified. Once the Lamb of God went to the cross scorned and with a crown of thorns. Now He sits upon the heavenly throne in Kingly dress and is worshipped.

Background

It is significant to note here that this multitude of Gentiles who are saved during the Tribulation carry palms in their hands.

There appears to be a distinction between this group and the Christians earlier caught up in the Rapture. This group apparently has no crowns at this point...yet they hold palms, a symbol of rejoicing and gladness.

Because this assemblage in white robes is gathered from out of the Tribulation Period, many will consequently suffer martyrdom and wear the crown of martyrs. Those who were previously caught up in the Rapture seem to be represented by those sitting AROUND the throne (Revelation 4:4). Those, however, who are saved in the Tribulation Period are here seen standing BEFORE the throne (Revelation 7:9).

These verses make it evident to us that worldwide preaching will somehow occur during the Tribulation for this "multitude, which no man could number of all nations" will come to Christ.

PAST	PRESENT	RAPTURE	FIRST 3½	LAST 3½	ARMA-GEDDON	MIL-LENNIUM	NEW HEAVENS & EARTH
			TRIBULATION				

11 And all the angels stood round about the throne, and *about* the elders and the four beasts, and fell before the throne on their faces, and worshipped God,
12 Saying, Amen: Blessing, and glory, and wisdom, and thanksgiving, and honour, and power, and might, *be* unto our God for ever and ever. Amen.

Psa. 29:2;95:6;John 4:23

Commentary

11-12. "On their faces...worshipping God...Saying, Amen: Blessing...glory...wisdom...thanksgiving...honour...power...might...unto our God for ever and ever. Amen." Here we have a wonderful portrait of *true worship* which certainly includes adoration to God, thanksgiving, and prayer. Each of us should meditate from time to time on the praises and attributes here assigned to God. While we would not deny the precious truth that the Lord is indeed our ever present friend; yet at the same time we should not fall into the opposite error of constantly thinking of God in so casual a manner that we fail to *worship* Him as we ought.

Background

The Book of Revelation mentions three groups of believers who will be saved during this period.

First: The Martyred remnant which is saved during the first half of the Tribulation. See Revelation 6:9-11.

Second: The 144,000 Jews who are saved during the first half of the Tribulation. God gives them His seal for protection (Revelation 7:2-8). And with this protection they are physically preserved from *God's* judgments which will fall on a wicked world during the Tribulation.

Third: The Gentiles described in Revelation 7:9-14 as the "great multitude, which no man could number." These are saved probably chiefly in the last half of the Tribulation.

Both the entire First and many—if not all—out of the Third Group suffer martyrdom. Many die by being beheaded for the witness of Jesus (Revelation 20:4).

Will the guillotine again become a common method of execution in the Tribulation Period?

PAST	PRESENT	RAPTURE	FIRST 3 1/2 TRIBULATION	LAST 3 1/2	ARMA-GEDDON	MIL-LENNIUM	NEW HEAVENS & EARTH

13 And one of the elders answered, saying unto me, What are these which are arrayed in white robes? and whence came they?

14 And I said unto him, Sir, thou knowest. And he said to me, These are they which came out of great tribulation, and have washed their robes, and made them white in the blood of the Lamb.

Jer. 30:7; Dan. 12:1; Matt. 24:21. Rev. 12:11

Commentary

13-14. The elder seeks to instruct John on the origin of this Second Saved Multitude, and as good teachers often do, he introduces his subject by a question. John's, "Sir, thou knowest," means, "Sir, I don't know but surely you must know and can tell me."

"Came out of great tribulation" in the Greek is literally, *"...These are the ones coming out of the great tribulation."* Notice that the verb is in the present tense and that the definite article "the" is clearly included. The significance of the Greek article is one of *identification.* Thus these have not come out of the general tribulation of this life—of which the Christian has much (Rom. 5:3; 8:35)—but rather these have *emerged from out of THE* GREAT TRIBULATION.

What is THE GREAT TRIBULATION spoken of in scripture? The answer is clear: Jer. 30:5; Dan. 12:1; Matt. 24:21,29. It is that end-time period which will end this age, Daniel's Seventieth Week, especially its final 3 1/2 years when Antichrist breaks the covenant and launches his worldwide persecution. Thus here we are taught that an immense number from all tribes and nations will be saved during the Great Tribulation. Again, this is the significance of the rainbow which surrounded the throne of judgment (Rev. 4:3).

Christ himself, in his Olivet Discourse, gave us the name "Great Tribulation when He spoke of this period, saying,

"For then shall be great tribulation, such as was not since the beginning of the world to this time, no, nor ever shall be."

(Matthew 24:21)

PAST	PRESENT	RAPTURE	FIRST 3½	LAST 3½	ARMA-GEDDON	MIL-LENNIUM	NEW HEAVENS &EARTH
			TRIBULATION				

15 Therefore are they before the throne of God, and serve him day and night in his temple: and he that sitteth on the throne shall dwell among them.
16 They shall hunger no more, neither thirst any more; neither shall the sun light on them, nor any heat.
17 For the Lamb which is in the midst of the throne shall feed them, and shall lead them unto living fountains of waters: and God shall wipe away all tears from their eyes.

Rev. 22:1; Zech. 13:1
Rev. 21:1

Commentary

15-16. It is plain that at the time contemplated in this vision this second saved multitude is safe with Christ. "Therefore are they before the throne, and serve him..."—They are seen now having come out of the Great Tribulation. This gives rise to the question, "Did they die as martyrs during the Tribulation?" for 14:13 and 20:4 indicates that many will indeed be slain for Christ during this time.

I would like to suggest that the answer is not made clear as to exactly when and how all of these came to be in the presence of the Lord. What is made clear, however, is that in the end all of those who do accept Christ during this period—who wash their robes in the blood of the lamb —end up with Christ in eternal safety and bliss. That is the important truth here.

17. Verse 17 speaks of those blessings promised as part of the life of the redeemed in the eternal state, *viz.*, living fountains and no more tears forever (Rev. 22:1; Zech. 13:1; Rev. 21:1). Thus John by this vision is given a sight of all those saved during The Great Tribulation and he sees them safe with the Lamb. Many no doubt arrived here through martyrdom; others survived the period and were saved from Antichrist's Armageddon slaughter by the timely coming and rescue of Christ (Matt. 24:22,31).

So much for chapter 7's visions. The church will be raptured and the wicked earthlings judged, but yet amid the Tribulation's fury God will call many many to faith out of both the Jews and the Gentiles. There is indeed a rainbow about the throne! Halleluia!

▼

PAST	PRESENT	RAPTURE	FIRST 3 1/2 LAST 3 1/2 TRIBULATION		ARMA-GEDDCN	MIL-LENNIUM	NEW HEAVENS & EARTH

CHAPTER 8

And when he had opened the seventh seal, there was silence in heaven about the space of half an hour.

Psa. 39:2; Hab. 2:20

2 And I saw the seven angels which stood before God; and to them were given seven trumpets.

3 And another angel came and stood at the altar, having a golden censer; and there was given unto him much incense, that he should offer *it* with the prayers of all saints upon the golden altar which was before the throne.

Rev. 5:8

CHAPTERS 8 AND 9: THE TRUMPETS

1. After the parenthetical visions of chapter 7 which revealed to us God's abounding mercy during this time of earthly plagues, the revelation of the judgments now continues. Chapter 6 closed with the releasing of the sixth seal, and we here continue with the seventh being opened.

John saw the seventh seal extracted from the scroll, and this was followed by half an hour of silence. Why? Apparently the contents of this seal were so strikingly awesom that even the celestial occupants were moved to silence. This silence in no way implies any questioning by the heavenly angels of the righteousness of loosing the contents of this seal upon a world which daily curses God; it, the silence, rather shows the gravity of the situation which has been wrought by man's sinfulness. Stern measures are needed; stern measures are to be used.

2. The contents of the seventh seal are revealed in the personages of the seven trumpet angels which now appear into view. The seal is pulled, there is a silence, and these seven appear. The awful plagues now to be released by these seven are described in chapters 8 and 9 and their fierceness fully justifies the period of silence in heaven.

Some suggest that the contents of the seventh seal *is* the half hour of silence—hence, silence is taken to represent peace on earth. Thus the seventh seal brings us to the appearance of Christ and the millennial peace. This must be rejected. The silence of vs. 1 is not described as the content of the seal; it is a by-product IN HEAVEN and not on earth.

3. The plagues on the earth brought by the trumpets will be the answer to many a prayer of the saints. These judgments will drive many to Christ, they will judge the sinners, and they will vindicate the testimony of the saints as to God's holiness, eventual judgment, and ultimate triumph.

SILENCE and then

THE SEVEN TRUMPETS

Background

Do you ever recall from your schooldays being in a class where suddenly the teacher stopped talking...and there was silence!

What happened? Those who were inattentive or talking suddenly stopped their activity and looked up, awaiting perhaps the anger or wrath of the teacher.

Sound is all around us...from the whispering wind to the jangling alarm clock. Much sound, such as that of jets, cars and some music, is causing sound pollution, threatening deafness even in the young.

A world without sound would be unpleasant and even dangerous. Yet perhaps no response could better declare the terror that lies ahead than this awe-inspiring silence.

The time of relative peace is short-lived. In this first 3½ years, Israel has been living under a false security that soon will end with terror and tragedy.

PAST	PRESENT	RAPTURE	FIRST 3½	LAST 3½	ARMA–	MIL–	NEW
			TRIBULATION		GEDDON	LENNIUM	HEAVENS &EARTH

Revelation 8

4 And the smoke of the incense, *which came* with the prayers of the saints, ascended up before God out of the angel's hand.

5 And the angel took the censer, and filled it with fire of the altar, and cast *it* into the earth: and there were voices, and thunderings, and lightnings, and an earthquake.

Lev. 16:12; Nu. 16:46

Exod. 19:16; 20:18
Rev. 4:5; 11:19; 16:18

Definition:

Altar—a raised platform upon which sacrifices were offered to God. These were of two kinds. The Lay Altar was made of earth or of uncut stones. Here laymen, as opposed to priests, could sacrifice to God as was done in the patriarchal age (Exod. 20:24-26). The Temple Altar (including the altar in the Tabernacle) was made of brass, cut stones, and other materials into a definite rectangular shape. Four prongs, or "horns," jutted out and above the altar from its four corners; one horn from each corner. A Main Altar for the animal sacrifices was in the court outside of the sanctuary, and a smaller Altar of Incense was within the Holy Place of the sanctuary.

Commentary

4-5. In this heavenly ceremony which was shown to the Apostle certain spiritual realities are being manifested to us by visual aids—as, for example, in the case of water baptism. Here through the golden censer, or small incense bowl, first the prayers of the saints are offered to God and then the heavenly fire is cast upon the earth with thunderings being heard seemingly as the holy flames strike the ground beneath. What does this represent? It seems to portray the truth that God is sending the coming trumpet judgments down upon the earth in answer to the accumulated prayers of his people. How many Christians have suffered even tortures at the hands of those who hated Christ! How many have prayed that the day would come when God would vindicate His people and His holy name! Now that day has come, and the thunders of judgment crackle as the fire from the holy altar strikes ground so long desecrated by feet "swift to shed blood" (Rom. 3:15).

The 6-Day War, contrary to popular belief, never ended! It soon became the Yom Kippur War and Israel was lulled into a semblance of normalcy by couriers of peace. One day, in the midst of agonizing war . . . peace will suddenly come.

Background

The Antichrist has fulfilled his promises in bringing peace to the land and protecting the Jews — perhaps from the onrushing armies of Russia and her allies. Some would believe they are approaching Utopia.

The unified church will be instrumental in helping to bring about the union of the Western Democratic Powers (Rev. 17:3), working towards peace...a peace without God. And soon the Great Tribulation will be ushered in.

You will recall that during World War 2 conventional weaponry was used on Japan for several years. But then suddenly, without warning, the most destructive force ever devised by man was unleashed on two cities reducing them to ashes. This was the atomic bomb. Its ratio of death and destruction far surpassed previous tribulations on the Japanese people.

In far greater magnitude...as the first 3½ years of the Tribulation Period brought judgments...the period to follow will be much more devastating.

▼

PAST	PRESENT	RAPTURE	FIRST 3½	LAST 3½	ARMA-GEDDON	MIL-LENNIUM	NEW HEAVENS & EARTH
			TRIBULATION				

6 And the seven angels which had the seven trumpets prepared themselves to sound.

7 The first angel sounded, and there followed hail and fire mingled with blood, and they were cast upon the earth: and the third part of trees was burnt up, and all green grass was burnt up.

Exod. 9:23-25:
Ezek. 38:22

Commentary

6. More plagues now begin to fall upon the earth during this Tribulation Period already beset with false prophets, wars and revolutions, famine, death, martyrdom, and astounding signs in the sky. The seals begin the seven years and the bowls of wrath (chapters 15-16) are almost—as we shall later see—at the close of the seven years. It is the trumpets which fall in the middle. Thus commentators disagree as to which half of the period the trumpets should be assigned.

At present I am inclined to think that the trumpets occur in the latter half of the first 3 1/2 years. I *think* this to be so because they are introduced to us *before* the great parenthetical break of chapters 10 through 14 which reveals the worldwide kingdom of the Antichrist WHICH BEGINS ESSENTIALLY AT THE MIDPOINT OF THE SEVEN YEARS WHEN THE ABOMINATION OF DESOLATION IS COMMITTED.

7. A heavenly fire falls as the first *trump sounds both a warning* to those in rebellion against God and gives *a signal* for the attack to the heavenly forces. God's judgments are now galloping forward.

A third of the trees and all of the green grass are burned as a result of this first trumpet. The Greek word *ge* can mean "earth" or "land," and so the account does not clearly specify whether one third of all of the trees in the world will be burned or whether what is seen burned is a third of the grass and trees in the area of Eur-asia and Palestine. In any case, end-time godless man claims that he can control the natural environment and here God rains fire from heaven to destroy grass and trees and humanistic man looks on helplessly.

From the description, a supernaturally originated physical calamity seems to be described. Could this be when Ezek. 38:22 is fulfilled???

THE FIRST TRUMPET

HAIL, FIRE, BLOOD
⅓ Earth on Fire
⅓ Trees Burned
All Grass Burned

Background

You will note that all these plagues have the element of fire in them.

These initial plagues cause destruction of only a third part which would seem to indicate that God is still dealing with His people in mercy.

Fire is the heat and light that comes from burning substances. Three conditions must exist before fire is produced. There must be a fuel or substance that will burn. The fuel must be heated to its *kindling temperature.* There must be plenty of oxygen. How often have you read where people have died...not because of the flames of the fire but rather because the fire consumed the available oxygen in a room?

In 1968 in the United States alone there were 115,344 forest fires burning 2,787,328 acres of land!

Imagine the fury of God's judgment upon nature. God is cursing the earth because it is the scene of man's display of lawlessness.

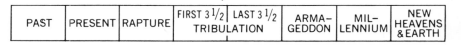

PAST	PRESENT	RAPTURE	FIRST 3 1/2 LAST 3 1/2 TRIBULATION	ARMA-GEDDON	MIL-LENNIUM	NEW HEAVENS &EARTH

8 And the second angel sounded, and as it were a great mountain burning with fire was cast into the sea: and the third part of the sea became blood;

Exod. 7:14-25; Rev. 16:3

9 And the third part of the creatures which were in the sea, and had life, died; and the third part of the ships were destroyed.

Exod. 7:21

Commentary

8-9. At the second trump John sees a great mountain mass aflame which is hurled into the sea turning one third of the sea to blood. The exact nature and origin of the mountain is not specified. We can speculate—and speculations are permissible so long as we do not confuse them with plainly taught truth. Is this a supernaturally activated volcano which has its upper mass, its crown, exploded into the air? Perhaps so—perhaps not?

The third part of the sea becomes blood. Clearly we are dealing with judgments which are yet *partial*—"a third"—but later the final Bowls of Wrath will be more thoroughly devastating. Then the second bowl will turn the waters entirely to blood (16:3). "The sea" may well indicate the Mediterranean Sea which washes Patmos Isle, Ephesus (where John lived before and after the vision), and the Holy Land. Perhaps it refers to the oceans also? Some are dogmatic on this—some one way and some the other—but since their dogmatism is not based on additional knowledge it is of little value. "Blood" surely at least signifies water that has turned to the color of blood. We must recall that John speaks in the *language of appearance;* he did not run a microscopic analysis on the water. What is described seems to be a *literal* turning of the water to a deep red which can honestly be described by the word "blood." This literally occurred in Egypt at the First Plague (Exod. 7:14-25) so we may expect it to take place again only now on a wider scale. The fish die in both cases (Exod. 7:21; Rev. 8:9). Here as part of the concomitant events a third of the ships are destroyed—perhaps by the tidal effect of the mountain striking the water.

FALLING METEOR

**THE
SECOND
TRUMPET**

Destroys
⅓ Ships
⅓ Fish
⅓ Sea filled with Blood

Background

The world's merchant fleet totals about 45,000 ships. This does not include military ships such as destroyers, aircraft carriers, and submarines.

The United States has plans now to spend over $20 BILLION for new sophisticated ships for its Navy.

Along with the merchant fleets of 45,000 ships one must add the navies of the world with about 3000 more ships, a total of 48,000 vessels. If a third of these ships were destroyed it would approximate 16,000 ships.

It must also be kept in mind that the 3000 ships of the navies are manned by approximately 1,527,000 personnel. This could mean that perhaps as many as ONE-HALF MILLION men will perish at sea with their ships.

This disaster plus one-third of the fish dying will truly create a sea red with blood.

PAST	PRESENT	RAPTURE	FIRST 3½	LAST 3½	ARMA–	MIL–	NEW
			TRIBULATION		GEDDON	LENNIUM	HEAVENS
							&EARTH

10 And the third angel sounded and there fell a great star from heaven burning as it were a lamp, and it fell upon the third part of the rivers, and upon the fountains of waters;

11 And the name of the star is called Wormwood: and the third part of the waters became wormwood; and many men died of the waters, because they were made bitter.

Rev. 16:4-6

Deut. 29:18; Prov. 5:4;
Jer. 9:15; 23:15;
Lam. 3:15, 19;
Amos 5:7

Commentary

10-11. The Greek word, *aster,* "star," refers to any heavenly light-emitting body, and anything fitting this description could be meant. What is here described seems to be a burning falling meteor—but a fiery space ship descending or a parachuted illuminated bomb could also fit. We have the description and we can be certain that when the event comes to pass it will appear exactly as here described. The precise nature of the star, however, is not revealed beyond this visual account.

The effect produced gives this star its name, *wormwood.* As ancient wormwood *(apsinthos),* a bitter substance, this falling star causes the rivers and reservoirs to become bitter and undrinkable. Here again the judgment is partial—a third—compared to the later Third Bowl of Wrath which will ruin the drinking water of the rivers everywhere (Rev. 16:4-6).

Look now at the mass of men who deny the supernatural and who claim in their exultant humanism that they control their world and destiny. God has judged them in His fury and yet they are loathe to acknowledge either His existence or their own frailty. Have you ever seen a sinner utterly helpless but still not ready to turn to the One who can save? This trumpet will produce multitudes like this—but some will come.

THE THIRD TRUMPET

FALLING STAR

Poisons
⅓ of all
Water on Earth

Background

Perhaps you remember the near disaster that occurred in Skull Valley, Utah.

On March 13, 1967 a jet plane flown by an Air Force pilot released 320 gallons of "nerve gas" that had been recently developed by the United States.

A sudden shift in winds caused perhaps less than 5% of the released load to fall accidentally 20 to 30 miles from the planned clear target. This small percentage of nerve gas settled on thousands of grazing sheep killing almost instantly 6400 of these sheep.

This accident awakened Americans to the fact that already catastrophic biological weapons of destruction exist...which can wipe out millions in seconds.

The "flaming star" from heaven could well be a falling spaceship whose nuclear or biological weapons poison one-third of all water on earth. Only time will tell. This judgment is in God's hands.

PAST	PRESENT	RAPTURE	FIRST 3½ TRIBULATION	LAST 3½	ARMA–GEDDON	MIL–LENNIUM	NEW HEAVENS & EARTH

12 And the fourth angel sounded, and the third part of the sun was smitten, and the third part of the moon, and the third part of the stars; so as the third part of them was darkened, and the day shone not for a third part of it, and the night likewise.

13 And I beheld, and heard an angel flying through the midst of heaven, saying with a loud voice, Woe, woe, woe, to the inhabiters of the earth by reason of the other voices of the trumpet of the three angels, which are yet to sound!

Rev. 16:8

*Exod. 10:21-23;
Matt. 27:45*

Rev. 9:12; 11:14

Commentary

12. Now something occurs that beclouds the light of the sun and moon. It is dark for part of the day; it is dark for part of the night. When the light is shining a third of the sky is still obscured.

Supernaturally caused darkness—whether God used secondary causes or not—came to pass in the Ninth Plague of Egypt (Exod. 10:21-23), at the crucifixion (Matt. 27:45), and at the *Fifth* Bowl of Wrath which is yet to come near the end of the Tribulation Period (Rev. 16:10-11). Since the darkness in Egypt and at the crucifixion were literal physical phenomena we should expect the same to occur here at the Fourth Trump. Since the Egyptian plague had real darkness, why should this similar plague judging a World-Egypt of rebellious sinners speak merely of *spiritual* darkness?

How will those earthlings who deny God explain this darkness? Will it perhaps be caused partially by human atomic weapons? In any case the darkness will come and multitudes will be chaotic—but will they now look up in belief and in repentance to Him who is the Light of the World?

13. Just as the first four seals were segregated from the others by their being pictured as horses because of their swiftness, so now the last three trumpets are called "Woes" because of their intense severity. The judgments—from seals to trumpets to bowls—get progressively worse in their destructive effects. *This alone should show that these three sets are not three different descriptions of the same events.*

THE FOURTH TRUMPET

SUN, MOON & STARS

⅓ of Sun, Moon & Stars DARKENED

Background

This can be the most terrifying of the judgments so far. Imagine if today the sun were darkened for one-third of the day. One would probably with the darkness experience extreme or unusual cold one-third of the day. Then when the sun shines...the heat would be intense.

The effects of climate and weather on man are considerable. Climate determines the clothes people wear, the style of their houses, the food they eat, the plant and animal life that surrounds them.

With the sun dimmed and darkened the way of living for everyone will be drastically disrupted. This will cause great alarm and fear.

There are many who already believe that minor climatic changes are occurring. In the summer we sometimes experience power blackouts caused by overloading due to air conditioners. Imagine the power failures that will someday occur when more and more electricity is used for longer and longer periods of time...to light, then to cool, then to heat!

PAST	PRESENT	RAPTURE	FIRST 3½ TRIBULATION	LAST 3½	ARMA-GEDDON	MIL-LENNIUM	NEW HEAVENS & EARTH

CHAPTER 9

And the fifth angel sounded, and I saw a star fall from heaven unto the earth: and to him was given the key of the bottomless pit.

2 And he opened the bottomless pit; and there arose a smoke out of the pit, as the smoke of a great furnace; and the sun and the air were darkened by reason of the smoke of the pit.

VERSES 1, 2

Rev. 12:4

Psa. 55:23; Nu. 16:30, 33

Rev. 19:3; Isa. 34:10

CHAPTER 9: THE FIFTH AND SIXTH TRUMPETS

1. Here at the fifth trump John sees a light descending rapidly from heaven. Apparently when the light reaches the ground John observes that this is not merely a burning meteor, but rather some personage to whom is given the key of "the bottomless pit" (Greek: *tou phreatos tes abussou; literally: "the shaft of the abyss").*

The one to whom the key is given is not identified for us by name despite our great desire to know who exactly this is. Some insist that it must be an evil being—Satan, a fallen angel, or a demon—but others say that only a good angel would be given this turnkey function. In either case it is God's permissive will that opens this door and the caged beings will rush out in a frenzy.

2. The apostle next beholds the opening of the shaft and he at once sees a mass of smoke pour out. This visionary glimpse into the unseen world corresponds with Luke 16:24 in the particular that the unseen chambers of the ungodly are characterized by things associated with intense heat and fire. Here it is smoke; in Luke 16:24 it is flames.

The sun and the air being darkened by the smoke demonstrates to us that this "shaft of the abyss" is an extremely awful place which may not have been opened for a long time—for the smoke seems to have collected in quantity and it now gushes out.

Each night, except during the winter months, out of the caves of Carlsbad Caverns National Park, New Mexico, emerge several million bats. The sky is blackened for two hours as thousands follow thousands into the air at twilight for their nightly food gathering vigil. They come as "a smoke out of the pit, as the smoke of a great furnace."

| THE FIFTH TRUMPET | LOCUSTS
5 Months of Torture by Scorpion Stings |  |

Background

It is difficult to imagine a bottomless pit which, when uncapped, gushes forth smoke that darkens the sun and air.

The pit is an abyss. And an abyss is a great shaft like a well. Abyss means "bottomless." This word occurs seven times in Revelation. It occurs twice in other parts of the New Testament. In Luke 8:31 the demons pleaded with Jesus not to command them to "go out into the deep." This pit or abyss is the intermediate place of punishment of the fallen angels and demons.

And when this pit is opened...everything goes...so to speak. We are now no doubt seeing a little of what is yet to come...with permissiveness, pornography, and obscenity all allowed to run rampant today in the name of "freedom."

| PAST | PRESENT | RAPTURE | FIRST 3½ LAST 3½ TRIBULATION | ARMA-GEDDON | MIL-LENNIUM | NEW HEAVENS & EARTH |

Revelation 9

3 And there came out of the smoke locusts upon the earth: and unto them was given power, as the scorpions of the earth have power.

Exod. 10:4-20

4 And it was commanded them that they should not hurt the grass of the earth, neither any green thing, neither any tree; but only those men which have not the seal of God in their foreheads.

Exod. 10:15

Exod. 8:22-23

Commentary

3. Now amid the smoke John beholds locusts *(akris:* locusts, grasshoppers) pouring out of the now opened shaft. These are given the power of scorpions *(scorpios).* The scorpion is a large member of the class arachnida, 4 to 7 inches in diameter including the leg spread, which is fairly common in the southern latitudes. These have a fierce sting and are greatly feared for this. Thus here these INFERNAL LOCUSTS have the mobility of the grasshopper and the horrible sting of the dread scorpion!

4. "It was commanded them"—That is, this is the ability and limitation which they are given to accomplish God's permissive will and they will instinctively obey it. There need have been no verbal command given to them.

Here we see the strange command given to these locusts. Locusts thrive by devouring rapaciously that which grows and is green; but here these Infernal Locusts will not eat grass or tree leaves. They will, rather, sting and bite humans as do mosquitoes. Yet amid the seemingly indiscriminate biting done by these, there is an unseen discrimination! They will in some divine way not be able to bite those who have been sealed. This, however, need not surprise the Bible believer. In Egypt the flies of the Fourth Plague swarmed only upon the Egyptians and not upon the Israelites. Thus will God have mercy even during this awful Tribulation Period upon those who turn from their sins to trust in Him. Yet, alas, most will harden their hearts as did Pharaoh (Exod. 8:32).

A rare photograph of the "walking catfish." Can jump 4 feet out of water, moves overland at will, virtually impossible to handle, kills everything it comes across.

Background

Some of the deepest areas in the world are found in the oceans. These especially deep areas are called trenches. The deepest discovered trench in the Pacific Ocean is the Mariana Trench which is 36,198 feet or almost 7 miles deep! While in the Atlantic Ocean the deepest discovered trench is the Puerto Rico Trench which is 28,734 feet deep.

While the locusts described in these verses may appear strange...one must remember that even today scientists are baffled by some strange new breeds of insects and animals.

In the summer of 1969 suddenly 17-year "locusts" emerged 4 years ahead of schedule. In some areas of Chicago there was discovered a million and a half locusts per acre! A plague of locusts can go on for 20 years—until it is killed off by the locusts being blown into a cold climate.

Florida wildlife experts are worried about the "walking catfish" which threatens to upset the balance of nature. And now, the influx of the especially ferocious Formosan termite into the U.S. poses a peril here.

▼

PAST	PRESENT	RAPTURE	FIRST 3 1/2 TRIBULATION	LAST 3 1/2	ARMA–GEDDON	MIL–LENNIUM	NEW HEAVENS & EARTH

5 And to them it was given that they should not kill them, but that they should be tormented five month: and their torment *was* as the torment of a scorpion, when he striketh a man.

6 And in those days shall men seek death, and shall not find it; and shall desire to die, and death shall flee from them.

Rev. 11:10; 14:10; 20:10

Job 3:21
Rev. 6:15-17

Commentary

5. Here we are informed of the exact length of this locust plague, five months (We will consider the nature of these locusts in connection with verses 7-10). We are not told as to why the plague ceases after the fifth month. Perhaps these locusts die off naturally, or it may be that those on earth at this time finally discover some chemical or mechanical way to annihilate them?

In a book by a wise Ohioan named Shadduck entitled, *Mistakes That God Did Not Make,* he points out the fact that the theory of organic evolution is inadequate to explain why a bee did not evolve with the sting of a black widow and soon destroy all of the mammal life from the globe. Here now in this Fifth Trumpet the omniscient God is here described as doing something of this very sort. These locusts shall be armed with the fearful sting of a scorpion. Those on earth will certainly be in torment with such creatures roving.

6. The natural consequences of such torments among fallen humanity is total despair. Men should see, as did some of the Egyptians, that, "This is the finger of God," and they should be driven to turn to Christ (Exod: 8:19).

The sting of the locusts, it appears, will be much like that of a scorpion even to the point that it yields torment and agony, but generally not death. People stung will be in extreme misery and they will wish to end it all, but the stings will not prove fatal. This lingering torment, as in the Egyptian plagues, will force men to face God's power over themselves and the earth—but will they react like Pharaoh (Exod. 10:7)?

PAST	PRESENT	RAPTURE	FIRST 3 1/2 LAST 3 1/2 TRIBULATION	ARMA- GEDDON	MIL- LENNIUM	NEW HEAVENS & EARTH

Revelation 9

VERSES 7, 8, 9, 10

7 And the shapes of the locusts *were* like unto horses prepared unto battle; and on their heads *were* as it were crowns like gold, and their faces *were* as the faces of men.
8 And they had hair as the hair of women, and their teeth were as *the teeth* of lions.
9 And they had breastplates, as it were breastplates of iron; and the sound of their wings *was* as the sound of chariots of many horses running to battle.
10 And they had tails like unto scorpions, and there were stings in their tails: and their power *was* to hurt men five months.

Dan. 7:19

Commentary

7-10. The apostle now describes for us the appearance of the locusts which he saw in the vision. Note the repeated usage of the comparison words "like" and "as," showing that the things described here are related in terms of what they looked like. Thus these were "like horses," but not really horses... "as...crowns" but not necessarily crowns, etc.

Exactly what are these? Answer: We do not yet know for sure. No one knows. We can read the biblical descriptions and make our calculated guesses, but until that day comes it is a prophetic mystery. There are three chief hypotheses as to the exact nature of these locusts, *viz.,* (1) they are a new species of the grasshopper family similar to the periodic appearing Seventeen Year Locust; (2) they are some form of demon spirits which God permits loose and which enter the bodies of locusts— just as the demons entered the herd of swine in Luke 8:33; and (3) they are in reality a modern army described in a figurative manner. Wearing gas masks and perhaps in helicopters and with bayonets, John might well describe them in the terms used in verses 7-10.

From the fact that the Egyptian plagues included lice and flies (Exod. 8:16, 21) we might favor theory (1); J. D. Pentecost in his excellent book, *Things to Come,* favors (3). Other commentators lean to (2). At present I incline to (3). What is your conclusion???

In any case when it comes to pass it will be a tormenting plague and men will seek death because of it—and it will come to pass.

PAST	PRESENT	RAPTURE	FIRST 3 1/2 LAST 3 1/2 TRIBULATION		ARMA-GEDDON	MIL-LENNIUM	NEW HEAVENS & EARTH

11 And they had a king over them, *which is* the angel of the bottomless pit, whose name in the Hebrew tongue is A-bad-don, but in the Greek tongue hath *his* name A-pol-ly-on.

Job 26:6; 28:22.

12 One woe is past; *and,* behold, there come two woes more hearafter.

Rev. 8:13; 11:14

Commentary

11. The name of the King of these Locusts is given. In the Hebrew it is *Abaddon* which means "destroyer," or "destruction" as it is used in Job 28:22 (*"Destruction* and death say,..."). The equivalent Greek word is *Apollyon* and it too means, "The one who is destroying." This word appears only once in the Greek New Testament, here in 9:11.

Now the text does not say that the King of these locusts is himself a locust. So the Commander-in-chief of many military forces is not a soldier, but a civilian. Thus the King of the locusts may well be Satan who personifies in reality the purpose of doing evil and rebelling against God.

If the King is Satan then these locusts are some group of insects, demons, or armed military men who are determined to do great evil. God, however, will not permit his sealed ones to be hurt by these (vs. 4). The locusts will be used of God in His permissive will to torment other evil beings—the unrepentant humans alive during this Tribulation Period (Psa. 76:10).

12. Here we see that these trumpet woes come not all at once, but one after another in time. The locust plague of the fifth trumpet was filled with more horror than were the earlier trumpets, hence it was called a "Woe." Two more awful woes are yet to come upon the rebellious earthlings. These infidels looked at the creation and said, "My how luckily everything worked out through evolution;" during the coming Tribulation they will have opportunity to say, "My how unluckily everything is working out now." Yet behind it all, even their seared consciences and blinded eyes cannot fail to see the spectre of a holy God sitting in judgment of a wicked world!

Background

These "locusts" may be of the insect or animal variety. Or they may be men...perhaps an army being unleashed from an underground complex.

Our fighting men in Vietnam have already witnessed how the enemy has built huge underground complexes with as many as 500 interconnecting rooms. Some rooms house hospital and operating quarters... others house ammunition and soldier's quarters.

There already has been invented a flying jet belt. When worn it can fly men at various speeds and altitudes. These men can carry a cylinder on their back which can emit a chemical substance from their exhaust openings. If one of the biological chemicals were used—from this tail area could be sprayed a substance which could cause painful stings.

PAST	PRESENT	RAPTURE	FIRST 3½	LAST 3½	ARMA-GEDDON	MIL-LENNIUM	NEW HEAVENS & EARTH
			TRIBULATION				

13 And the sixth angel sounded, and I heard a voice from the four horns of the golden altar which is before God,

14 Saying to the sixth angel which had the trumpet, Loose the four angels which are bound in the great river Eu-phra-tes.

15 And the four angels were loosed, which were prepared for an hour, and a day, and a month, and a year, for to slay the third part of men.

I Kg. 1:50-53; 2:13-25.

Rev. 16:12; Gen. 2:14.

Eph. 1:11; Isa. 46:8-11.
Rev. 9:18; 6:8.

Commentary

13. Here at the trumpet sound of the sixth angel a voice comes from the horns of the altar. The altar was a place of sacrifice for sin and to the horns of the altar victims were sometimes tied (Psa. 118:27). Fugitives would clasp a horn of the altar and ask for mercy (1 Kg. 1:50-51). Can you think of the reason for them doing this?

The voices from the horns would here seem to signify a cry for the judgment of sin; the time for mercy has elapsed. Perhaps the angelic cry is to the effect that, "Let the sixth judgment fall upon the wicked for they do not yet come to the horns of the altar through trust in Christ in order to ask God for mercy!"

14. Here the coming of the army of 200 million horsemen is somehow associated with the river Euphrates (See Rev. 16:12 which speaks of this river being dried up in order to make way for the armies of the East which will at the end of the Tribulation be marching toward Armageddon.). Thus it may be that here too what is portrayed is a gigantic land army coming somehow across the Euphrates River.

Look at the Euphrates on a globe. An army from Russia, Iran, Red China, or India marching into either the Holy Land or Africa could hardly avoid crossing the Euphrates. The same is true for an African army going into Asia. Thus we may well here have pictured an army or a group of confederated armies moving from Asia into Palestine or Africa. It could also, of course, be the other way around, but at present this seems remote.

15. This, when it happens across the world scene may seem to be all of man's doing, but here we are told that God had foreordained it to come to pass long long before. The death toll will be frightful. One-third of men will be killed! Thus either a third of the world's population will be slain—or what seems more likely from the localizing label of the "Euphrates," a third of those in the battle region will be slain!

THE SIXTH TRUMPET

SATAN'S ARMY
200 Million Warriors Kill ⅓ of Mankind

Background

Imagine an army of 200 million men destroying one-third of the world's population. Soon the population of our present world will approach 6 billion people. It is now 3 1/2 billion but by the year 2000 experts believe it will zoom to 6 billion.

If one-third of all men were killed at that time...this would be 2 BILLION dead. The United States presently has only a little over 206 million. Such destruction as described here could leave all of the United States population dead. One-third or 2 BILLION could kill everyone in Asia, as Asia's present population is 2 billion people!

The most densely populated state in the United States is New Jersey where there are on the average 774 persons for every square mile! Europe is the most densely populated continent with 159 persons per square mile; Asia has only 119 persons to the square mile.

PAST	PRESENT	RAPTURE	FIRST 3 1/2	LAST 3 1/2	ARMA– GEDDON	MIL– LENNIUM	NEW HEAVENS & EARTH
			TRIBULATION				

16 And the number of the army of the horsemen *were* two hundred thousand thousand: and I heard the number of them.

17 And thus I saw the horses in the vision, and them that sat on them, having breastplates of fire, and of jacinth, and brimstone: and the heads of the horses *were* as the heads of lions; and out of their mouths issued fire and smoke and brimstone.

18 By these three was the third part of men killed, by the fire, and by the smoke, and by the brimstone, which issued out of their mouths.

19 For their power is in their mouth, and in their tails: for their tails *were* like unto serpents, and had heads, and with them they do hurt.

Rev. 9:7-10

Rev. 9:15

Rev. 9:10

Commentary

16. 200,000 x 1000 equals 200,000,000 or 200 million! An army such as this, if a human army, would best fit a population giant such as Red China.

17-19. Here is an amazing description much like that of the locusts of vss. 7-10. Again as in the case of the locusts we are perplexed as to whether these will be (1) some sort of animal or insect plague here figuratively described. In Egypt frogs, then lice, then flies, and later locusts came one after another, Exod. chapters 8-10; so these 200 million could well follow the locusts; (2) a demon or fallen angel army could perhaps also be here described; or (3) a great human army may be intended. No one knows which it is for sure; John is describing the creatures in terms of his experience and his vocabulary—though without error as they looked just that way. But what are they??? What do you think? I am *today* inclined to think that they are a human army with weapons and gas masks. They are either an organized army *or* a spontaneous army, such as 200 million communists taking to arms suddenly in various parts of Asia. What an awful time in which to live!

▼

PAST	PRESENT	RAPTURE	FIRST 3 1/2 LAST 3 1/2 TRIBULATION	ARMA-GEDDON	MIL-LENNIUM	NEW HEAVENS & EARTH

20 And the rest of the men which were not killed by these plagues yet repented not of the works of their hands, that they should not worship devils, and idols of gold, and silver, and brass, and stone, and of wood: which neither can see, nor hear, nor walk:

Exod. 8:32; 10:7; 11:9.

Isa. 46:5-7;
I Cor. 10:20-21.

21 Neither repented they of their murders, nor of their sorceries, nor of their fornication, nor of their thefts.

Luke 16:29-31.

Commentary

20. The mass of those on earth at this time who have been spared death reveal the hardness of their sinful hearts by their continued refusal to repent despite the awful evidence of God's judgment which now lurks everywhere around them. They are like Pharaoh, Exod. 8:10; 10:7.

These who remain adamant in their unrepentence continue to worship devils (Greek: *daimonia,* literally "demons"). That is, they follow and give allegiance to those false prophets and doctrines which are inspired by Satan and his demonic emissaries. The scriptures show this to be especially the case in the latter days of this age (I Tm. 4:1). The Antichrist himself, called "The Beast," shall be inspired of Satan (Rev. 13:4); thus he who follows the Antichrist will be worshipping the Devil.

The unrepentent worship gold and silver, that is, worldly wealth is their idol which replaces the One True and Living God. They worship that which is made—brass, stone, and wood. Do not the Communists make their scientific and engineering achievements their god??? Yet these cannot see or move of themselves any more than could the ancient Baals and Dagons.

21. The earthlings even amid these tortures do not repent of "their murders" (they are filled with violence and hate), "their sorceries" (occultism, astrology, and narcotic euphoria is on the increase), "their fornication" (immorality reigns again as it did in the days of the Fall of the Roman Empire), nor of "their thefts" (dishonesty in charging fees is today embraced by civic leaders and professional men alike as well as by the average man who cheats on taxes). Read Romans 1:18-32; 3:10-18. Thus after the holocaust of the seven seals and of the first six trumpets the world as a whole yet stands fast in its sin.

PAST	PRESENT	RAPTURE	FIRST 3 1/2	LAST 3 1/2	ARMA-GEDDON	MIL-LENNIUM	NEW HEAVENS & EARTH
			TRIBULATION				

CHAPTER 10

And I saw another mighty angel come down from heaven, clothed with a cloud: and a rainbow *was* upon his head, and his face *was* as it were the sun, and his feet as pillars of fire:

Dan. 10:5-6
Dan. 10:6

2 And he had in his hand a little book open: and he set his right foot upon the sea, and *his* left *foot* on the earth,

Dan. 10:4; 12:7

3 And cried with a loud voice, as *when* a lion roareth: and when he had cried, seven thunders uttered their voices.

CHAPTER 10: THE SUN-FACED ANGEL

1-3. Chapter 10 now gives us the parenthetical vision of THE SUN-FACED ANGEL AND THE LITTLE SCROLL. Just as the opening of the sixth seal (6:12-17) was followed by the parenthetical visions contained in chapter 7, so here too following the sixth trumpet (9:13-21) we now have a series of parenthetical visions before the blowing of the final trump in 11:15.

The vision here at hand in chapter 10 shows the coming of a powerful angel—perhaps even one of the archangels such as Michael or Gabriel (Dan. 8:16; 9:21; Luke 1:19, 26; Dan. 12:1). This angelic appearance occurred when the Apostle John saw the vision centuries ago; it does not depict a future angelic visitation during the Tribulation Period.

It would appear certain that this is not the same book as the one which Christ is opening during this period (5:1ff). The book which Christ is opening was the Seven Sealed Scroll (*Biblos*—5:1) while here it is a Little Scroll (*Biblaridion*). This little book, or scroll, apparently contained additional details of the events which were to occur in the latter half of the Tribulation Period which our Book of Revelation now begins to enter in chapters 12-19 and parts of 11.

Background

How refreshing after a raging storm to see a peaceful sky with the arch of brilliant colors which we call a rainbow. If the rain has been especially heavy the rainbow may spread all the way across the sky, and its two ends seem to rest on the earth.

You will recall that God originally placed a rainbow in the clouds as a token of His covenant. This covenant with Noah was that He would never again destroy this world by a flood (Genesis 9:11-13).

And while the world has passed through awesome judgments God is still a God of mercy to those who will call upon Him.

Here we see an angel with a rainbow on his head, a face bright as the sun, and feet as pillars as fire.

This angel well pictures Christ's dealings with men at this time. He comes with mercy, yet with power, and with feet as pillars of fire—ready to mete out judgment to those who are still ignoring His previous judgments.

PAST	PRESENT	RAPTURE	FIRST 3 1/2	LAST 3 1/2	ARMA-GEDDON	MIL-LENNIUM	NEW HEAVENS &EARTH
			TRIBULATION				

Revelation 10

4 And when the seven thunders had uttered their voices, I was about to write: and I heard a voice from heaven saying unto me, Seal up those things which the seven thunders uttered, and write them not.

Dan. 12:4

5 And the angel which I saw stand upon the sea and upon the earth lifted up his hand to heaven,

Dan. 12:7

6 And sware by him that liveth for ever and ever, who created heaven, and the things that therein are, and the earth, and the things that therein are, and the sea, and the things which are therein, that there should be time no longer:

Dan. 12:7

7 But in the days of the voice of the seventh angel, when he shall begin to sound, the mystery of God should be finished, as he hath declared to his servants the prophets.

Dan. 12:7; 9:24, 27

Commentary

4. The seven thunders here described no doubt are additional judgments from God upon those on earth who stand fast in their rebellion against Him. The number "seven" shows that there is here another *complete cycle* of judgments awaiting the wicked, and the details of this cycle have been sealed up and hidden from us. Since, however, thunders are portents of divine judgments in the Book of Revelation, we can be certain that when these seven thunders come to pass their effects will be fierce and devastating.

Seventh Day Adventist works profess to know the contents of the thunders, but they err for these things have been sealed up!

5-7. *These verses find their parallel in Daniel 12:7 and 10:4-6* (which see)! Daniel 10:5-6 gives the description of Daniel's "Man clothed in linen" who is the speaker and actor of the words and deeds of Daniel 12:7. The description, words, and action found here in Daniel seem to be essentially the same as that of Rev. 10:5-7. Both show resplendent angels of great power. Both stand apparently by the water's edge—claiming God's ownership and sovereignty over His land and water creation. Both lift a hand to heaven and sware by God. But, where the angel in Daniel declares that there are yet coming 3 1/2 years ("times") to complete God's judgment of this age, here the angel in Revelation announces "Time no longer." That is, the time for the judgments of the Great Tribulation have at last come at this point in the vision. Thus, it would seem, at the blowing of the seventh trump (11:15) we reach the midpoint of the week and then begin to enter that awful period described in Matthew 24:15, 21.

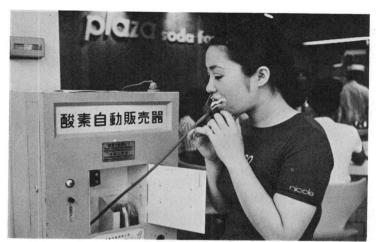

In Tokyo oxygen vending machines in coffee shops dispense a whiff for 25 cents.

Background

TIME IS NO LONGER...what a dreadful sound. Yet this is what these verses tell us. The world has gone on its merry way unheeding the previous judgments.

Now time is catching up with them. And soon the terrible vial judgments will be unleashed.

In spring, 1970 a great stir was made about Earth Day. For a brief moment people seemed concerned about the dangers that could come from our polluting the earth. But soon it was forgotten.

Some scientists predict that starvation and pollution will cause man to virtually become extinct within the next 30 years. Others fear a severe oxygen shortage will occur because our pollutants are killing oxygen-producing plants. In Japan already there are oxygen dispensing machines. Fertilizers high in nitrates are further polluting our water systems.

Men of scientific renown are issuing dire warnings that time is running out. One day...God tells us that TIME will be no longer. Then come judgments. It is too late!

PAST	PRESENT	RAPTURE	FIRST 3 1/2 LAST 3 1/2 TRIBULATION		ARMA- GEDDON	MIL- LENNIUM	NEW HEAVENS & EARTH

8 And the voice which I heard from heaven spake unto me again, and said, Go *and* take the little book which is open in the hand of the angel which standeth upon the sea and upon the earth.

9 And I went unto the angel, and said unto him, Give me the little book. And he said unto me, Take *it,* and eat it up; and it shall make thy belly bitter, but it shall be in thy mouth sweet as honey.

10 And I took the little book out of the angel's hand, and ate it up; and it was in my mouth sweet as honey: and as soon as I had eaten it, my belly was bitter.

11 And he said unto me, Thou must prophesy again before many peoples, and nations, and tongues, and kings.

Jer. 15:16-18

Ezek. 2:9-10; 3:1-4, 14

Commentary

The idea that verse 6 teaches that there is coming a time when "time shall not be" is, I believe, quite unsubstantiated. This goes along with the dogma of some that the future eternal life will be one big "now" as everything and nothing seem to be forever happening at once. Such unsupported hypotheses about heaven need not alarm us when they spring from those who have never been there. As Dr. Herman Hoyt of Grace Seminary has said, "Time had a beginning when God began his creation; but it will never have an ending." We are temporal creatures, and we have been promised eternal—ever continuing time—life through Christ.

8-11. Here the book tasted sweet at first, but then in the stomach it was bitter. The significance of this would seem to be that this new revelation of the prophetic details of the final half of the Tribulation Period would be at first welcomed with delight, but then when the horrible martyrdoms and sufferings were described, especially of those who would be then turning in faith to God, the reaction would be one of bitterness. Is not this something akin to our own reaction to the entire Apocalypse? When we at first begin to understand some of its mysteries we are filled with delight; but then when we latter comprehend the sufferings to be yet endured by those who turn to God during those days we find ourselves feeling sick in the stomach. Our medicine is, however, the good news of God's final salvation and deliverance (Rev. 19)!

Kakhk, a village in Iran where 6000 of a village population of 7000 were killed by an earthquake. A man who had witnessed this said: "I have seen so many crushed and heard so much wailing that I can neither eat nor sleep."

Background

Those who write or speak on God's prophetic portions of His Word are sometimes referred to as "Doomsday Prophets."

For while many Christians like to sing about Heaven...and while many Pastors choose to preach about every subject in God's Word except prophecy...nevertheless these judgments are there.

And while the expectation of the Millennium and the New Heavens and New Earth are wonderful beyond words...sweet as honey. Yet in a further study of prophecy we suddenly discover that His Word also tells of awful judgments. Terrible judgments will kill one-third of the world's population, turn rivers into blood, scorch mankind with intense heat, and plunge the earth into darkness!

Many church groups preach a God of love but forget to remind their congregations that God is also a God of judgment. How often have you heard the question which begins..."How can a God of love (do this or do that)?"

PAST	PRESENT	RAPTURE	FIRST 3½ TRIBULATION	LAST 3½	ARMA-GEDDON	MIL-LENNIUM	NEW HEAVENS & EARTH

Revelation 11

And there was given me a reed like unto a rod: and the angel stood, saying, Rise, and measure the temple of God, and the altar, and them that worship therein.

Zech. 2:2; Ezek. 40:5

2 But the court which is without the temple leave out, and measure it not; for it is given unto the Gentiles: and the holy city shall they tread under foot forty *and* two months.

Rev.11:3; 12:6,14;13:5.

CHAPTER 11: THE TWO WITNESSES AND THE SEVENTH TRUMPET

1. Here in verses 1 and 2 we have the parenthetical vision of THE MEASURING OF THE TEMPLE. In Zech. 2:2 the prophet Zechariah beholds an angelic being going forth in order to measure the city of Jerusalem. The significance of that act is then revealed in Zech. 2:4 when it is explained that Jerusalem shall in the future yet be inhabited by the people of God. Thus the measuring depicted God's intention of possessing the city fully in the future. So also with Ezekiel 40:5ff where Ezekiel measures the millennial temple.

Thus here in Rev. 11:1 the measuring informs us that God will yet possess and control the temple and those who go with it, Israel.

2 Thess. 2:3-4, Matt. 24:15, and Dan. 9:27 show that a Third Temple will yet be constructed and that in the middle of the Tribulation Antichrist will desecrate it by that infamous act known as the Abomination of Desolation (Matt. 24:15). God, however, will in the end occupy His Temple.

2. The temple had its innermost court accessible only to *Priests*; then there was a court open only to Hebrew *Men*; next came the *Women's* Court or the Treasury—here Hebrew women could come as well as Hebrew men and priests. Here Jesus did much of his teaching.

Here it is announced that the Gentiles, the nations,—not Israel—shall yet dominate the temple's outer court and Jerusalem for 3 1/2 years (42 months) during the Tribulation. This must refer not to the first 3 1/2 years of this period for then Antichrist will be still honoring his covenant with Israel and guaranteeing their security in Jerusalem (Dan. 9:27). It rather refers to the last half of the seven years when Antichrist shall disannul his agreement with the Israelites and persecute them (Dan. 9:27; Matt. 24:15,21). Thus we find that Israel shall eventually have their temple, but they shall be dispossessed for the final half of the Tribulation.

▼

PAST	PRESENT	RAPTURE	FIRST 3 1/2 LAST 3 1/2 TRIBULATION		ARMA-GEDDON	MIL-LENNIUM	NEW HEAVENS & EARTH

Revelation 11

3 And I will give *power* unto my two witnesses, and they shall prophesy a thousand two hundred *and* threescore days,
clothed in sackcloth:

Isa. 8:2; 43:10; 55:4

Gen. 37:4; 2 Kg. 19:1.

Definitions:
The Tribulation Week—*This refers not to a week of days, but to the
seven year duration of the end-time Tribulation Period (Dan. 9:27;
see Gen. 29:27).*
Beast-Antichrist—*This is the coming evil "prince" of Dan. 9:27 who will
be Satan's world ruler. He is the final and ultimate antichrist (1 Jo. 2:18),
the counterfeit Christ, and in Revelation he is called "the Beast" (Rev.
11:7; 13:1ff).*

Commentary

3. Revelation 11:3-13 now gives us the parenthetical vision of THE
TWO WITNESSES. During the days of the Tribulation God will cause
two mighty prophets to arise. These two shall give a worldwide testimony to God's salvation and they shall denounce the wickedness of the
day. They shall thus be His "two witnesses." Their dress of sackcloth
shows them to be prophets in an evil age calling not for rejoicing but
rather for repentance and judgment. The span of their ministry is clearly delineated as 3 1/2 years (1,260 days at 30 days to the month).

It seems to me that the time of the ministry of these two must be during
the first half of the Tribulation's seven years. This best fits the situation
and the available evidence. Their 3 1/2 year ministry surely must coin-
cide with one of the two clearly defined 3 1/2 periods of the Tribulation
(Dan. 9:27; Rev. 11:2,3; 12:6,14; 13:5; Dan. 7:25). Then, *if the time of
the Beast-Antichrist's persecution is placed in the second half* of the
seven year week—*and it surely is* (Dan. 9:27; Mt. 24:15ff; Rev. 13:5 &
19:20)—*then the Two Witnesses must prophesy in the first half.* This is
true because at the end of the second half of the week all of God's Foes
are destroyed and the Kingdom is inaugurated; but in contrast to this,
at the end of the Two Witnesses' 3 1/2 year testimony the Two Witnesses are still lying dead in the street while God's foes make merry (Rev.
11:7-10). Thus the Two Witnesses are dead at the midpoint of the week,
and consequently their ministry was in its first half.

▼

PAST	PRESENT	RAPTURE	FIRST 3 1/2 LAST 3 1/2 TRIBULATION	ARMA-GEDDON	MIL-LENNIUM	NEW HEAVENS & EARTH

4 These are the two olive trees, and the two candlesticks standing before the God of the earth.

5 And if any man will hurt them, fire proceedeth out of their mouth, and devoureth their enemies: and if any man will hurt them, he must in this manner be killed.

Zech. 4:3, 11
John 5:35

2 Kg. 1:9-14

Definitions:
Second Temple—*The Babylonians tore down the Solomonic First Temple in 586 B.C. The Jews who returned from Babylon rebuilt the Temple, the Second Temple, from 536 to 516 B.C. under Zerubbabel and Joshua.*

Candlestick-Lampstand—*The Greek word in 11:4, as well as that in chapters 2 and 3, is* luchnia. *The translation given as "candlestick" in the King James Version of 1611 would have been better rendered as "lampstand." This was a stand upon which was fastened a lamp which burned olive oil.*

Commentary

4. Zechariah 4 gives a similar vision. There the two olive trees represent God's "two anointed ones" who are Zerubbabel, the Governor, and Joshua, the High Priest, who were then especially endued with the Spirit in order to accomplish the building of the Second Temple. Olive trees give olive oil, which was the fuel for the temple lights (Ex. 27:20). They thus symbolize those who are filled abundantly with God's spirit.

Here, during the early half of the Tribulation, God's "two witnesses" (vs. 3) will appear and they shall be two men who will be filled with the Spirit of God as was John the Baptist when he entered the scene. These will be two bright lamps, burning and shining lights for God amid a diabolical age.

5. Here we learn that for the course of their ministry as it has been predetermined by the counsel of God, forty-two months (vs. 2), they will have their lives supernaturally protected. That "fire proceedeth out of their mouth..." indicates, it would seem, that at their command fire from heaven will slay their would-be assassins just as was the case for Elijah (2 Kg. 1:9-14).

The President Rides in an Armored Car.

Background

In the United States the President requires fortress protection. For the most part he must ride in a $500,000 automobile designed to withstand small military attacks.

The car has a fighter plane canopy...and more than 2 tons of armor. This shielding is designed to stop a 30 caliber rifle bullet. The window glass and plastic bubble-top canopy, all bullet-proof, are thicker than the glass and plastic used in air force fighter planes.

The limousine runs on 4 specially designed truck tires. Within each tire is a hard steel disc with a hard rubber tread which would allow the limousine to be driven up to 50 miles at top speed with all four tires flat.

Today the Secret Service has more than twice as many agents (760) protecting the President as it had when John F. Kennedy took office. While today it takes all kinds of measures to protect one of importance... yet, in the days of the Two Witnesses, during the God-ordained period of their witness, no man will be able to hurt these messengers of God. The one who attempts to do so will suffer death in the attempt.

▼

PAST	PRESENT	RAPTURE	FIRST 3 1/2 TRIBULATION	LAST 3 1/2	ARMA-GEDDON	MIL-LENNIUM	NEW HEAVENS & EARTH

Revelation 11

6 These have power to shut heaven, that it rain not in the days of their prophecy: and have power over waters to turn them to blood, and to smite the earth with all plagues, as often as they will.

7 And when they shall have finished their testimony, the beast that ascendeth out of the bottomless pit shall make war against them, and shall overcome them, and kill them.

1 Kg. 17:1
James 5:17-18

Exod. 7:20; Rev. 8:8; 16:4

Rev. 13:1-8

Rev. 12:11

Commentary

6. Not only is the element of fire devouring those who would kill them like the power given to Elijah, but also here their ability to stop the rain can remind us of no other beside that same prophet (1 Kg. 17:1). Power to turn waters to blood and to smite with plagues, however, calls to mind Moses. Thus these two will have the powers of both Elijah and Moses—not in themselves, of course, God will be the One manifesting the power. What days are yet ahead! Apostasy and wickedness at its zenith; but God's messengers again appearing with fullness of the Spirit to inspire faith and to rebuke sin—and with the power once again to pray and see God work miracles of judgment!

Are these two men Elijah and Moses raised from the spirit world? Elijah's body was taken directly to heaven (2 Kg. 2:11) and God kept Moses' body from Satan (Jude 9). Also, these were the two who appeared alive at Christ's transfiguration (Mt. 17:3)! We can affirm that without doubt these two shall be Elijah-like (Mt. 11:14; Lk. 1:17) and Moses-like; but to dogmatically assert that the Two Witnesses will be Elijah and Moses brought back to the earth—as some do—seems to be passing off human theory as the teaching of Scripture. We must wait for the answer.

7. God permits His Two Witnesses to be slain only when their appointed ministry is finished. What a lesson there is for us here!

The Beast slays them. We will examine the identity and characteristics of this personage more when we arrive at chapter 13, *his chapter.* For now, however, let us merely note that this Beast is the final evil European-Mediterranean Empire *and* its supreme dictator, the Antichrist. The Antichrist, the "man of sin" of 2 Thess. 2:3-4, rises to world power, rules for the 3½ final years of the Tribulation, persecutes those who turn to God and is finally destroyed by Christ at Armageddon at the close of the Tribulation (19:19-20). It is he who in fierce hatred has the two witnesses of God killed!

Background

Imagine the power that these Two Witnesses will have. At their command they will be able to make the rains cease during a span of 3 1/2 years. During this time they are invincible. No one can assassinate them. Those that try are killed.

They come dressed in sackcloth. In the Bible such attire was one that depicted distress and mourning. While judgments do occur during their stay on earth...they come not primarily to bring judgment but to turn men to Christ.

In that day many in Israel will be converted.

This must outrage Antichrist as he sees his leadership being threatened. Perhaps missiles will be aimed at these Witnesses...only to return somehow to their source causing death and injury. After many attempts to destroy them, Antichrist may even fling an entire army at them...not realizing that the Witnesses finally die only because their time of 3 1/2 years is finished. Little does Antichrist know that this is a hollow victory.

PAST	PRESENT	RAPTURE	FIRST 3 1/2	LAST 3 1/2	ARMA-GEDDON	MIL-LENNIUM	NEW HEAVENS & EARTH
			TRIBULATION				

8 And their dead bodies *shall lie* in the street of the great city, which spiritually is called Sodom and Egypt, where also our Lord was crucified.

9 And they of the people and kindreds and tongues and nations shall see their dead bodies three days and an half, and shall not suffer their dead bodies to be put in graves.

I Sam. 31:9-10

10 And they that dwell upon the earth shall rejoice over them, and make merry, and shall send gifts one to another; because these two prophets tormented them that dwelt on the earth.

Cp. Isa. 14:20; Jer. 8:2

Cp. Isa. 14:16

Commentary

8. The city called "Sodom and Egypt" is identified as the city wherein our Lord was slain. Thus it is beyond all cavil Jerusalem. Consequently we are again brought to the realization that many of the events winding up this age will again center in the "Holy Land." Perhaps the Two Witnesses will live all their lives in Israel? Or perhaps one will witness in Africa and the other in Australia—God only knows. Yet their place of final ministry and death will be in Palestine. Placing their ministry during the initial 3 1/2 year half of the Tribulation, their death will come at the middle of the period. The killing of these may well occur in connection with the Abomination of Desolation when Antichrist claims to be the god of this world (2 Th. 2:3-4)!

9. The Antichrist who is Satan indwelt will hate with choler the Two Witnesses and he will curse the effects on many of their holy testimony. Now that at last he has slain them, how can he demonstrate their error? the futility of following them? the end of all who believe in the One called God? Answer: He shall leave their dead bodies to decay publically in the street so that all can behold their end and learn the obvious lesson.

This will be a world news event, and cameras shall by satellite transmit TV pictures of their decaying bodies the world over.

10. This verse has aptly been called, "The Devil's Christmas." Sinners the world over rejoice with unbridled joy to see the two who condemned their every desire now dead. Gifts are given in celebration— perhaps upon the decree or suggestion of the Antichrist. From this we must ask ourselves a profitable question, *viz.*, In a sinful era what will be the world's general reaction to true prophets of God? Then, "Are those today who call themselves God's prophets and who are *chummy* with the modernists not condemned by this verse?" Lesson?

Background

Some may wonder at the thought that the dead bodies of the Two Witnesses will be allowed to lie in a street of Jerusalem for three and a half days.

But similar actions are occurring even today. In Bagdad, the capital of Iraq, many who the government termed "spies" were executed and their bodies were left hanging in the city square for several days. This did not occur hundreds of years ago but in 1969.

And such an exhibition drew thousands who came...many in a frivolous spirit...rejoicing in the fact that the executions had taken place.

So it is not difficult to understand that during the time when the Two Witnesses are present...many will be further hardened against the Gospel...and will proclaim a holiday when their death at last occurs. Because the Witnesses pronounced condemnation upon the unbelievers ...their deaths will cause many to celebrate by giving each other gifts!

So instead of repentance...there is rejoicing.

▼

PAST	PRESENT	RAPTURE	FIRST 3 1/2	LAST 3 1/2	ARMA–	MIL–	NEW
			TRIBULATION		GEDDON	LENNIUM	HEAVENS &EARTH

Revelation 11

11 And after three days and an half the Spirit of life from God entered into them, and they stood upon their feet; and great fear fell upon them which saw them.

Mt. 27:54

12 And they heard a great voice from heaven saying unto them, Come up hither. And they ascended up to heaven in a cloud; and their enemies beheld them.

Acts 1:9
2 Kg. 2:11

Commentary

11. Here amid the derision of the wicked, the boasts of Antichrist, and the despondency of many whose hope was in God a wonderful miracle occurs. After eighty-four hours of death—when swooning or revivication were beyond grasp—God miraculously brings His Two Witnesses back to life just as He had brought Christ from death to life. As these two climb to their feet the world stands by gaping in hushed amazement. This is the greatest testimony of the careers of these Two Witnesses!

12. The heavenly voice calls and these two ascend into heaven! The world fears as they behold the irrefutable power and glory of God. Enoch, Elijah, Christ, and now these Two Witnesses along with the raptured host have now ascended to God miraculously. This time the wicked see the event with their own eyes and cannot deny it. God, as always, eventually has the last word.

Do the words, "Come up hither," here indicate that the rapture will be at the middle of the Tribulation—when these things take place—at the same time as the ascension of the Two Witnesses? Or did the words, "Come up hither," in 4:1 spoken to John prove the rapture to have been then? Obviously, any conclusion from such sayings must be regarded as pious theorizing. Pious theorizing is certainly not wrong as long as we keep in mind that we must never equate our theories as equal in value or certainly to that which the Scriptures clearly teach.

Background

Do you remember how the entire world was able to watch as man first landed on the moon? And how the world watched television for days as commentators gave a step by step account of the crippled Apollo's 13's flight back to earth?

Think of the television, radio and news coverage that this event will receive. Two Witnesses, upheld by many as the reason for all the world's troubles, finally dead. Not even buried...but allowed to lie on the street exposed to the ridicule of men, the hunger and ravaging of birds and beasts.

The whole world is in jubilation. But God intervenes. Imagine the disbelief in the voices of the reporters as they report that the dead Witnesses suddenly are standing on their feet!

Over the television screen, on the radio, people will hear as the voice of the Lord says, "COME UP HITHER." And the Two Witnesses will ascend!

God allows those living in the Tribulation Period to see the resurrection and ascension of the Two Witnesses. There can be no doubt now as to exactly what happened. It cannot be explained away!

PAST	PRESENT	RAPTURE	FIRST 3 1/2 LAST 3 1/2 TRIBULATION	ARMA-GEDDON	MIL-LENNIUM	NEW HEAVENS &EARTH

13 And the same hour was there a great earthquake, and the tenth part of the city fell, and in the earthquake were slain of men seven thousand: and the remnant were affrighted, and gave glory to the God of heaven.

14 The second woe is past; *and,* behold, the third woe cometh quickly.

Commentary

13. Within an hour of the time of the ascension of God's Two Witnesses there occurs a catastrophic earthquake. "The city" can hardly be any other than that referred to in verse 8 wherein these events occur, *viz.,* Jerusalem. A tenth of the city falls and 7,000 persons ("of men"—that is, 7,000 of the human race) are killed. While this is no small disaster, yet the earthquake of Yokohama and Tokyo, Sept. 1, 1923, killed 200,000 and destroyed Yokohama entirely and half of Tokyo. In June of 1970, 50,000 died in the Peru earthquakes.

There was an earthquake after Christ was crucified (Mt. 27:51), and here in Rev. 11:13, as there, God broadcasts by such His holy displeasure at sin. At this calamity the survivors fear and, at least for the time, recognize that God is behind the earthquake. He is proclaiming His anger at the murdering of His Witnesses.

14. Now we return again to the main sequence of the judgments of chapters 6 through 19. Seven seals to seven trumpets to seven bowls (vials) is the pattern. *The Fifth Trumpet was the "First Woe"* and this was the five month locust plague described in 9:1-11. *The Sixth Trumpet was the "Second Woe"* and this was the 200,000,000 horsemen of 9:12-21. Then came the parenthetical visions of chapters 10 and 11.

Now it is announced that the *"Third Woe"* is coming quickly. This will be the sounding of the *Seventh Trumpet* which brings forth the *Heavenly Temple* (11:15, 19) out of which—after more parenthetical visions in chapters 12-14—come the *Seven Bowls of Wrath* (15:5-8). Thus the Third Woe is the Seventh Trumpet, and its contents are the Heavenly Temple which gives forth the seven last plagues, the awful bowls of wrath! The diagram given at the beginning of Chapter 6 makes this order of succession clear.

A man wrinkled with age holds the body of a child killed in an earthquake that shook a village in North Iran in 1968.

Background

Two news events occur almost simultaneously. First the Two Witnesses are resurrected in front of everyone's eyes. Then, within the hour the television screens flash the news of an earthquake in Jerusalem. For unbelievers this is one of their blackest hours.

In this century alone ONE MILLION PEOPLE have already died in earthquakes and their attendant floods, fires and famines.

And more than 100,000 of these deaths have occurred in the last decade with Iran the victim three times.

PAST	PRESENT	RAPTURE	FIRST 3 1/2 LAST 3 1/2 TRIBULATION	ARMA-GEDDON	MIL-LENNIUM	NEW HEAVENS & EARTH

Revelation 11

15 And the seventh angel sounded; and there were great voices in heaven, saying, The kingdoms of this world are become *the kingdoms* of our Lord, and of his Christ; and he shall reign for ever and ever.

16 And the four and twenty elders, which sat before God on their seats, fell upon their faces, and worshipped God,

17 Saying, We give thee thanks, O Lord God Almighty, which art, and wast, and art to come; because thou hast taken to thee thy great power, and hast reigned.

Rev. 19:16
Dan. 7:14

Psalm 2

Definition:

Proleptic (adjective)—*That which regards future events as so certain so as to speak of them as already having been accomplished. Isaiah 53:3-9 is an example of prophetic proleptic speech. Although written 700 B.C. the words of the prophecy speak of Christ's sufferings as having already been accomplished.*

Commentary

15-17. THE SEVENTH ANGEL BLOWS THE SEVENTH TRUMPET and mighty shouts of acclamation and praise to God are lifted. Why here, but not at each of the previous trumpets? Answer: Because the seventh trump gives forth the Heavenly Temple which in turn gives forth the "Seven last plagues" and in them "is filled (completed) the wrath of God" (15:1). It is as when onlookers shout for joy upon seeing a police car enter a scene where a crime is being perpetrated. Oh yes, until the police actually get out of the car the judgment upon the robbers is not completed. Yet, when the police car is spotted turning onto the scene, at that very instant, the cries of relief and jubilation go up because the onlookers realize that the struggle is virtually now settled, or will be in a matter of a short time. So it is here! When the seventh trumpet is blown the heavenly citizens, knowing that it contains the final decisive bowl judgments, shout for joy that, "The kingdoms of this world are become the kingdoms of our Lord." With the blowing of this seventh trump God is clearly now the conqueror; the battle is seen as won— though it yet rages on earth—and the joy is unspeakable. The expressions given are *proleptic.*

THE SEVENTH TRUMPET

EARTHQUAKE

7000 Die in Jerusalem People Run to Mountains

Background

Man, who has so often placed his faith and trust in mortal Kings...has always been disappointed.

It was only after the unprecedented disaster of military defeat in 1945 that the Japanese, with profound shock, learned from their emperor—(supposedly a direct descendant of the sun-god) that he was no longer divine.

In early Egyptian days this posed a problem. If even the superior gods could die, how could the frail flesh of the king escape? Thus when the king grew old, they believed it was much better to kill him, so that "the divinity in him could be transferred to his successor."

Some kings were killed at the end of a fixed time, some at a certain age, some when they fell ill and some as the result of an annual lottery.

Soon, as these verses relate, Satan's power is to come to an end and God, our King which IS and which WAS and which IS TO COME will reign forever and ever in great power.

PAST	PRESENT	RAPTURE	FIRST 3½ TRIBULATION	LAST 3½	ARMA-GEDDON	MIL-LENNIUM	NEW HEAVENS & EARTH

Revelation 11

18 And the nations were angry, and thy wrath is come, and the time of the dead, that they should be judged, and that thou shouldest give reward unto thy servants the prophets, and to the saints, and them that fear thy name small and great; and shouldest destroy them which destroy the earth.

19 And the temple of God was opened in heaven, and there was seen in his temple the ark of his testament: and there were lightnings, and voices, and thunderings, and an earthquake, and great hail.

VERSES 18, 19

Psalm 2

Rev. 15:5-8

Ex. 19:16; 20:18

Commentary

18. This verse continues with the proleptic proclamations that view God as having judged sinners now that the 7th trump has sounded.

19. Suddenly the Heavenly Temple is seen. This temple comes from the seventh trump and out of it will come the final bowl judgments which are described in chapter 16. The earthquake and thunderings show that the time for the judgment of sin is again coming nigh. God comes forth in holy and righteous anger. The earthquake and great hail, in addition to their symbolical presence, probably cause additional havoc upon the earth. The identification of this earthquake with the one of verse 13 seems to lack evidence. They may or may not be the same. Seiss, in his classic, *The Apocalypse,* magnificently describes this scene wherein the gold covered acacia wood ark is now seen in the Heavenly Temple. He relates that the sight of this sacred box can only signify that in God's prophetic time-clock "Jewish things" have again come into view. Thus here at the middle of the seven years the "Great Tribulation" proper now begins (Mt. 24:15). Antichrist will now seek to destroy the Jews and all others who are turning to God, but they shall be saved by the God of Israel.

The time of "Jacob's trouble" (Jer. 30:7; Dan. 12:1) has arrived. And, just as we are about to see Israel, Jacob, plunged into its hour of "trouble" the blowing of the seventh trump and the appearance of the Ark assures us of God's ultimate triumph and of His not forgetting His covenant promises. He will save His remnant (Jew and Gentile)—the Ark mutely testifies to us of this (Rom. 11:26-27).

▼

PAST	PRESENT	RAPTURE	FIRST 3 1/2 LAST 3 1/2 TRIBULATION		ARMA– GEDDON	MIL– LENNIUM	NEW HEAVENS & EARTH
			FIRST 3 1/2	LAST 3 1/2			

Revelation 12

CHAPTER 12

And there appeared a great wonder in
heaven; a woman clothed with the sun,
and the moon under her feet, and upon
her head a crown of twelve stars:
2 And she being with child cried, travail-
ing in birth, and pained to be delivered.

Gen. 37:9-10

CHAPTER 12: THE WOMAN AND THE DRAGON

1. Concerning this controversial chapter, The Woman and The Dragon,
much has been written. Is the woman here described the apostate
church out of which comes her child, the true church (Buswell)? Is she
the church out of which comes her child, the Christ (Seiss)? Or is she
Israel out of whom comes the Messiah, her child of verse 2?

While I have many doubts concerning the interpretation of this detail or
that in the Apocalypse, I am persuaded that here without doubt the only
correct interpretation is that this woman with sun, moon, and twelve
stars is Israel, and that her child of verse 2 is the Messiah, Christ. Thus
the parenthetical vision here given in chapter 12 is that of the Dragon
persecuting the Woman for 3 1/2 years, that is, SATAN'S PERSECU-
TION OF ISRAEL DURING THE FINAL HALF OF THE TRIBULATION.
Matt. 24:15-21; Jer. 30:7ff; and Dan. 12:1 are some of the passages
describing this period.

The confirmation that this woman is Israel lies in Gen. 37:9-10. There
in Joseph's dream the then incipient nation of Israel is revealed. Jacob
the father is the sun; Rachael, Joseph's mother is the moon; and the
brothers are pictured as eleven stars, Joseph himself being here the
twelfth star. The sun, moon, and twelve stars match nothing else in
Scripture. The woman is Israel. The interpretations which make her anything else are far-fetched. Truly, I do not think that Seiss ever had
Gen. 37:9-10 called to his attention concerning this passage; if it had
been I believe that he too would have agreed that the woman is Israel.

2. The child that springs from Israel is the Messiah. Romans 9:4-5 declares, "Who are Israelites...of whom as concerning the flesh Christ
(Messiah) came." This confirms the interpretation. The woman is Israel,
and out of her after centuries of travail came the Christ child, the Messiah.

(With a flashback to the birth of Christ)

PAST	PRESENT	RAPTURE	FIRST 3 1/2 / LAST 3 1/2 TRIBULATION	ARMA–GEDDON	MIL–LENNIUM	NEW HEAVENS & EARTH

3 And there appeared another wonder in heaven; and behold a great red dragon, having seven heads and ten horns, and seven crowns upon his heads.

Rev. 13:1; 17:3, 10,11;
Cp. Dan. 7:6

Commentary

3. The woman, Israel, was the first "wonder" and here the Dragon is the second. The word translated "wonder" is *semeion* which literally means "sign." Thus God is in this chapter, as in others, telling us of significant world events through John's seeing "signs." Thus by the showing of a dragon persecuting a woman, God is revealing Satan's final persecution of Israel and all who turn to God.

The dragon is clearly Satan; verse 9 states this (see vs. 9). He is pictured as a dragon because he is voracious, powerful, and vicious. He is red because he is dripping with the blood of the martyrs who have been slain by his human workers.

The ten horns upon the dragon are familiar to students of prophecy. Daniel 7:7, 20, 24 and Rev. 17:12ff show these *same* horns. In these two passages they are declared to represent ten kings, and here as well as in Rev. 13:1, they represent a confederation of ten end-time rulers who give their support to the Antichrist and his persecution of Israel. See Dan. 7:7, 20, 24 and Rev. 17:12-16. These ten horns in Daniel 7 correspond with the *ten toes* of Dan. 2:42, 44. They are the final rulers of the fourth and last of Daniel's prophesied world empires (Dan. 2 and 7). Thus they are the rulers of the Roman Empire of the last days, the Revived Roman Empire. Thus they are some sort of a Euro-Medeterranean Confederation of the end-times. The fact that these ten horns appear on Satan shows that during the Tribulation Satan's political henchmen shall be these TEN KINGS OF THE REVIVED ROMAN EMPIRE. Satan shall be the real persecutor, the behind the scene master, but the actors upon the world's stage will be these ten political rulers. WILL COMMUNISM BE THEIR CREED??? (I think yes!)

We will postpone a discussion of the seven heads until 13:1 and 17:3, 10, 11.

Emblem above, a frequent sight on European cars, promotes a United States of Europe.

Background

We are already seeing evidences of the "ten horns" coming into focus. These refer to the ten-nation empire that will be in power during the Tribulation Period.

Presently we are seeing many European countries seeking to combine their economic efforts. Their goal—EUROPE UNITED. Travelling through Europe you will see this emblem on many cars. Already it is planned, before 1982, that all of Europe will be using a single currency. Possibly these 10 nations will include England, France, West Germany, Italy, Belgium, Norway, Sweden, Finland and perhaps the United States and Canada???

They will give their support to Antichrist and his persecution of Israel. These ten horns described in this verse are the same ten horns described in Daniel 7:7, 20, 24 and Rev. 17:12 ff. They correspond to the ten toe-nations of Daniel 2:42,44.

Satan will be the real persecutor in those days...but his puppets upon the world's stage will be these ten political rulers.

(With a flashback to the birth of Christ)

PAST	PRESENT	RAPTURE	FIRST 3 1/2	LAST 3 1/2	ARMA-GEDDON	MIL-LENNIUM	NEW HEAVENS & EARTH
			TRIBULATION				

4 And his tail drew the third part of the stars of heaven, and did cast them to the earth: and the dragon stood before the woman which was ready to be delivered, for to devour her child as soon as it was born.

Commentary

4. "His tail drew the third part of the stars..."—This seems to be an allusion to the fall of Satan and his subsequent leading of a third of the angelic beings into their fall into sin. Angels are sometimes, after all, signified by stars in the Scriptures (Job 38:7; Rev. 1:20; 9:1).

The dragon stood...to devour her child as soon as it was born." Here we learn that again it was Satan who was the master strategist who so directed events so as to cause Herod the Great to seek to slay the Christ child newly born in Bethlehem. Herod was the murderer of the infants as we see history, but in the eyes of God that diabolical being which urged Herod was even more guilty (Jn. 8:44).

In fact, just as God prepared Paul the Apostle from the womb for his eventual apostolic mission; so too was Herod prepared by Satan. Time after time Herod had to run to Rome to preserve his crown—in 37 B.C. to Antony; in 31 B.C. to Octavian. Herod slew his wife and his sons to preserve his throne. He systematically hunted out the last of the Hasmonean line in order to eliminate them from claiming the throne. Then when Jesus came, Satan's man was ready to preserve his throne by slaughtering the Bethlehem babies.

Potter's field where it is believed Judas hanged himself.

Background

Satan's original name was Lucifer, "The Light Bearer" or "The Brilliant One" (Ezekiel 28:11-13). He was created by God. In Ezekiel 28, we are told that (A) he was the height of *wisdom* and *beauty* (verse 13), (B) he was the *wisest* of all God's created beings (verse 12) and (C) the *administrator* of the affairs of the Angelic realm (verses 14, 15).

Lucifer's glory was a reflected glory...God being the Creator and SUN. His pride would not let him admit his righteousness was nothing. And in Isaiah 14:12-15 we read the 5 "I WILL" statements of Lucifer, who is now Satan:

1. I WILL ASCEND into HEAVEN (Lucifer perhaps dwelt in the Second Heaven...intersellar space... and while he had access to the Third Heaven...he wanted direct control there.)
2. I WILL EXALT MY THRONE ABOVE THE STARS
3. I WILL SIT UPON THE MOUNT OF THE CONGREGATION IN THE SIDES OF THE NORTH (He wanted to administer the affairs of earth and universe)
4. I WILL ASCEND ABOVE THE HEIGHTS OF THE CLOUDS
5. I WILL BE LIKE THE MOST HIGH

In his rebellion we are told that "the third part of the stars of heaven (angels)" followed him. Since Satan is not omnipresent his angels (demons) work 24 hours a day to do his evil bidding. How important it is for each of us to know Satan's purposes and his methods!

PAST	PRESENT	RAPTURE	FIRST 3 1/2	LAST 3 1/2	ARMA-GEDDON	MIL-LENNIUM	NEW HEAVENS & EARTH
			TRIBULATION				

(With flashbacks to the Fall of Satan and to the Birth of Christ)

5 And she brought forth a man child, who was to rule all nations with a rod of iron: and her child was caught up unto God, and *to* his throne.

Psalm 2

6 And the woman fled into the wilderness, where she hath a place prepared of God, that they should feed her there a thousand two hundred *and* threescore days.

Rev. 12:16

Rev. 12:14

Commentary

5. The man child was Christ and He will rule all nations as Psa. 2:7-9 teaches. The "rod of iron" is described in Psa. 2:9 and it denotes Christ's rule, after His Second Advent, in the millennial age (Rev. 20:6). It pictures Him with an iron scepter, the symbol of His reign. This can only teach us that Christ's millennial rule will deal severely with any open sin or rebellion which appears. He will strike those who rebel, if there should be such out of those then born, with His hard iron rod. So Psa. 2:10 shows that at His coming and during His reign He breaks into pieces all who oppose Him. He will yet be King of Kings and Lord of Lords (Rev. 19:16).

"Caught up unto God..."—This refers to Christ's ascension into heaven. Stephen in Acts 7:55 saw Christ standing "on the right hand of God."

6. The woman flees into the wilderness and is fed there for 1,260 days. This length of time equals 3 1/2 years at 30 days per prophetic month. Thus we are taught here that Israel will be persecuted for 3 1/2 years. This is during the last half of the Tribulation, and as has already been pointed out, such texts as the following describe these awful days and show them to be in the final half of the seven years: Mt. 24:15, 21 (from the Abomination of Desolation at the middle of the seven years to Christ's coming at Armageddon); Jer. 30:7ff; Dan. 12:1, Dan. 9:27 (from Antichrist's breaking of his covenant to protect Israel in the middle of the seven years to the end of the seven years).

Zechariah 13:8-9 shows that only ONE-THIRD OF ISRAEL SHALL SURVIVE THIS ORDEAL—this shall be the remnant which, along with the gentiles who have turned to Christ, will accept Christ as their Messiah when He appears to them on the Mount of Olives after the Battle of Armageddon (Zech. 12:9-14; 14:1-4ff).

Is the "wilderness" to which Israel flees the natural rock fortification south of Israel called Petra? Many pamphlets claim this to be so; but only time will reveal the answer.

PAST	PRESENT	RAPTURE	FIRST 3 1/2 LAST 3 1/2 TRIBULATION		ARMA- GEDDON	MIL- LENNIUM	NEW HEAVENS & EARTH

Revelation 12

7 And there was war in heaven: Michael and his angels fought against the dragon; and the dragon fought and his angels,

8 And prevailed not; neither was their place found any more in heaven.

Eph. 6:12

9 And the great dragon was cast out, that old serpent, called the Devil, and Satan, which deceiveth the whole world: he was cast out into the earth, and his angels were cast out with him.

Gen. 3:1ff

Definition:

Michael.—*One of the archangels mentioned in Scripture (Dan. 10:13, 21; 12:1; Jude 9; Rev. 12:7). He seems to bear a special protective mission in connection with Israel. His name is Hebrew:* Mi-ca-el *which is a three word combination which asks a question of adoration, "Who-is* (Mi) *like* (ca) *God (El)?"*

Commentary

7-9. Here we have a parenthetical element in verses 7-13 within this parenthetical vision of chapter 12. Verses 7-13 show that there is a spiritual war in heaven and that it culminates with the casting of Satan to the earth. When this happens Satan, knowing his time is short, unleashes his fury upon Israel. When this angelic war began we are not told. It may have began at the start of the Tribulation, or it may have started when Satan and his angelic followers first fell. In any case, the time of Satan's being cast to the earth in some special way seems clear. Verses 13-14 show that upon his being cast out Satan begins to immediately persecute Israel for 3 1/2 years ("times" 1 + 2 + 1/2 = 3 1/2). Thus he is cast out of heaven at the middle of the Tribulation.

It is interesting to note that Dan. 12:1 tells of the fierce "time of trouble, such as never was since there was a nation." This is the 3 1/2 years of "Great Tribulation" (Mt. 24:21). *In the same verse, Dan. 12:1, wherein Daniel speaks of this final end-time persecution* HE ALSO SPEAKS OF MICHAEL STANDING UP FOR DANIEL'S PEOPLE, ISRAEL! Do you see the connection here with Revelation chapter 12? Here too in Revelation when we reach the chapter describing the final anti-Israel persecution, we find Michael fighting a war with Satan! Both match— Daniel 12:1 and Revelation chapter 12. Thus we are confirmed in our belief that the woman is Israel and we see that Michael in some special way defends the remnant of Israel in the heavenly unseen realms.

The calling of Satan by the title "that old serpent" can only be an allusion to Gen. 3:1ff wherein Satan deceived Eve. Thus Christ, the author of Revelation, asserts afresh that the Genesis account of the Fall is authentic and not a myth.

▼

PAST	PRESENT	RAPTURE	FIRST 3 1/2	LAST 3 1/2	ARMA-GEDDON	MIL-LENNIUM	NEW HEAVENS & EARTH
			TRIBULATION				

Revelation 12

10 And I heard a loud voice saying in heaven, Now is come salvation, and strength, and the kingdom of our God, and the power of his Christ: for the accuser of our brethren is cast down, which accused them before our God day and night.

11 And they overcame him by the blood of the Lamb, and by the word of their testimony; and they loved not their lives unto the death.

12 Therefore rejoice, *ye* heavens, and ye that dwell in them. Woe to the inhabitants of the earth and of the sea! for the devil is come down unto you, having great wrath, because he knoweth that he hath but a short time.

Job 1:6-12; 2:1-7
Rev. 2:7, 11, 17, 26;
3:5, 12, 21
Ex. 12:3, 13

Mt. 8:29

Commentary

10. "The accuser of our brethren".—Here the word "accuser" is *kategor,* "an accuser; one who brings charges against another." In vs. 9 the word "Devil" is *diabolos* and this literally means "slanderer." Both words convey a similar idea and they corroborate the description of Satan's work which is found in Job 1:6-12 and 2:1-7. There he has a permitted access to God in heaven and he then *accuses* and *slanders* the people of God.

11. Here is a key biblical verse in content, although because of its clarity we will treat it only briefly. There are at this time during the Tribulation many martyrs. They love God more than life; yet they die. But still they *overcome!* How? By "the blood of the lamb," that is, by Christ's atoning for their sins on the cross and by His giving to them eternal life (John 3:16). They thus testify to this salvation and to the righteousness of God; they condemn sin. By this "word of their testimony" they show outwardly the reality of the inner work of the Spirit. Thus Romans 10:9-10 likewise connects the inward faith in Christ's death with the outward verbal testimony of belief: "If thou shalt confess with thy mouth the Lord Jesus, and shalt believe in thine heart...thou shalt be saved."

12. Satan now has 3 1/2 years until his imprisonment (Rev. 20:1-3). He, like the demons, knows that his end approaches. The demons asked Christ, "Art thou come hither to torment us before the time?" (Mt. 8:29). Now with the end coming fast he is a cornered animal and begins to persecute those in Israel and those of the Gentiles who are turning to the Lord during the Tribulation as was pictured in Revelation chapter 7. *The greatest persecution of the history of the world yet lies ahead.* Read Jer. 30:7; Dan. 12:1; and Mt. 24:15, 21ff and see if this bitter truth is not clearly taught.

Riots, lawlessness and guerrilla-type sneak bombings are creating more havoc in the United States than ever before. Control is becoming increasingly difficult.

Background

There are approximately 6 million Jews in the United States of which over one-third or 2 million reside in the New York City area alone!

Thus there are twice as many Jews in the United States as there are presently in Israel!

Therefore, if persecution for the Jews lies ahead (the greatest persecution of the history of the world)...then it is reasonable to assume that even here in the United States Jewish persecution will be rampant.

If six out of every 10 Jews were killed in Europe during the days of Hitler...and if the persecution in these Last Days will be greater...the death of 3 million or more Jews in America is within the realm of possibility.

Time will tell what causes will bring about this persecution. Will it involve a rebellion of the Jews against the excesses of Antichrist, the "Lawless one" (2 Thessalonians 2:8)?

▼

PAST	PRESENT	RAPTURE	FIRST 3½ TRIBULATION	LAST 3½	ARMA-GEDDON	MIL-LENNIUM	NEW HEAVENS &EARTH

Revelation 12

VERSES 13, 14, 15

13 And when the dragon saw that he was cast unto the earth, he persecuted the woman which brought forth the man *child.*

Zech. 13:8-9

14 And to the woman were given two wings of a great eagle, that she might fly into the wilderness, into her place, where she is nourished for a time, and times, and half a time, from the face of the serpent.

Rev. 12:6; Dan. 7:25

15 And the serpent cast out of his mouth water as a flood after the woman, that he might cause her to be carried away of the flood.

Mt. 7:25, 27

Commentary

13-14. Satan's persecution of Israel lasts, we are again here told, 3 1/2 years. In fact, vs. 14 takes off where vs. 6 stopped with the intervening vss., 7-13, parenthetically telling of the War in Heaven.

Here the word "time" is *kairon* which could also be translated, "a season." When it is paralleled to the other time designations in the Book of Revelation (11:2, 3; 12:6; 13:5) which uniformly designate either half of the Tribulation as 3 1/2 years, it is seen that here too 3 1/2 years must be represented. With a "time" representing a year we see pictured 1 + 2 + 1/2 = 3 1/2 times or years. This *perfectly* duplicates Dan. 7:25 which also speaks of 1 + 2 + 1/2 times = 3 1/2 times or years. So too in Dan. 4:25, 32 a "time" seems to represent one "year." Thus Antichrist will rush to destroy Israel and the Gentiles who seek after God in the final 3 1/2 years of the Tribulation (Dan. 9:27). Those who persecute, whatever be their pious excuse, will be emissaries of the Dragon. Chairman Mao Tse-Tung of Red China, for example, has said, "In order to end war, one must wage war."

15. The overwhelming tide of persecution is pictured as a flood of water. Psa. 32:6; 69:2,15 paint overwhelming troubles as a flood.

A father brings his sons to the Western (Wailing) Wall to pray. How long will Israel dwell in safety?

Background

Do you recall when the Apollo 13 was in deep trouble and the nation feared for the safety of her crew? At this time, it was permissible to pray. Indeed prayers were offered by people of many nations during this critical hour. And God answered prayer.

Now, in these verses, we find Israel burdened as never before from persecutions of the greatest intensity. No longer do her people boast of their own strength and military might. Israel has been brought down to the depths of degradation. Her enemies are gloating in their victory.

Now Israel starts turning to God...not everyone...but a large number. And they pray. Where does their flight take them? To Petra or somewhere in the Sinai peninsula?

Naturally an army follows them to persecute them. Perhaps Antichrist directs the march from the Mount of Olives? Scriptures do not say. We are told that a "flood" swallows up the opposition. This may be an earthquake...with the pursuing army swallowed up. Could it be another Red Sea miracle?

PAST	PRESENT	RAPTURE	FIRST 3½ TRIBULATION	LAST 3½	ARMA-GEDDON	MIL-LENNIUM	NEW HEAVENS & EARTH

Revelation 12

16 And the earth helped the woman, and the earth opened her mouth, and swallowed up the flood which the dragon cast out of his mouth.

17 And the dragon was wroth with the woman, and went to make war with the remnant of her seed, which keep the commandments of God, and have the testimony of Jesus Christ.

Gen. 8:13, 14;
Cp. Nu. 16:28-33!

Jer. 23:3

Commentary

16. Just as the earth absorbs a great rain which covered it in rivulets hours before, so here the earth will absorth the persecution of the Dragon to help the faithful. Perhaps this denotes that there will be such a state of confusion and chaos among the nations at this time that the systematic persecution of the godly is made difficult. Does not one who seeks to escape often run into a crowd? There he can slide away amid the confusion. So here, God produces chaos amid the nations—wars, population movements, countless refugees—so that the fleeing ones can survive the Antichrist's reign of terror.

17. The target of Satan is the "remnant of her seed." The "remnant" in Scripture refers to the faithful ones who remain true after the mass have proven their unfaithfulness. So 1 Kg. 19:14,18 speaks of 7,000 in Israel who have not yet bowed the knee to Baal.

Zechariah 13:8-9 shows that out of end-time Israel one-third will survive the Great Tribulation. These will turn to Christ in faith at His coming at Armageddon or prior (Zech. 12:9-10ff). They shall see His feet "stand in that day upon the Mount of Olives" (Zech. 14:4).

"But how can God save these end-time Israelites?" one asks. Answer: Rev. 12:17—They "have the testimony of Jesus Christ." He saves them as elect ones who have turned or who do turn to Himself by the close of the Tribulation. Another asks, "After all these years of unbelief, do Jews deserve to be saved?" Answer: No one has ever deserved to be saved, therefore, these end-time Jews do not deserve to be saved—nor do any of the end-time Gentiles who are saved during the Tribulation (Rev. 7:9-17). "Then," it is asked, "why does He save them?" Answer: Why does God save anyone? Because He is rich in mercy and exceedingly gracious. Also He saves them because He is true to His promises. He promised to bless Abraham's seed and to eventually give them Palestine, and centuries of sin on the part of Israel still has not nullified that promise. *Romans 11* explains this!

Finally, let us end this chapter with this question: If Satan is the one who seeks to destroy Israel and God is the One who seeks to save and convert Israel to Christ, how can any born-again Christian justify those false prophets who in the name of Christ publish monthly anti-semitic magazines, etc.???

U.S. and Peace Flags march side by side in Beverly, Massachusetts 1970 Memorial Day parade.

Background

We have seen how the Two Witnesses will preach in Jerusalem for 3 1/2 years. And this must have great impact upon the Jews...even those who still not believe. They will be impressed by what they see... just as the yet unconverted Paul was impressed by the testimony of dying Stephen.

Then, the 144,000 Jews who testify during this same time undoubtedly will cause a greater concern and questioning from those in Israel.

Suddenly Israel turns against the united World Governments...realizing that in this action...terrible trials will befall her. Again the odds are against her...just as in the Arab-Israeli war. Now they must look to God.

Do you remember Revelation 12:11? "...they loved not their lives unto the death." Those Israelites devoted to Christ determine to remain true...even if such devotion means death.

Look at our Christian church today. How many in your congregation would be this faithful to Christ faced with the same situation? Are they more concerned with self, rather than service...with pleasures, rather than prayer?

PAST	PRESENT	RAPTURE	FIRST 3 1/2 LAST 3 1/2 TRIBULATION	ARMA-GEDDON	MIL-LENNIUM	NEW HEAVENS & EARTH

Revelation 13

CHAPTER 13

And I stood upon the sand of the sea, and saw a beast rise up out of the sea, having seven heads and ten horns, and upon his horns ten crowns, and upon his heads the name of blasphemy.

VERSE 1
Dan. 7:7, 24
Rev. 12:3, 17:3

CHAPTER 13: THE BEAST

VERSE 1. THE IDENTITY OF THE BEAST (ONE OF THE KEYS TO THE BOOK OF REVELATION)

MANUSCRIPTS
Some of the leading manuscripts (p47, Aleph, A, C) have, "And he stood" (estathe) instead of "And I stood" (estathen). If it is "he," then it is *the Dragon,* the subject of the final verse of the previous chapter, who is now looking out into the sea—looking for his final evil monster to arise from out of the angry waves.

Here, as in almost all cases where there is some question about the exact text of a word or verse, the doctrinal difference is nil.

THE SEA
The sea, as in the similar case of Daniel 7:2-3, refers to the sea of nations which is troubled like an ocean with roaring and crashing waves—as empires rise and fall. So too, in Revelation 17:15, the "waters" of the sea are explicitly declared to be nations and peoples.

ANIMALS REPRESENT EMPIRES
In Daniel 7 and 8 various "beasts," wild animals, proved to be great empires often headed by certain individuals. And the horns atop the beasts represented various notable kings of those empires. In fact, both Daniel 7:24 and Revelation 17:12, tell us plainly that the horns represent kings.

THIS IS DANIEL'S FINAL EMPIRE
Thus here in Revelation 13:1 John is seeing an end-time empire rise up out of the political struggles amid the nations. As we too see it ascend out of the waters we stand amazed—for it is an empire that we have seen before in the past prophetic visions of the scriptures! It is the Fourth Beast of Daniel 7 (Dan. 7:7-8, 19-28). See the chart on a nearby page, "A Comparison Between Daniel's Fourth Beast and the Beast of Revelation." PLEASE examine this chart now.

A COMPARISON BETWEEN DANIEL'S FOURTH BEAST AND THE BEAST OF REVELATION

Daniel's Fourth Beast:

Comes up out of the sea
(7:3)

Ten horns—ten kings
(7:7, 24)

Another horn (Antichrist)
becomes dominant ruler
(7:24-26)

Stamped with the feet
(7:7)

Great iron teeth
(7:7)

Blasphemous (7:25)

Persecutes saints (7:21)

Power for a time, times, and
a dividing of a time
(1 + 2 + 1/2 = 3 1/2
years) (7:25)

Defeated by God who then
sets up the Kingdom
(7:21-22, 26-27)

Revelation's Beast:

Comes up out of the sea
(13:1)

Seven heads (13:1)

Ten horns—ten kings
(13:1; 17:12)

The beast as a person (cf. 19:20)
becomes dominant ruler
(17:12-13)

Like a leopard (13:2) — This beast has characteristics from each of Daniel's first three beasts, viz., lion, bear & leopard (Dan. 7:4-6).

Feet of a bear (13:2)

Mouth of a lion (13:2)

Scarlet color (17:3)

Blasphemous (13:5)

Dragon gives him power (13:2)

Persecutes saints (13:7; 11:7)

Power for 42 months (3 1/2 years)
(13:5)

Defeated by God who then
sets up the Kingdom
(19:11—20:6)

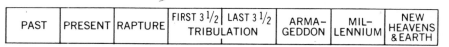

PAST	PRESENT	RAPTURE	FIRST 3 1/2 LAST 3 1/2 TRIBULATION		ARMA-GEDDON	MIL-LENNIUM	NEW HEAVENS & EARTH
			FIRST 3 1/2	LAST 3 1/2			

CHAPTER 13: THE BEAST

VERSE 1. THE IDENTITY OF THE BEAST (ONE OF THE KEYS TO THE BOOK OF REVELATION) (Continued)

IT IS THE REVIVED ROMAN EMPIRE

Daniel 7's Fourth Beast was the Roman Empire which was seen to linger in the world in some way until the time of Christ's Second Coming (Dan. 7:23-27). So likewise, this Beast of Revelation lingers until it is destroyed by Christ at His coming at the end of the Tribulation at the Battle of Armageddon (Rev. 19:19-20). Thus clearly this Beast of Revelation must be the final manifestation of the Roman Empire which will be in the world at the times of the end. Thus some have called it the "Revived Roman Empire." (Students of prophecy who have studied Daniel 2 will also realize that this chapter too shows that the Roman Empire will in some sense survive until Christ comes. The iron which represents Rome, in Dan. 2, lasts until the end—although it becomes mixed with clay.)

IT IS END-TIME EUROPE

But, someone asks, "Didn't the Roman Empire fall away? Then how can it be in existence at the end when Christ comes?" Answer: Yes, it did fall away in name; but its constituents, the European nations which made it up still linger in the cracked up divided continent of Europe. In fact, Daniel 2 pictures the Roman Empire—the iron in the image of Daniel 2—as being eventually divided into two legs (the E and W empires, divided by Emperor Diocletian in 300 A.D.) and then latter cracking into pieces (into the present divided Europe)! Thus this Beast represents the final state that Europe and the Mediterranean world will be in during the end-times.

It is definitely the *final* manifestation of this empire as it, the Beast, meets its end at Christ's Armageddon coming (Rev. 19:19-21). Its period of power and persecution is brief, "one hour" (Rev. 17:12)—that is, the 42 months (3 1/2 years) which make up the awful last half of the Tribulation Period (Rev. 13:5).

IT WILL HAVE 10 CONFEDERATED RULERS

This end-time wicked empire will be some sort of a confederation of 10 rulers, "kings." Here Revelation 13:1 shows them as horns as does Dan. 7:7,24, while Dan. 2:41-44 portrays them as the toes of Nebuchadnezzar's dream-image. It is these toes which the rock, Christ, strikes at His Armageddon Coming (Dan. 2:34,44).

Revelation 17:12-13 (which see) shows us plainly that the 10 horns will in some manner form a coalition, and together give their power to the Beast. Thus we await a time when the European nations will band together into some type of 10 nation confederacy—and in this way REVIVE THE ROMAN EMPIRE. Is the present European Common Market the precursor of this coming empire???

The Image of Daniel 2

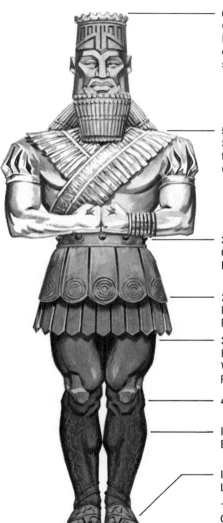

606 ± B.C.
Gold — Nebuchadnezzar's Babylon (Unquestioned obedience to one absolute sovereign)

536 ± B.C.
Silver — The dual Empire of the Medes & Persians (The 2 arms!)

336 B.C.
Copper — The Greek Empire

200 ± B.C.
Iron Legs United — Roman Republic & Empire

300 ± A.D.
Iron Legs Divided — Western & Eastern Roman Empire

476 & 1453 A.D. (They fall)

Iron Legs Cracking — European States

Iron & Clay Feet — End-time Lawlessness (Communism)?

10 Toes — Revived Rome Confederacy

A.D.?

AN 11TH HORN, THE ANTICHRIST, WILL ARISE
Here read Dan. 7:8,20-21,24-28. These verses show that another leader will arise, and this new horn will be victorious in a power struggle with three of the kings. Then this new horn will blaspheme God and persecute the saints intensely for 3 1/2 years. This 11th horn is the Antichrist! It is he who will commit the Abomination of Desolation in the rebuilt Jerusalem temple (2 Thess. 2:3-4; Matt. 24:15). It is he who will lead the armies to Armageddon on some diabolical mission—and here he will be cast directly into the Lake of Fire by Christ (Rev. 19:19-21).

ANTICHRIST TO BE DICTATOR OF THE BEAST-EMPIRE
Since this 11th horn, the Antichrist, is shown to be the persecutor of the Tribulation Saints during the final 3 1/2 years of the Tribulation (Dan. 7:20-28) it is seen that THIS 11TH HORN OF DANIEL, THE ANTI-CHRIST, AND THE ENTIRE BEAST OF REVELATION DO THE SAME THINGS (Rev. 13:4-7); AND LIKEWISE BOTH PERISH AT THE COMING OF CHRIST AT ARMAGEDDON TO ESTABLISH HIS KINGDOM. Why? Answer: The 11th horn, the Antichrist, when he becomes the leader of the ten nation Mediterranean-European Confederation, asserts his will over the entire BEAST empire, so that the mind of the Antichrist (the person; the 11th horn) becomes synonymous with the mind of the entire evil Beast empire.

THE BEAST BOTH A PERSON AND AN EMPIRE
It is this relationship which the Antichrist as a person has to the Beast-empire which he dominates (as Christ will someday dominate His Kingdom) that explains why the Beast of Revelation seems to be at the same time a person and a nation! Thus the Beast is an end-time empire as the animals in Daniel 7 are empires; but the Beast is also a *person* who is cast at the end into the Lake of Fire at Christ's coming (Rev. 19:19-21; and here the Beast *cannot* be the entire empire for the armies, part of the empire, merely die and go to Hades while the Beast goes directly to the Lake of Fire).

In this same way in Dan. 2:38, the golden head of the image stood both for the nation Babylon and at the same time for its notable king, Nebuchadnezzar. So too, it was said of Adolf Hitler, *"Der Furhrer ist Deutschland und Deutschland ist der Fuhrer,"* "The Leader (Hitler) is Germany and Germany is the Leader (Hitler)." Hitler was introduced this way in a great rally in the late 1930's. So too will the BEAST be the final European-Medeterranean Confederacy as well as its supreme evil mind and leader, the 11th horn dictator, the Antichrist!

THE 7 HEADS REPRESENT WORLD DOMINION
The heads? In Daniel 7:6 the beast representing the Greek Empire's period of domination had FOUR HEADS, one head for each of the four geographical sections of the post-Alexander Greek Empire. After Alexander had made his conquests and died (336-323 B.C.) his empire was divided into four regions by his generals, and with slight adjustments this was the status quo until the rise of Rome.

CHAPTER 13: THE BEAST

VERSE 1. THE IDENTITY OF THE BEAST (ONE OF THE KEYS TO THE BOOK OF REVELATION) (Continued)

If the heads of this Beast of Revelation are interpreted similarly, then the 7 heads must represent geographical regions. The fact that there are SEVEN heads, the number used everywhere in this book to represent total completeness of an item, can only indicate that these 7 heads signify some type of universal dominion. Since Rev. 13:3-7 informs us that the Beast will eventually have world control, the 7 heads must represent a dominion over all of the geographical regions of the globe! And...interestingly enough, the *Readers Digest Atlas* (1963) tells us that there are SEVEN continental land masses on our globe: North America, South America, Europe, Asia, Africa, Australia, and Antarctica!

Thus this final world empire to be controlled by the Antichrist will not only be the Revived Roman Empire, but the evil system which emanates from this empire will in some way achieve world domination. Just as the leaders of the Soviet Union today dominate much of the world outside of Russia, so in the last days the European Confederacy will through some diabolical system eventually rule the world! (I am indebted to Jim Springett, Glendale, Calif., for his ideas concerning the 7 heads.)

IT IS AN EMPIRE OF BLASPHEMY
That the word "Blasphemy" (anti-god speech) appears on each head of the Beast shows that this will be a world system based on wicked principles. Its leader, the 11th horn, the Antichrist, shall blaspheme, curse God, and persecute those who would turn to Christ during the entire awful final 3½ years of the Tribulation Period (Dan. 7:20, 21, 25). In fact, Rev. 13:4 clearly tells us that Satan himself is the unseen power behind this Beast system. This is why the Beast is identical in appearance to Satan, the Dragon (Rev. 12:3; 13:1)! Compare John 14:9.

In Rev. 12:3 Satan is the Dragon *and his 7 heads are crowned.* In 13:1, however, Antichrist is the Dragon *and his 10 horns are crowned.* Why the difference? Answer: Satan comes as the ruler of all of the geographical regions (the 7 heads) of this earth; while Antichrist comes as the ruler of the 10 nation Revived Roman Empire!

THE CLAY OF DANIEL 2 PERVADES THIS EMPIRE
In Daniel 2:40-44 the fourth and final world empire, the Roman Empire is shown as the iron legs of Nebuchadnezzar's dream image. Since it comes immediately after the ancient Greek Empire, which it replaces, and lasts until Christ's Second Coming, we know that this is the Roman Empire which will in some form survive unto the end of the age. If in the image vision the top of the iron legs are unified by having a garment covering the upper thighs then the history of the Roman Empire was to be as follows:

Background

First, the unified upper legs denote a unified Rome which displaced the Greeks as the world power by the 2nd century B.C.; *Second,* the two iron legs show the division of the empire into two states, the Eastern and Western Roman Empires, by Diocletian in 300 A.D.; *Third,* the cracked feet signify in later days the empire's cracked and broken condition as the separate nations of Europe; *Fourth,* the ten toes are declared to be 10 kings (Dan. 2:41, 42, 44), and since Christ strikes these at His Coming we know that these are the 10 kings of the last days who give their allegiance over to the Antichrist (Rev. 17:12-13); and *Fifth,* a "miry clay" separates the strong Roman iron in the feet.

THIS CLAY (DAN. 2:41-43) IS DESCRIBED AS SOME DIVISIVE FORCE OR SYSTEM WHICH SHALL PERVADE THE REVIVED EMPIRE IN ITS LAST DAYS– for it is mingled with the iron in the FEET which Christ smashes at His appearance at Armageddon.

THE IDENTITY OF THE CLAY—INTERNATIONAL LAWLESSNESS (COMMUNISM?)
This final clay-system is divisive, it tends to perpetuate divisions. What could this be??? What causes and perpetuates divisions among nations? Answer: Sin—treaty breaking, lying, undermining governments, false propaganda, attempting to gain unfair advantage, starting wars, causing revolutions, persecuting, etc. All of this in the world scene is a form of international LAWLESSNESS. Communism is the system that by both policy and practice perfectly fits this evil description!

31 WAR AREAS IN ONE YEAR

Generally, only the major wars ever come to our attention. We fail to realize that each year there are many conflicts where lives are lost and nations conquered. In 1970, as an example, there were at least 31 places that were fields of war or insurgencies — in Asia, Africa, the Middle East and Latin America.

NAME/LOCALE	PARTICIPANTS
Middle East War	Israel vs. Egypt, Libya, Sudan, Syria, Iraq, Jordan, Algeria, Saudi Arabia, South Yemen, and other Arab states
Jordan	Jordan vs. Palestinian guerillas.
Cyprus	Greek vs. Turkish Cypriots
Lebanon	Lebanese government vs. Syria Saeqa guerillas
Iraq Iranian border	Iraq vs. Iran (Kurdish guerila operations)
South Arabia	Dhofar Liberation Front vs. Muscat and Oman
Sudanese civil war	Southern vs. northern Sudanese
Angola	Portuguese vs. African insurgents
Mozambique	Portuguese vs. African insurgents
Portuguese Guinea	Portuguese vs. African insurgents
Rhodesia	Zambian guerillas vs. Rhodesia/S. Africa
Mozambique-Angola	Zambian guerillas vs. Portuguese
Kenya	Somalian "Shifta" bandits vs. Kenya
Ethiopia	Eritrean Liberation Front insurgents vs. Ethiopia
Chad	Civil war between local factions combined with anti-French insurgency
Ruanda	Batusi guerillas vs. ruling Bahuti tribe
Vietnam	South vs. North Vietnamese and Viet Cong; U. S. and allies vs. North Vietnam
Thailand	Thai government vs. Meo, Chinese-Malaysian and North Vietnamese insurgents
Malaysia	Chinese insurgents vs. Malaysia
Burma	Chinese and indigenous insurgents vs. Burma
Tibet-Nepal-N. E. Frontier of India	Chinese and indigenous insurgents vs. Nepal and India
Cambodia	Kmer Serai and North Vietnamese vs. Cambodian forces; U. S. troops vs. North Vietnamese forces
Laos	Laotian factions and U. S. vs. North Vietnamese and other insurgents
Mongolia-Manchuria	China vs. USSR
Korea	North Korean incursions vs. South Korea
Philippines	Huk insurgency, Luzon
Guatemala	Communist insurgents vs. Guatemala
Venezuela	Castroite guerillas vs. Venezuela
Colombia	Castroite guerillas vs. Colombia
Uruguay	Irban insurgents vs. Uruguay
Honduras-El Salvador	Border hostilities following "Soccer War"

VERSE 1. THE IDENTITY OF THE BEAST (ONE OF THE KEYS TO THE BOOK OF REVELATION) (Continued)

In 2 Thess. 2:3 the Antichrist is called, "the man of sin"—which in the Greek literally translated would be, *ho avthropos tes anomias,* "the man of LAWLESSNESS." Thus Antichrist and the Beast Empire will be characterized by lawlessness, as well as by blasphemy and persecution (2 Thess. 2:3, 4; Rev. 13:1; Dan. 7:20-25). It will be Satan's empire and its persecution and blasphemy will be directed against Christ and His people (Rev. 13:4). Thus it is a "scarlet Beast" because it is red with the blood of the saints (Rev. 17:3).

Again, COMMUNISM is the system which fits. It is at its own admission anti-God, anti-Christ, anti-law, revolutionary and divisive. This Satanic system has sprung into life in 1917 with Lenin and already it has devoured a billion people, a full one-third of the world! It has persecuted the saints already to a degree unparalleled in history sending more martyrs to their deaths in this century alone than have been slain in all the previous 19 centuries since Christ. It is growing wildly today across the world, and soon this 7 headed Beast may have a hand of control over every continent of the globe. Its appitite remains unsatiated as it openly announces its desire to slay and devour all in the world who confess God.

SUMMARY: ON THE BEAST

Thus the Beast in its final form will be some sort of European Confederacy of 10 nations, a Revived Roman Empire. Its head is the Antichrist, the 11th horn, whose personality and mind will become synonomous with that of the empire which he rules. This man and empire will grow until it has at least some degree of control over every region of the world. It will ferociously persecute those who will confess Christ and during the final 3½ years of the Tribulation it will slaughter them amid the greatest persecution the world has ever seen. Today there is a system which fits this Beast, it is atheistic materialistic diabolical anti-Christ world COMMUNISM with its divisive spirit of revolution and its terrifying record of murder. We yet await the center of power to shift somehow from Moscow to a European Confederation, and then finally to "the man of lawlessness"—the Antichrist who is to arise.

Truly I think the above to be quite accurate—though the name of the system and even its emphasis may in the coming years be somewhat changed. We shall see—God knows. We, however, rather look forward to the Coming of Christ at the Rapture (1 Thess. 4:13-18), and we remember our Saviour's words of Luke 21:28,

> And when these things begin to come to pass, then look up,
> and lift up your heads; for your redemption draweth nigh.

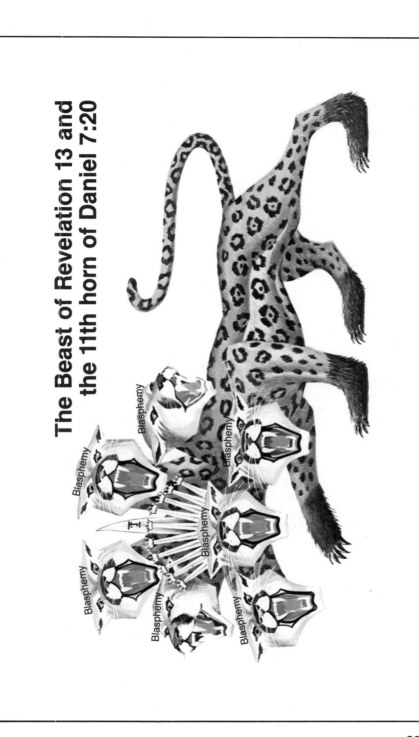

The Beast of Revelation 13 and the 11th horn of Daniel 7:20

207

2 And the beast which I saw was like
unto a leopard, and his feet were as *the
feet* of a bear, and his mouth as the
mouth of a lion: and the dragon gave him
his power, and his seat, and great
authority.

Dan. 7:7
Dan. 7:6,
Dan. 7:5,
Dan. 7:4,
Jn. 5:30

Commentary

2. The Beast has the fierce qualities of the Daniel 7's previous beast
nations as Rev. 13:2 shows. It has the Babylonian "mouth of a lion"
(Rev. 13:2; Dan. 7:4)—lust to consume victims; great power. It has the
Persian "feet...of a bear" (Rev. 13:2; Dan. 7:5)—great size; armies able
to crush rebellions. It has the Greek body of a "leopard" (Rev. 13:2;
Dan. 7:6)—agility, swiftness; a capacity for military mobility and speed
of strike. The future Beast will have all of these qualities. And lest we
forget, it is a Beast—in God's sight a monster that consumes rapaciously. Since the Dragon, Satan, gives it its power, the Beast—both the empire and the man, Antichrist—will be exceedingly anti-god, against all
who turn to God, and wicked in every way.

PAST	PRESENT	RAPTURE	FIRST 3 1/2 / LAST 3 1/2 TRIBULATION	ARMA-GEDDON	MIL-LENNIUM	NEW HEAVENS &EARTH

Revelation 13

VERSES 3, 4

3 And I saw one of his heads as it were wounded to death; and his deadly wound was healed: and all the world wondered after the beast.

4 And they worshipped the dragon which gave power unto the beast: and they worshipped the beast, saying, Who *is* like unto the beast? who is able to make war with him?

2 Thess. 2:6-12
John 12:44

Dan. 3:15b

Commentary

3. The fatal wound of the head may be something that befalls the Antichrist as an individual as the leader of the then dominent European head of the final Satanic government. Verses 12 and 14 do not speak of merely one head being fatally wounded; on the contrary, they speak of "the Beast" as a whole having been slain. This fits some sort of assassination of the Antichrist, and verse 14 says "by a sword."

Yet the "deadly wound" (Greek: "wound of death"—a fatal wound) was healed! This causes all the world to "wonder," that is, not "to question" or "to wonder how it happened," but "to marvel over" (Greek: *thaumadzo).*

Something so amazing occurs that all the world (literally in the Greek "the whole earth") marvels. This seems to be the Antichrist's counterfeit of the resurrection of Christ! How will it occur? No one knows. Perhaps it will be accomplished by modern freezing techniques??? Antichrist may be stabbed, pronounced dead, frozen, operated upon, unfrozen, given an electric shock—and then be ALIVE AGAIN! RESURRECTED!

ANOTHER VIEW, however, was suggested to me by Jim Springett, of Jet Propulsion Lab, Glendale, Calif. If this head refers to one of the geographical regions—IT MAY BE THAT THE RUSSIAN ARMIES ARE DESTROYED HERE IN THE BATTLE OF EZEK. 38:1-39:16???

4. Just as we worship God the Father when we worship Jesus the Son, so also when the world follows Antichrist they will be following and worshipping Satan, the Dragon.

By this time the Beast apparently has become a strong military factor with his confederation of ten kings behind him, and so the question will be then asked, "Who is able to make war with him?" This is especially fitting after his revivication from death has shown him to be undefeatable. There now comes a Satanically inspired charismatic auora around the Beast—Who can resist such a one?

PAST	PRESENT	RAPTURE	FIRST 3 1/2	LAST 3 1/2	ARMA– GEDDON	MIL– LENNIUM	NEW HEAVENS & EARTH
			TRIBULATION				

Revelation 13

5 And there was given unto him a mouth speaking great things and blasphemies; and power was given unto him to continue forty *and* two months.

6 And he opened his mouth in blasphemy against God, to blaspheme his name, and his tabernacle, and them that dwell in heaven.

Rev. 12:6, 14; Dan. 7:25

Rev. 17:3

Commentary

5. *The revived Antichrist now will continue for 42 months* or 3 1/2 years. This 3 1/2 year period corresponds with the other Biblical references which show the final Tribulation Period, the Seventieth Week of Daniel 9:27, to be a period of seven years in length divided clearly in the middle into two 3 1/2 year sections by the blasphemous breaking of the covenant and Abomination of Desolation by Antichrist (Dan. 9:27; 7:25; Rev. 11:2, 3; 12:6,|14).

The reviving unto life of the Antichrist and *the Abomination* of Desolation wherein he *defiles the temple* (Dan. 9:27; and Mt. 24:15; 2 Thess. 2:3-4) and *breaks his covenant* with Israel (Dan. 9:27) would both seem to occur in the middle of the seven years. Dan. 9:27 shows that the Abomination and its resultant breaking of the treaty with Israel happens at the mid-point of the seven years. And here, Rev. 13:5, shows, as it follows the description of his death and reviving, that Antichrist's 3 1/2 year period of power actually follows this event. Thus all of these items —death, resurrection, abomination, defiling the Temple, and covenant breaking—seem to occur as one integrated group of related events.

6. Now all can see the true nature of Antichrist; the mask of "an angel of light" has been torn off! He now boldly curses God and all heavenly powers. Now the final half of the Tribulation, that final 3 1/2 year period called "the Great Tribulation," has started.

Here the persecution of Israel and of all Gentiles who turn to Christ begins. Rev. 12:6, 14 show that this persecution lasts 3 1/2 years, the 42 months of Antichrist's power (13:5). Now begins the period whereof Jesus in Mt. 24:15 said, "When ye therefore shall see the abomination of desolation . . . Then let them which be in Judaea flee . . . For then shall be great tribulation, such as was not since the beginning of the world..." (Mt. 24:15, 16, 21).

And these events did not occur when Titus and the Romans captured Jerusalem in A.D. 70, for the events described in Mt. 24:22-31 which were to follow "immediately after" (Mt. 24:29) not only did not occur in A.D. 70, but they have not yet occurred!

Will this be the scene as world leaders meet with Antichrist?

Background

Revelation 13, Daniel 2 and Daniel 7 are three chapters which blend perfectly. They teach that at the end-time when Christ finally comes to destroy the rebels upon earth there shall be some human empire or government system ruling at least in the European-Palestinian region that will be a confederation of ten leaders in an Antichrist government.

One thing is certain from the many references found regarding the Antichrist in the Scriptures: He will be a counterfeit and a clever imitation of a true Christ.

His rise will be sudden.

This also will be an imitation of Christ. For 30 years Christ remained in obscurity in his home in Nazareth.

Do you remember in John 5:43 when the Lord Jesus Christ said,
I am come in my Father's name, and ye receive me not: if another shall come in his own name, him ye will receive.

This is a prophetic reference to Antichrist.

PAST	PRESENT	RAPTURE	FIRST 3 1/2 LAST 3 1/2 TRIBULATION	ARMA-GEDDON	MIL-LENNIUM	NEW HEAVENS & EARTH

7 And it was given unto him to make war with the saints, and to overcome them: and power was given him over all kindreds, and tongues, and nations.
8 And all that dwell upon the earth shall worship him, whose names are not written in the book of life of the Lamb slain from the foundation of the world.

Rev. 14:9-10
Rev. 20:12, 15

Definition:
Saints—*Greek,* hagioi, *literally "the holy ones." This term speaks of those who have been justified, declared forgiven of their sins and righteous, on the basis of their faith in Christ's death having paid the just penalty for their sins. This salvation is "by grace (bestowed as a free gift) through faith." In 1 Cor. 1:2, for example, the Corinthian believers are called "saints." It is interesting that nowhere does the Bible speak of any lone individual as a "saint." The latter day canonization of saints is a practice unknown to the Scriptures.*

Commentary

7. The Beast during the final 3 1/2 year Great Tribulation is allowed by God's permissive will to achieve some sort of universal dominion—perhaps the Antichrist shall be made the head of the United Nations? He is permitted to persecute the saints (Rev. 12). Jesus said concerning this persecution, "And except those days should be shortened, there should no flesh be saved: but for the elect's sake those days shall be shortened" (Mt. 24:22).

8. The mass of humanity shall follow the Antichrist and by so doing they "shall worship him"—the "him" being Antichrist. And the worship of Antichrist will for that day and age constitute the worship of the One behind him, Satan, the Dragon.

Those whose names are written in the Book of Life—the saved, the elect—these shall not worship the Beast. Someone asks: "Why won't they?" Answer: God's Holy Spirit will keep them from doing it. "But didn't He, the Holy Spirit, depart from the earth at the rapture of the church?" Answer: Yes, this seems so, but...just as He was present in the Old Testament even before Pentecost, so too He will be present at this time even after the rapture.

You recall Jesus was led by the Spirit into the wilderness where He was tested by the devil. When Christ fasted 40 days and 40 nights, He was naturally hungry. Satan suggested he command the stones to be turned to bread.

The photograph at right taken at Bethany is a familiar Holy Land scene. In today's world the counterfeit Trinity often offers as an enticement, "stone" bread in the form of money, seductive love, material gain. Many never realize this "bread" is Satan's stone that sinks man into deeper sin.

Background

Note these interesting comparisons. The Antichrist is part of the Satanic Trinity just as Christ is part of the Heavenly Trinity.

The Heavenly Trinity is made up of the:
1. Father
2. Son
3. Holy Spirit

The counterfeit Trinity is made up of:
1. Satan - sometimes referred to as the Dragon. He imitates the work of God the FATHER.
2. Antichrist - sometimes called the Beast. He imitates the work of God the SON.
3. The False Prophet - sometimes called the Second Beast. He imitates the work of God the HOLY SPIRIT.

At this present time the vast majority of the Jews have rejected Jesus Christ as their Messiah. Yet when Antichrist comes they, along with most of those left on earth, will be at first deceived by him and accept him...welcoming him with open arms as their human king and saviour.

PAST	PRESENT	RAPTURE	FIRST 3 1/2 LAST 3 1/2 TRIBULATION		ARMA- GEDDON	MIL- LENNIUM	NEW HEAVENS & EARTH

9 If any man have an ear, let him hear.   *Rev. 2:7*
10 He that leadeth into captivity shall go
into captivity: he that killeth with the
sword must be killed with the sword.
Here is the patience and the faith of the   *Rev. 12:11*
saints.

Definitions:
Trinitarianism—*the belief that the Godhead is revealed in Scripture to
be a tri-unity. One God in three co-equal, co-divine, co-eternal persons,
the Father, Son, and Holy Spirit (Mt. 28:19).*
Unitarianism—*the belief that only the Father is God, and that the Son
and Holy Spirit are not part of the godhead. This is a modern form of the
heresy of Arius condemned by the first great ecumenical council of the
Church, the Council of Nicea, 325 A.D.*

Commentary

9. Here is an admonition to us to heed these things, both those already
said and those to follow. These things will occur, let us listen with the
ear of faith and so speak and live.

10. This is a difficult verse, and commentators vary on it. Some say that
it is an admonition telling us that when these things come to pass it is
futile for the Christian to take up arms to resist. Thus he that wields the
sword will only end up slain. This is akin to Jeremiah's message to Israel,
that resistance to the invading Babylonians would be useless.

Others, however, take this to be teaching that the wicked who at this
time are capturing and slaying will eventually under the sure judgment
of God themselves end up captive and slain. Thus the saints who must
endure with "patience" may take hope by knowing this.

Both views are possible. Let the reader choose.

PAST	PRESENT	RAPTURE	FIRST 3½ TRIBULATION	LAST 3½	ARMA-GEDDON	MIL-LENNIUM	NEW HEAVENS & EARTH

11 And I beheld another beast coming up out of the earth; and he had two horns like a lamb, and he spake as a dragon.

12 And he exerciseth all the power of the first beast before him, and causeth the earth and them which dwell therein to worship the first beast, whose deadly wound was healed.

Rev. 19:20

John 16:13, 14

A SECOND BEAST (13:11-18)

11. This second wild-beast is in 19:20 called the "False Prophet." He and his ministry prove to be a counterfeit of the Holy Spirit and of his ministry. He seems to be a person rather than an empire. He comes as a beast to show his parallel and complicity with the Beast-man, the Antichrist. Remember, the Beast of Revelation 13:1-10 with its 10 horns, etc., is the same as Daniel 7's FINAL world empire. Thus this new two-horned beast cannot be any later world empire. No, it is a man, a False Prophet.

Do you see the "Infernal Trinity" which tries to duplicate the "Eternal Trinity"? The Dragon is the Father. The Beast, the Antichrist, is the Son—he is the earthly image of the Father, he dies and is raised again. The Second Beast, the False Prophet, is the Holy Spirit—he causes all to worship the Son, and he puts his seal upon all of his children, and once these are sealed they may eat in communion fellowship with him!!!

This second beast comes "up out of the earth" (Greek: *ge*, earth, ground, land). This would seem to mean that he rises out of the "land," that is, the land of Palestine. Maybe he will be an Israeli? Maybe not? But it would seem that he will be a Palestinian.

"Two horns like a lamb, and he spake as a dragon"—What does this fully mean? That day will reveal it. The two horns must represent two kingly, i.e., rulership, functions. Perhaps he will be the head of a World Church Council and at the same time be the Head of a Denominational or Regional Church Council? Perhaps...??? In any event, his lamb-like appearance shows us that he will, as did the Antichrist, come at first as humanity's friend; but his dragon voice shows that his true inner nature is corrupt and Satanic.

12. Like the true Holy Spirit, this imposter—though probably on a more human vane—will not direct adoration to himself, but rather to the Antichrist, the Imposter-Christ. This seems to come to past, as it is here described, *after* the death-resurrection cycle of the first beast.

▼

PAST	PRESENT	RAPTURE	FIRST 3 1/2 LAST 3 1/2 TRIBULATION		ARMA- GEDDON	MIL- LENNIUM	NEW HEAVENS & EARTH

Revelation 13

VERSES 13, 14

13 And he doeth great wonders, so that he maketh fire come down from heaven on the earth in the sight of men.

2 Kg. 1:9-16

14 And deceiveth them that dwell on the earth by *the means of* those miracles which he had power to do in the sight of the beast; saying to them that dwell on the earth, that they should make an image to the beast, which had the wound by a sword, and did live.

John 16:13, 14

Dan. 3

Definition:
Obelisk—*This is a commemorative pillar of which there abound multitudes from the ancient world. See them still today in Rome and Egypt. They memorialize men, events, and battles. They are carved or plain, but usually tall and slender with a point on the top. Example, the Washington Monument.*

Commentary

13. Malachi said that Elijah would come before the coming of the day of the Lord (Mal. 4:5). So Jewish people traditionally leave a seat vacant at the Passover meal for Elijah who is to come at the time of the advent of the Messiah.

Here the doing of wonders and the making of fire to come down from heaven reminds us of Elijah. John the Baptist, called Elijah in Mt. 11:14 and 17:12, was filled with the Holy Spirit. Here the False Prophet, the second beast, somehow does wondrous feats. Perhaps they will be modern scientific technological marvels which glorify man as opposed to God? Or perhaps they will be Satanic enablements such as gave Pharaoh's magicians power to duplicate the sign of Moses

14. The False Prophet "deceiveth" while the true Holy Spirit "will guide you into all truth" (Jn. 16:13). Yet the False copies the true in that "He shall glorify me" (not Himself, Jn. 16:14). Here the False Prophet by "miracles"—"lying wonders" 2 Thess. 2:9—deceives the earthlings and causes them to adore and give allegiance (worship) to the Antichrist.

The image of the Beast, what shall it be? Again, we do not know; that day will declare it. It seems akin to Nebuchadnezzar's tall golden obelisk image of the plain of Dura which was 60 cubits high and 6 cubits wide. Death was the punishment for refusal to worship...and the righteous refused! (Dan. 3)

This image may be a giant computer used by Antichrist's governmental coalition, it may be an obelisk, or it may be an automated statue of the Antichrist which gives his prerecorded answers to standard questions when the proper button is pushed.

PAST	PRESENT	RAPTURE	FIRST 3½ TRIBULATION	LAST 3½	ARMA-GEDDON	MIL-LENNIUM	NEW HEAVENS & EARTH

15 And he had power to give life unto the image of the beast, that the image of the beast should both speak, and cause that as many as would not worship the image of the beast should be killed.

Dan. 3:6
Mt. 5:10-12

Commentary

15. Somehow the False Prophet will give life to the image. This does not require that he, as God did with Adam, breathe life into the inanimate image. He may perform that which is described by merely activating a button that turns on an electronic robot which is equipped with some type of speaking apparatus.

Obeisance to this image becomes tantamount to saluting a nation's flag. Respect and honor given to it signifies loyalty to the Beast and to the Satanic system which he comes to represent. This explains why 14:9-10 declares that those who "worship" (honor, bow to, reverence) this image are doomed to receive the wrath of God. Failure to honor the image—as in the case of the early Christians' refusal to offer incense to the Roman gods—will bring upon the one refusing a martyr's death.

PAST	PRESENT	RAPTURE	FIRST 3 1/2 LAST 3 1/2 TRIBULATION		ARMA– GEDDON	MIL– LENNIUM	NEW HEAVENS & EARTH

16 And he causeth all, both small and great, rich and poor, free and bond, to receive a mark in their right hand, or in their foreheads:

17 And that no man might buy or sell, save he that had the mark, or the name of the beast, or the number of his name.

Rev. 7:3; 2 Cor. 1:22
Rev. 14:9-10

Commentary

16. There is instituted under the regime of the False Prophet, who serves the Antichrist, some system of overt labeling. Loyalty to the Beast must now be outwardly affirmed. Since there will be a great persecution of God's people during this time (Mt. 24:15-22; Rev. 12), the Antichrist and False Prophet apparently have a disloyalty problem. This marking method would at least bring to the surface the deep-seated hardened rebels to the Beast's rule. Those who hate the Beast, who think him to be Satanic, will not submit to a mark. Here, the False Prophet, imitates the Holy Spirit by sealing his followers (Rev. 7:3; Eph. 1:13).

The places for the mark are the right hand and forehead, two difficult-to-conceal easily-seen open locations. Perhaps the choice is permitted between the two places, as has been suggested by Kirban in his book *666,* so as to allow the super-loyal to be sealed boldly on their foreheads while permitting the women and those more beauty orientated to avoid marring their facial appearance by having their mark put on the hand. This suggestion certainly seems to fit the facts.

The mark, however, may yet be one invisible to the naked eye under normal light—one that requires a black light to reveal it. Some years ago I was marked as having paid my admission at Marineland of the Pacific by a stamp. I could not see any mark. Then when I commented on this, I was told to put my *right hand* under a special lamp. The black square mark appeared boldly!

17. This loyalty mark which by a number (v. 18) signifies the name of the Antichrist now becomes the Key to Survival in the Beast's Kingdom. You can neither buy nor sell unless you have the mark. To survive, humanly speaking, one must either be loyal to the Beast or at least profess loyalty outwardly.

Already some have suggested that universal credit cards should replace cash. As this more and more goes into effect it becomes increasingly easier to comprehend how those without the Beast's Mark can be deprived in one stroke of all of their buying and selling power. The invalidation of their card would lead to instanteous poverty.

To complete his blasphemy it would not be surprising if Antichrist used churches as centers to apply the Mark.

Background

The Mark which will be employed during the Great Tribulation may be the numbers "666" or it may take another form.

Since we have just also read where possibly the image of Antichrist will be unveiled in the Temple, it is also in the realm of possibility that those showing loyalty to Antichrist will initially have their mark applied in the Temple—or in a local Church.

What greater way to show disrespect to the true God!

One who had lived in Bulgaria remarked in the presence of Dr. W.A. Criswell,

> You cannot understand and you cannot know that the most terrible instrument of persecution ever devised is an innocent ration card. You cannot buy and you cannot sell except according to that little, innocent card. If they please, you can be starved to death, and if they please, you can be dispossessed of everything you have...

What a tragedy!

PAST	PRESENT	RAPTURE	FIRST 3 1/2 TRIBULATION	LAST 3 1/2	ARMA-GEDDON	MIL-LENNIUM	NEW HEAVENS &EARTH

18 Here is wisdom. Let him that hath understanding count the number of the beast: for it is the number of a man; and his number *is* Six hundred threescore *and* six.

Commentary

18. In ancient Greek there was no indefinite article ("a," "an") so the words "the number of a man" may just as well be translated "the number of man." Thus the number may represent *man* as opposed to *God.* In Daniel 3:1 Nebuchadnezzar's human-oriented statue was 60 by 6 cubits. If it was an obelisk of the usual type it would have had a square base, and hence it would be 60 x 6 x 6 cubits. Thus the number in this verse, Rev. 13:18, "600,60,6" (as it appears in the Greek) may represent *man* in general as opposed to God. Man falls short of God. God is eternal and infinite and these qualities are often in Scripture represented by the number 7, which also represents a completed cycle of God's work (Gen. 1:1-2:4, the seven days of creation; Rev. 2:1; 3:1). Thus the Trinity might well be represented as 777; and then the counterfeit trinity with a human-Christ (Antichrist) could be 666!

Gematria was the ancient system of number coding and of spelling out numbers by letters. Any alphabet can be used. The code uniformly runs like this, here using English: a = 1; b = 2; c = 3; d = 4; e = 5; f = 6; g = 7; H = 8; i = 9; j = 10; k = 20; l = 30; m = 40; n = 50; o = 60; p = 70; q = 80; r = 90; s = 100; t = 200; u = 300; v = 400; w = 500; x = 600; y = 700; z = 800. Thus the name "Fox" would yield 6 + 60 + 600 or 666. It *may* be that the *name* of the Antichrist, or the name of his system, will be marked upon his followers, and that when this name is *counted* (as this verse commands) the total will yield 666.

Sufficient to say here is that no one will know how this prophecy will come to its fulfillment until the time arrives...but someday that hour will come.

Background

Numbering or identifying systems are not new. And in this complex age with a rapidly growing population...numbering identifications are becoming more widely used.

In contacting someone by telephone you must know their number. If you are calling long distance it can involve 11 numbers! People are also identified by a social security number of at least 9 digits. Your operator's number of about 8 digits gives you the right to drive. The town in which you live is now designated by a 5-digit zip code number.

An unusual machine already exists which leases for about $15 a month and which can identify an individual by his right hand. The individual places his credit card and right hand in the machine. The machine reads both, compares the two, then flashes an "accept" or "reject" light. Through this automatic verification the individual can then buy...or is denied credit.

PAST	PRESENT	RAPTURE	FIRST 3½ LAST 3½ TRIBULATION		ARMA-GEDDON	MIL-LENNIUM	NEW HEAVENS &EARTH

Revelation 14

CHAPTER 14

And I looked, and, lo, a Lamb stood on the mount Sion, and with him an hundred forty *and* four thousand, having his Father's name written in their foreheads.

Heb. 12:22
Rev. 7:1-8
Rev. 7:3

CHAPTER 14: VISIONS SHOWING FOR THE 144,000— DELIVERENCE; FOR THE WICKED—DESTRUCTION

Definition:

Mount Sion—this is identical to Mt. Zion, the sacred mountain-hill of Jerusalem upon which David built his city (2 Sam. 5:7). Hebrews 12:22 speaks of a heavenly Mt. Zion.

THE 144,000 ON MT. ZION (14:1-5)

1. Chapters 11, 12, and 13 have shown to us the awful conditions upon the earth during the last 3 1/2 years of the Tribulation Period. The two witnesses are murdered (but then raised); those turning to God out of Israel and the nations are hunted; and the Antichrist and his henchman, the False Prophet, are marking the masses with their number—this was the story of Revelation chapters 11-13. There are now two sets of people marked—God's 144,000 (7:1-8) and the Beast's followers!

Questions, therefore, naturally arise: "Through all of this evil what will be the fate of the 144,000 who were sealed in 7:1-8? Did they get killed? Did they, perhaps, somehow deny their faith and accept the mark of the Beast?"

Here the answer is supplied for us by God. Indeed, to answer these naturally arising questions, seems to be the purpose of these verses. What is the answer? It is simply this: At the end of their lives, the 144,000 which were sealed by God are found to be with Christ. This is what sets to rest our hearts. Whether some die during the first half of the Tribulation, whether many—or all of them—die during the final half of the Tribulation, despite it all and through it all they are found at the end *all* safe with Christ. Many questions that we are curious about are not answered, but the chief one is. Just as the news "Arrived Safely" does not tell the whole story, but yet it relates the vital point, so here God has soothed our doubts about the fate of the 144,000 and their coming through the Tribulation. They arrive safely with Jesus!

"Could this be another 144,000?" someone asks. The answer is *No!* Look at verses 6, 8, and 9. John makes differences clear: "And I saw another angel" (v. 6)..."And another, a second angel," (Greek, v. 8)... "And another angel, a third" (Greek, v. 9). John does not call this, "Another 144,000," although he uses this word over and over in this book. No, it is the same 144,000, and they have come through the Tribulation safely (whether they were martyred or stayed alive) and now they are finally safe with the Lamb! What lessons are there here for us?

Mt. Zion is where David brought the Ark, built his palace and was buried. See Nehemiah 12:37; 2 Samuel 6:12,17 and 1 Kings 2:10.

Background

There are some interesting facts here.

Christ is spoken of as the "Lamb" 27 times in the book of Revelation.

And this verse tells of Christ standing on Mount Zion. The earthly Mount Zion, which is a mountain-hill in Jerusalem, was the seat of government for Israel from the time of David. It is mentioned 156 times in the Bible. Jerusalem is mentioned 828 times. These two terms are sometimes used interchangeably.

In chapter 13 we have just witnessed the corruption of the earth as Antichrist introduces idolatry and persecution.

Chapter 14 tells us about the worship of the true God.

And what a reunion this is at Mount Zion. From our reading of Psalm 126:1, Isaiah 1:26-27, we see that Zion represents the whole city of Jerusalem.

Both archaeology and Scripture confirm the fact that Zion (Jerusalem) is a holy site. It was here that Solomon built his temple.

PAST	PRESENT	RAPTURE	FIRST 3 1/2 TRIBULATION	LAST 3 1/2	ARMA–GEDDON	MIL–LENNIUM	NEW HEAVENS & EARTH

Revelation 14

2 And I heard a voice from heaven, as the voice of many waters, and as the voice of a great thunder: and I heard the voice of harpers harping with their harps:
3 And they sung as it were a new song before the throne, and before the four beasts, and the elders: and no man could learn that song but the hundred *and* forty *and* four thousand, which were redeemed from the earth.

Psa. 107:2

Definition:
Redeemed—*This word used in verse 3 is the Greek word* agoradzo *which means "to buy; to purchase." Christ "purchased" the believer in that when he was lost in sin and had not the infinite price to buy back his soul from its justly deserved eternal damnation, Christ "redeemed" him by paying for him upon the cross the infinite price necessary to satisfy divine justice (1 Cor. 7:23).*

Commentary

2-3. Here we see that these 144,000 who were "redeemed" from the earth are admitted to special heavenly privileges. They alone are here seen able to learn the new song which proceeds from the heavenly harpers. Why are these so privileged, and not others? We are not given the answer. It is God's sovereign will, we know this, and that is enough.

This is a heavenly scene—for the four beasts, the twenty-four elders, and the throne belong to the celestial chambers and not the earthly (chapters 4-5). This is part of the Heavenly Mount Zion and the Heavenly Jerusalem (Heb. 12:22). The words, "redeemed from the earth" (v. 3), also fit this being a heavenly picture.

▼

PAST	PRESENT	RAPTURE	FIRST 3 1/2 LAST 3 1/2 TRIBULATION	ARMA- GEDDON	MIL- LENNIUM	NEW HEAVENS & EARTH

Revelation 14

4 These are they which were not defiled with women; for they are virgins. These are they which follow the Lamb whithersoever he goeth. These were redeemed from among men, *being* the firstfruits unto God and to the Lamb.
5 And in their mouth was found no guile: for they are without fault before the throne of God.

1 Cor. 7:24-40

Lev. 23:9-16;Jn. 1:47
Isa. 6:5-7;

Commentary

4. We live in a day of rising immorality; what will the last days be like? They will be Sodom and Gomorrah days! Despite such evil days and temptations, the 144,000—by God's gracious enablement—"have not made themselves impure" (Greek; *moluno*, "to make one's self impure; to stain; to defile"). These did not join the world in committing adultery and other defiling iniquities.

These, in fact, "are virgins." Does this mean that spiritually they are virgins in that they have not joined the world in its sinfulness? Or does it mean that these, all 144,000, are unmarried? Personally I find it hard to be sure. In any event, marrying is no sin (1 Cor. 7:28). Dean Alford (commenting *in loc.* this passage) declared that, "The married are more like the Lord intended man to be, but these [the 144,000] are more like the Lord Himself was."

These are the "firstfruits." How? These are not the first saved men starting from Adam...or starting from Pentecost. The 144,000, however, could be (and must be) the first saved out of Israel during this period

Revelation 7:1-8 showed us that the 144,000 were Israelites; and Zech. 12:10 prophecies of the mass of Israel turning to Christ at His appearance at the end of the 7 years. These 144,000, however, are Israelites who are sealed, not at the end of the seven years, but early in the period (7:3—before the 7th seal and the trumpets). They are the "firstfruits" of those out of Israel who are to be saved during this period. This was the symbolism of Lev. 23:9-16 with its (a) Feast of the Firstfruits, and then (b) fifty days later at Pentecost the initial sampling of the gathered harvest. First the *firstfruits,* and then the *harvest.* The 144,000 are saved as *firstfruits;* then the mass of Israel are saved as the harvest by the end of the Tribulation (Zech. 12:10ff; Rom. 11:26-27).

5. In a day of enlarged cursing and blaspheming, these 144,000 have kept their tongues pure. Now glorified, safe with Christ, they are faultless and before His throne. "ARRIVED SAFELY" is the message to us here in 14:1-5.

PAST	PRESENT	RAPTURE	FIRST 3 1/2 TRIBULATION	LAST 3 1/2	ARMA-GEDDON	MIL-LENNIUM	NEW HEAVENS & EARTH

6 And I saw another angel fly in the midst of heaven, having the everlasting gospel to preach unto them that dwell on the earth, and to every nation, and kindred, and tongue, and people.

Mt. 24:14

7 Saying with a loud voice, Fear God, and give glory to him; for the hour of his judgment is come: and worship him that made heaven, and earth, and the sea, and the fountains of waters.

Rom. 1:21

Rev. 8:7-12; 16:1-9

Commentary

THREE ANGELIC MESSAGES (14:6-13)

6. "...another angel fly...having the everlasting gospel to preach..."— John saw this angel with its contents and proclamation for this time, the last 3 1/2 years of the Tribulation. We should not think that this means that an angel, instead of man, will preach the message of salvation at this time. No, rather John's seeing the angel with the Gospel shows that now, during the Tribulation, as before, is the time for the Gospel message to be given out.

"To every nation..."—Christ gives us His comment in Mt. 24:14, "And this gospel of the kingdom shall be preached in all the world for a witness unto all nations; and then shall the end come."

7. The four items listed here as those made by God, the heaven, earth, sea, and fountains of waters (rivers, etc), are those which the first four trumpets and first four bowls smite in chapters 8 and 16 (with the heavens smitten fourth, instead of first as it is here mentioned). God's judgment manifests itself here by His depriving the *unthankful* of their use of those things which He has in love given to man. They thank him not for the rivers, saying that these are merely lucky-evolutionary-breaks, therefore He smites the rivers, etc. Romans 1:18-32 reveals this pattern of equitable judgment. Romans 1:21 says, "...they glorified Him not...," and this verse of judgment commands them to "give glory to Him."

"The hour of His judgment is come"—the Tribulation Period is this hour!

PAST	PRESENT	RAPTURE	FIRST 3 1/2 LAST 3 1/2 TRIBULATION		ARMA-GEDDON	MIL-LENNIUM	NEW HEAVENS & EARTH
			FIRST 3 1/2	LAST 3 1/2	ARMA-GEDDON	MIL-LENNIUM	NEW HEAVENS & EARTH

8 And there followed another angel, saying, Babylon is fallen, is fallen, that great city, because she made all nations drink of the wine of the wrath of her fornication.

Rev. 16:10; 18:2

Definition:
The Unpardonable Sin—*See Mt. 12:22-32, especially vs. 31-32. This is the sin of blaspheming the Holy Ghost by willfully crediting the clearly manifested works of God to be the work of evil and of Satan. The sinner who so hardens his heart so as to call once-and-for-all the prodings of the Spirit "evil," can no longer be reached by the Spirit, who alone can bring a man to repent, and consequently he will forever remain in his lost state.*

Commentary

8. Greek: "And another, a second angel, followed...." This announcement of the fall of the city of Babylon, the leading city in Antichrist's political and commercial empire, is proleptic. That is, it is a proclamation of something certain to happen in the future as if it had already happened. Isaiah 53 speaks of Christ's death in this way—as already accomplished although another seven centuries would pass by until actual fulfillment.

The Antichrist's city of Babylon will soon fall at the pouring out of the seventh and last Bowl of Wrath (16:17, 19). The fall of this city will then be described in detail in chapter 18. Suffice it for now, however, for us to note that after the calamitous state of the world in Revelation chapters 11-13, this chapter, 14, is now proclaiming the safety of the 144,000 and the final doom of all that pertains to iniquity and Antichrist. Of great importance, then, in setting the final picture straight after the awful scenes of the last 3 1/2 years is this certification of the Fall of Babylon. The details of this fall shall be studied in chapter 18.

▼

PAST	PRESENT	RAPTURE	FIRST 3 1/2 LAST 3 1/2 TRIBULATION	ARMA– GEDDON	MIL– LENNIUM	NEW HEAVENS & EARTH

Revelation 14

VERSES 9, 10, 11

9 And the third angel followed them, saying with a loud voice, If any man worship the beast and his image, and receive *his* mark in his forehead, or in his hand.

10 The same shall drink of the wine of the wrath of God, which is poured out without mixture into the cup of his indignation; and he shall be tormented with fire and brimstone in the presence of the holy angels, and in the presence of the Lamb:

11 And the smoke of their torment ascendeth up for ever and ever: and they have no rest day nor night, who worship the beast and his image, and whosoever receiveth the mark of his name.

Mt. 26:39

Gen. 19:24
Isa. 66:24
Rev. 20:15
Lk. 16:23-28

Commentary

9-11. Greek: "And another angel, a third, followed...."

These verses as a unit teach, through the message of the third angel, that if anyone worships the Beast and receives the mark then he is one whose soul will be lost forever. This conclusion is inescapable. "This sin constitutes the Unpardonable Sin for the Tribulation Age" (R. J. Dunzweiler).

This sin here remarkably matches those circumstances of Mt. 12:22-32 wherein Christ describes the unpardonable sin. There it was the crediting of a clearly miraculous and divine healing by Christ to be the work of "Beelzebub," here it is the crediting of the clearly evil work of the Beast, Antichrist, to be that of God—with the concomitant rejecting of God's true witnesses as evil ones. The acceptance of the Beast as Saviour of this world and the taking of his mark signify this end-time blasphemy against the Spirit of Truth, the Holy Ghost, and the seal makes certain the eternal doom of the lost who take the mark.

It may be that in order to receive the mark one may have to recite some blasphemous oath or commit some blasphemous act. In any case, we may be sure, a believer could never do such and God will not allow one of His children, even amid so great temptation, thus to fall away. That was the message of the 144,000 safe on Zion! Someone asks, "But what if one of the 144,000 takes the mark?" Answer: God will not allow this. The 144,000 *all* end up safe with Christ, while those who take the mark *all* "shall be tormented with fire and brimstone."

▼

PAST	PRESENT	RAPTURE	FIRST 3 1/2 LAST 3 1/2 TRIBULATION	ARMA-GEDDON	MIL-LENNIUM	NEW HEAVENS & EARTH

Revelation 14

12 Here is the patience of the saints: here *are* they that keep the commandments of God, and the faith of Jesus. 13 And I heard a voice from heaven saying unto me, Write, Blessed *are* the dead which die in the Lord from henceforth: Yea, saith the Spirit, that they may rest from their labours; and their works do follow them.

2 Cor. 5:6-8; Rev. 1:18

1 Cor. 15:58

Commentary

12. In a time of extended persecution, here at its height for 3 1/2 years—and even today in Communist countries—a saint (a believer) needs the gift of patience from the Lord. He or she needs patience so as not to capitulate and fall into obedience of the wicked so as to save the body. Christ said, "And fear not them which kill the body, but are not able to kill the soul: but rather fear him which is able to destroy both soul and body in hell" (Mt. 10:28).

Christ further said, "Blessed are ye, when men shall revile you, and perseculte you...Rejoice, and be exceedingly glad: for great is your reward in heaven, for so persecuted they the prophets which were before you" (Mt. 5:11-12).

13. A man is truly blessed if his final reward is one of blessing, despite the temporary persecutions of this life. This verse now brings out the fact that those who "die in the Lord" are blessed.

This would surprise many, and, in fact, it is only by the eye of faith that we can apprehend it. Whoever of the sons of this earth thought that someone was "blessed" when he died? Death is viewed as the opposite of blessing. It is the final and irreversible calamity—it is the end of everything! But this is only the view of human eyes before one has come to the cross for forgiveness, life, and enlightenment. Death for the believer is the gateway to being forever with Christ. This is joy and life, not sadness.

This proclamation of the blessed who die is made in light of the troubles portrayed in chapters 11-13. It is made in light of the world's worst and "Great Tribulation" (Mt. 24:21). It is timely and it is wonderful. Those who die for Christ during the final 3 1/2 years of the Tribulation, though they perish in great numbers, are: (a) *blessed*—in a happy state; (b) they are at *rest* from the pains of persecution; and (c) they will be *rewarded* for their works which do not perish but rather follow them to the Judgment Seat of Christ (2 Cor. 5:10).

PAST	PRESENT	RAPTURE	FIRST 3 1/2	LAST 3 1/2	ARMA-GEDDON	MIL-LENNIUM	NEW HEAVENS & EARTH
			TRIBULATION				

14 And I looked, and behold a white cloud, and upon the cloud *one* sat like unto the Son of man, having on his head a golden crown, and in his hand a sharp sickle.

Rev. 19:11-21;
Isa. 63:1-6

Commentary

THE HARVEST: ARMAGEDDON (14:14-20)

14-20. Here in 14:14-20 we have a vision of Armageddon. The imagery is that of the ancient Palestinian farmer who first gathers together his ripe grapes into the winepress and then smashes them with his bare feet in order to release their red juice.

Here the portrait is essentially the same as that found in those two remarkable prophecies, Isaiah 63:1-6 and Joel 3. Zechariah 12 and 14:1-7 also speak of this. The wicked armies of the end-time are depicted as ripe grapes. The winepress of God—the place where He will smash the armies—is the great Armageddon Pass (which is the great Plain of Esdraelon and the Jezreel-Jordon Valleys). This is the 10 by 40 mile northwest-to-southeast gateway to Jerusalem through the mountains; and it will be the latter-day winepress of God. The red juice of the ancient Palestinian grape well represents visually the blood of the wicked which will here be shed.

14. Here in the context of the above explanation we see Christ, the Son of Man, coming as the Judge. We now understand plainly that it is He that is the grand subject of Isa. 63:1-6 and of the other Old Testament visions which are parallel to this one. The crown shows Him coming now not as the Lamb, but as the King. The sickle shows that He is ready to judge with the cutting instrument already in His hand. It is a *sharp* sickle! Why?

And the sky was split apart like a scroll... (Revelation 6:14)

Background

Notice that verse 14 refers to a sharp sickle. This would appear to indicate that not only will God's judgment be swift but it will be a terrifying holocaust—the most frightful ever witnessed by man.

The day of patience and mercy has ended! Now comes the time for judgment.

Today, many leading churchmen are leading their congregations towards a socialized gospel. One clergyman stated: "...the Bible is just as dated as anything else. It is first century theology."

Another remarked, "I feel sorry for laymen who are caught between the idea that these may be the last days of the world...I think the pains of this era are the pangs of a better world."

A news magazine reported: "Among Protestants, radical theologies are causing many to wonder whether religion any longer has a worthwhile mission of its own to the world at large."

Soon those who turn their back on God will suddenly feel His full wrath.

PAST	PRESENT	RAPTURE	FIRST 3 1/2 LAST 3 1/2 TRIBULATION	ARMA-GEDDON	MIL-LENNIUM	NEW HEAVENS & EARTH

15 And another angel came out of the temple, crying with a loud voice to him that sat on the cloud, Thrust in thy sickle, and reap: for the time is come for thee to reap; for the harvest of the earth is ripe. 16 And he that sat on the cloud thrust in his sickle on the earth; and the earth was reaped.

Joel 3:1-3, 9-16
Zech. 12; 14:1-7

Definition:
To reap—*Greek:* therizo, *to gather in the harvest.*

Commentary

15-16. Here we must not think that the angel is *commanding* the Lord; the angel in loyal excitement implores Christ to destroy the wicked—the hour of visitation has come to its fulness.

"The earth was reaped"—Here Christ, the Lord of All will gather the armies of Antichrist to Armageddon. Revelation 16:13-16 shows that wicked voices bring the evil armies to Armageddon; here we see that Christ the sovereign Lord has Himself gathered them for DESTRUCTION! His cutting the grapes down with the sickle (reaping) portrays His mobilizing the wicked armies for battle. His throwing them into the winepress pictures his gathering them into Armageddon in Palestine. Then, His crushing the grapes depicts Christ's destroying the armies of the Antichrist in a great slaughter from above.

PAST	PRESENT	RAPTURE	FIRST 3½ LAST 3½ TRIBULATION	ARMA–GEDDON	MIL–LENNIUM	NEW HEAVENS & EARTH

17 And another angel came out of the temple which is in heaven, he also having a sharp sickle.

18 And another angel came out from the altar, which had power over fire; and cried with a loud cry to him that had the sharp sickle, saying, Thrust in thy sharp sickle, and gather the clusters of the vine of the earth; for her grapes are fully ripe.

Joel 3:1-3, 9-16

Rev. 19:11-21;
   Zech. 12; 14:1-7
Isa. 63:1-6;
   Rev. 16:13-16

Definition:
Winepress—*A dug-out and lined usually-rectangular trench in the ground in which ripe grapes were gathered and there crushed for their red juice.*

Commentary

17-18. "From the altar"—Here in verse 18 the angel comes from the Heavenly Brazen Altar, the place where sacrifice for sin is signified. Christ has paid for sin once and for all, but yet the imagery of this ancient altar speaks to us of God's holiness and justice. Sin must be paid for—thus the angel coming from this site crys out desiring to see the rebellous sinners pay the just penalty for their sins.

"Her grapes are fully ripe"—Genesis 15:16 shows God telling Abraham that He would not yet destroy the Amorites for their iniquity was "not yet full." God, in history, in His sovereignty often allows an error or wicked group to wax into a fullness of evil in order that their iniquity might be fully manifest. He did this finally with the Amorites; and He had them destroyed for their sins by Israel under Joshua. He did this with ancient Egypt, Babylon...with Hitler, and He will do this with Antichrist and his system (which may be Communism). That the grapes are fully ripe indicate that Antichrist's government and his world has fully manifested their utter corruption—they have become ripe for destruction.

PAST	PRESENT	RAPTURE	FIRST 3 1/2	LAST 3 1/2	ARMA–GEDDON	MIL–LENNIUM	NEW HEAVENS & EARTH
			TRIBULATION				

Revelation 14

VERSES 19, 20

19 And the angel thrust in his sickle into the earth, and gathered the vine of the earth, and cast *it* into the great winepress of the wrath of God.
20 And the winepress was trodden without the city, and blood came out of the winepress, even unto the horse bridles, by the space of a thousand *and* six hundred furlongs.

Joel 3:1-3, 9-16

Isa. 63:1-6

Commentary

19. This winepress is Armageddon as 16:16 clearly shows, as do the Old Testament similar visions, viz., Isa. 63:1-6; Joel 3.

20. "Blood...unto the horse bridles"—Many feel compelled on the basis of this verse to demand that at Armageddon the blood of the wicked will flow into a stream which will become about 6 foot deep. While I do not doubt that God could perform such a miracle, yet I think this to miss the imagery.

The farmer, or more often some young hired boy, jumps up and down in the winepress. In Isa. 63:1-6, which also speaks of Armageddon, we see Christ doing this with such a fury that He stains all of his garments red with the juice from the grapes. Here Rev. 14:20 depicts such a furious crushing from within the winepress which is below ground level that the red juice splashes upwards as high as a horse bridle—about six feet above ground. Thus this verse doesn't attempt to give us a reading on the exact depth of blood flowing; rather, I think, it indicates to us the terrible fury in which the Son of God will destroy those armies gathered behind the Beast and against Jerusalem at the end-time.

Matthew 24:22 tells us, "And except those days should be shortened, there should no flesh be saved...." Antichrist and his armies would have their way except Christ interivened. No wonder Christ comes with a sickle in righteous fury!

PAST	PRESENT	RAPTURE	FIRST 3 1/2 LAST 3 1/2 TRIBULATION		ARMA-GEDDON	MIL-LENNIUM	NEW HEAVENS &EARTH

CHAPTER 15

And I saw another sign in heaven, great and marvellous, seven angels having the seven last plagues; for in them is filled up the wrath of God.

Commentary

CHAPTERS 15 & 16:
THE SEVEN LAST PLAGUES

1. Now we again continue on in the main sequence of events. The seven Seals, then the seven Trumpets, and now the final seven Bowls of Wrath constitute the chief pre-Armageddon Tribulation judgments. The initial two series have been sent, and their turmoil lingers. Here is the final and most severe series. Just as chapters 4 & 5 showed us the heavenly scene before the Tribulation period began, so likewise here chapter 15 shows us the celestial scene before the Bowls are poured out in chapter 16.

The very fact that this series, as will be seen in chapter 16, so transcends the previous two in severity, shows us that they cannot be contemporaneous series—that is, that the seals, trumpets, and bowls do not all fall at the same time. No, a child is not struck easy, medium, and hard all at once. First comes the easy, then if there is no change the medium, and finally the hard. Thus it is not: Seal 1 Trumpet 1 Bowl 1; S2 T2 B2; etc., but SSSSSSSTTTTTTTBBBBBBB.

"Last plagues...filled up the wrath of God"—Neither of the other series are called "last plagues." Why? Because only these Bowls of Wrath are *last;* the others are loosed prior to these.

These are "last" in the relative sense of God's pre-Armageddon castigations of a wicked generation upon the earth. It is clear, however, that the awful Armageddon destruction comes after these bowls for here the Beast's Kingdom is attacked (16:2, 10, 19), but at Armageddon the Beast and all of his are forever destroyed (19:11-21).

"The wrath of God"—Only those who reject the Bible deny the fact that the Holy God is wrathful against sin and rebellious sinners. These, as the idol makers of old, carve out their own gods according to their imaginations. Of these Romans 1:32 declares: "Who knowing the judgment of God, that they which commit such things are worthy of death, not only do the same, but have pleasure in them that do them."

▼

PAST	PRESENT	RAPTURE	FIRST 3 1/2	LAST 3 1/2	ARMA-	MIL-	NEW
			TRIBULATION		GEDDON	LENNIUM	HEAVENS & EARTH

Revelation 15

2 And I saw as it were a sea of glass mingled with fire: and them that had gotten the victory over the beast, and over his image, and over his mark, *and* over the number of his name, stand on the sea of glass, having the harps of God.

3 And they sing the song of Moses the servant of God, and the song of the Lamb, saying, Great and marvellous are thy works, Lord God Almighty; just and true *are* thy ways, thou King of saints.

4 Who shall not fear thee, O Lord, and glorify thy name? for *thou* only *art* holy: for all nations shall come and worship before thee; for thy judgments are made manifest.

VERSES 2, 3, 4

Rev. 21:21

Rev. 12:11

Ex. 15:1-21

Zech. 8:22

Commentary

2-4. Here is a wonderful triumph anthem sung in heaven (v. 3) by those saved by faith in Christ during the Tribulation. It is rich with meaningful adoration of the Wonderful and Holy God who is now again about to stretch forth His hand to deliver His people and to punish the wicked. Those who sing this would appear to be the *victorious martyrs* of this period.

The fact that they sing both the song of Moses and the song of the Lamb shows, despite various theories to the contrary, that the New Testament never sees an opposition between Moses-and-the-Old-Testament and Christ-and-the-New-Testament (e.g., Lk. 16:31).

Students of Greek will see in v. 3 that Granville Sharp's Rule does not apply, so that the songs are not one, but two. Not: "the song of Moses even the song of the Lamb," but, "the song of Moses...and [another song] the song of the Lamb."

Exodus 15:1-21 shows us the glorious Song of Moses which was given to commemorate the deliverance from the Egyptian armies. How well this fits the Tribulation Period! There the enemy was wicked, rebellious against God, the situation was desperate, all seemed lost, but then God intervened in might and miracle. Is not this the case in the Tribulation (Mt. 24:21-22)?

Exodus 15:11 in the Song of Moses is a glorious verse. It is the theme and title of an ancient Hebrew hymn, *Me-ca-mo-cah,* "Who is like unto thee?" The song goes just as the verse reads, "Who is like unto thee, O Lord, among the gods? Who is like thee, glorious in holiness?"

PAST	PRESENT	RAPTURE	FIRST 3 1/2 \ LAST 3 1/2 TRIBULATION	ARMA– GEDDON	MIL– LENNIUM	NEW HEAVENS & EARTH

5 And after that I looked, and, behold, the temple of the tabernacle of the testimony in heaven was opened:
6 And the seven angels came out of the temple, having the seven plagues, clothed in pure and white linen, and having their breasts girded with golden girdles.

Rev. 11:15, 19;
Ex. 31:7-11;
Nu. 11:24; 14:10

Commentary

5-6. Notice at this appearance of the Temple in Heaven how the sequence of the book is continuing. In 11:15 the Seventh Trumpet finally blew and at this the Heavenly Temple was revealed (11:19). Now after the parenthetical visions of chapters 12-14, which showed us how evil would reign during the last half of the Tribulation, we again are returned to the contents of the Seventh Trumpet, namely, the Heavenly Temple with the final "Seven Plagues" coming out of it.

Angels bring the plagues out of the Heavenly Temple; the angels are clad in white and bound by golden "belts" (v. 6—"girdles" in the KJV; Greek *zone*, "belt"). These circumstances show that these coming plagues will be holy and righteous judgments. The Temple with its altars, etc., speaks of God's holiness and the necessity that sin be dealt with; the white clothed angels speak further of holiness. Even the golden belts remind us of God's righteousness and faithfulness (Isa. 11:5).

"The temple of the tabernacle of the testimony"—Greek: "the sanctuary-temple of the tent of the testimony"—reminds us of God's Tent ("Tabernacle") of the Testimony which Israel under Moses carried with them in their wilderness journeys. This is significant, for Rev. 7:1-8; ch. 12; Joel ch. 3; and Zech. chs. 12-14 show that God will again fight for and rescue the believing remnant of Israel of the last days who turn to Christ.

"After that"—Greek, *meta tauta*, literally "after these-things." This is one of John's favorite expressions, and his constant usage of it shows his continual desire to inform us as to precisely when various events occur *(Meta tauta*—1:19; 4:1; 7:1; 7:9; 15:5; 18:1; 19:1; and in John's Gospel 2:12; 3:22; 5:1; 6:1; 7:1; 19:28, 38; 21:1. / Rev. 7:1; Jn. 2:12; and 19:28 being *meta touto*, "after this-thing.").

PAST	PRESENT	RAPTURE	FIRST 3 1/2 TRIBULATION	LAST 3 1/2	ARMA-GEDDON	MIL-LENNIUM	NEW HEAVENS & EARTH

Revelation 15

VERSES 7, 8

7 And one of the four beasts gave unto the seven angels seven golden vials full of the wrath of God, who liveth for ever and ever.

8 And the temple was filled with smoke from the glory of God, and from his power; and no man was able to enter into the temple, till the seven plagues of the seven angels were fulfilled.

Rev. 8:8

Isa. 6:1-4

Commentary

7-8. The fact that "one of the four beasts" (Greek, *zoon,* "living-creatures") gave these vials of wrath to the seven angels again shows us that the holiness of God demands that the great sin of the earth meet with these great punishments. This is so because each of the "Four Living-Creatures" continually was occupied night and day in praising God's holiness, saying, "Holy Holy Holy, Lord God Almighty..." (Rev. 4:8).

"...smoke...the glory of God...no man was able to enter..."—all of this declares to us that the matter was now irreversibly initiated, the Seven Bowls of Wrath are now about to be poured out upon the Antichrist and the world following him.

The Bowls (or "vials" as in the KJV; Greek, *phiale)* of Wrath convey to us the image of God's wrath against sin being stored up in bowls, higher and higher, until they are at last full and overflowing with judgment (as in Gen 15:16). I think that the picture which we ought to here see is not that of large angels pouring out seven little *thimbles* of judgment upon the corrupted earth, but rather seven angels pouring out *gigantic* bowls—much larger than the angels themselves—filled with boiling and smoking acid-wrath against the rebel sinners who will not come to Christ for forgiveness, but who rather curse God and rejoice in their iniquities.

PAST	PRESENT	RAPTURE	FIRST 3 1/2	LAST 3 1/2	ARMA-GEDDON	MIL-LENNIUM	NEW HEAVENS &EARTH
			TRIBULATION				

Revelation 16

CHAPTER 16

And I heard a great voice out of the temple saying to the seven angels, Go your ways, and pour out the vials of the wrath of God upon the earth.

VERSE 1

Rev. 1:15; 14:15

Jer. 42:18; 44:6;
Dan. 9:11, 27

Commentary

1. *Seven* angels with *seven* bowls signifies that this will be a full and complete cycle of judgments—just as the prototype, the *seven* days of creation, constituted the full and entire creation period.

A voice command begins the judgment. No voice is necessary, but for our sakes, so that we will understand that these things come from God, a voice comes from the holy Heavenly Temple to begin these plagues. So in Genesis 1 at the Creation, no voice was necessary, but for our sakes God spoke a command...and it was done. John 11:41-42 further illustrates this, as Christ openly declared that the reason that he prayed outloud before raising Lazarus was *for the sake of* those watching—that all people might understand that this raising originated with the Father and was performed through the mediation of the Son.

PAST	PRESENT	RAPTURE	FIRST 3½ LAST 3½ TRIBULATION	ARMA–GEDDON	MIL–LENNIUM	NEW HEAVENS & EARTH

2 And the first went, and poured out his vial upon the earth; and there fell a noisome and grievous sore upon the men which had the mark of the beast, and *upon* them which worshipped his image.

Rev. 13:15-17

THE
FIRST
VIAL

BOILS

Malignant
Sores affect
those with
Mark of Antichrist

Commentary

2. These "last plagues" (15:1) are poured out in the last half of the Tribulation Period, near its end, but yet before the final gathering together at Armageddon which closes the period (Rev. 19:11ff). This *first plague* is poured out, as we see from this verse, after the image to the now-risen Beast has been erected and after the Beast's followers have been marked (13:15-17).

"A noisome and grievous sore"—Greek, *elkos kakon kai poneron,* literally, "an-ulcerated-sore bad and evil." How this will occur we can only speculate; however, it will occur. Perhaps the mark of the Beast will involve something very similar to the modern tatoo which, after its initial drawing, becomes a sore, forms a scab, and requires a few days to heal. If this be so, God in someway may allow these tatoos to become infected en masse across the earth. Maybe the ink formula will irritate the human blood system? Perhaps God will on a strictly supernatural basis cause the infections? Perhaps God will cause some earthly gas to become suddenly abundant and this gas will cause the wild inflammations on these Beast marks? In any case, the ulcerating of these marks is true justice at the hands of the rejected Great Physician!

PAST	PRESENT	RAPTURE	FIRST 3½ TRIBULATION	LAST 3½	ARMA-GEDDON	MIL-LENNIUM	NEW HEAVENS & EARTH

3 And the second angel poured out his vial upon the sea; and it became as the blood of a dead *man:* and every living soul died in the sea.

Rev. 8:8-9; Ex. 7:20-25

THE SECOND VIAL

SEA of BLOOD
Everything in Ocean Dies

Commentary

3. The *second bowl* affects the sea and "it became blood as of-a-dead-man" (literally from the Greek). The *sea* here may represent only the Mediterranean Sea—the sea of the Bible world—or it may involve all of the earth's oceans.

God supernaturally touches the waters and they turn red and fish die in abundance. Again, this is the *language of appearance,* and the inspired text does not demand that the reddened sea be actually turned from hydrogen and oxygen (H_2O) into that unfathomably complex blood molecule with all of its many elements.

In 8:8-9 the second trumpet turned the sea one-third to blood and one-third of the fish died. Here, however, the 2d bowl is not partial; it is universal in magnitude. It will sweep the sea, and the fish not in aquariums or otherwise separated from the sea will perish. Alas, sinful man denies God and boasts that he controls the oceans—that he is the master of his fate. God's plagues will, as in the case of Pharaoh, show all that God alone rules the world!

Since Exodus 7:20-25 shows that the turning of the Nile into blood at the touch of Moses' rod was an event that actually occurred in the real world, I do not doubt for a moment that this second bowl judgment will also literally take place. Here we do not have a mere parabolic-fairy story that is intended to teach us the lesson that God will own the seas in the end; but one which will never actually happen. No, the second bowl will be poured forth and the sea will become blood. It has been spoken; it will come to pass.

Revelation 16

4 And the third angel poured out his vial upon the rivers and fountains of waters; and they became blood.

5 And I heard the angel of the waters say, Thou art righteous, O Lord, which art, and wast, and shalt be, because thou hast judged thus.

6 For they have shed the blood of saints and prophets, and thou hast given them blood to drink; for they are worthy.

7 And I heard another out of the altar say, Even so, Lord God Almighty, true and righteous *are* thy judgments.

Rev. 8:10-11;
Ex. 7:20-25

Rev. 4:8

Mt. 23:32-36

Gen. 18:23-33;
Rom. 9:14

Commentary

4. This *third bowl* is essentially similar to the second, except instead of the seas, here the rivers and water-sources of mankind are ruined for drinking and for fresh water fish because of this blood plague. Just as the Nile was turned, now there shall be a thousand polluted red Niles on earth (Exod. 7:20-25).

In the third trumpet, 8:10-11, a third part of the rivers were infested; here the judgment is again universal and all of rivers are turned. Chaos and thirst will reign on earth.

5-7. These angelic voices ring out the cry that the murderous earthlings deserve this horrible plague because they have shed the righteous blood of the prophets and of the saints, that is, of those who trusted in God and in His Christ.

This is retribution in kind, and it is righteous and holy (despite what some modern-day sinners may say about all retribution being evil to their sinful and fallen minds). If God does it and if the holy angels say that it is just, let us have done with men who snivel and who say that God is unrighteous when He judges the wicked (Gen. 18:23-33; Rom. 9:14-24).

THE THIRD VIAL

RIVERS of BLOOD

Rivers and Springs Turn to Blood

Background

It may be difficult for you to imagine the disaster that these Second and Third Vial judgments create.

One must remember that the vast' oceans and rivers constitute a system which act as God's great air conditioner...sweeping away the impurities of the air...balancing nature.

Also the oxygen-giving phytoplankton (the organisms in the tiny green plankton plants), which are found in water, supply a majority of the earth's oxygen to man.

With suddenly the oceans and rivers and springs turning to blood - possibly because of billions of fish dying - what happens?

1. Waters become poisonous and putrid, and foul smelling air sweeps across the world as decay takes place.

2. Fish, an important source of food, becomes unobtainable. The fishing industry collapses...starvation of people accelerates.

3. People will rush to dig wells...only to have them gush forth blood!

4. Man's oxygen supply will diminish.

Possibly we will see blood-red snow. Imagine fouled reddish ice-cubes in your soft drinks! This is a picture of disaster, confusion and death.

PAST	PRESENT	RAPTURE	FIRST 3 1/2 LAST 3 1/2 TRIBULATION	ARMA-GEDDON	MIL-LENNIUM	NEW HEAVENS & EARTH

8 And the fourth angel poured out his vial upon the sun; and power was given unto him to scorch men with fire.

9 And men were scorched with great heat, and blasphemed the name of God, which hath power over these plagues; and they repented not to give him glory.

Rev. 8:12; Ezek. 8:16

Jer. 8:6

Definition:
Synechtoche—*This is a figure of speech wherein the whole is represented by a part, or wherein a part is represented by the whole. For example, in Judges 8:6 the question is asked as to whether or not the "hands of Zebah and Zalmunna" have been captured by Gideon. Here the "hands" represent the whole persons of the two fugitives.*

Commentary

8. In this *fourth bowl* the sun itself is affected and men are scorched with its intense heat. In the fourth trumpet (8:12) the heavenly bodies were also affected—but there one-third of the sun was *darkened* and presumably a cooling effect would take place, not to mention the alarm. Here, however, men are burned.

Men have from the ages tended to worship the sun, that which has been created, rather than the creator (Rom. 1:18-23; Ezek. 8:16). Even today, when scientists lecture on the effects of solar heat and on photosynthesis the sun, rather than God, is usually made into the worshipped world Santa Claus who gives us everything. Now with this plague God shows the Antichrist and his earth full of followers, that He, not the sun, is the Sustainer of the earth (Col. 1:16-17). God here, as in the other judgments, shows all who follow the Beast the utter futility of depending on any one but God to control the world in which we dwell.

9. As in the case of Pharaoh, the mass of mankind in further rebellion against God chooses not to repent of their sins, but prefers rather to curse and blaspheme God (Ex. 9:34-35). Here too, as then, as the wicked rise higher in blasphemy against God and His children, God more and more displays His power and glory and gets praise unto Himself (Ex. 6:1,6).

OPPRESSIVE HEAT

THE FOURTH VIAL

Sun Scorches all Mankind

Background

I can remember when my daughters, Doreen and Diane, and I visited the Dead Sea and Jericho in May, 1969. We will never forget the scorching sun that beat down unmercifully on us. Our guide told us that ordinary thermometers could not measure the heat because they would burst. He estimated the heat at 125° F. in the *shade!* It was easy to see how anyone lost in this desert area would die very quickly.

Unless someone has been in heat so oppressive, they cannot appreciate what they take for granted - WATER!

Water is symbolic of LIFE. Yet we have just seen in the Third Seal judgment that the water of the earth has become blood-red. And now those living in this day have also the HEAT of the sun...added to their prior loss of fresh water to quench their thirst.

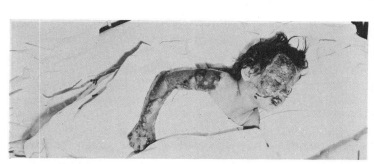

Man-created napalm victim (pictured above) gives you some idea of how heat can destroy flesh. The temperature of a napalm flame can approach 2060° C. Napalm burns are deep and extensive, with burns that result in severe scars. What will a severe burn be like in that coming day when pure water will not be on hand?

PAST	PRESENT	RAPTURE	FIRST 3 1/2 LAST 3 1/2 TRIBULATION	ARMA-GEDDON	MIL-LENNIUM	NEW HEAVENS & EARTH

10 And the fifth angel poured out his vial upon the seat of the beast; and his kingdom was full of darkness; and they gnawed their tongues for pain,

11 And blasphemed the God of heaven because of their pains and their sores, and repented not of their deeds.

Ex. 10:21-23

Rev. 16:9

DARKNESS

THE
FIFTH
VIAL

Earth
Plunged into
Darkness

Commentary

10-11. The *fifth bowl*, like the fifth trumpet (9:4), is primarily directed against wicked men—here against the Beast's followers.

"...the seat of the Beast...his kingdom...their sores..."—These things show us that this plague of darkness accompanied by some pain causing agent is aimed (a) against the capital city of the Beast's empire, his "seat" of government; (b) against his entire "kingdom" which by this time extends across continents as 13:7-8 shows; and (c) it further aggravates the sores caused by the first bowl, 16:2.

The fact that the sores of first bowl upon the Antichrist's followers are further agitated here in the fifth bowl would suggest to us that the falling of the bowls may come in short succession

"They gnawed their tongues for pain"—the pain must be fiercely intense to cause this. They who used their God given tongues to curse and blaspheme (vss. 9,11) are now again suitably punished—let them chew on their tongues to divert the pain. Yet with all this, these, like Pharaoh, repent not.

Since the "darkness which may be felt" actually fell upon the land of Egypt in the Nineth Mosaic Plague (Ex. 10:21-23), we may be confident that this plague described here in the Book of Revelation will likewise physically and actually come to pass.

▼

PAST	PRESENT	RAPTURE	FIRST 3 1/2 TRIBULATION	LAST 3 1/2	ARMA-GEDDON	MIL-LENNIUM	NEW HEAVENS & EARTH

12 And the sixth angel poured out his vial upon the great river Eu-phra-tes; and the water thereof was dried up, that the way of the kings of the east might be prepared.

Exod. 14:21-22;
Josh. 3:15-17
Mt. 2:1

THE
SIXTH
VIAL

RIVER Euphrates
DRIED UP

Army Marches
on Israel

Commentary

12. The *sixth bowl,* like the previous five bowls, is similar in certain respects to its corresponding trumpet, the sixth (9:13-16ff). In the sixth trumpet the four angels were loosed who were bound to the RIVER EUPHRATES; here the EUPHRATES is dried up! In the sixth trump the army of 200 million horsemen was started on their march to slay a third of men; here also armies are set to marching—the armies headed by the Kings of the East.

Thus the trumpets and the corresponding bowls each involve the same basic area, but each yet differs, and always where the trumpet judgment is partial, the bowl is more universal. Thus we can expect that here the Kings of the East with their armies will involve greater multitudes than even the 200 million of the sixth trump; and verses 13-16 of this chapter will show that this expectation will not be in vain.

"The kings of the east" is a synectoche for the armies of the East which are led by them. This is made clear in the next few verses.

In order to truly fathom what is here involved the reader ought to consider the verse at hand while looking at a globe (a globe is here preferred over a flat projection map). The Euphrates River, that great and renowned stream of antiquity which cradled early civilizations such as the Babylonian and Assyrian, winds some 1700 miles flowing southeast into the Persian Gulf. On a globe one can see the strategic intercontinental position of this river. Africa, Palestine, and Arabia are to the southwest of this river; and Russia, China, India, and Iran (Persia) are to its northeast. The Euphrates is the wet line which separates these two

PAST	PRESENT	RAPTURE	FIRST 3 1/2 | LAST 3 1/2 TRIBULATION	ARMA-GEDDON	MIL-LENNIUM	NEW HEAVENS & EARTH

13 And I saw three unclean spirits like frogs *come* out of the mouth of the dragon, and out of the mouth of the beast, and out of the mouth of the false prophet.

14 For they are the spirits of devils, working miracles, *which* go forth unto the kings of the earth and of the whole world, to gather them to the battle of that great day of God Almighty.

Exod. 7:10-13, 22

Joel 3:2, 9-12

Commentary

13-14. Following the pattern already set, here in verses 13-16 there is a parenthetical interlude between the sixth and seventh bowl judgments. Previously, amid both the seals and trumpets there also were such interludes—the vision of 7:1-17, the "Two Saved Multitudes" came between the opening of the sixth and seventh seals; and between the sixth and seventh trumpets were interjected the sights of 10:1 to 11:13.

In each case, God seems to desire that we realize some truth or set of truths before each series is completed. Here in the bowl set, before we arrive at the final bowl, by this vision of THE THREE FROGS God makes us realize that these bowls are leading up to the final showdown battle at Armageddon.

In verse 13 we see that from the Infernal Trinity there goes out a clamor for the armies of this world to gather together in northern Palestine, the approach valley-plain to Jerusalem, Armageddon (verse 16). Why? We do not yet know the Satanic reasons that these three will give to the world. Some have suggested that the western world will desire to have a showdown against the eastern armies marching to take Palestine. This may be it. Perhaps both east and west are coming as a United Nations force to once and for all settle the Middle East by totally annihilating Israel; and representative armies from all over the world are to participate in this necessary "for the good of mankind" genocide? This would certainly fit the circumstances of Joel 3 and Zechariah 12-14.

"Frogs"—Did you ever sit in the dark in a quiet rowboat in the middle of a lilypad covered lake? Suddenly there is a noise closeby from a frog on one side. Then one croaks from far away on the other side. From here, there, over here, over there the noises come! So the Antichrist, Satan, and the False Prophet will jump around the world croaking forth their propaganda stirring up the world to Armageddon.

PAST	PRESENT	RAPTURE	FIRST 3½ LAST 3½ TRIBULATION		ARMA-GEDDON	MIL-LENNIUM	NEW HEAVENS & EARTH

Revelation 16

15 Behold, I come as a thief. Blessed *is* he that watcheth, and keepeth his garments, lest he walk naked, and they see his shame.

Mt. 24:42-51

Rev. 3:18

Definition:

Phases of the Second Coming—*One Second Coming is prophesied throughout the Scriptures. This one coming, however, involves many complex events as God sets in order a wicked earth.*

Commentary

15. "I come as a thief"—What does the coming of Christ share in common with the arrival of a wicked thief? Answer: A sudden surprising unexpected and unannounced appearance!

Therefore we are admonished to "keep our garments," that is, to be ready for the occasion by being always fitly dressed. This is an obvious speech figure, the point of which is that we are to be living for God constantly—and not living in sin—so that when Christ suddenly comes we will not be ashamed at what he finds us doing.

This admonition speaks of what coming? Christ's coming at the rapture (1 Thess. 4:13-18) or at Armageddon at the close of the seven year Tribulation (Rev. 19:11ff)? I think that the answer lies in our comprehending the truth that the *Second Coming of Christ* will be one grand event with many parts over and beyond the Tribulation Period.

Just as the first coming of Christ involved many phases over a 33 year period from the Annunciation to the Ascension, the Second Coming likewise encompasses at least four phases which take place before, during, and beyond the 7 year Tribulation Period. These are: Phase One—*Christ comes for the believers at the Rapture (1 Thess. 4:13-18);* Phase Two—*Christ judges the rebelious nations remaining on earth during the Tribulation. He does this by the seal, trumpet, and bowl plagues of Rev. 6-18;* Phase Three—*Christ destroys the Antichrist and his massed armies at Armageddon (Rev. 19:11ff);* Phase Four—*Christ establishes on earth the prophesied millennial Kingdom of God (Mt. 25:31ff; Rev. 20:1-6; Dan. 2:44; 7:13,14,27).*

The admonition here to be prepared for His coming would, I think, apply to all who shall await Christ's revelation out of heaven—whether they now look for Him at the Rapture, or whether they await the brightness of His coming at Armageddon at the close of the seven year Tribulation.

PAST	PRESENT	RAPTURE	FIRST 3 $\frac{1}{2}$ / LAST 3 $\frac{1}{2}$ TRIBULATION	ARMA-GEDDON	MIL-LENNIUM	NEW HEAVENS & EARTH

Revelation 16

VERSES 16, 17, 18

16 And he gathered them together into a place called in the Hebrew tongue Ar-ma-ged-don.

Joel 3:2, 9-14

Rev. 14:14-20; 19:11ff.

17 And the seventh angel poured out his vial into the air; and there came a great voice out of the temple of heaven, from the throne, saying It is done.

Rev. 15:8
Exod. 19:16

18 And there were voices, and thunders, and lightnings; and there was a great earthquake, such as was not since men were upon the earth, so mighty an earthquake, *and* so great.

Rev. 11:13
Mt. 24:21

Commentary

16. Here, as is described in Joel 3:2, 9-14, the armies of Antichrist are assembled at the huge Armageddon Esdraelon-Jezreel-Jordon valley-plain (See comments on 14: 14-20). The Kings of the East bring their armies across the now dried Euphrates, the Beast and False Prophet are coming with their armies (16:12; 19:19). God's providence has allowed it to come to pass. The stage is set; the harvest is ripe!

17. "It is done"—This signifies that the Seal-trumpet-and bowl cycles of judgment have now been completed; Armageddon is ahead!

The early seals were providential calamities for the earth—war, famine, etc. Then the trumpets had the marks of the supernatural, but these were partial in their destructions as noted by the repeated usage of the words "one-third" in connection with them. The bowls, however, are both supernatural and *universal.* Here, in verses 17-21, the seventh bowl concludes these devastations with gigantic hail, worldwide earthquakes, and the destruction of the Antichrist's Babylon capital! The end is rushing upon us.

18. The lightnings and thunders, God's ancient signs of displeasure and judgment of sin, here abound (Exod. 19:16). Just as the rainbow is God's sign of His covenant with Noah and his seed (Gen. 9:13) despite the fact that we today can explain its colors by alluding to the reflection and refraction of light; so too these thunders *here* show God's displeasure at sin despite electro-static and electro-kinetic explanation. This "great earthquake" is unmistakeably described as the greatest earthquake "since men were upon the earth." This must, I would think, include the man made atomic bomb earthquakes! Today scientists tell us—and multitudes tremble—that geologic fault lines extend through Palestine's Jordan Valley down into Africa and through the California coast. At the pouring out of this final bowl of wrath these and others may give way underneath a world of sinners who claim that they do not need God to hold them up.

THE SEVENTH VIAL

HAIL
Cities
Crumble

Background

Now at the end of this 7 year Tribulation Period, all the events of the past focus together into one tremendous battle between the forces of good and the forces of evil.

This is called the Battle of Armageddon.

This area was the scene of many decisive battles in the history of Israel. Since Mt. Megiddo commands the Jezreel Valley and the Plain of Esdraelon the name Armageddon (Hebrew for: "Mount Megiddo") represents this entire strategic valley area in North Israel.

This quiet and peaceful Valley of Jezreel soon will have all the eyes of the world focused upon it.

PAST	PRESENT	RAPTURE	FIRST 3½ LAST 3½ TRIBULATION	ARMA– GEDDON	MIL– LENNIUM	NEW HEAVENS &EARTH

19 And the great city was divided into three parts, and the cities of the nations fell: and great Bab'-y-lon came in remembrance before God, to give unto her the cup of the wine of the fierceness of his wrath.
20 And every island fled away, and the mountains were not found.

Isa. 14:4
Rev. 18:5

Commentary

19. "The great city was divided"—This city is at first unnamed, however, its identity we know. The Antichrist's capital city, called "Babylon," is called "great" in 18:2,10,18,19,21! It is in chapter 18 described as the commercial emporium of Antichrist's empire. There may be many great cities of the end-time, but from chapter 18 it is clear that this one alone is "The Great City." Will this be Rome or rebuilt Babylon or...? we shall consider this in 17:9. In any case it is called, "Babylon." The very word "Babylon" in Scripture represents a composite of the continuing corrupt world system led by the unseen arch-spirit of evil, Satan. The earthquake is sent by God—not merely by seismic activity—and it will split the Beast's capital into three.

"Babylon came in remembrance"—In 18:5 we read of Babylon's destruction in the words, "...and God hath remembered her iniquities." What occurs here is that 16:19 shows that at the time of the seventh bowl God destroys the capital city of the Beast along with his satanic system and empire, and then chapters 17-18 describe this destruction in detail. This is basically the same pattern that we find in Genesis 1 and 2 describing the creation of man. In Genesis 1 comes the brief description of man's creation on the sixth day; then in Genesis 2 we are provided with a more detailed description of these events. So it is here. In 16:19 amid the catastrophic happenings of the seventh bowl we are told that Babylon is remembered for destruction; then in chapters 17-18 we have the full details of this ruination given.

20. Not only is Antichrist's capital city devastated, but here we see that every island and the mountains are affected. The whole wicked world is convulsed by an indignant and righteous God because the world has harkened willingly to the iniquitous man of sin and his satanic ent-time system!

Tanks and trucks still clutter the landscape in the Holy Land from the Six Day War. What greater disaster lies ahead when Russia battles Israel and it takes 7 years to collect the debris (Ezekiel: 39:9).

Background

It is quite possible the Battle of Armageddon may start as a series of conflicts and wars capping themselves into one mighty invasion attempt against Palestine.

Imagine as this verse tells us of a catastrophe so great that every island "flees" (Greek: *pheugo*) - sinks into the waters. And the mountains are flattened out! This earthquake may take place the moment Jesus' feet rest upon the Mount of Olives. It will surpass all earthquakes that have ever before occurred!

Every portion of the globe will be affected!

Spoken centuries before, the Second Psalm gives us some of the fullest description of what will occur at this particular time. While Psalm 2 applies to all rebellion against God throughout the ages - its meaning reaches its apex of fulfillment at the time of Antichrist.

We find Antichrist declaring that he will not permit God to set up his King on David's throne to reign over the world. God actually laughs at the vain boasting of Antichrist. Read Psalm 2:4-6.

▼

PAST	PRESENT	RAPTURE	FIRST 3 1/2 LAST 3 1/2 TRIBULATION	ARMA- GEDDON	MIL- LENNIUM	NEW HEAVENS & EARTH

21 And there fell upon men a great hail out of heaven, *every stone* about the weight of a talent: and men blasphemed God because of the plague of the hail; for the plague thereof was exceeding great.

Exod. 9:22-26;
   Josh. 10:11
Rev. 16:9, 11

Commentary

21. A talent is estimated at various weight figures, and this need not surprise us when we consider that the modern concept of having a standard gram, kilogram, or a platinum meter kept at zero degrees centigrade had not pervaded the ancient world. Suffice it to say that it was probably in the vicinity of 95 pounds.

Hail of such magnitude, weighing as much as a 155mm howitzer shell or almost as much as a 100 lb. bomb, would indeed be an unquestionably lethal weapon. To be struck on an arm or foot would mean certain severe damage, and a strike landing more directly would bring instant death. The property damage to buildings, cars, and planes would be incalculable.

The wicked followers of Antichrist, however, choose even with this to blaspheme rather than repent!

That this plague will literally take place I have no doubt. In Exodus 9:22-26 essentially this same plague took place. Fire and hail fell as the ice plunged down from heaven upon Egypt and with it came lightning bolts creating fires over the land. Just as the other bowls with their sores, darkness, and waters turning to blood were similar to those that fell upon Egypt, so too is this plague of hail. The Egyptian judgments truly came to pass in the physical world; so will those here prophesied to be levied upon Antichrist and his human hosts.

It is evident throughout Scripture, men either by faith repent and turn to Christ who has paid for their sins, or they cling to unbelief, follow Satan, and perish in their iniquity. The choice is clear.

Photograph shows how New York City earthquake may look.

Background

In this Seventh Bowl or vial judgment cities actually crumble. Visualize the town or city in which you live...with its buildings crumbling.

Try to envision the giant skyscrapers of New York suddenly tumbling down like a bunch of toy blocks. Think of the devastation, the terror, and the death that will occur. Yet man still will not turn to God!:

Think of the majestic Rockies reaching from Alaska to the southern tip of South America suddenly disappearing...and Mt. Everest sinking into a flatland.

All the church buildings, long since devoted to worshipping Antichrist, are now in shambles. The visible assets of todays American churches are nearly $80 billion - better than twice the worth of the top five business corporations in the nation. Within moments...they are reduced to NOTHING!

All this coupled with a hail storm the like of which the world has never seen!

PAST	PRESENT	RAPTURE	FIRST 3 1/2 / LAST 3 1/2 TRIBULATION	ARMA-GEDDON	MIL-LENNIUM	NEW HEAVENS & EARTH

CHAPTER 17

And there came one of the seven angels which had the seven vials, and talked with me, saying unto me, Come hither; I will shew unto thee the judgment of the great whore that sitteth upon many waters:

Hosea 2:1ff; 3:1ff
Rev. 17:15

CHAPTERS 17 AND 18: THE JUDGMENT OF THE BABYLON SYSTEM OF THE END-TIMES

Chapter 17: THE JUDGMENT OF THE BABYLON RELIGIOUS SYSTEM—THE GREAT HARLOT

1. After seeing the vision of the bowl judgments of chapter 16, John next speaks with one of the angels of judgment. This angel now proceeds to show the apostle in detail just how the false system of the end-times will be destroyed. This was a natural thing to do since the previous vision ended with the words, "And great Babylon came in remembrance before God, to give unto her the cup of the wine of the fierceness of his wrath..." (16:19).

We will in these next two chapters, 17 and 18, now see in detail how the antichrist Babylon of the last days meets its end just as 16:19 has already briefly shown us. This method, of first showing in brief the entire picture and then repeating *in detail* the chief events, is used often in the Bible. In Genesis 1 first the entire creation is viewed, then in Genesis 2 the creation of man is again described, but this time in great detail: So too, in Revelation 21:1-2 the new creation is shown, then in 21:9 to 22:5 New Jerusalem is redescribed in full detail.

"The great harlot"—Here the end-time false religious system is represented as an unfaithful and wanton woman. Because of the duty of faithfulness to a husband, the imagery of a woman is often used in Scripture to represent a religious system. In Isaiah 54:5 Israel is pictured as the wife of Jehovah; in Hosea 2:1ff and 3:1ff she is portrayed as an adulterous woman. In Revelation 12 the persecuted woman is end-time Israel. The church at Corinth is a "chaste virgin" (2 Cor. 11:2); and in Revelation 19:7-9 the Church of Christ as a whole is the "Bride."

"...Sitteth upon many waters"—This is explained by vs. 15 which declares that these waters are "peoples and multitudes, and nations, and tongues." Thus we see that there are two rival women at the end-time. Both claim to love Christ. One is the true Church, the "Bride" (19:7-9); and the other is the apostate false church, this "Great Harlot" of Babylon.

▼

PAST	PRESENT	RAPTURE	FIRST 3½ / LAST 3½ TRIBULATION		ARMA-GEDDON	MIL-LENNIUM	NEW HEAVENS & EARTH

Revelation 17

VERSES 2, 3

2 With whom the kings of the earth have committed fornication, and the inhabitants of the earth have been made drunk with the wine of her fornication.
3 So he carried me away in the spirit into the wilderness: and I saw a woman sit upon a scarlet coloured beast, full of names of blasphemy, having seven heads and ten horns.

Isa. 23:17

Rev. 17:15

Rev. 12:6, 14
Mt. 27:28

Rev. 12:3; 13:1;
Dan. 7:7, 19, 20

Commentary

2. The "kings of the earth have committed fornication" with this woman. This tells us that the False Church of the end-time will have a great influence on the nations and rulers of the world. Sinfully these have come together. This church loves the world and the world loves her (1 Jn. 2:15!).

"The inhabitants of the earth...made drunk..."—The false doctrines and teachings of the apostate church through its member churches and denominations make the people of the earth insensible to the call and commands of God. The false church fills the people with unbelief and encourages immorality. Its wine corrupts the earth. Are you in a congregation which is part of the growing apostate world church? 2 Cor. 6:14-7:1 tells you to "Come out." Or...have you been made drunk by her wine so that you now say. "Oh I can stay a little while longer"?

3. The woman sitting upon the Beast! What does this mean? The description of this Beast shows it to be Antichrist and his wicked end-time system ("blasphemy...seven heads...ten horns"—12:3; 13:1). Thus here the false church is seen riding upon the political system of Antichrist. Is the rider controlling the beast, or is the beast running his own way while the one atop holds on tightly? We do not know; but they are together. Thus the apostate church and the antichrist with his ten nation confederation (the ten horns—See 13:1) will for a time mutually support one another. The church will hail the Antichrist and his system as that which can save the earth, and for this the Antichrist shall permit the church to share his rise into power and glory. They ride together to pollute the world.

Could today's APOSTATE CHURCHES and their flirtation with diabolical COMMUNISM be the beginning of the ride seen here?

"The wilderness"—In 12:6 the wilderness seems to be the chaotic world into which the Israelites flee in order to escape the Beast's persecution.

PAST	PRESENT	RAPTURE	FIRST 3½ LAST 3½ TRIBULATION		ARMA- GEDDON	MIL- LENNIUM	NEW HEAVENS & EARTH

4 And the woman was arrayed in purple and scarlet colour, and decked with gold and precious stones and pearls, having a golden cup in her hand full of abominations and filthiness of her fornication:

Jer. 51:7; Mt. 23:25-26

5 And upon her forehead *was* a name written, MYSTERY, BABYLON THE GREAT, THE MOTHER OF HARLOTS AND ABOMINATIONS OF THE EARTH.

Rev. 3:12; 7:3; 13:16
2 Thess. 2:7

Commentary

4. From this verse we see that this Great Harlot has a royal external appearance, one of grandeur, but her cup—that which she offers to her companions—is filled with abominations. Thus the false church system will deceive many by its impressive appearance, but its cup—its teachings and pronouncements—will be spiritually and morally corrupt. That the cup is "golden" shows that her teachings may outwardly seem to be godly and moral, but yet from out of that glistening cup comes only filth. Are many of today's denominations, churches, and councils already like this?...Yes! They praise communism and immorality and condemn the Bible and believers.

5. Here the "mystery" *(musterion)* of this woman is partially made clear to us by this name upon her forehead. Since the earliest Greek manuscripts were written in uncials, a style of using all capital letters, we cannot be entirely positive as to whether or not the word "mystery" is the apostle John's comment or part of the title on the forehead. That is, does John say, "...a name written, a mystery, BABYLON THE GREAT..., or is it, "...a name written, MYSTERY, BABYLON THE GREAT..."? (Greek has no word for the indefinite article, the word "a", and translators insert it or omit it as they see fit. So there is no clue here.) This, however, makes no difference, for in any case here the sacred word—be it from John's remark or from the name on her head—shows that this woman is a "Mystery."

The identity of this mystery woman is well explained to us by the summary paraprase given to her name by Grant D. Shattuck ("A Critical Investigation of Revelation 17:5," Unpublished B.D. Critical Monograph, Grace Theological Seminary, Winona Lake, 1956). His paraphrase of the verse is on the next page.

			FIRST 3½	LAST 3½	ARMA-	MIL-	NEW
←DISTANT PAST ➡				▼			
PAST	PRESENT	RAPTURE	TRIBULATION		GEDDON	LENNIUM	HEAVENS &EARTH

Revelation 17

6 And I saw the woman drunken with the blood of the saints, and with the blood of martyrs of Jesus: and when I saw her, I wondered with great admiration.
7 And the angel said unto me, Wherefore didst thou marvel? I will tell thee the mystery of the woman, and of the beast that carrieth her, which hath the seven heads and ten horns.

Mt. 23:32-36

2 Thess. 2:7

*Rev. 12:3; 13:1;
Dan. 7:7, 19, 20*

Commentary

6. That the Great Harlot is called "Babylon the Great" teaches us that the final apostate world church system has its roots way back into the satanic false religions of antiquity. Satan's anti-god religions have been vieing against Jehovah for the ages. Thus this Great Harlot is guilty of all the blood of the martyred saints of the past as well as of the blood of those who will be slain during the awful final Tribulation Period. Just as the blood of the prophets from Abel to Zachariah was demanded from Jerusalem in A.D. 70 (Matt. 23:32-36), so the blood of the saints, including that of the prophets, will be demanded from this Babel Church System of the last days.

What will the final Great Harlot be like? Time will tell. At present it appears that we may be heading for a United World Church—with the Catholic Church and Ecumenical Protestantism playing major roles of leadership—and this Babylonian amalgam seems headed toward fully endorsing communism, immorality, lawlessness, and unbelief...and all this in, they say, Christ's holy name...no wonder she is called, "The Great Harlot."

7. Now the angel tells John that he will further explain this "mystery" of the Harlot riding upon the Beast—the final False Church riding upon the final False Saviour of the political and economic world.
Basically, "Babylon" refers to two systems in the endtimes. One refers to the final ecumenical religious system (Ecumenical Protestantism plus Catholic Church). It also refers to the great political and commercial system during the Tribulation.

Generally speaking, Revelation 17 describes the ecclesiastical Babylon. Revelation 18 describes the political-commercial Babylon.

▼

PAST	PRESENT	RAPTURE	FIRST 3 1/2	LAST 3 1/2	ARMA-GEDDON	MIL-LENNIUM	NEW HEAVENS & EARTH
			TRIBULATION				

8 The beast that thou sawest was, and is not; and shall ascend out of the bottomless pit, and go into perdition: and they that dwell on the earth shall wonder, whose names were not written in the book of life from the foundation of the world, when they behold the beast that was, and is not, and yet is.

Isa. 14:4-27

Commentary

8. The angel now in verses 8-18 explains to John concerning the Harlot and the Beast. In 8 to 11 we have verses as mysterious and as difficult of interpretation as any in the entire Bible. While many views on these are manifestly false, yet until these events actually occur their interpretation may not be fully understood. But when they happen in the world, it will be again clear—just as it was concerning some of the difficult prophecies of Christ's first advent—that God from the beginning knew all! Praise to His name!

This Beast, from the verse, (a) existed in the past; (b) he cannot now be seen; (c) he shall appear again having ascended from the nether world; and (d) he shall be returned to perdition, hades and the Lake of Fire.

Since only spirits and the spirits of men can go into or come out of hades—nations cannot really do this except in a general figurative sense—it seems that here we have in view primarily the Beast, the Antichrist, as a person. Who can this be?

I think that the answer is none other than Satan! He existed in the past (Isa. 14:12-15; Gen. 3); and he cannot now be seen—he "is not." That is, as a spirit we cannot see him as a human personage or as a world ruler today though he controls the hearts of many. When he entered Judas for a time there was a certain sense when we could see him, but now Judas is gone and to our eyes Satan "is not." Yet this one whose ultimate habitation is hell will again appear on the world scene—and in this sense he "shall ascend out of the bottomless pit." This will take place when Satan, as in the case of Judas, enters into the Antichrist. Then to see the Antichrist will be to see Satan! Thus Antichrist is described in 13:1 as the Beast—identically as Satan is described in 12:3,9! Finally, Antichrist will be cast at Christ's coming into the Lake of Fire (19:20).

"...the beast...was, and is not, and yet is."—This may be explained as above, or it may be an allusion to Antichrist's being alive, being slain, and yet being revived from the dead in the mock-resurrection (13:3).

PAST	PRESENT	RAPTURE	FIRST 3 1/2 TRIBULATION	LAST 3 1/2	ARMA-GEDDON	MIL-LENNIUM	NEW HEAVENS & EARTH

9 And here *is* the mind which hath wisdom. The seven heads are seven mountains, on which the woman sitteth.

10 And there are seven kings: five are
fallen, and one is, *and* the other is not yet
come; and when he cometh, he must
continue a short space.

Rev. 12:12

Commentary

9. "And here is the mind which hath wisdom."—That is, here comes a
true answer concerning the Beast and the Woman who sits upon him.

*The Harlot is apparently somehow sitting astride the seven heads of the
Beast.* Now we are told that this represents her sitting upon "seven
mountains" *(oros)* or "high hills."

These could be the 7 continents (see remarks on 13:1), or—the seven
hilled city of Rome! Rome, as the "Eternal City of Seven Hills" was the
capital of the Roman Republic during the epoch from 754 to 31 B.C.
Then from 31 B.C. it became the capital of the Roman Empire until
1890 A.D. (Discounting the moving of the capital of the Eastern Empire
to Constantinople in 325 A.D., etc.)

This fits with that which has already been concluded from this book. Is
it possible that the false World Church System of the endtimes could
have its capital anywhere else than in this city, "Roma," the city of the
Caesars, the Emperors, the Councils, and the Popes? Time will tell.
Perhaps at first it will not be the capital, but, it seems, eventually it will.
Some contend that the ancient city of Babylon in Iran will be rebuilt.
Time alone will tell. In either case the same Babylon spirit will be there.

*That the Harlot sits on this city indicates clearly that false religion has
and will dominate it.*

10. Here the mystery continues. The Greek for the words, "And
there are seven kings" can also be translated *just as easily,* "And they
[that is, the seven heads and mountains] are seven kings." The same
word, *eisin,* means "they are" as well as "there are."

PAST	PRESENT	RAPTURE	FIRST 3 1/2 TRIBULATION	LAST 3 1/2	ARMA- GEDDON	MIL- LENNIUM	NEW HEAVENS &EARTH

Revelation 17

11 And the beast that was, and is not,
even he is the eighth, and is of the seven,
and goeth into perdition.

Commentary

THE SEVEN HEADS—HISTORIC VIEW (Also see comments on 13:1)

For a thorough investigation of the identity of the Beast's seven heads see H. Keith Binkley, "Meaning of the Seven Heads in Revelation 17:9" (Unpublished B.D. critical monograph, Library, Grace Theological Seminary, 1959).

Binkley, pp. 46-49, concludes that the seven heads represent "seven kingdoms which have been influenced by paganism (false religion, religious harlotry) throughout the course of their history." He names these kingdoms as Egypt, Assyria, Babylon, Medo-Persia, Greece these are the five which have "fallen"—Rev. 17:10), Roman Empire (this is the head that "is"—Rev. 17:10), and the Revived Roman Empire (this is the head yet to come which will only last a short while—Rev. 17:10).

The Beast "that was and is not" who is the eighth, but one of the seven (Rev. 17:11), refers to the Antichrist and his kingdom in the last 3 1/2 years of the Tribulation period. After his resuscitation in the middle of the week, he becomes dictator of the Revised Roman Empire, and he and his kingdom become the "eighth" who "is out of the seven," i.e., this is simply another aspect of the seventh head, the Revived Roman Empire (Rev. 17:11; cf. 13:3).

Zahn, when speaking of the heads of the beast, says,

Since Revelation was written at the time of the Roman Empire, this is, according to xvii. 10, the sixth head; another seventh kingdom will follow it, but will not long reign. Upon this follows the eighth,—that of the antichrist,—which, however, is only a revivication of one of the five earlier kingdoms. Without question this is intended to be the Graeco-Macedonian and its typical ruler, the pre-Christian antichrist, Antiochus Epiphanes....The interpretation of the seven heads as the line of Roman emperors from Augustus or from Caesar onwards, which has confused many, is untenable. (See reference on next commentary page.)

Certainly the number of heads, seven, in company with the many sevens of the Book of Revelation, exhibits the totality of that which is signified. Thus the 7 heads may symbolize the entire run of historic Babylon-type Satanically led pagan kings and empires. That final one, that of the Antichrist, "is the eighth, and is of the seven" (Rev. 17:11).

PAST	PRESENT	RAPTURE	FIRST 3 1/2 TRIBULATION	LAST 3 1/2	ARMA-GEDDON	MIL-LENNIUM	NEW HEAVENS & EARTH

12 And the ten horns which thou sawest are ten kings, which have received no kingdom as yet; but receive power as kings one hour with the beast.
13 These have one mind, and shall give their power and strength unto the beast.

Dan. 7:24

Definition:
King (Greek: Basileus) *refers to a ruler or leader of a nation despite the particular title he holds,* viz, *President, Premier, Caliph, Prime Minister, etc. Thus the "Pharaoh" of Egypt was called its "king"* (Hebrew: Melech) *in Exod. 1:8,15.*

Commentary

12-13. The angel now explains to John the mystery of the ten horns which are upon the Beast. These are ten kings! Horns, the crown and glory of an animal—and its offensive weapon—often represented kings in the Old Testament. For example, in Dan. 8:8 the "Great Horn" clearly represents Alexander the Great, and the "little horn" in Dan. 8:9 pictures Antiochus IV Epiphanes, the persecuting Syrian monarch.

These ten horns are those ten kings portrayed in Dan. 2:42, 44 as the ten toes of the statue, that is, as the end-time manifestation of the Roman Empire. Since they are made partially of iron, the element in Dan. 2 which stood for the Roman Empire, and since they seem to be in some sort of a ten nation confederation these are often referred to as the "Revived Roman Empire."

Dan. 7:24-28 portrays these as ten horns which are "ten kings" (vs. 24). Dan. 7:24 speaks of the Antichrist coming as "another horn." This corresponds with our verses, Rev. 17:12, 13, which show that these ten kings follow the Antichrist and join him in his final "hour" of power.

"These have one mind..."—These ten end-time kings give complete allegiance to the Beast, the Antichrist. This is precisely why the Beast is constantly seen as having ten horns upon his head (12:3; 13:1; 17:3). It is this group of ten allied nations that form the Revived Roman Empire which eventually becomes headed by the evil being whose mind then becomes synonomous with the mind and will of the empire.

Is the European Common Market the precursor to a ten nation European Confederation???

(Theodore Zahn, "The Writings of John," *Introduction to the New Testament* (Vol. III. Translated by M. W. Jacobus, *et al.* Edinburgh: T & T. Clark, 1909), pp. 441-42).

▼

PAST	PRESENT	RAPTURE	FIRST 3 1/2 LAST 3 1/2 TRIBULATION		ARMA-GEDDON	MIL-LENNIUM	NEW HEAVENS & EARTH

14 These shall make war with the Lamb, and the Lamb shall overcome them: for he is Lord of lords, and King of kings: and they that are with him *are* called, and chosen, and faithful.

15 And he saith unto me, The waters which thou sawest, where the whore sitteth, are peoples, and multitudes, and nations, and tongues.

Rev. 12:11

Rev. 19:14

Rev. 17:2

Commentary

14. These, the ten kings and the Antichrist, shall make war with the Lamb, Christ, by the determined anti-god program of their kingdom. They shall persecute those who turn to Christ (Rev. 12:3ff; Dan. 7:25), and this persecution shall be especially fierce during the final 3 1/2 years of the Tribulation (Rev. 12:6, 14; 13:5-7; Dan. 7:25; Matt. 24:21).

Yet Christ, the Lamb, "shall overcome them." This is accomplished in many ways. *First,* the persecution of Antichrist and his kings is overcome by Christ's Blood sacrifice at Calvary atoning for the sins of those who turn to Him as their Saviour (12:11). To His followers Christ gives eternal life (14:13; 20:4; 7:14).

Second, by the Rapture of the Church Christ delivers the pre-tribulation believers from the "hour of temptation which shall come upon all the world" (3:10; 17:12; I Thess. 4:13-18).

Third, Christ keeps much of the remnant from death by preserving them during the Tribulation (12:6, 14). And *fourth,* Christ at the end of the seven year period comes at Armageddon and destroys the Antichrist, his followers, and his armies (19:11ff). And *fifth,* at the Judgment of the Nations after Armageddon, Christ does not permit the followers of Antichrist to enter the Millennial Kingdom (Matt. 25:31-46).

"And they that are with Him are Called-Ones, and Chosen-Ones, and Faithful-Ones." This is how the Greek reads. Note, it is not, "They are called Chosen...," but they "are Called-Ones..." Romans 8:28-31 sheds light on these descriptions of the "called" and "chosen" believer. With the great temptations of the Tribulation to deny the faith and to receive the Beast's mark the adjective "Faithful-Ones" is aptly added to those who turn to Christ during this awful period of history.

15. This was commented upon in connection with verse 2. The Harlot Church dominates by its false teachings the roaring oceans of people which cover the globe.

PAST	PRESENT	RAPTURE	FIRST 3 1/2 LAST 3 1/2 TRIBULATION	ARMA– GEDDON	MIL– LENNIUM	NEW HEAVENS & EARTH

16 And the ten horns which thou sawest upon the beast, these shall hate the whore, and shall make her desolate and naked, and shall eat her flesh and burn her with fire.

17 For God hath put in their hearts to fulfil his will, and to agree, and give their kingdom unto the beast, until the words of God shall be fulfilled.

18 And the woman which thou sawest is that great city, which reigneth over the kings of the earth.

Prov. 21:1; Exod. 4:21

Isa. 46:9-11

Rev. 17:5, 9

Commentary

16. Greek: "And the ten horns which you saw and ["and," *kai;* not "upon" which would be *epi*] the beast,...shall hate...."

This is the chapter which tells us of "The Judgment of the Great Harlot" (vs. 1), and now we learn how this judgment will occur. At the start of the chapter the Harlot and the Beast rode together; now the Antichrist *and* his ten underling kings hate the Harlot! Thus we can expect that the united apostate world church will support the evil Antichrist in his rise to power during the first 3 1/2 years of the Tribulation. However, somewhere along the line, the Antichrist and his kings will begin to hate even this apostate religious system. Perhaps this will occur in connection with the Abomination of Desolation and the persecution that follows? In any case there will be a break between the Great Harlot and the Antichrist, and the Harlot shall now be hated. Perhaps the Antichrist shall loathe the Harlot Church because she rivals him for power?

"...hate...make desolate and naked...shall eat her flesh...burn her with fire." We see a progressively worsening relationship and a thoroughly complete destruction—a purge. Thus during the final 3 1/2 years of the Tribulation this judgment will take place. Perhaps even today the seeds for these events are now blowing in the wind. Do you think so?

17. Here we see the divine side of the human events. The ten nations aligning themselves behind the Antichrist and then these destroying the apostate church, all of this is in accord with and determined by God's plan! (Eph. 1:11; Exod. 4:21; Isa. 10:5ff).

18. Again the woman, the False Church, is said to be in some sense synonomous with the ruling city of the earth. She is called, BABYLON, in verse 5. Thus this is the judgment of that religious system which in God's sight becomes basically the same as Babel-Babylon, a system of rebellion against God (Gen. 11:9).

PAST	PRESENT	RAPTURE	FIRST 3 1/2 TRIBULATION	LAST 3 1/2	ARMA-GEDDON	MIL-LENNIUM	NEW HEAVENS & EARTH

Revelation 18

CHAPTER 18

And after these things I saw another angel come down from heaven, having great power; and the earth was lightened with his glory.

2 And he cried mightily with a strong voice, saying, Babylon the great is fallen, is fallen, and is become the habitation of devils, and the hold of every foul spirit, and a cage of every unclean and hateful bird.

Rev. 14:8; Isa. 21:9; Jer. 51:8

Isa. 13:17-22

THE JUDGMENT OF BABYLON'S END-TIME CAPITAL CITY

1. Having just been shown in chapter 17 the destruction of the final manifestation of the Babylon anti-god religious system, now a mighty angel comes to show John the ruination of the Babylonian system's latter day metropolis, the commercial emporium of the world. The great power and glory of the announcing angel betokens the greatness of his proclamation.

2. This pronouncement is proleptic, that is, it speaks of a yet future event as already having taken place. This was the method used in Isaiah 53 when the prophet described the first advent of the Messiah as if already accomplished. Thus he wrote 700 years before Christ, "He was oppressed, and he was afflicted...."

Here we find the same basic language dealing with the fall of latter-day Babylon as Isaiah used 700 years B.C. to speak of the fall of the ancient Babylonian kingdom (Isa. 13:17-22; 21:9). BUT NOTE, these are different Babylons for the ancient Babylonian empire was vanquished by an invasion of the Medes and Persians in 536 B.C. (Isa. 13:17; Dan. 5:28-31), while the Babylon here destroyed in Revelation 18 is destroyed by a sudden devestation by fire at the time of the pouring out of the Seventh Bowl of Wrath (18:17-18; 16:19 compared with 18:5).

Ancient Babylon, once destroyed in 536 B.C. was never to be rebuilt and resettled. So say the Prophets in Jer. 50:1-3, 39-46; 51:26, 37, 44, 57,64; Isa. 13:17-22. Is this city of Revelation 18, then, ancient Babylon rebuilt—now to be destroyed again and forever? I *think* not; I rather *think* that another city called "Babylon," because Antichrist and his evils dominate it, is here spoken of. Rome with its seven hills corresponds to the seven hill-mountains of the city of 17:9...but New York fits the descriptions of the commerce of this city in chapter 18. Perhaps Antichrist's capital will be a 7 city complex...or will it be Rome...or Babylon rebuilt??? Just as Jerusalem is called "Sodom" in 11:8, this final center of Antichrist is called Babylon—and it is FALLEN, FALLEN.

▼

PAST	PRESENT	RAPTURE	FIRST 3½ / LAST 3½ TRIBULATION	ARMA-GEDDON	MIL-LENNIUM	NEW HEAVENS & EARTH
			FIRST 3½ | LAST 3½			

3 For all nations have drunk of the wine of the wrath of her fornication, and the kings of the earth have committed fornication with her, and the merchants of the earth are waxed rich through the abundance of her delicacies.

Jer. 51:7

Commentary

3. As in the case of the Great Harlot, the corruption of the system which resides in this city has affected "all nations." This city too is guilty of "fornication" and worthy of "wrath" because it loves Antichrist and Satan rather than the one true God.

"The merchants are waxed rich..."—With these words we begin the description which pervades this chapter of the singularly enormous commercial enterprise which captivates this city.

"For all nations have drunk of the wine"— These words inform us that this Babylon has provided a mind-affecting beverage to influence people dwelling throughout the entire world. Wine affects the mind, the thinking processes, as well as the emotions. Strong drink makes people desire what they ought not to desire and it lulls to sleep many of their right inclinations and cautions. It turns the mind, as it were, topsy-turvy. Sufficient strong drink will make a man fall in the gutter thinking it to be a sweet bed. And, to say the least, it robs a person of his or her god-ward inclinations for who has ever seen the drunken man who both desired and was capable of Bible study and prayer?

Thus here God's word in a figure tells us that the system which is characteristic of this city is bringing ruination to the peoples of the globe. This is the same system that pervades the Great Harlot-False Church since it too is called by the same name, "Babylon." This is none other than the Satanic system of the last days which will fill the Antichrist and his empire (Rev. 13), the final Harlot Church (Rev. 17), and the final capital city, or region of cities, which is devoted to Antichrist (Rev. 18). All this is and will be "Babylon."

▼

PAST	PRESENT	RAPTURE	FIRST 3 1/2 / LAST 3 1/2 TRIBULATION	ARMAGEDDON	MILLENNIUM	NEW HEAVENS & EARTH

Revelation 18

4 And I heard another voice from heaven, saying, Come out of her, my people, that ye be not partakers of her sins, and that ye receive not of her plagues.
5 For her sins have reached unto heaven, and God hath remembered her iniquities.

VERSES 4, 5

2 Cor. 6:14-7:1

Rev. 15:1; 16:19
Gen. 4:10
Rev. 16:19

Commentary

4. Some of those who have turned to God have, as is evident from the command here, nevertheless remained in this city amid its evil system. The heavenly voice outwardly demonstrates to the listening Apostle John what the Scriptures and the Spirit plead. "Come out" is the command, and the incentive to obedience is "that ye be not partakers of her plagues." She is about to be judged, therefore, "Come out." In 2 Cor. 6:14-7:1 we learn that God's will is that believers should, "Be not unequally yoked with unbelievers." Instead they should, "Come out from among them" and "Touch not the unclean thing...."

Despite these and other clear commands professed believers still today remain in modernistic churches shrouding their disobedience in the claim that somehow they are doing good. So too in the Tribulation Period some who have turned in their hearts to God will still be living in Babylon as did Lot in Sodom...God cries for them to come out just as the angel appealed to Lot (Gen. 19:12-25).

5. "God hath remembered her iniquities."—Here the word "remembered" *(mnemoneuo)* means that God has "remembered" them for judgment. This Babylonian-Antichrist system has reveled in sin, and it seemed as if God had forgotten it. With the sudden destruction of this megapolis it will be apparent that "God has remembered her iniquities."

In 16:19 at the pouring of the seventh bowl we read, "...and the cities of the nations fell: and great Babylon came in remembrance *(mimneskomai)* before God...." Note,

16:19—"Babylon came-in-remembrance (mimneskomai)..."
18:5 —"God hath remembered (mnemoneuo) her..."

The two Greek verbs used here are essentially identical. To give an English comparison we would say, "Babylon came-in-*remembrance*" and "God hath *recalled.*"

Thus the destruction of chapter 18 takes place at the time of the seventh bowl, near the end of the Tribulation. Chapter 18, we see, gives the detailed description of the fall of Babylon which occurs at 16:19 at the outpouring of the seventh bowl.

▼

PAST	PRESENT	RAPTURE	FIRST 3 1/2 TRIBULATION	LAST 3 1/2	ARMA-GEDDON	MIL-LENNIUM	NEW HEAVENS & EARTH

Revelation 18

6 Reward her even as she rewarded you, and double unto her double according to her works: in the cup which she hath filled fill to her double.

7 How much she hath glorified herself, and lived deliciously, so much torment and sorrow give her: for she saith in her heart, I sit a queen, and am no widow, and shall see no sorrow.

8 Therefore shall her plagues come in one day, death, and mourning, and famine; and she shall be utterly burned with fire: for strong *is* the Lord God who judgeth her.

VERSES 6, 7, 8

Contrast Mal. 3:10

Jer. 16:18; 17:18;
   Isa. 40:2

Jer. 7:18; 44:17;
   Acts 8:27
Rev. 15:1

Psa. 2:1-5, 9

Commentary

6. "...double...double...double..."—God assures us by these words that despite the delay, the eventual payment in judgment will more than adequately repay her for her transgressions.

7. This wicked system has lived for a time in splendor with her every whim gratified. This fits 13:5-8 which declares that Antichrist and his government will rule in absolute sway over this world for a 42 month period, the second 3 1/2 years of the Tribulation.
"...I...shall see no sorrow."—Humanly speaking the collapse and doom of this Beast could not be seen in the foreseeable future.

8. "Her plagues."—This word, "plague" *(plege)* is used here and in verse 4 in connection with the judgment of this city. It has just been observed that this city—along with other cities, 16:19—will be destroyed in connection with the seventh bowl judgment. It is thus significant that this bowl judgment, as well as the others, is referred to in 15:1 as a "plague." This constant calling of Babylon's judgment by the name "plague" harmonizes perfectly with our finding that the city's final end will culminate in the Seventh-Bowl-Plague.

"...in one day...utterly...burned with fire..."—Note the continuing reassertion of these three ideas as the chapter progresses. The destruction shall come suddenly and its duration will be very brief—"in one day" (vs. 8)..."in one hour" (vs. 10)..."in one hour" (vs. 17)..."in one hour" (vs. 19). It will be complete "utter" destruction (vss. 21-23, vs. 14). And it will take place by means of "fire" (vss. 8, 9, 18).

PAST	PRESENT	RAPTURE	FIRST 3 1/2 LAST 3 1/2 TRIBULATION		ARMA-GEDDON	MIL-LENNIUM	NEW HEAVENS & EARTH

Revelation 18

9 And the kings of the earth, who have committed fornication and lived deliciously with her, shall bewail her, and lament for her, when they shall see the smoke of her burning,

10 Standing afar off for the fear of her torment, saying, Alas, alas that great city Babylon, that mighty city! for in one hour is thy judgment come.

VERSES 9, 10

Psa. 2:2

Ezek. 26

Commentary

9. This city is destroyed at the outpouring of the seventh bowl which occurs before the final end at Armageddon. Thus the wicked rulers of this earth who have loved this city and its Antichrist will have time to witness the fiery conflagration that will engulf it.

10. The peoples of the world witness in abject terror and shock God's sudden visitation upon this populous den of iniquity.

The cry, "Alas, alas," in the Greek uses the identical word *(ouai)* which in 8:13 is translated, "Woe, woe, woe." The two factors of (a) the greatness of this city, and (b) the sudden flaming destruction has left the workers of iniquity who were not within the city at its conclusion in absolute stunned terror. This end-time Babylon was another Sodom, and God as in the former case again rained fire and brimstone upon it.

How does it happen? Will it be a completely supernatural judgment? Will God cause the city to catch on fire by some natural means which results from the supernaturally caused earthquake? The great fires of the past sometimes began in small ways. On September 2, 1666 the Great London Fire started in a baker's house and was not out until it had destroyed 89 churches, 13,200 houses, and had left 200,000 homeless. It burned from September 2nd to the 6th. Then too, the great Chicago fire began on Oct. 8, 1871 supposedly from Mrs. O'Leary's cow kicking over a lantern. It burned for two days killing 250, ruining 17,450 buildings and leaving 100,000 homeless. So too the city of Rome burned in 64 A.D. with ten of its fourteen precincts consumed by the flames. Nero was blamed for it because of his publicly stated desires of wishing to be able to rebuild the city. He wickedly blamed the Christians and thus began the first of the ten Imperial Roman persecutions.

Or could the great earthquake of the seventh bowl be an atomic weapon? We do not know how it will happen, but only what the result will be.

▼

PAST	PRESENT	RAPTURE	FIRST 3 1/2 / LAST 3 1/2 TRIBULATION	ARMA- GEDDON	MIL- LENNIUM	NEW HEAVENS & EARTH

11 And the merchants of the earth shall weep and mourn over her; for no man buyeth their merchandise any more:

Ezek. 27

12 The merchandise of gold, and silver, and precious stones, and of pearls, and fine linen, and purple, and silk, and scarlet, and all thyine wood, and all manner vessels of ivory, and all manner vessels of most precious wood, and of brass, and iron, and marble,

Ezek. 27

13 And cinnamon, and odours, and ointments, and frankincense, and wine, and oil, and fine flour, and wheat, and beasts, and sheep, and horses, and chariots, and slaves, and souls of men.

Commentary

11-13. We are informed that the merchants of the earth will mourn at the loss of this city, and then we are given a list of some of her divers commodities. From this we see that this Babylon has become a world commercial center. In fact, it would seem that it has become the center and hub of world commerce—for this inordinate bewailing of her trade capacity by merchants and seamen would hardly be fitting for even the cities of today—except possibly for New York or Chicago (verses 11, 15, 17-19, 22-23)...or Tokyo.

We should, therefore, expect that when Antichrist reigns in the Tribulation Period that his capital city—be it Rome, Babylon, or the United Nations Headquarters in *New York City*—will blossom into the commercial capital of the globe. Perhaps the system of distributing foodstuffs and goods only to those who have the Mark (13:17) will have something to do with this city's prominence? We shall yet note more on this subject, however, when we come to verse 23.

▼

PAST	PRESENT	RAPTURE	FIRST 3 1/2	LAST 3 1/2	ARMA-	MIL-	NEW
			TRIBULATION		GEDDON	LENNIUM	HEAVENS & EARTH

Revelation 18

14 And the fruits that thy soul lusted after are departed from thee, and all things which were dainty and goodly are departed from thee, and thou shalt find them no more at all.

I John 2:15-17

Eccl. 5:10-17; 2:1-11

Commentary

14. The treasures of the wicked are gone. This is the irony of iniquity. Sin deludes man into thinking that by sin he can have treasure and joy for evermore; but always the serpent lies and soon the ephemeral treasures of sin have gone and only gall, bitterness, disappointment, and death remain. This city served Mamon and therefore had to war against God—until God destroyed it. Read Matt. 6:19-24 as a dirge and lamentation over this city and its vanishing gold.

Lay not up for yourselves treasures upon earth, where moth and rust doth corrupt, and where thieves break through and steal:

But lay up for yourselves treasures in heaven, where neither moth nor rust doth corrupt, and where thieves do not break through nor steal:

For where your treasure is, there will your heart be also.

Matthew 6:19-21

PAST	PRESENT	RAPTURE	FIRST 3 1/2 LAST 3 1/2 TRIBULATION	ARMA– GEDDON	MIL– LENNIUM	NEW HEAVENS & EARTH

15 The merchants of these things, which were made rich by her, shall stand afar off for the fear of her torment, weeping and wailing,

16 And saying, Alas, alas that great city, that was clothed in fine linen, and purple, and scarlet, and decked with gold, and precious stones, and pearls!

Mt. 7:26-27

Rev. 17:4

Commentary

15. "...shall stand afar off for the fear..."—*Dia ton phobon,* literally, "on account of the fear...." The smoke and heat is so intense and the destruction so complete that the mourners neither attempt to save the city nor to salvage any of her treasures. Rather than be consumed within her borders they prefer to weep from a distance.

16. "Alas, alas" is *ouai, ouai* in the Greek, hence "Woe, woe" would also fit as in 8:13. As a sample of the textual observations which could be made from time to time, let us note the following: The second *ouai* is omitted in an 8th to 9th century manuscript kept in Rome and known as "046." Since, however, this word does appear in the older 4th century manuscripts Sinaiticus (Aleph), and Ephraemi Rescriptus (C) there is no real doubt that it belongs to the original text. It also appears in the valuable 5th century manuscript, Alexandrinus. Somehow, in some later copying this second "alas" was omitted.

This sort of interesting but actually insignificant textual observation could be made quite often. The only really significant thing is to note that all in all our text of the New Testament is better preserved than any book from the ancient world. We can have confidence that that which has come to us has been preserved by God and is the Word of God written.

▼

PAST	PRESENT	RAPTURE	FIRST 3 1/2	LAST 3 1/2	ARMA-GEDDON	MIL-LENNIUM	NEW HEAVENS & EARTH
			TRIBULATION				

17 For in one hour so great riches is come to nought. And every shipmaster, and all the company in ships, and sailors, and as many as trade by sea, stood afar off,

Ezek. 27:8-9,25-36

18 And cried when they saw the smoke of her burning, saying, What *city is* like unto this great city!

19 And they cast dust on their heads, and cried, weeping and wailing, saying, Alas, alas, that great city, wherein were made rich all that had ships in the sea by reason of her costliness! for in one hour is she made desolate.

Ezek. 27:8-9, 25-36

Commentary

17-19. These verses further accentuate to us the inordinate grief of the shipmasters. Those fortunate enough to be out in the water some distance from the city's harbors at the time of her doom—whether these ships were sailing in or departing—would see the flames and smoke for vast distances across the waves.

Sea trade still today accounts for far more cargo than the now burgeoning air transportation industry. Although the air has displaced the sea for passenger travel, nevertheless, it is not seen in the foreseeable future that this will happen in the cargo industry. In fact, the opposite is true. The cost per ton via plane is still high with only those valuing speed willing to pay so great a dollar premium. Then with the new gigantic tankers and transportation ocean vessels—often eight times as large as the former "largest" merchant ships—the cost of ocean shipping per ton is falling. Thus it will be no surprise to us that it is the sea merchants who weep at this calamity to Babylon.

If Babylon were to be rebuilt on its ancient site, 50 miles south of Bagdad in Iran, although on the Euphrates River, it still would take some 250 miles of sailing up the river against current to reach Babylon. Of course, Antichrist's city could expand to a megapolis and its bounds might reach the Persian Gulf, and then this difficulty would vanish. Rome, however, as well as New York (with its United Nations Headquarters) and Tokyo even now have ports suitable to these descriptions. If Berlin expanded north to the Baltic Sea in a megapolis it would qualify. Moscow never (see map)!

All that remains of the great palaces of ancient Babylon.

Background

The word "Babel" means confusion. And it was here at Babel that we find introduced the first recorded organized adulterous religious system in the world.

The tower of Babel must have been a tremendous structure. It may have consisted possibly, like its later Babylonian counterparts, of eight towers, each 75 feet high, rising one upon the other.

There was a chapel on the top which made the total height over 600 feet. This is equivalent to almost a 60 story building and it is as high as the modern $3½ million Space Needle of Seattle, Washington. It is estimated that one golden image alone in those days was valued at $17½ million. And that the sacred utensils which were used were worth approximately $200 million!

And those riches were made desolate! Now in the end of the Tribulation Period another Babylon is fallen and her riches also vanish.

PAST	PRESENT	RAPTURE	FIRST 3½ TRIBULATION	LAST 3½	ARMA- GEDDON	MIL- LENNIUM	NEW HEAVENS & EARTH

Revelation 18

20 Rejoice over her, thou heaven, and ye holy apostles and prophets; for God hath avenged you on her.
21 And a mighty angel took up a stone like a great millstone, and cast *it* into the sea, saying, Thus with violence shall that great city Babylon be thrown down, and shall be found no more at all.

Rev. 6:10; Rom. 12:19; Jer. 50:15

Judg. 9:53; Lk. 17:2

Mt. 24:37-39

Definition:
Megapolis.—*This modern 20th century term is from the Greek* mega, *"great," and* polis, *"city." It is hence a city of astounding size, such as one of our present U.S. states, but packed with population like a city. Los Angeles is predicted to engulf all of S. Calif. into one huge "megapolis."*

Commentary

20. The sense of justice within the followers of God rejoices *(euphraino* —to rejoice, be joyous) when at last the unrepentant murderers and workers of iniquity come to their rightful justice. The martyrs under the altar in the fifth seal (6:10) were anxious to see the unrepentant hardened ones who had murdered them in a cavalier manner punished by God. How long should they go on murdering the prophets and cursing God? God is longsuffering that the wicked might turn from their sins unto Him (2 Pet. 3:9), but the time eventually comes when those who hold to their love of iniquity must be judged (2 Pet. 2:4-14).

21. Picture a 300 pound stone being cast off of a bridge into the sea. It falls with increasing velocity, it strikes the water in a tremendous splash, and then almost instantaneously it sinks and fades from sight as if gone and forgotten without a trace forever. So it will be with this Babylon of the end-times. God will destroy it like Sodom. Archeologists wade into the south end of the Dead Sea searching for ruins from famed Sodom and Gomorrah, but alas they are gone as a millstone which struck the water. So it will be with Babylon—sudden earthquake and hail (16:17-21), fire and smoke, and then GONE FOREVER! What a picture in contrast to heaven and the New Jerusalem (21:1ff)!

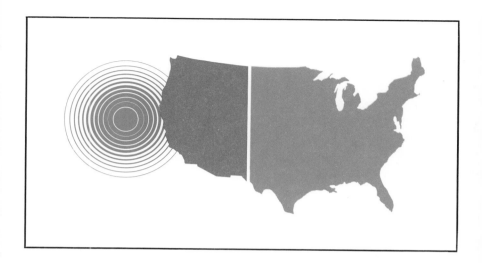

Background

Many people are unaware of the awesome methods of destruction that mortal man has created in the last 20 years.

They find it difficult to believe that a Great City...the most important city in this Tribulation Period...with a population of millions will just suddenly disappear from the face of the earth within one hour!

Yet scientists tell us that if a nuclear bomb were dropped about 100 miles off the shore line of California...its impact would generate a tidal wave such as man has never seen.

The tidal wave of destructive water would be 800 feet high and would not stop until it covered one-third of the United States!

Such a tidal wave could conceivably kill as many as 40 million people. Present U.S. population is approximately 205 million.

PAST	PRESENT	RAPTURE	FIRST 3 ½	LAST 3 ½	ARMA-GEDDON	MIL-LENNIUM	NEW HEAVENS & EARTH
			TRIBULATION				

22 And the voice of harpers, and musicians, and of pipers, and trumpeters, shall be heard no more at all in thee; and no craftsman, of whatsoever craft *he be,* shall be found any more in thee; and the sound of a millstone shall be heard no more at all in thee;

Rev. 14:2; 15:2

Commentary

22. Upon her demise all of those things associated with human earthly joy will be gone. As the millstone plunged beneath the ebbing tide so shall this metropolis sink into oblivion.

A close and striking analogy to this, besides that of Sodom and Gomorrah, would be the destruction of Pompeii. On August 24th throughout the 26th in 79 A.D. Mount Vesuvius suddenly erupted and with no essential warning buried the cities of Pompeii and Herculaneum, Italy, killing some 2000 people by the noxious gases, the falling soot particles, and the hot lava. Foods were still baking in the ovens, archeological excavation has shown. Life was going on as usual with no hint that these cities were to be seared with a hot steaming iron from out of the sky. Then it happened and the gases and the other effects slew the populace as swiftly as the dropping of the millstone.

It is interesting to note that there are drawings on some of the walls of Pompeii that demonstrate the abject immorality of some of its population. Only God knows the percentage. We only know that if there had been but only ten righteous men in Sodom it would have been spared (Gen. 18:23-33)! Will this same standard be applied to Babylon???

Against a midnight sky this hot lava flowing down a mountainside presents an awesome spectacle as its searing liquid burns everything in its path. This photograph taken in Iceland in a small way conveys the holocaust of the Great Tribulation period.

Background

The system we have described here is Babylon. It is that evil anti-god Satanic opposition to Jehovah which has been ever in rebellion against Him.

One commentator has remarked that the underground of the city of Babylon is composed of a type of combustible asphalt. As the earthquake breaks up the earth's crust, the city could easily be plunged into a devastating lake of fire. And all within the space of one hour.

Whether the foundation of the city actually rests on burning asphalt or not remains to be seen. We do know, however, that the city will disappear and so complete will be the destruction that it will "be found no more."

Like a bulky heavy millstone, it will sink below the earth's surface, quickly vanish!

▼

PAST	PRESENT	RAPTURE	FIRST 3½ TRIBULATION	LAST 3½	ARMA- GEDDON	MIL- LENNIUM	NEW HEAVENS &EARTH

Revelation 18

23 And the light of a candle shall shine no more at all in thee; and the voice of the bridegroom and of the bride shall be heard no more at all in thee: for thy merchants were the great men of the earth; for by thy sorceries were all nations deceived.

VERSE 23

Mt. 24:41

Mt. 24:38

Commentary

23. "...For thy merchants were the great men of the earth; for by thy sorceries [*pharmakeia*—compare with, "pharmaceuticals," drugs] were all nations deceived [*planao*—"caused to wander," as the *planets* seem to wander through the zodiac in the sky].

It is here made clear that Babylon is the deceiver of the nations. A city is often associated with a deception. So we can say that "Moscow (communism) is deceiving the world." In the Second World War one could remark, "Berlin has led the world astray." Today one can utter, "New York (the United Nations) is proclaiming folly to the earth's continents." Thus the commercial success of the final Babylon is merely the by-product of Babylon's deceiving the world. *(Could chapter 18's description be figurative representing the buying and selling of vice—1:20?).*

The system which shall reside here is Babylon. This Babylon at the end of the age, however, will be the Antichrist capstone of the entire evil pyramid—and God will smash it in His fury with fire from heaven.

PAST	PRESENT	RAPTURE	FIRST 3½ TRIBULATION	LAST 3½	ARMA-GEDDON	MIL-LENNIUM	NEW HEAVENS & EARTH

24 And in her was found the blood of prophets, and of saints, and of all that were slain upon the earth.

Mt. 23:29-38
Rev. 6:9-11

Commentary

24. The best commentary upon this verse is Matt. 23:35 wherein Jesus declares that upon the Jerusalem of His day would "come all the righteous blood shed upon the earth, from...Abel...to Zachariah...." The Jerusalem of Christ's day was rejecting the Messiah and Saviour. In doing this the Christ rejectors of that day showed that they were morally one with all those who in generations past had slain the innocent, holy, and righteous prophets of God. Finally God's patience had run out and He destroyed the city for all of its past and present sin (See Matt. 22:2-7!).

Likewise here with Babylon. The wicked within this endtime system which is in rebellion against God—and at this moment the system of the end appears to be communism—by embracing such a system which curses God and murders His saints align themselves with all of the rebels against God of all the ancient past since (and before) Babylon. Those in the endtime Babel—be it in Rome, New York, or in rebuilt Babylon—are merely wearing the up-dated uniforms of Satan's age old army.

Jerusalem brought on the deluge of judgment by the Romans in A.D. 70 by its murder of the Christ, its acropolis of its ages of wickedness. Likewise, the latter-day Babylon will bring on its judgment by its own acropolis of wickedness—the devoting of itself completely to Satan and His Antichrist in the last days! Thus this Babylon will again slaughter God's people (chapter 12; 6:10; Matt. 24:15, 21). And in this attempt to annihilate Christ and Christianity from the globe by lie and by knife it will bring upon its own head God's fury of fire!

PAST	PRESENT	RAPTURE	FIRST 3 1/2 | LAST 3 1/2 TRIBULATION	ARMA- GEDDON	MIL- LENNIUM	NEW HEAVENS & EARTH

Revelation 19

CHAPTER 19

And after these things I heard a great voice of much people in heaven, saying, Alleluia; Salvation, and glory, and honour, and power, unto the Lord our God;

Psa. 150:1,6

2 For true and righteous *are* his judgments: for he hath judged the great whore, which did corrupt the earth with her fornication, and hath avenged the blood of his servants at her hand.

Psa. 149:1,7-9
Rev. 17:1,15
Rev. 17:6

3 And again they said, Alleluia. And her smoke rose up for ever and ever.

Isa. 34:10

CHAPTER 19 THE CLIMAX OF THIS AGE: ARMAGEDDON

This chapter comes to us in three parts,

19:1-6	THE FOUR ALLELUIAS
19:7-10	THE MARRIAGE OF THE LAMB
19:11-21	ARMAGEDDON

19:1-6 THE FOUR ALLELUIAS

1-2. Here we have the first "Alleluia" of the Revelation "Alleluia Chorus." This word is written in Greek in the New Testament, but it is a pure Hebrew word which is actually a combination of words. The Hebrew *Haleluya,* as in Psalm 146:1, is composed of *Halel* ("Praise"), *u* ("Ye"), and *ya* ("the Lord"). Thus the word literally means and says, "Praise-ye-the Lord."

This first Alleluia, as we can observe from verses 1 and 2, is shouted in praise of the Lord because He has now at last judged and destroyed the Great Harlot, the Apostate Harlot Church, whose false teachings have corrupted the people of the earth. God is further praised because He has "avenged" *(ekdikeo—*take vengeance upon, or for) His martyred servants whom apostate religion has murdered.

If the heavenly hosts praise God for His utter destruction of the end-time false religious system, then how can some Christians remain in and cooperate with already apostate denominations???

3. The second "Alleluia" is shouted, and we are told of the smoke of the harlot church's burning rising "for ever and ever" (Greek: "unto the ages of the ages").

A "church" *(ekklesia)* in the New Testament refers to a body of "called out" believers *(ek—*out of; and *kaleo—*call). Unlike our modern English word "church," it does not also refer to a building. Thus by analogy the "smoke rose up" need not point us to the destruction of the buildings of the Harlot Church, but rather to the everlasting destiny of the lost souls who comprised this false church.

Pilgrims climb Holy Stairs on their knees at church in Rome. They receive 28 years off purgatory for each step. Stairs are supposedly the front steps to Pontius Pilate's Judgement Hall and Palace in Jerusalem. At top of steps are relics revered by pilgrims.

Background

Babylon about 600 B.C. was proud of its hanging gardens. And they are considered one of the Seven Wonders of the Ancient World.

On the Ziggurat (tower) of Eanna the Babylonians built the Temple of Ishtar, goddess of sensual love. The Babylonians believed that this goddess Ishtar told the king: "I will protect you as a mother protects her children. I will shelter you between my breasts like a jewel on a necklace." And the king told his city, "I love you, Babylon, as I love my own precious life! May all the kings of the world and all mankind pay you tribute. May you endure for all eternity."

But as Isaiah prophesied...Babylon fell (Isaiah 13:19). This city with its two highways, three canals, eight city gates and twenty-four streets, with its fifty-three temples to the great gods and hundreds of chapels to Ishtar..WAS NO MORE!

And now as the Tribulation Period comes to an end the final Babylon also falls - and there is great rejoicing in Heaven.

PAST	PRESENT	RAPTURE	FIRST 3 1/2 LAST 3 1/2 TRIBULATION	ARMA-GEDDON	MIL-LENNIUM	NEW HEAVENS & EARTH

Revelation 19

4 And the four and twenty elders and the
four beasts fell down and worshipped
God that sat on the throne, saying, Amen;
Alleluia.

Rev. 4:8

5 And a voice came out of the throne,
saying, Praise our God, all ye his servants, and ye that fear him, both small
and great.

Psa. 148:11-12

6 And I heard as it were the voice of a
great multitude, and as the voice of many
waters, and as the voice of mighty thunderings, saying, Alleluia: for the Lord
God omnipotent reigneth.

Rev. 1:15: 14:2

Psa. 146:10

Commentary

4-5. Now the twenty-four elders, representing the "Church Triumphant," and the four "living creatures" *(zoon)*, who continually glorify
around the Throne God's holy government of the universe, together
worship God and give their "Alleluia." This is the third.

6. *"...the voice of many waters..."*—This same expression is used in 1:15
and 14:2. In 1:15 it clearly is used to describe the omnipotent sound and
authority of Christ's own voice of deity. In 14:2 it may well be Christ's
voice also, but it is difficult to be dogmatic here. In the verse at hand,
19:6, this voice which is "as" a great multitude, "as" many waters, and
"as" mighty thunderings may be the voice of Christ Himself. It utters
forth in a sound transcending any voice which our human ears hear—
and John describes it with these various accolades of praise. And this
great voice ushers forth the fourth "Alleluia"—"Because the Lord God,
the Omnipotent has reigned."

The verb "has reigned" *(ebasileusen)* is here in the aorist (past) tense.
This usage of the past tense seems to be in light of God's now having
destroyed the Great Harlot System. Now He has reigned (that is,
"He has demonstrated His reign") by destroying the apostate church
and Kingdom—Alleluia!

If the Scriptures did not here plainly declare "Alleluia"—or "Praise the
Lord"—at the destruction of the Harlot System some would no doubt
say that such a sentiment represented an awful and an unloving attitude.
That this is not so, is shown by the fact that the four living creatures also
proclaim "Alleluia" at this event (verse 4); and these are ever glorifying
God's eternal holiness (4:8). Let no one belittle God's infinite love and
mercy; but there comes a time when the *holiness* of God demands that
the unrepentant be judged. This time has come for the deceiving and
murdering members of the Harlot Church and Kingdom, and at their
destruction the heavenly hosts can say nought but "Alleluia!"

United Nations pictured at extreme left on New York City skyline. Headquarters building is now guarded like a fortress. The public has been barred since its 25th anniversary. Parcels are x-rayed. The guard force has been increased to over 200. About 2000 New York city police watch not only U.N. Headquarters but also hotels and diplomatic missions where notables from foreign countries stay.

Background

It was the Babylonian army that destroyed the city of Jerusalem and its temple. Nebuchadnezzar had the eyes of Zedekiah, the King of Judah, put out and led the Jewish people into captivity in Babylon (2 Kings 25:7; Jeremiah 39:7). The Jews of that day saw the power and the glory and riches of Babylon, the city on the Euphrates. They read what Nebuchadnezzar had ordered to be written:

> Babylon, the city of my royal glory, I completed her walls. At her gates I set mighty bulls and terrible dragons. I laid her foundations firmly on the bosom of the underworld, I built up her summit as high as a mountain...I rebuilt the step-tower of Babylon.

Doesn't this proud boasting remind you of the boasting of many godless leaders in the world today. Their wealth and power to them seems invincible...but soon these too, as Babylon of old, shall crumble!

PAST	PRESENT	RAPTURE	FIRST 3 1/2 TRIBULATION	LAST 3 1/2	ARMA–GEDDON	MIL–LENNIUM	NEW HEAVENS & EARTH

7 Let us be glad and rejoice, and give honour to him: for the marriage of the Lamb is come, and his wife hath made herself ready.

Eph. 5:25-27; 2 Cor. 11:2

Commentary

19:7-10 THE MARRIAGE OF THE LAMB

7. We are now told to be glad and to rejoice "for the marriage of the Lamb is come...."

The Church is portrayed as the Bride of Christ in Ephesians 5:25-27 ("Husbands, love your wives, even as Christ also loved the church...that he might present the church to himself a glorious church...") and in 2 Corinthians 11:2 ("...for I espoused you to one husband, that I might present you as a pure virgin to Christ").

Thus the "marriage of the Lamb" speaks of an eternal union between Christ and the Church. This marriage has evidently not yet taken place for all three passages (Eph. 5:25-27; 2 Cor. 11:2; Rev. 19:7-9) uniformly treat it as an event yet future. This fits the facts as we know them. The Church, composed of the believers, is not yet fully united with Christ. Although there is a true sense in which He abides with us today on earth; yet in another sense He is in heaven and many of us are still here on the earth separated from our loved One. Thus, following the imagery of a marriage, the "marriage of the Lamb" must speak to us of that event which will mark our finally and permanently coming to be forever together with Him.

Together forever with Christ—what a theme! This, has already occurred at least to some extent with those believers who have died—they are forever with the Lord (2 Cor. 5:6-8). At the rapture of the Church all of the believers who "are alive and remain" will be taken up to be forever with Christ (1 Thess. 4:15).

"...the marriage...is come..."—or from the Greek, *elthen*, "...the marriage ...has arrived...." Personally I think that this speaks of Christ's coming with His people (His Bride) and to His people when He comes at Armageddon at the end of the Tribulation (Zech. 12:10; Matt. 25:31,34). This is a time that will indeed mark Christ forever being with His beloved Church; and she with Him. He will then rule the earth upon David's throne (Isa. 9:7). The locating of this event here also fits in perfectly with the movement of the Book to this point. Thus 19:1-6 sees rejoicing at the destruction of the rival of the Bride! The Harlot apostate church is now destroyed, so all is clear for the public union of Christ with His true Church! Then the wedding is announced in 19:7-10; and then Christ comes with His saints to abide upon the earth with all who love Him after He destroys the wicked at Armageddon (Rev. 19:11-20:4).

Background

"His wife hath made herself ready."—Dr. Herman A. Hoyt, President of Grace Theological Seminary, Winona Lake, suggested to our class in 1965 that this referred to the raptured church's purification which she experienced in heaven (during the Tribulation Period upon the earth) at the Judgment Seat of Christ (2 Cor. 5:10). I have never heard a better suggestion.

In Revelation 17 we saw the Great Harlot of false religion, Babylon, destroyed. This occurs after the middle of the Tribulation Period.

Then in Revelation 18 we read how the Great City (commercial and political Babylon) was destroyed. This occurs near the end of the Tribulation Period.

Now both religious Babylon and political Babylon - the two powerful anti-God forces - have met their final doom on earth.

And countless people will be able to witness this destruction. For Scriptures tell us that "Her smoke rose up for ever and ever" (verse 3).

In verse 4 of this present chapter we have the last mention of the 24 elders. From now on the raptured church in Heaven is called the Bride - for the marriage of the Lamb is coming near.

PAST	PRESENT	RAPTURE	FIRST 3½	LAST 3½	ARMA-GEDDON	MIL-LENNIUM	NEW HEAVENS & EARTH
			TRIBULATION				

8 And to her was granted that she should be arrayed in fine linen, clean and white: for the fine linen is the righteousness of saints.
9 And he saith unto me, Write, Blessed *are* they which are called unto the marriage supper of the Lamb. And he saith unto me, These are the true sayings of God.

Rom. 3:21-28; Rev. 19: 14; 4:4.

Luke 14:15

Commentary

8. Yes, her righteousness "was granted" or "given" *(edothe)* to her. Believers are declared to be righteous, although they once were sinners, by God on the basis of Christ's having paid the penalty for their sins upon Calvary's cross (Rom. 3:21ff).

9. *"Blessed are they which are called unto the marriage supper of the Lamb."*—Salvation and eternally remaining in the presence of God is pictured as a Great Supper in the parables of Matthew 22:1-14 and Luke 14:15-24. Both of these parables run chronologically in time and place the supper at the end after all of those who will come have been gathered. This fits the passage at hand. It would then seem that the celebration supper which rejoices at the permanent union of the believers with their Lord takes place during the Millennial (1000 year) Kingdom (Rev. 20:4); that is, right after the marriage.

Perhaps this supper shall take place in some literal vast and blessed ceremony at the start of the millennium? Or perhaps the "supper" speaks to us of our communion with Christ during the entire millennium and after? I think that both are true here.

"These are the true sayings of God."—The Spirit knows our infirmity and weakness, our tendency since the Fall not to believe eagerly God's good promises, so for our benefit we are assured that these wonderful prophecies are true. Alleluia!

When do you think that these events will occur? Will you be there?

Doreen adjusts tie for Duane at brother Dennis Kirban's wedding.

Background

If you have ever had a wedding in your family you know the excitement that prevails in all the planning.

The climax comes on the day of the wedding. Oftentimes I have heard brides say as they waited in a side room just prior to walking up the aisle, "I don't feel a bit nervous."

And this is true. The attendants and mother and dad are usually more nervous than the bride. Suddenly she appears the picture of beauty and serenity. The time for her marriage has come.

Remember the tears of joy as the marriage ceremony finally takes place. Then everyone sits down to the marriage table. The whole wedding party is at ease. There is happiness...complete joy.

How much greater anticipation of joy as we come to the marriage supper of the Lamb!

PAST	PRESENT	RAPTURE	FIRST 3½ TRIBULATION	LAST 3½	ARMA-GEDDON	MIL-LENNIUM	NEW HEAVENS & EARTH

Revelation 19

10 And I fell at his feet to worship him.
And he said unto me, See *thou do it* not:
I am thy fellowservant, and of thy brethren that have the testimony of Jesus:
worship God: for the testimony of Jesus
is the spirit of prophecy.

*Contra Rev. 1:17-18;
Lk. 5:8,10*

*Definition:
Second Coming of Christ
This is one of the most prominent doctrines in the Bible. In the New
Testament alone it is referred to over 300 times. His First Coming was
over 1900 years ago when He came on earth to save man from sin. The
Second Coming is an event starting at the Rapture and comprehending
four phases: First, at the Rapture Christ takes the believers out of this
world to be with Him (1 Thessalonians 4). Second Christ pours out His
judgments on the world during the 7 year Tribulation Period. Third,
Christ at the end of the 7 year Tribulation destroys the Antichrist and
his wicked followers (Revelation 19). Fourth, Christ sets up His millennial Kingdom prophesied so often in the Old Testament.*

Commentary

10. No good angel will accept worship. These uniformly ascribe the
glory to God and they direct that only He is to be worshipped. Satan,
however, that fallen arch-angel, desires to be worshipped as God (Isa.
14:12-14; Matt. 4:8-10).

Jesus, however, accepts worship in Revelation 1:17-18 and in Luke
5:8,10. At the very least in these passages Jesus never is recorded as
making any attempt to correct His would be worshippers. No, He continues to speak and thus by His silence on the subject He accepts the
worship. This makes Jesus either a blasphemer or God! We must either
stone Him or bow before Him! But, praise God, the matter is clear. He is
deity; He is God! The prophets prophesied that the Messiah would be
both human and God! In the Old Testament Christ also accepted the
worship that God alone could accept (Isa. 9:6; Micah 5:2; Josh. 5:13-15;
Dan. 3:14; Zech. 12:10—notice the pronouns).

(Left) Tranquil scene at Sea of Galilee. It is sometimes referred to as the Sea of Tiberias (John 6:1, 21:1) and the Lake of Gennesaret (Luke 5:1) and in four instances in Luke, "the lake." While this scene is one of calm the Sea is subject to violent storms because of differences in temperature of the mountains and tableland surrounding it.

(Right) Faithful Palestinian guide, Charles Yasmineh, sits down with author at Ein Gev kibbutz outdoor dining area on the shore of Sea of Galilee. Tourists who have visited this area will remember the wonderful "feast" of St. Peter's fish freshly caught right in Galilee and tasty cucumber and tomato salad.

Background

When will this marriage feast take place? And who will be present?

From Scriptures it is fairly clear that the wedding feast will take place at the beginning or during the Millennium. There are some who believe that it may last throughout the entire Millennium of 1000 years (Revelation 21:9,10).

Those present will certainly include the Old Testament saints (Luke 13:29, 29). There will also be those believers who will be martyred during the Tribulation period (Revelation 20:4).

Then, too, the redeemed of Israel will be there. Those Israelites who are believers and living on earth at the end of the Tribulation Period will enter the Millennium and join the wedding feast (Matthew 25:1-13).

Believing Gentiles, saved during the Tribulation, will also be present (Matthew 25:31-34).

And, of course, the Christians, previously raptured will be there.

▼

PAST	PRESENT	RAPTURE	FIRST 3½ TRIBULATION	LAST 3½	ARMA-GEDDON	MIL-LENNIUM	NEW HEAVENS & EARTH

Revelation 19

11 And I saw heaven opened, and behold a white horse; and he that sat upon him *was* called Faithful and True, and in righteousness he doth judge and make war.

12 His eyes *were* as a flame of fire, and on his head *were* many crowns; and he had a name written, that no man knew, but he himself.

13 And he *was* clothed with a vesture dipped in blood: and his name is called The Word of God.

Zech. 14:1-4ff
Rev. 2:18
Rev. 4:4,10

Rev. 3:12; 2:17

Isa. 63:1-6

Commentary

19:11-21 ARMAGEDDON

11-12. The person astride this mount is Christ coming now at the end of the seven year Tribulation as the Lion of the Tribe of Judah (Rev. 5:5).

He is coming to "judge and make war." Let us face it, the Christ which the modernists have carved out for themselves is a non-existent idol and the modernists worship a god of their own making just as did the ignorant pagans of antiquity. They tell us of a Christ who forgives and who will forgive everyone in the world—with no exceptions—because he is so loving. This god they have chiseled out of their own stony hearts. The Scriptures tell us of "the terror of the Lord" (2 Cor. 5:11) and of a Christ who is coming again to save those who have trusted in His blood and to destroy those who have rejected Him and His words (Matt. 25:41-46; 7:21-23).

His crowns of triumph, glory, and deity and His omniscient flaming eyes here show Christ to be God coming to judge the world in holiness.

13. *"...clothed with a vesture dipped in blood."*—It has been made blood red by His own blood which He shed for us who believe when He died for us by crucifixion upon the cruel cross. His vesture will be further now dipped in the blood of His enemies here at Armageddon. Isaiah 63:1-6 shows this latter statement to be true; it speaks of Armageddon.

"His name is called the Word of God."—The best commentary on these sublime words is found in John 14:7-11. There Jesus explains to Philip that He, Jesus, is the visible and audible expression (word!) of the unseen God! Just as the spoken word is the outward manifestation of the unseen spirit which dwells within the body of a man; so is Jesus the outward manifestation—the LIVING WORD—of the unseen God. The Bible, on the other hand is the WRITTEN WORD of God!

Suddenly the skies will open and reveal His glory!

Background

Believers (those who have accepted Christ as personal Saviour and Lord) who have lived in this present age will be resurrected at the Rapture (1 Thesselonians 4:13-18).

Those saved (believers) during the Tribulation Period and who have died will be resurrected by the end of the Tribulation. By this time all of those who have been redeemed will be raised - Old Testament saints, New Testament saints, and Tribulation saints.

Thus the Marriage Supper of the Lamb takes place after all of these component groups of the First Resurrection have been raised.

In verses 11, 12 and 13 we find the climactic moment at last arriving -- the time when Christ will quickly destroy the powers of sin at Armageddon.

At Christ's First Coming, Christ came riding on a donkey - an animal of peace.

But now at His Second Coming, Christ rides on a white horse - a regal horse to make war against the evil on earth.

PAST	PRESENT	RAPTURE	FIRST 3 1/2 TRIBULATION	LAST 3 1/2	ARMA- GEDDON	MIL- LENNIUM	NEW HEAVENS &EARTH

VERSES 14, 15

14 And the armies *which were* in heaven followed him upon white horses, clothed in fine linen, white and clean.
15 And out of his mouth goeth a sharp sword, that with it he should smite the nations: and he shall rule them with a rod of iron: and he treadeth the winepress of the fierceness and wrath of Almighty God.

*Isa. 64:6; Matt. 22:11-14
Rev. 1:16; 2 Thess. 2:8
Isa. 11:4*

*Psa. 2:9; Rev. 12:5
Isa. 63:1-6; Joel 3:13;
    Rev. 14:14-20*

Commentary

14. Here the believers of the ages, having been gathered together into one group at the rapture (1 Thess. 4:16-17), come with Christ dressed in those white robes of declared-righteousness which He alone can give to the rag-clad sinner.

15. Christ here comes as God and thus His word of judgment is immediately translated by His deity into the performance of that word. Thus "God said, Let there be light: and there was light" (Genesis 1:3). Hence, His omnipotent word is shown as a sharp sword that will smite the nations.

"He shall rule ... with a rod of iron."—Here in the language of Psalm 2:9 Christ's coming millennial rule is pictured. After Armageddon during the 1000 year millennial period which is described in Revelation 20 and Isaiah 11 Christ's rule will be so absolute and authoritative that it is placed before our eyes as an "iron rule." For, you see, although Christ will then reign sinners will still be born during that time and thus authority and power will still be necessary (Zech. 14:16-21; Rev. 20:7-10).

That Armageddon is pictured in numerous places as a winepress—where grapes are squashed and red liquid splatters everywhere—has already been thoroughly shown in the comments on 14:14-20. Such passages show that wicked nations will for some diabolical cause gather themselves together on the great Armageddon-Esdraelon-Jezreel-Jordon plains and valleys which connect together in forming the huge land pass through the mountains into Jerusalem and Israel. This vast assemblage is likened to grapes in the winepress because here they will be stamped and tread upon in an unsparing judgment. The blood of the wicked will splatter up just as did the juice of the grapes. Isa. 63:1-6; Joel 3:13; Rev. 14:14-20; Zech. chapters 12-14.

Matthew 24:29-31 ("...immediately after the tribulation of those days...") shows that this scene of Armageddon occurs immediately at the end of the seven year Tribulation Period.

Background

Look at the picture above. Can you in your own mind's eye picture the splendor, the majesty, the awesome power that will dumbfound those on earth?

Suddenly, perhaps while watching on their television screens...or looking up at the sky, they see a strange phenomena, they hear rumblings in the heavens.

Soon a majestic figure on a white horse is apparent...and behind him a vast and numberless throng all on white horses.

We are told that this is not an army...but, rather, *armies!*

Thus, perhaps, more than just the raptured Saints (you and I, as believers) are in this multitude. Perhaps even the legions of angels are also included!

Imagine the shock as people of earth look up and see millions upon millions of Christians converging on them from the sky, all riding on white horses!

▼

PAST	PRESENT	RAPTURE	FIRST 3 1/2 LAST 3 1/2 TRIBULATION	ARMA- GEDDON	MIL- LENNIUM	NEW HEAVENS & EARTH

16 And he hath on *his* vesture and on his thigh a name written, KING OF KINGS, AND LORD OF LORDS.

Rev. 3:12; 2:17

Commentary

16. As I write these words I cannot but sing out the Halleluia Chorus of Handel's "Messiah"...

KING OF KINGS, AND LORD OF LORDS...
And He shall reign forever and ever...
....
Alleluia, Alleluia...Alleluia Alleluia...Alleluia!

This name depicts the true nature of its wearer, Jesus. Jesus is the rider for the description of this rider is essentially identical to the description given of Jesus in chapter 1 (19:12 compared to 2:18; and 19:15 compared to 1:16). Thus Jesus is Lord of Lords; Jesus is divine—the conclusion is inescapable.

Let the Jehovah witnesses come with their riddles, over and over again this Book of Revelation asserts unmistakeably the deity of Christ. No, faint Christian, the entire true Church throughout the centuries has not erred—the Jehovah Witnesses and all of the others who deny the deity of Christ are the ones who err...and their error is grievous.

Let us rejoice when current events discourage us; Christ is coming again in power and glory to rule the earth as King of Kings, and Lord of Lords.

Many tourists overlook seeing the inside of the Golden Gate. Its double arched entrance has been blocked since 1530. Perhaps Christ with His army will enter through these gates to Jerusalem. It is the only gate that leads directly to the temple area!

Background

As we believers join with Christ in this descent to earth...there will be no problem as to what to wear.

How often on earth have you heard your wife or daughter say when an important event was coming up, "But, dear, I haven't a thing to wear!"

Here in Revelation 19:15 we find our wardrobe will be:

1. A Royal Garb
   We are clothed in fine linen...the ancient symbol of wealth and the attire of kings and queens.

2. Flawless
   No worry about short or long hemlines, unpressed pants or missing buttons or color harmony. Our garments will be white, the symbol of purity and perfectness.

3. Clean
   No worry with laundry or dry cleaners. We will have a spotless, clean attire.

Have you ever ridden on a horse? You will when Christ beings you as a believer with Him to pronounce judgment at the battle of Armageddon! And it will be a stately white horse. What a picture!

PAST	PRESENT	RAPTURE	FiRST 3 1/2 LAST 3 1/2 TRIBULATION	ARMA-GEDDON	MIL-LENNIUM	NEW HEAVENS &EARTH

17 And I saw an angel standing in the sun; and he cried with a loud voice, saying to all the fowls that fly in the midst of heaven, Come and gather yourselves together unto the supper of the great God;
18 That ye may eat the flesh of kings, and the flesh of captains, and the flesh of mighty men, and the flesh of horses, and of them that sit on them, and the flesh of all *men, both* free and bond, both small and great.

Ezek. 39:17-24

Commentary

17-18. Here an angel standing with the sun as his background invites the carion of the sky to "THE SUPPER OF THE GREAT GOD." Thus this chapter speaks of two end-time contrasting suppers. In 19:9 we read of "THE MARRIAGE SUPPER OF THE LAMB" which will be a feast of unbounding joy as the redeemed partake of this feast together with their wonderful Lord. The armies of the redeemed who come with their Lord (19:14) will have a part in this grand banquet.

The armies of the wicked nations that in the end-time choose to follow Antichrist, the Beast, shall at this Revelation appearance of Jesus Christ be involved in this other supper (19:17-18). These shall be slain by "the brightness of His coming" and their dead bodies shall lie upon the ground lifeless to be picked at by the crows, hawks, and vultures 2 Thess. 2:8. This is a *Supper of Death* to which the followers of Antichrist will attend; while those who love Christ will attend the *Supper of Life!*

The description here in verses 17-18 perfectly matches that of Ezekiel 39:17-24, and the two passages I think must speak of this same Armageddon battle. Ezekiel 38:1-39:16, however, speaks of an earlier Russian invasion of Israel. The prophet, Ezekiel, first sees the Northern confederation's (Russia and her allies) invasion of Israel and then his vision moves right into this latter Armageddon. In both battles God in the latter days defeats a satanically inspired group of armies in the land of Palestine. Thus Ezekiel sees them both amid chapters 37-39 wherein the theme is the end-time deliverance and conversion of Israel by God.

Israeli Cavalry unit on patrol on horses! Will horses play an important role in the Tribulation period?

Background

At the end of the 7 year Tribulation Period there will occur the endtime Battle of Armageddon when evil armies from all over the world come up against Jerusalem for a diabolical purpose (Joel 3; Revelation 14 and 19).

While this is clear, all the details leading up to this battle have not been revealed to us. Antichrist, under the great coalition of western nations, may set up a headquarters in Jerusalem to reign over Israel. Not only will he reign over Israel and Europe but he will also control the entire world (Revelation 13:7,8)!

It will be at the close of the Tribulation Period that Israel will find itself under an invasion by an Army probably numbering into the millions of men - quite possibly this final armada will include the army of 200 million from the Sixth Trumpet (Revelation 9:16). These are those who must cross the River Euphrates (Revelation 9:14, 16; 16:12) - hence they come from ASIA!

▼

PAST	PRESENT	RAPTURE	FIRST 3 1/2 TRIBULATION	LAST 3 1/2	ARMA-GEDDON	MIL-LENNIUM	NEW HEAVENS & EARTH

19 And I saw the beast, and the kings of the earth, and their armies, gathered together to make war against him that sat on the horse, and against his army.

20 And the beast was taken, and with him the false prophet that wrought miracles before him, with which he deceived them that had received the mark of the beast, and them that worshipped his image. These both were cast alive into a lake of fire burning with brimstone.

Rev. 16:12-16

Dan. 7:11
Rev. 13:1,11,14

Rev. 13:15-18

Rev. 20:11-15

Commentary

19. The Book of Revelation teaches that the Antichrist, the Beast, and his end-time ten kings, along with his armies from all the world, come to the Armageddon region of Palestine at the end of the Tribulation Period for some arch-diabolical purpose (Joel 3:2, 9-16: Rev. 16:12-16; 14:14-20). Thus we have this continually repeated winepress theme denoting masses of wicked armies gathered to one place for destruction (Isa. 63:1-6).

Both Zechariah chapters 12-14 and Matthew 24:15-31, as well as Revelation 12, show that at least *part* of the purpose of this march to Armageddon will be a satanic final effort to annihilate the remnant of Israel as well as those gentiles who are turning and who have turned to Christ during the Tribulation. Just why this will be we can still only guess—but the details will be filled in when the time comes.

Matthew 25:40,45 shows that what men do to Christ's brethren they do to Christ Himself! Thus when the Antichrist and his armies make war against those who turn to Christ, they make war against Christ Himself. This explains how the Antichrist at Armageddon with his armies is "gathered together to make war against him that sat on the horse" (vs. 19).

20. The Antichrist (the Beast) and the False Prophet are thrown directly into the Lake of Fire; they are not merely slain as are the multitudes which follow them. Their followers are cast into hades (Greek: *hades*— literally: *ha*, "not" and *ides*, "seen," thus the unseen world of the dead) wherein they await their final judgment (20:11-15). Such a formality of a final judgment is not accorded to these two Beasts of inquity; they are cast directly into the Lake of Fire.

The Beast's 42 months of power (Rev. 13:5) began at the Abomination of Desolation in the middle of the Tribulation and it extended for 3 1/2 years until now, at Armageddon. The length of the period of power for the wicked has ever been determined by God, and as in this case, the end of that span always arrives.

Armageddon...now peaceful...but soon a blood-soaked battleground!

Background

Are all those marching against Palestine united at the start of the Battle of Armageddon? Perhaps so. Yet — maybe not. It may be that the armies of Asia (Revelation 9:14, 16; 16:12) are marching against the Antichrist and his western forces. If this later theory should be the one that comes to pass, then events *might* occur something like this:

With 200 million men marching on Israel...Antichrist becomes alarmed and decides he is going to meet this 200 million man army.

However, his intent is to fight them on a battleground which will be to his advantage. Therefore, he will set himself up in the Mountains of Judea where he will have the advantage of some natural defenses.

Suddenly something unusual happens. The Heavens open.

The two opposing forces - Antichrist and his force and the invading Asiatic forces - realizing God is moving in...unite forces. By so uniting they hope to devote all their energies to wiping out the Lord Jesus Christ and His followers.

Suddenly Christ and His armies appear. Within a short time...all is over. Sinners and evildoers are conquered. The Lord is victorious. Antichrist and the False Prophet are thrown into the Lake of Fire. Their followers are cast into hades to await their final judgment...after which they too will be cast into the Lake of Fire.

PAST	PRESENT	RAPTURE	FIRST 3 1/2	LAST 3 1/2	ARMA– GEDDON	MIL– LENNIUM	NEW HEAVENS & EARTH
			TRIBULATION				

21 And the remnant were slain with the sword of him that sat upon the horse, which *sword* proceeded out of his mouth: and all the fowls were filled with their flesh.

Ezek. 39:17-24

Definition:
Remnant.—*Hebrew,* shear *(Isa. 10:20-22) and Greek,* hupoleimma *(Rom. 9:27), the "remaining ones." Thus the "remnant" often denotes the few who are faithful to God amid a general apostasy—such as the 7000 of Elijah's day (1 Kgs. 19:18). It often stands for those from Israel and the nations whom God will save in the latter days out of a world that rejects God. Here in 19:21 it is ironically used for the perishing wicked armies at Armageddon.*

Commentary

21. Isaiah 10:20-22 (quoted in Romans 9:27) and Zech. 13:8-9 speak of a "remnant" which will believe in the Lord amid the general apostasy. This remnant is the REMNANT UNTO LIFE; they turn to God and He saves them from perishing.

Here at Christ's appearance Zech. 12:9-10 will be fulfilled as the REMNANT OF ISRAEL looks to Christ as their deliverer and Messiah!

In Revelation 19:21, however, we see a REMNANT UNTO DEATH. That is, all those of the armies which followed the Antichrist who were not at once thrown into the Lake of Fire, as were their two supreme leaders, are the "remnant" who are slaughtered by Christ at His coming.

Which remnant are you headed for???

Note:
This smiting of the world powers by Christ at His coming will be a fulfillment of that awesome and wondrous prophecy of Daniel 2. Here "the stone cut without hands" (Christ) smashes into the statue of human governments, hitting the ten-toe kings who follow the Antichrist, and ruins them completely at Armageddon. Christ next establishes His kingdom which lasts forever (Rev. 20—The kingdom lasts forever despite the uprising at the end of the 1000 years and despite the creation of the new heavens and earth after this.). Daniel 2, especially verses 42, 44-45.

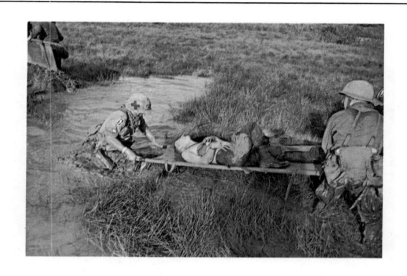

Background

In reading this verse can you actually fathom the number of people that will be killed during this Armageddon battle?

On the basis of the 200 million size force described in Revelation 9:16, let us theorize a possible projection.

First, the armies of possibly 200 million men coming from Asia will be slain. Then, Antichrist's western forces, perhaps equal in size, of 200 million or more will also be slain.

During World War 2 there were approximately 16 million Americans serving in the Armed Forces. Presently there are about 3½ million.

But let's take the higher figure of 16 million. This represented about 10% of the entire U.S. population at that time.

For the purpose of very rough estimates...If a combined army of 400 million men represents about 10% of the population in Antichrist's day...then the balance of the population may number as high as 4 BILLION. With the present day population explosion such figures - which once may have been considered wildly astronomical - are now modest and easily conceivable! Thus, it is *possible* that at Armageddon there *may* be as many as 400 million casualties.

PAST	PRESENT	RAPTURE	FIRST 3½ LAST 3½ TRIBULATION		ARMA- GEDDON	MIL- LENNIUM	NEW HEAVENS & EARTH

These stone steps could very well be the very same stones on which Jesus walked to be tried by Caiaphas (Matthew 26:57). This path is at the Palace of Caiaphas. Caiaphas was the high priest at the time of Jesus' arrest and crucifixion.

(Matthew 25:32)

JUDGMENTS and their DISTINCTION

There are 4 judgments in Scripture of which you should be aware:

1. Judgment of the Church ("The Judgment Seat of Christ")
   2 Corinthians 5:10-11

Here we have the judgment of the believer's works...not his sins. Hebrews 10:17 tells us that the Christian's sins and iniquities will be remembered no more. But Matthew 12:36, Romans 14:10, Colossians 3:24-25 remind us that every work must come to judgment. This judgment **occurs at the return of Christ for His church** (Rapture)...immediately after the Rapture but before the marriage supper of the Lamb.

2. Judgment of individual Gentiles
   Verse 32 of Matthew 25 refers to this.

This event is fully anticipated in the Old Testament. See Psalm 2:1-10, Isaiah 63:1-6, Joel 3:2-16; Zephaniah 3:8 and Zechariah 14:1-3.

Here the sheep (believers) are separated from the goats (unbelievers). This **occurs after the Tribulation Period** when those Gentiles who have come to Christ during this perilous period will be ushered into the kingdom and eternal life. The goats (unbelievers) will be cast into everlasting fire for their sins.

3. Judgment of Israel
   Ezekiel 20:33-38

When Christ returns **after the Tribulation Period** He will regather the Jews and purge those who rebelled. This will be accomplished after He first delivers the whole nation from its persecutors. Those who, like the sheep among the Gentiles, are believers in Jesus Christ will be ushered into the kingdom.

4. Judgment of the Wicked
   Revelation 20:11-15

For this judgment we look to the time **after the Millennium** (1000 years). This last judgment comes to all unbelievers of all ages at the Great White Throne. The Holy God, the Sovereign Judge, will be seated on the throne. These unbelievers will be judged according to their sinful works. And because not one of them has his name written in the Lamb's book of life...they will be cast into the lake of fire. There will be no escape forever!

VERSE 1

CHAPTER 20
And I saw an angel come down from
heaven, having the key of the bottomless
pit and a great chain in his hand.

Rev. 1:18; 9:1
2 Kg. 25:7

Commentary

*CHAPTER 20: THE 1000 YEARS AND THE GREAT WHITE
THRONE JUDGMENT*
 20:1-10 THE 1000 YEARS
 20:11-15 THE GREAT WHITE THRONE

20:1-10 THE 1000 YEARS
1. Chapter 19 concluded the seven year Tribulation Period with Christ's
coming "with power and great glory" at Armageddon (Matt. 24:29-30;
Rev. 19:11-21). There He slew the armies of the Antichrist, and cast into
the Lake of Fire both the Antichrist and the False Prophet, the "Son"
and the "Holy Spirit" of the Infernal Trinity.

The initial sights of chapter 20 continue the events of chapter 19—and
no time interval between the events of the two chapters should be im-
agined. Christ at His glorious Armageddon appearance *deals with all of
the wicked forces on the earth...*

a. He casts the Beast and False Prophet into the Lake of Fire (19:20);

b. He slays the armies of the Beast gathered at Armageddon (19:21);

c. He, through an angel, imprisons Satan—the "Father," the third member of the False Trinity—for 1000 years (20:1-3);

d. He has the people of all nations gathered before Him (those left alive
at His coming at the close of the Tribulation), and He does not permit
the wicked to remain alive to enter the Kingdom which He is now inau-
gurating upon the earth (Matt. 25:31-46).

"...an angel..."—That on the command of God one angel can imprison
Satan shows the power of God and of His angels. "...the key...a great
chain..."—We know little of the physics concerning that which is able to
imprison a mighty spirit such as Satan. Despite this lack of knowledge,
however, the result is perfectly clear—Satan is absolutely confined and
able to deceive no one.

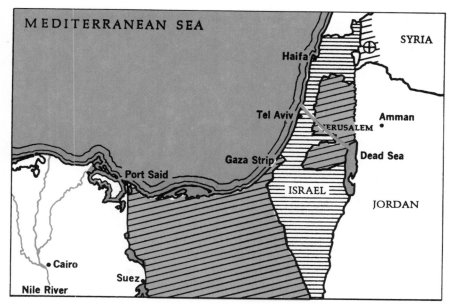

Map shows how waters will go out from Jerusalem to Mediterranean and Dead Seas.

Background

The Millennial Kingdom

The 1000 year reign of Christ is ushered in by the Lord himself. This is sometimes referred to as the Millennial Kingdom.

This 1000 year reign will take place right here on earth.

In the battle of Armageddon, which occurs at the end of the 7 year Tribulation Period, Christ will come down from Heaven and His feet will stand upon the Mount of Olives. Here's what will happen:

> And His feet shall stand in that day upon the mount of Olives, which lies before Jerusalem on the east, and the Mount of Olives shall be split in two from the east to the west by a great valley; and half of the mountain shall remove toward the north, and half of it toward the south...
>
> (Zechariah 14:4 Amplified Bible)

> ...that living waters shall go out from Jerusalem, half of them to the eastern (Dead) Sea, and half of them to the western (Mediterranean) Sea; in summer and in winter shall it be.
>
> (Zechariah 14:8 Amplified Bible)

This, in itself is a marvel to anyone who has seen the Dead Sea!

PAST	PRESENT	RAPTURE	FIRST 3½	LAST 3½	ARMA-GEDDON	MIL-LENNIUM	NEW HEAVENS & EARTH
			TRIBULATION				

Revelation 20

2 And he laid hold on the dragon, that old serpent, which is the Devil, and Satan, and bound him a 1000 years.
3 And cast him into the bottomless pit, and shut him up, and set a seal upon him, that he should deceive the nations no more, till the thousand years should be fulfilled: and after that he must be loosed a little season.

Rev. 12:9

Dan. 12:4; Matt. 27:66
I Pet. 5:8
Isaiah 11:1-10

Commentary

2-3. Look at the succession of steps here narrated to bring to our attention how securely God will imprison Satan for the 1000 years...

> "laid hold on"..."bound him"..."cast him into"..."bottomless pit"... "shut him up"..."set a seal upon him...."

"That he should deceive the nations no more."—During the millennium Satan will be absolutely out of the picture and will not be able to deceive the nations upon the earth—although, of course, those born during this period to the ones admitted after Armageddon to the earthly kingdom will still be born with the Adamic nature and able to sin (Matt. 25:31-46; Zech. 14:16-21; etc.).

The Amillennialists who affirm that the 1000 year kingdom is taking place on earth TODAY and that Satan is bound TODAY—with all their oft displayed erudition—are shown to be in error by this single verse, 20:3! Two characteristics of this period will be that *Christ will be ruling the nations* with a rod of iron (19:15) and *Satan will not be deceiving the nations* (20:3). Numerous scriptures as well as countless newspapers and history texts show that during this present age this simply is not true, nor was it ever true since the crucifixion.

Satan—contrary to the amillennial claims—was not imprisoned at the time of the cross in the sense taught here, *viz.,* "that he should deceive the nations no more." During the early centuries of Christianity with their persecutions, during the medieval centuries with their "Dark Ages," and now in modern times with the converting of whole nations to diabolical communism—during all of the course of this age, Satan has been deceiving the nations "as a roaring lion" (1 Pet. 5:8).

Amillennialism simply is not in accord with Revelation 20:3, nor with such passages as Isaiah 11:1-10 which show a universal state of peace on earth among the nations during the millennial age.

"After that he must be loosed a little season."—(Greek; "it is necessary for him to be loosed") This imperative is due solely to the sovereign will of God. God desires to show us the true sinful nature of man. God will show us that even after 1000 years of peace when sin is held down and when Christ is ruling, when given an opportunity SOME will rebel.

In the Millennium the trees will always bear fruit.

Background

The Dead Sea at present has no exit for its waters except by evaporation. The present Dead Sea is 53 miles long, 9 to 10 miles wide and its surface lies 1286 feet below sea level.

The Jordan River, which is the main body of water which feeds the Dead Sea, flows SOUTH to the Dead Sea. When it reaches here - there is no exit!

But look at this! On the previous page we quoted Scriptures that tell us that these waters will go out from Jerusalem - half of them EAST to the Dead Sea and half of them WEST to the Mediterranean Sea.

And we are further told in that same verse (Zechariah 14:8) that these waters shall go out from Jerusalem.

In today's Jerusalem THERE IS NO RIVER!

But at the ushering in of the Millennial 1000 year age not only will there be a river in Jerusalem, but also then the death-giving Salt Sea - the Dead Sea - will come ALIVE. It will be alive with its banks lined with all kinds of trees for food, ALWAYS fruit bearing, and fishermen on its sides.

Take a minute to read Ezekiel 47:8, 9, 10, 12. The Dead Sea comes alive!

▼

PAST	PRESENT	RAPTURE	FIRST 3 1/2 TRIBULATION	LAST 3 1/2	ARMA- GEDDON	MIL- LENNIUM	NEW HEAVENS & EARTH

4 And I saw thrones, and they sat upon them, and judgment was given unto them: and I *saw* the souls of them that were beheaded for the witness of Jesus, and for the word of God, and which had not worshipped the beast, neither his image, neither had received *his* mark upon their foreheads, or in their hands; and they lived and reigned with Christ a thousand years.

Dan. 7:9,22,27
I Cor. 6:2-3

Rev. 7:13-14

Rev. 13:15-17
Luke 22:30

Commentary

4. *"Thrones...judgment was given unto them."*—Here, and in the next two verses, we are given a glimpse into the position and privileges which will be enjoyed by the redeemed in the millennial kingdom. Here "judgment was given unto them" is an expression signifying that they shall be granted authority to judge; and likewise the thrones would indicate that they will also have some authority under Christ to rule. This is in accord with other Biblical teachings, for example: 1 Cor. 6:2-3, "Do you not know that the saints shall judge the world?...we shall judge angels...;" and Luke 19:17,19, "...have thou authority over ten cities...Be thou also over five cities."

"I saw the souls of them that were beheaded...and they lived and reigned with Christ a thousand years."—From the description here we see that those who come out of the Tribulation having refused to worship the Beast, but who rather turned in faith to Christ, will be given life again and they will rule with Christ during the millennium. Verses 5 and 6 which follow shed light here. They show that the subject at hand is a resurrection. Thus these who were beheaded—in light of verses 5 and 6 —will rule and reign with Christ during the millennium *in their new resurrected bodies;* and not merely as disembodied spirits.

Since the saints of the present inter-advent age (between the cross and the Second Coming) are not here specifically mentioned as ruling during the millennium, some might wonder if perhaps only the Tribulation saints will rule here. But this could hardly be the case since verses 5 and 6 which follow show that ALL of the redeemed are raised by the start of the 1000 years in the "first resurrection." The lost are not raised— but they await the second resurrection 1000 years later. Thus it would seem that all of those who have died in Christ will rule and reign during the 1000 years—yet verse 4 only speaks of those beheaded in the Tribulation as the representative sample of all the multitudes who have been faithful to Christ through the ages.

Vassar seniors wear peace symbol on mortarboards at June, 1970 graduation day protest.

Background

In today's world we have witnessed an ever growing spiral of student rebellions. Some are peaceful demonstrations, others are quite violent. Student deaths have occurred. There have been charges and countercharges. We have witnessed student radicals using 4-letter words, and at the same time we have heard professors and even government officials using language not much better - as demagogues and false prophets dominate today's news.

Basically, when it comes right down to the issues, both hawks and doves are claiming to be seeking peace. But both sides have their own ideas as to how best this peace can be achieved.

The fact is, however, that on this earth despite the herculean efforts of even some who deny Christ as Saviour and Lord...peace will NEVER be achieved!

Even when conditions are ideal and people find themselves living in a perfect environment in the Millennial Kingdom...still people will not be content.

PAST	PRESENT	RAPTURE	FIRST 3 ½ TRIBULATION	LAST 3 ½	ARMA– GEDDON	MIL– LENNIUM	NEW HEAVENS &EARTH

5 But the rest of the dead lived not again until the thousand years were finished. This is the first resurrection.

John 5:28-29

Commentary

5. Here we are clearly shown that there are to be two resurrections separated by the 1000 years. The first will be the RESURRECTION UNTO LIFE and it would include:

All of those "dead in Christ" who were raised at the rapture (1 Thess. 4:13-18);

The tribulation saints who died after the rapture and who are raised at the end of the Tribulation Period (20:4);

All of the pre-deluvian and post-deluvian Old Testament saints. (Even though it is absolutely clear that these are "in Christ" in the sense that their salvation was purchased solely by Christ's blood, whether these are raised at the rapture or at the end of the seven year Tribulation is hotly disputed by some Bible believers.)

Any believer who may die in the millennial period—if indeed this be the case—will be part of the First Resurrection whether they are raised individually at death or later (See Isa. 65:20).

But the lost, "the rest of the dead," are not raised for another 1000 years. That is, their disembodied spirits are kept in hades ("the unseen world") awaiting the RESURRECTION UNTO DEATH wherein they are cast into the Lake of Fire forever at the Great White Throne Judgment (20:11-15).

The amillennial claim, on the basis of such verses as John 5:28-29, that there is to be only one final general resurrection of both the saved and the lost is completely refuted by the clarity of this verse. Let the Greek student secure a copy of the commentary of that great scholar of yesteryear, Dean Alford, and read his vehement declaration on this subject in his commentary on Revelation 20.

Let no one suppose a contradiction between John 5:28-29 and Revelation 20. The former seems to teach a general resurrection of both saved and lost, while here we clearly see that these two will be separated by 1000 years—and both the first and the second may have their own subparts. Compare to this the Old Testament affirmations that there is only one God (Deut. 6:4), with the later New Testament clarifications that this one Godhead is actually a tri-unity (trinity), one God composed of three co-equal divine persons! A true generalization does not deny later true and clear clarifications! Thus there will be a resurrection of all the dead; but the justified dead will be raised a thousand years before the unregenerate dead.

Background

What will life be like in the Millennium? David will be brought back in a ruling capacity (Ezekiel 37:24—though the "David" in this verse may represent the final Davidic king, Jesus).

With Satan imprisoned during this time (Revelation 20:1-7)...the Millennium Period will be one of:

1. PEACE
There will be no war. See Isaiah 11:6-9, Isaiah 2:4.

2. HAPPINESS
See Isaiah 11:6-9 and 12:3. Also Revelation 20:3.

3. LONG LIFE and HEALTH
Read Isaiah 65:20 and Isaiah 33:24. Sickness will virtually be removed.

4. PROSPERITY
This will be a time of unequalled prosperity. See Isaiah 35:1,2.

5. JOY IN LABOR
Read Isaiah 65:21,22

Sexual reproduction will still exist in the Millennium. Those saints who live through the Tribulation Period and enter the 1000 year Millennium in their natural bodies will be able to have children (Matt. 25:31-40). Thus Isaiah 11:6 and 8 speak of little children living during the Millennial Age.

▼

PAST	PRESENT	RAPTURE	FIRST 3 1/2 TRIBULATION	LAST 3 1/2	ARMA-GEDDON	MIL-LENNIUM	NEW HEAVENS & EARTH

6 Blessed and holy *is* he that hath part in the first resurrection: on such the second death hath no power, but they shall be priests of God and of Christ, and shall reign with him a thousand years.

Rev. 1:3; 14:13; 16:15; 19:9; 22:7,14

1 Pet. 2:9; Exod. 19:6

Commentary

6. Truly the redeemed are "blessed." We were lost in sin and deserving of the second death, eternal irrevocable separation from God. But God in His love, turned our hearts around and called us unto Christ for forgiveness of sin and everlasting life (Romans 8:28-30). Now the second death no longer has power to destroy us. Romans 8:33-34 beautifully explains why, once we have been saved, we can no longer be condemned to death for our sins:

> Who shall lay anything to the charge of God's elect? It is God that justifieth.

> Who is he that condemneth? It is Christ that died, yea rather, that is risen again, who is even at the right hand of God, who also maketh intercession for us.

"They shall be priests."—Peter in his first epistle in 2:9 speaks of believers as "a royal priesthood." All believers are priests in that they may pray directly to God without any human mediator in a position of a "priest." Christ is the one mediator between God and man (1 Tim. 2:5), and so shall it be in the millennial age also.

Like an outdoor country picnic...every need supplied.

Background

The general outward obedience of the nations during the Millennial Period unfortunately does not mean that every last individual will come to Christ and accept Him as personal Saviour and Lord during the 1000 years.

Remember, during the Millennium Period living saints will give birth to children. Those children must individually decide either to accept Christ or reject Him.

Some will reject Him. This is possible because sin will still be possible during this 1000 years! See Zechariah 14:17-19.

Imagine, living in the 1000 year Millennium Period with every need supplied, all sorrows erased, lasting joy, virtually no sickness...abundant harvests...and yet there will still be some who will not be content!

This is the picture we have here as the 1000 year Millennial Period draws to a close. Soon those who are unhappy will be given their opportunity to make a choice.

PAST	PRESENT	RAPTURE	FIRST 3 1/2 TRIBULATION	LAST 3 1/2	ARMA-GEDDON	MIL-LENNIUM	NEW HEAVENS & EARTH

7 And when the thousand years are expired, Satan shall be loosed out of his prison,

8 And shall go out to deceive the nations which are in the four quarters of the earth, Gog and Ma-gog, to gather them together to battle: the number of whom *is* as the sand of the sea.

Rev. 20:3

Commentary

We would not have expected what we here read; but it is clear. Although Christ will rule the nations during the millennium, sin will yet be present upon earth (Zech. 14:16-21; Isa. 65:20). Those born during the 1000 years will be born with sinful hearts which need regeneration just as ours do today. And although the majority of those born during the millennium will no doubt follow Christ, yet other multitudes will not believe. They will be like the pharisees who saw the miracles but yet refused to accept Him as their Lord (John 11:47).

"As the sand of the sea."—With the population explosion we are now accustomed to hear vast population statistics. On the millennial earth the population may be staggering in size since wars and devastations will not ruin the crops. With so large a population, the number of those who follow Satan may be vast—while being at the same time only a fraction of the earth's population.

"Gog and Magog."—In Ezekiel 38:1-39:16 we read of Gog and Magog (38:2) coming out of the *north* to invade Israel. God intervenes and miraculously saves Israel. Thus the names "Gog and Magog" come to represent any large assemblage of people who wickedly war against God and who are suddenly destroyed by Him. Compare Isaiah 1:10.

The Gog and Magog war of Ezekiel 38:1-39:16 is an *anti-Israeli* invasion from the *north;* Revelation 20:7-10 is an *anti-Christ* onslaught by people gathered from *all over the earth.* They are not the same events.

PAST	PRESENT	RAPTURE	FIRST 3 1/2 LAST 3 1/2 TRIBULATION		ARMA-GEDDON	MIL-LENNIUM	NEW HEAVENS & EARTH

Revelation 20

9 And they went up on the breadth of the earth, and compassed the camp of the saints about, and the beloved city: and fire came down from God out of heaven, and devoured them.
10 And the devil that deceived them was cast into the lake of fire and brimstone, where the beast and the false prophet *are*, and shall be tormented day and night for ever and ever.

2 Kgs. 1:10,12;
Numb. 16:31-35
1 Tm. 2:14; Rev. 12:9;
13:14; 19:20
Rev. 19:20

Commentary

9. In Genesis 3 Satan deceived our first parents into believing that they could rebel against God and by so doing improve their lot; he also convinced them that they might not incur the awful promised penalty of death for their sin. So too, at the end of the 1000 years, Satan will somehow by some means lure huge numbers into rebellion against Christ. These "compassed the camp of the saints;" that is, since Jerusalem is the capital—Zech. 8:22—the rebellious multitudes come up against it.

God destroys them suddenly and miraculously—these have sinned wickedly in the face of the great millennial light. Such is the nature of sin.

10. Now, God's purposes having been achieved, Satan is rewarded according to his iniquity. He is cast into the Lake of Fire where the Beast and the False Prophet are. The Greek then reads literally: "And they [all three of them] shall be tormented [this is not annihilation] unto the ages of the ages [eternal separation from God]."

It should be made clear, before leaving this subject, that the visible kingdom of God inaugurated at Christ's Second Coming at Armageddon is not in any way stopped or destroyed by this "brief rebellion" at the close of the thousand years. Indeed, Daniel 2:44 prophesies that the kingdom that will be inaugurated at Christ's second coming will "never be destroyed...and it shall stand forever and ever." This kingdom continues on despite the rebellion at the end of the millennium and it continues directly into the creation of the New Heaven and Earth and forever after.

PAST	PRESENT	RAPTURE	FIRST 3 1/2 LAST 3 1/2 TRIBULATION		ARMA- GEDDON	MIL- LENNIUM	NEW HEAVENS & EARTH

Revelation 20

11 And I saw a great white throne, and him that sat on it, from whose face the earth and the heaven fled away; and there was found no place for them.

John 5:22,27-30
Luke 5:8; Isa. 6:5

Commentary

20:11-15 THE GREAT WHITE THRONE

11. Verse 5 ("But the rest of the dead lived not again until the thousand years were finished") shows us that this Great White Throne judgment scene, wherein the "rest of the dead" are raised, takes place directly after the 1000 years and the final rebellion have run their course.

Now finally all who offend and who have ever offended, the unrepentant sinners, will be forever put out of the picture by God. This will make way for the making of the New Heavens and Earth which have never nor will ever be tainted by a drop of sin.

This is a *thronon megan leukon* (Greek); a "Throne great white." That it is a *throne* reveals to us the fact that great authority resides here in this judgment—that of God Almighty. It is *great* because of the infinite majesty of God and because of the enormity of the business to be transpired—the judgment of the unsaved dead of the ages. Finally, it is *white* symbolizing the absolute spotless holiness of God—the standard by which the dead shall be judged for their sins.

J. Oliver Buswell, Jr. has suggested in his *Systematic Theology* that this verse, in connection with 21:1, speaks of the departing of the present earth and its atmospheric heavens (2 Pet. 3:10) in preparation for the coming of the New Heaven and New Earth. That the earthy scene of sin should be burned away at the same time that the sinners are forever put away sounds quite reasonable. The timing also fits, as next, in 21:1, we do see the former earth gone and the new present.

Dear Reader: If you are not certain that you are a child of God, even now as you read this pray a prayer to God and ask the risen Christ to be your Saviour from sin. He died on the cross to pay for the sins of all who would believe in Him. Make your sinful soul *white* by the blood of the Lamb (Rev. 7:14). Do it right now. Why should you someday stand before this terrifying Great White Throne and be condemned forever for your sins? Jesus is standing and waiting, knocking at your heart's door (Rev. 3:20). Why should you perish in the judgment when there is eternal life to be had?

PAST	PRESENT	RAPTURE	FIRST 3 1/2 LAST 3 1/2 TRIBULATION		ARMA- GEDDON	MIL- LENNIUM	NEW HEAVENS & EARTH

12 And I saw the dead, small and great, stand before God; and the books were opened: and another book was opened, which is *the book* of life: and the dead were judged out of those things which were written in the books, according to their works.

13 And the sea gave up the dead which were in it; and death and hell delivered up the dead which were in them: and they were judged every man according to their works.

Rev. 17:8; 21:27
Dan. 7:9-10

Rev. 6:8

12-13. In this day of sending waves and beams to the planets and farther...of lasers and potential matter transmission...why should men think it impossible for God to restructure the atom-electron pattern that once made up the bodies of men? That is, why do men doubt that God can raise the dead? (See Mt. 22:23-33).

The Bible, despite what the skeptics dogmatically declare and prattle, here and in other places tells us that God will indeed raise the dead... and that there will be a final judgment. Jesus, furthermore, has demonstrated that God can actually raise the dead (John 11:25-26, 43-44; Rev. 1:18; Lk. 8:49-56; 7:11-17; 1 Kg. 17:17-24).

Here all of the lost are raised unto the judgment. The redeemed believers were already raised at the Rapture and after the Tribulation, a 1000 years before, at the First Resurrection—they are not the ones spoken of here (1 Thess. 4:13-18; Rev. 20:4-6).

All the lost dead are here raised. "Death and hell" [Greek: *hades*—the unseen world] give up its dead. The "sea" is specifically mentioned showing us that those whose bodies were destroyed or devoured by voracious fish into thousands of little bits will still be raised at this scene —God is able!

The dead are judged out of the Book of Life "according to their works."

"According to their works."—All are judged fairly; but, alas, "All have sinned and come short of the glory of God" and thus at this judgment all are condemned (Rom. 3:23). Believers would also have been condemned—but, Christ paid the penalty for their sins upon the cross.

> For the wages of sin is death; but the gift of God
> is eternal life through Jesus Christ our Lord (Rom. 6:23).

PAST	PRESENT	RAPTURE	FIRST 3½ LAST 3½ TRIBULATION		ARMA-GEDDON	MIL-LENNIUM	NEW HEAVENS & EARTH
			FIRST 3½	LAST 3½			

14 And death and hell were cast into the lake of fire. This is the second death.
15 And whosoever was not found written in the book of life was cast into the lake of fire.

Rev. 20:6

Rev. 3:5; 13:8; 17:8; Phil. 4:3

Commentary

14. *"...cast into the Lake of Fire."*—The Bible clearly tells us that the fate of the wicked will be a horrible one. Jesus said the same thing (Matt. 7:21-23; 5:22,29-30).

Some get involved in trying to fathom the chemistry of the oxidation, or burning, which takes place in the Lake of Fire. Will this be an immense pool of burning liquid? Will it be a heavy fiery white dwarf star—a spheroid pool of ever burning liquid—cast forever out into the depths of space???

We must confess that the full chemistry of the matter has not been disclosed; and it actually matters little. All that a child need know is that a coffee pot has contents which can horribly burn and scald his skin. He need not necessarily fathom the phenomena of percolating or how the ten amperes of alternating 110 or 220 volt current passes through a coil resistor giving heat.

So too here—God has given us sufficient information for our eternal welfare. The Lake of Fire is a terrible doom—that is all we need to know to run away from it in terror to Christ who with love abounding at the foot of the cross seeks to save us from our sin's just penalty (John 3:16; 6:37; Matt. 23:37).

This is the "second death." Spiritual death is *separation* from God just as physical death is the separation of the soul from the body. All of us of the race of Adam, unless we have Christ, are "dead in trespasses and sins" (Eph. 2:1). We are separated from God. Now in the scene before us the lost who have both previously been spiritually dead and physically dead are made alive at the Second Resurrection. They are given resurrection bodies and they are brought into the presence of God for this judgment. Then because of their sinfulness they are cast forever into the Lake of Fire. They have made an irrevocable life-decision to cling to their sinful estate despite all of God's warnings and pleadings. This involves an eternal *separation* from the God before whom they now stand, and it is hence called the "Second Death."

15. *"...not found written in the Book of Life..."*—It is interesting to note that Revelation 3:5 says of the believer that his name will not be *blotted out* of the Book of Life (Compare Psa. 69:28; 109:13). No...for the believer, his sins will be *"blotted out"* (Acts 3:19).

No earthly gods will be able to save those who have rejected Christ as Lord!

Background

So now it is finished...or rather just beginning...for the dead - the unbelievers.

Now comes a judgment related in only 18 words in our English Bible that will condemn them forever to a real, everlasting Hell:

> AND WHOSOEVER WAS NOT FOUND WRITTEN IN THE BOOK OF LIFE WAS CAST INTO THE LAKE OF FIRE.
>
> (Revelation 20:15)

And here at last, many may wish that they had put their good intentions to accept Christ into action...but it will be too late! There is no second chance.

Remember this important fact:

> It does NOT require a new decision to go to Hell
>
> but
>
> It DOES require a decision to go to Heaven!

Thus ends...and begins...the most tragic moment in history...a moment that for the unbeliever will begin an eternity in constant torment in Hell. For the unrepentent...Doomsday has finally arrived. Oh sinner—flee from the wrath to come...flee to Christ who will forgive and cleanse you.

PAST	PRESENT	RAPTURE	FIRST 3 1/2 LAST 3 1/2 TRIBULATION		ARMA-GEDDON	MIL-LENNIUM	NEW HEAVENS & EARTH

(Mark 9:44)
The Characteristics of Hell
THE FIRE THAT NEVER SHALL BE QUENCHED

Many people jokingly refer to Hell as a place where they will be busy greeting all their friends. Unfortunately, this is far from the Scriptural picture in the sense that they will not be greeting their friends but rather they will be in eternal torment.

All the non-believers, with Satan, with Antichrist and with the False Prophet and Satan's angels will be together in the final Lake of Fire. (Could a super-heavy liquid-fire white dwarf star be the location of the Lake of Fire???)

Hell will be:

1. A PLACE OF CONSCIOUSNESS

You will recall in Scriptures a message concerning a certain rich man and Lazarus, a beggar. The rich man was conscious in Hell and he was in torment:

> And in Hades (the realm of the dead, Hell), being in torment, he lifted up his eyes...and cried out...
> *(Luke 16:23,24 Amplified Bible)*

This Scripture indicates that the unsaved dead are CONSCIOUS.

2. A PLACE OF TORMENT

Both in the above verse just quoted and in verse 28 of Luke 16:

> ...warn them (the rich man's 5 brothers)...lest they too come into this place of torment.

we have an indication from God that Hell is a real place of torment....Also Hell, from these Scriptures, is shown as a hot place for the rich man asks that Lazarus (the beggar who went to Heaven) "dip the tip of his finger in water and cool my tongue; for I am in anguish in this flame" (Luke 16:24 Amplified Bible).

Can you imagine the intense suffering from an unbearable heat? Anyone who has been to Vietnam or other hot climates where the suffocating humidity envelops you along with the intense heat can appreciate this scene.

Also picture the desperateness of the occasion when the rich man would welcome the beggar Lazarus to get water on his finger to alleviate the suffering!

Hell is truly a place of real torment!

3. A PLACE OF DARKNESS

We are told in Matthew that the unsaved

> ...will be driven out into the darkness outside, where there will be weeping and grinding of teeth.
>
> *(Matthew 8:12 Amplified Bible)*

Also

> ...throw him (the unsaved) into the darkness outside (of Heaven); there will be weeping and grinding of teeth.
>
> *(Matthew 22:13 Amplified Bible)*

And in Jude 13 we are told that the "gloom of darkness" has been "reserved forever" for those outside of Christ. What a picture of hopelessness!

4. ETERNAL SEPARATION FROM LOVED ONES

Think about this for a moment. If you are an unbeliever and some of your best friends and loved relatives...perhaps even a husband or wife are BELIEVERS...they will go to Heaven...and you will be eternally separated from them!

> There shall be weeping and gnashing of teeth, when ye shall see Abraham, and Isaac, and Jacob, and all the prophets, in the kingdom of God, and you yourselves thrust out.
>
> *(Luke 13:28 King James Version)*

What a tragedy to enter Hell and then to realize that you are now eternally separated from those whom you loved so much on this earth!

5. NOT THE SLIGHTEST HOPE OF RELEASE

Many places in Scripture tell of Hell being a place of eternal judgment from which there is no turning back. In Hebrews 6:2 we learn that Hell is a place of "eternal judgment." In Matthew 25:46 it is revealed that the unbeliever will "go away into everlasting punishment...."

6. THE TORMENT OF MEMORY IN HELL

This, perhaps could be the most agonizing aspect of those in Hell...the torment of a memory...a memory that will evoke continual anguish. This is brought out so clearly in Luke 16:27,28 where the rich man implores Abraham to:

> ...send him (Lazarus, who is in Heaven) to my father's house:

> For I have five brethren; that he may testify unto them, lest they also come into this place of torment.
>
> *(Luke 16:27,28 King James Version)*

What an insight into Hell! Imagine if those unsaved dead right now could speak to us for just a moment...what a warning they would give...and yet, sad to say, would anyone pay attention?

How pointedly Abraham replied...and how prophetically when he said,

> ...If they hear not Moses and the prophets, neither will they be persuaded, THOUGH ONE ROSE FROM THE DEAD.
>
> *(Luke 16:31 King James Version)*

Thus, the unbeliever in Hell must go through an eternity in torment with a searing, ever-present memory!

7. THE TORMENT OF UNSATISFIED LUSTFUL CRAVINGS

In Hell the unbeliever will **never gain satisfaction.** Sin will continue in Hell but it will be a constant craving...without fulfilling. Thus we read,

> He who is unrighteous (unjust, wicked) let him be unrighteous still, and he that is filthy (vile, impure) let him be filthy still....
>
> *(Revelation 22:11, Amplified Bible)*

These words here are referring to the activity in Hell. Can you imagine the surprise that awaits the filth peddlers who on this earth are having a heyday distributing pornographic films and literature.

At least, here on earth this activity brings them barrels of cash while they influence negatively the lives of others.

But in Hell, these filth peddlers will have their cravings and lusts...but these will be unfulfilled cravings. Can you imagine the intensity of suffering this will cause!

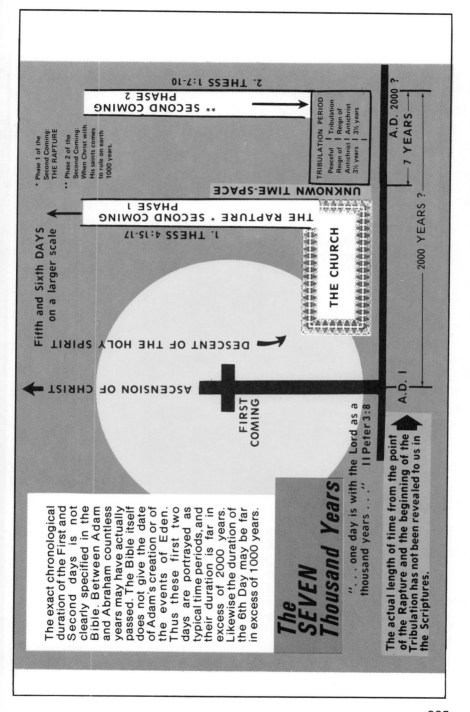

The exact chronological duration of the First and Second days is not clearly specified in the Bible. Between Adam and Abraham countless years may have actually passed. The Bible itself does not give the date of Adam's creation or of the events of Eden. Thus these first two days are portrayed as typical time periods, and their duration is far in excess of 2000 years. Likewise the duration of the 6th Day may be far in excess of 1000 years.

The SEVEN Thousand Years

". . . one day is with the Lord as a thousand years . . ."
II Peter 3:8

The actual length of time from the point of the Rapture and the beginning of the Tribulation has not been revealed to us in the Scriptures.

Fifth and Sixth DAYS on a larger scale

* Phase 1 of the Second Coming: THE RAPTURE

** Phase 2 of the Second Coming: When Christ with His saints comes to rule on earth 1000 years.

2. THESS 1:7-10

** SECOND COMING PHASE 2

TRIBULATION PERIOD
| Peaceful Reign of Antichrist 3½ years | Tribulation Reign of Antichrist 3½ years |

UNKNOWN TIME-SPACE

THE RAPTURE * SECOND COMING PHASE 1

1. THESS 4:15-17

THE CHURCH

DESCENT OF THE HOLY SPIRIT

ASCENSION OF CHRIST

FIRST COMING

A.D. 2000 ?

7 YEARS

2000 YEARS ?

A.D. 1

CHAPTER 21   *VERSE 1*

1 AND I saw a new heaven and a new
earth: for the first heaven and the first
earth were passed away;

*2 Pet. 3:12-13; Isa. 66:22
Isa. 65:17**

Commentary

21:1-22:5 *THE NEW HEAVEN AND THE NEW EARTH*

1. Now after the thousand year Millennial Age God at last brings forth
the New World. The chief characteristic of this New Creation is that it is
entirely free from any taint of sin—and therefore the resultant effects of
sin are absent. Here there is neither death, sorrow, tears, pain, nor
separation from God (vs. 4).

This New Creation comes into being after the 1000 years, and after the
rebellion and the Great White Throne Judgment which follow the 1000
years. This is eminently plain. Look at the order of events:

    Rapture (1 Thess. 4)
    Tribulation (Rev. 6-19)
    Armageddon (Rev. 19)
    Imprisonment of Satan (Rev. 20)
    Inauguration of the Millennial Kingdom (Mt. 25)
    The Millennial Kingdom (Rev. 20; Isa. 11)
    Satan Is Loosed (Rev. 20)
    The Brief Rebellion (Rev. 20)
    Great White Throne Judgment ("Second Death," Rev. 20)
    New Heaven and New Earth (Rev. 21-22)
    New Jerusalem (Rev. 21-22)

Since the characteristic of the New Heaven and Earth is an utter freedom from the stain of sin (vss. 1-5), how could this be true if the New
Heaven and Earth were created at the start of the Millennium as some
have suggested? For there will yet be sin during the Millennium (Zech.
14:16-21) and there will be that awful rebellion which is specifically declared by Scripture to take place at the end of the 1000 years (20:7-9).
Then too, the Second Death takes place at the end of the 1000 years
(20:6). It is clear—sin, rebellion, and death are *not* done away with fully
until *after* the Millennial Kingdom. Thus the New Heaven and Earth with
its lack of any sin, rebellion, and death cannot begin until *after* the 1000
years. Thus the grand events of chapters 21 and 22 follow those of 20
just as the ordinary reader would here presume.

* Verses 18-25 speak of the Mil. Kgm., while vs. 17 goes beyond to the final state.

THE STAGES OF EARTH

THIS PRESENT EARTH

ETERNITY

ORIGINAL EARTH

"In the beginning God created the heaven and the earth."
(Genesis 1:1)

EARTH CURSED MAN SINS

Genesis 3

ANTEDELUVIAN Before the Flood AGE WICKEDNESS INCREASES

"And (God) spared not the old world, but saved Noah the eighth person, a preacher of righteousness, bringing in the flood upon the world of the ungodly."
(II Peter 2:5)

FLOOD JUDGMENT

". . . I will cause it to rain upon the earth . . . and every living substance that I have made will I destroy from off the face of the earth."
(Genesis 7:4)

PRESENT EVIL AGE

"(Christ) Who gave Himself for our sins, that He might deliver us from this present evil world . . ."
(Galatians 1:4)

TRIBULATION PERIOD JUDGMENT

"Then shall the Lord go forth, and fight against those nations . . . and His feet shall stand . . . upon the Mount of Olives . . ."
(Zechariah 14:3,4)

1000 YEAR MILLENNIAL AGE

". . . and they lived and reigned with Christ a thousand years."
(Revelation 20:4)

EARTH DESTROYED BY FIRE

". . . the elements shall melt with fervent heat, the earth also and the works that are therein shall be burned up."
(II Peter 3:10)

ETERNITY

THE NEW HEAVENS AND NEW EARTH

"And I saw a new heaven and a new earth: for the first heaven and the first earth were passed away; and there was no more sea."
(Revelation 21:1)

And there was no more sea.   Psa. 102:25:26

Commentary

"No more sea."—This may mean the absence of the Mediterranean, or of the vast oceans which now cover some seventy percent of the present earth's surface. All waters, in any event, shall not be done away with as John describes at least one river upon the New Earth (22:1-2). Perhaps this river will be akin to that of Eden (Gen. 2:10-14). There the "river" seems to be descriptive of a far-flung Mediterranean-oceanic system with its "heads" (sub-parts) being what we today call "rivers."

Perhaps the New Earth will be made as large as Jupiter???

Some commentators have enumerated SEVEN NEW THINGS within this new world, *viz.,*

> A New Heaven (21:1)
> A New Earth (21:1)
> A New Jerusalem (21:2, 10)
> A New People (21:3)
> A New Temple (21:22)
> A New Light (21:23)
> A New Edenic Paradise (22:2)

Background

It may be difficult for some to see how small and relatively insignificant the earth is until they see its position in our observable universe.

The top illustration shows the earth's size and position in relation to the Solar system.

The second drawing shows the Solar system (which includes the earth) in relation to the Milky Way. The Solar system is identified by an arrow.

The third picture shows the Milky Way in relation to the supercluster of 2500 galaxies.

And the last illustration shows the supercluster of galaxies in relation to our observable universe.

NOW READ PSALM 8:3,4 and these words will have greater depth of meaning to you.

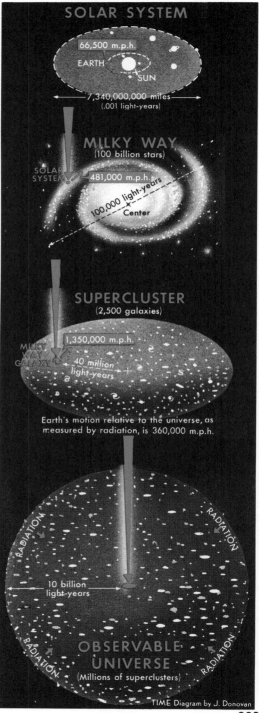

SOLAR SYSTEM

66,500 m.p.h.

EARTH

SUN

7,340,000,000 miles
(.001 light-years)

MILKY WAY
(100 billion stars)

SOLAR SYSTEM

481,000 m.p.h.

100,000 light-years

Center

SUPERCLUSTER
(2,500 galaxies)

MILKY WAY GALAXY

1,350,000 m.p.h.

40 million light-years

Earth's motion relative to the universe, as measured by radiation, is 360,000 m.p.h.

OBSERVABLE UNIVERSE
(Millions of superclusters)

RADIATION

RADIATION

RADIATION

RADIATION

10 billion light-years

TIME Diagram by J. Donovan

329

Revelation 21

2 And I John saw the holy city, new Je-ru-sa-lem, coming down from God out of heaven, prepared as a bride adorned for her husband.
3 And I heard a great voice out of heaven saying, Behold, the tabernacle of God *is* with men, and he will dwell with them, and they shall be his people, and God himself shall be with them, *and be* their God.

VERSES 2, 3

Rev. 3:12

Rev. 19:7

1 Chr. 17:5,6; Exod. 25:8,

2 Cor. 6:18
Gen. 17:7

Commentary

2. 2 Peter 3:12-13 describes the New Heavens and Earth as coming forth after the former ones have had their "elements melt with fervent heat." This causes some to wonder lest anything might happen to those believers on earth at the close of the millennial kingdom. After God saved the "Beloved City" and "the camp of the saints" from destruction by the rebellious hordes following Satan (20;9), would He somehow allow the saints to be consumed in the final earth consuming conflagration? The answer is obvious, and here in 21:2,3 is the proof.

The believers are preserved in the Holy City, and after the earth is burned and re-newed the believers descend safely in the Holy City. The physics of this we are not told. Yet we are told the wonderful results— the New Jerusalem descends in glory as a bride. She is the bride of Christ by virtue of her housing His people whom He loves and for whom He died. Notice: With the coming of the New Heaven and Earth and the descent of New Jerusalem, believers now spend their eternity "in heaven" UPON THE NEW EARTH!

I once heard a Rev. John Ashbrook, Jr. suggest that it was "not lawful" for Paul to tell what he had seen when he was "caught up into Paradise" because the people would not believe it. They would consider such things—because they were too marvelous for human credibility—to be mere imagination (2 Cor. 12:4; Isa. 64:4). They would be like that King of Siam who once said to the American ambassador, upon hearing the former tell of frozen white water upon which men could walk..."Before I thought you told lies; now I know that you tell lies." Perhaps this is one of the reasons for God withholding from us many of the details concerning the New Jerusalem and its origin.

3. *"Behold the tabernacle of God is with men."*—The Greek word for "Tabernacle" is *skene,* meaning "tent." It is the word from which we get the English word "scene," since in the Greek dramas the actors changed costumes in the painted tent at the stage.

No more sin; God will "tent" with man. He will manifest Himself in this city just as He now does in Heaven. No wonder this announcement was preceded with the startling word, "Behold!"

Close-up of section of Dome of the Rock reveals intricate mosaic inlay. Yet the new Jerusalem coming down from God will be beyond human description in beauty.

Background

It may be difficult at first to understand how a city can come down from Heaven to earth. But anyone living through the Tribulation Period would not be surprised. For during this period they witnessed many most unusual judgments occur and this phenomena will not be unbelievable when it occurs.

The mechanics of how this comes about we are not told. We have many questions...but God has chosen at this time not to reveal the answers. Yet we are shown the glorious result...and that is really what is important! The New Jerusalem descends in glory housing God's people whom He loves and for whom Christ died.

Believers now spend their eternity "in heaven" UPON THE NEW EARTH dwelling forever in happiness with God. Here at last there is a city and people wherein perfect love and peace dwells. The initial joy of a newly married couple often fades after time passes; here, however, the joy of the redeemed will never fade nor find disappointment.

PAST	PRESENT	RAPTURE	FIRST 3 1/2 TRIBULATION LAST 3 1/2		ARMA-GEDDON	MIL-LENNIUM	NEW HEAVENS & EARTH
			FIRST 3 1/2	LAST 3 1/2			▼

4 And God shall wipe away all tears from their eyes; and there shall be no more death, neither sorrow, nor crying, neither shall there be any more pain: for the former things are passed away.

Isa. 65:19*

5 And he that sat upon the throne said, Behold, I make all things new. And he said unto me, Write: for these words are true and faithful.

Rev. 3:14

Definition:
Glorified *(from the Greek:* doxazo, *"I glorify;" compare: Doxology).*
When applied to the final state of the believer this word refers to God's making the believer perfect...justified, having eternal life, and not able to sin—yet free. Hence the prayer, "In Thy service is perfect freedom; in Thy presence is fullness of joy forevermore."

Commentary

4. In the New Creation sin is no more, Alleluia! Sin always has its evil and damaging effects on both the sinner himself and upon others nearby who are also injured. When God permitted man to sin the gate for the entrance to immense suffering, of course, was also opened. The sister of Sin is Suffering; the two are inseparable companions. The sorrow, pain, and death in this world of agony all come because of sin. This is true, despite the skeptics attempting to show that suffering is merely a result of lack of education...or a necessary rung on the evolutionary ladder to perfection.

In the world to come, after the 1000 years and the White Throne Judgment, sin will be gone forever. The saints who have been given everlasting life will be "glorified" and they will have a nature confirmed in doing righteousness. As the Latin theologians put it, they will be *Posse non peccare et non posse peccare* ("Able not to-sin and not able to-sin").

With the passing away of sin, the awful effects of sin depart. Gone will be the "tears...death...sorrow...crying...pain." Could it be said more completely? Could it be spoken more tenderly..."God shall wipe away all tears from their eyes."

5. God announces that in the world to come all things will be new... never contaminated by sin...therefore perfect.

"Write...these words are true and faithful."—Just as we sigh that these things are too grand to be true, God again assures us by His sacred unbreakable word that these descriptions are "true and faithful."

* 65:20, however, refers to the Millennial Age. In 65:17-21 Isaiah sees the millennium and the eternal state together.

Special wide angle view shows Gethsemane in foreground. In background is Inner City wall of Jerusalem with Golden Gate. Dome of Rock slightly visible is next to Golden Gate.

Background

No earthly pen can hope to convey the completeness of joy and the fullness of peace that will be ours as Christians, born-again believers, in God's New Heaven and New Earth!

But some day, God will reveal our Heavenly inheritance and it will be beyond human words...

> The false and empty shadows
> The life of sin, are past -
> God gives me mine inheritance
> The land of life at last.

One of the first inklings that God gives us about His Divine inheritance for us is found in the Old Testament book of Isaiah:

> For, behold, I create new heavens and a new earth: and the former shall not be remembered, nor come into mind (Isaiah 65:17).

I wonder if you can grasp the full significance of this verse? What God is revealing to us is that not only is He going to create a New Heaven and a New Earth...but it will be so wonderful, so breathless in sight that it will occupy all of our thoughts and we will not even remember this old world which we now call Earth!

> For since the beginning of the world men have not heard, nor perceived by the ear, neither hath the eye seen, O God, beside thee, what He hath prepared for him that waiteth for Him (Isaiah 64:4).

PAST	PRESENT	RAPTURE	FIRST 3 1/2 / LAST 3 1/2 TRIBULATION	ARMA- GEDDON	MIL- LENNIUM	NEW HEAVENS & EARTH

Revelation 21

6 And he said unto me, It is done. I am Al-pha and O-meg-a, the beginning and the end. I will give unto him that is athirst of the fountain of the water of life freely.
7 He that overcometh shall inherit all things; and I will be his God, and he shall be my son.
8 But the fearful, and unbelieving, and the abominable, and murderers, and whoremongers, and sorcerers, and idolaters, and all liars, shall have their part in the lake which burneth with fire and brimstone: which is the second death.

Rev. 1:8; 22:13

*Mt. 6:33; Rom. 8:32;
   Mk. 10:29*
2 Cor. 6:18

Gal. 5:19-21

Definition: Universalist.—*This is one who holds to the unbiblical teaching that eventually all of mankind, including those who have died unrepentant, will be saved.*

Commentary

6. Here as in 1:8 and 22:13, Christ (who is the apparent speaker as a comparison between 22:13 and 22:16 shows) calls Himself the Alpha and the Omega. As has been said before, this must be seen as a claim of deity. If as the early Arian heresy claimed—which heresy was settled at the First Council of Constantinople in 325 A.D.—Jesus was created by the Father after the Father had already been eternally in existence, then Jesus would not be the alpha, but the beta. He would be the second letter; but not the first. But He is the Alpha, and hence the first in existence as well as being first in every sphere.

As God, Jesus can give eternal life, here pictured as water since water is a vital life necessity. The only requirement here mentioned is that one must be "athirst" (Greek: *dipsao*). To be athirst a person must need water badly and at the same time desire it. This aptly depicts the human dead in sin who desires eternal life. To this one Christ promises to give salvation freely. What a grand promise for the SINNER! For you???

7. The reward for overcoming sin by asking Christ for mercy at the cross is to "inherit all things." Christ promises to this one all of the glories of the eternal kingdom.

8. The unrepentant sinners, however, will have their portion in the Lake of Fire. In verse 6, the thirsty one who will turn to Christ for forgiveness is given a PROMISE OF LIFE; here in verse 8 the unrepentant is assured of his fate by a PROMISE OF DEATH. Let the Universalists say what they will; the unbelieving will not receive eternal life.

Background

One of the wonderful promises the Christian can look forward to is a *new body.* Scriptures indicate that we will be the same person having the same soul as we now have. At our resurrection, however, our body is replaced with a new glorified body.

The characteristics of this new body will no doubt bear a relationship to our former body much like the qualities of Christ's resurrection body bore to His same pre-resurrection body.

You will recall that the final relationship between Christ and His saints is partially revealed in Christ's prayer of intercession in Gethsemane when He prayed:

> Father, I will that they also, whom thou hast given me, be with me where I am; that they may behold my glory, which thou hast given me....

(John 17:24)

"The fearful." - Greek, *deilos.* In this context (verse 8) these can only be those who are afraid to confess God and to come to Christ for forgiveness of their sins because they fear human persecution or ridicule (Luke 12:8-9).

★ ★ ★ ★ ★

PAST	PRESENT	RAPTURE	FIRST 3 1/2 TRIBULATION	LAST 3 1/2	ARMA– GEDDON	MIL– LENNIUM	NEW HEAVENS & EARTH

Revelation 21

9 And there came unto me one of the seven angels which had the seven vials full of the seven last plagues, and talked with me, saying, Come hither, I will shew thee the bride, the Lamb's wife.

10 And he carried me away in the spirit to a great and high mountain, and shewed me that great city, the holy Je-ru-sa-lem, descending out of heaven from God,

Rev. 22:17

Mt. 4:8; Ezek. 40:2

Commentary

9. One of the angels, which in chapters 15-16 was prophetically seen pouring down destruction upon the unrepentant world, now carries John away "in the spirit" to see the new city of the eternal state, New Jerusalem.

That the same angel who destroys the wicked also brings blessings to the righteous is altogether consistent with the unified biblical teachings concerning God and His angels. The modernists, however, claim that when the Bible speaks of the distribution of blessings, God can be given the credit; but when judgment is poured out they say that "a later writer must have added this element which is not compatible with the nature of a good God."

In 21:1-2 in a brief panorama John saw the New Heaven and Earth come into being and the New Jerusalem descend. Now from 21:9 to 22:5 the angel takes John and us for a more detailed gaze at this wonderful new city. This process of first describing the major events briefly and then returning to examine important details is also followed in Genesis 1 and 2. In Genesis 1 the entire creation is rapidly, though majestically, narrated; then Genesis 2 returns and gives us a detailed account of the creation of man. So here too. The coming of the New World was given in Rev. 21:1-2 and now in 21:9-22:5 we return to see the New Jerusalem in detail. Neither here, nor in the opening chapters of Genesis, are there "traces of two distinct and contradictory creation stories."

10. In Matthew 4:8 Satan carried away Jesus to a great and high mountain to show Him the kingdoms of this world. He wished to entice Jesus to sin in order that He, Jesus, might obtain these kingdoms "easily" and without enduring the cross. Jesus, however, would not yield to Satan, and now in God's own time from a high mountain God's eternal kingdom-city is seen coming into being. It comes as the Lamb's Bride and it far surpasses anything that Satan could have promised (Dan. 7:13-14). So it is always. If we will but resist temptation and turn to Christ, God's eternal reward will outshine the glitter of Satan's illusory promises.

All that is left of the grandeur that was once Hisham's Palace built in 724 A.D. during the Omayyad dynasty. Man's cities soon crumble. The NEW JERUSALEM will be eternal.

Background

It is important to remember that this New City, NEW JERUSALEM, will not be the identical city on this present earth that we know as Jerusalem.

God reveals to John, the author of this God-inspired Book of Revelation in the Bible, that great city, Jerusalem, descending out of Heaven.

This New City, Jerusalem, is suspended over the earth as John initially sees it in the future!

One of the very interesting aspects of these new things is that while God chose to reveal to us in one single verse the creation of the New Heavens and Earth...there are at least 25 verses which describe in very great detail the "great city, the holy Jerusalem" (Revelation chapters 21 and 22).

Note this. The Heavenly City descends from out of heaven. Man does not create it; not even millennial man. So too, the stone of Daniel 2:34, 35,45 which inaugurates the earthly Kingdom of God is described as a stone "cut without [human] hands."

PAST	PRESENT	RAPTURE	FIRST 3½ LAST 3½ TRIBULATION		ARMA– GEDDON	MIL– LENNIUM	NEW HEAVENS &EARTH

11 Having the glory of God: and her light
was like unto a stone most precious, even
like a jasper stone, clear as crystal;

Definition:
Anthropomorphic.—*This word comes from the Greek* anthropos, *"man,"*
and morphe, *"outward form." It thus means "man shaped," that is, some-*
thing described or viewed in terms of the language, experiences, and
knowledge of man.

Commentary

11. Here John attempts to describe in anthropomorphic terms what the
holy city looked like to him. Her light is "like unto" (Greek: *homoios)* the
light coming from a dazzling crystalline jasper. A jasper reflects a green-
white light. From this and what follows we get a glimpse, a peek, into the
glories of heaven. John here attempts to tell us what cannot be fully told
(Isaiah 64:4!).

May we compare him to a primitive native blindfolded while yet in his
jungle, and then after being transported having the blind removed at
night when he stands amid Chicago's O Hare International Airport. His
description of this glimpse would then, on his return to his native
friends, have to be "Junglepocentric"—or in terms of the jungle life
which his companions could comprehend. For him to say, "Then we saw
a Boeing 747 land with full flaps down," would be meaningless. He
might have to describe this as a gigantic flying elephant. Thus the Apostle John tells us of New Jerusalem; but since his account is inspired of
God we know that it is not only helpful but trustworthy and accurate.

Background

In this New Jerusalem there will be no more tears...no more pain.
There will be no more sorrow, no crying. There will be no more death
(Revelation 21:4). What a glorious transformation...when His blessed
face I see...no more pain and no more sorrow...O what glory that will
be!

As the Eisenhower family looks on representatives from each of the Armed Forces bear the casket of General Eisenhower to the National Cathedral in Washington.

PAST	PRESENT	RAPTURE	FIRST 3 1/2 TRIBULATION	LAST 3 1/2	ARMA-GEDDON	MIL-LENNIUM	NEW HEAVENS & EARTH

Revelation 21

VERSES 12, 13, 14, 15
Isa. 56:5; 60:18

12 And had a wall great and high, *and* had twelve gates, and at the gates twelve angels, and names written thereon, which are *the names* of the twelve tribes of the children of Is-ra-el:
13 On the east three gates; on the north three gates; on the south three gates; and on the west three gates.
14 And the wall of the city had twelve foundations, and in them the names of the twelve apostles of the Lamb.
15 And he that talked with me had a golden reed to measure the city, and the gates thereof, and the wall thereof.

Rev. 11:1-2;
Ezek. 40:2-3

Commentary

12-14. The wall of the city manifests its eternal security. It will radiate through the eons the message that there is security only with God.

There are twelve gates named for the twelve tribes of Israel, and twelve foundations named for the apostles stand alternately between each two gates. It is difficult to escape the fact that here we have in this eternal city a togetherness of both the believers of Old Testament Israel and of the New Testament times. One group is not exalted above the other; neither is one group inside engaged in Bible study while the other group is outside plowing the earth—as some might have us believe. They are now together in eternity with Christ. How wonderful! Similarly see 15:3 where both the Songs of Moses and of the Lamb, Christ, are song.

15. The measurements are made with a golden measuring stick. It is fitting that precious things be measured and handled with apropos equipment.

In Hell there will be no refreshing stream of water to cool parched lips.

Background

While believers are enjoying their inheritance in the New Jerusalem... all non-believers with Satan with Antichrist and with the False Prophet will have their part in the Lake of Fire.

Contrary to popular belief, that will *not* be a time for grand reunions. It *will* be a time for eternal torment!

It will be:

1. A Place of Consciousness (Luke 16:23,24)
2. A Place of Torment (Luke 16:23,24,28)
3. A Place of Darkness (Matthew 8:12)
4. Eternal Separation from loved ones who are believers (Luke 13:28)
5. Not the Slightest Hope of Release (Matthew 25:46, Hebrews 6:2)
6. The Torment of Memory in Hell (Luke 16:27,28)

Think of the suffering those in Hell will go through as they remember the opportunities to accept Christ that they rejected.

PAST	PRESENT	RAPTURE	FIRST 3 1/2	LAST 3 1/2	ARMA-GEDDON	MIL-LENNIUM	NEW HEAVENS & EARTH
			TRIBULATION				

16 And the city lieth foursquare, and the length is as large as the breadth: and he measured the city with the reed, twelve thousand furlongs. The length and the breadth and the height of it are equal.

1 Kgs. 6:19-20

Commentary

16. This description of the city's size shows that it has a square base and that its length, breadth, and height are all equal in measurement. Thus the city may either be a cube or a square-based pyramid. The suggestion that the entire city is a huge Holy of Holies, cubical in shape as was the sacred inner sanctuary of the Temple (1 Kg. 6:20), perfectly fits the truth that this city will be the very place in which God makes His dwelling (verse 22).

The city's dimension of 12,000 furlongs (Greek: *stadion,* hence "stadium") has every aspect of being the literal size of the city despite its obvious symbolical use of the "governmental number" 12 (There were 12 tribes and 12 apostles).

If the 12,000 stadia is the length of merely one side, then at 607 feet per Attic Stadium, the city will be 1380 miles to a side with an area of 1,900,000 square miles.

If the 12,000 stadia are the circumference, then each side will be 3000 stadia or 345 miles, and the area of the city will be 119,000 square miles. This is an immense area for a city even if it is only 1/16th of the former figure. Previous to the modern "Megapolis" concept, a city of such proportions was but a dream.

For population let us compare this city with the 117 square mile City of London which contained in 1956 3,273,000 inhabitants (Not to be confused with Greater London with its 8 million in 1956). By slide rule I calculate that with a similar population density as London, New Jerusalem (3000 stadia to a side) will have a population of 3,330,000,000 or 3 1/3 billions of *redeemed* people! If the city is a full 12,000 stadia to a side, then the population reaches the astounding figure of 53 billion!

"For since the beginning of the world *men* have not heard, nor perceived by the ear, neither hath the eye seen, O God, beside thee, *what* he hath prepared for him that waiteth for him." Isaiah 64:4

Background

6% of world's population lives in North America yet they devour

35% of its annual production of raw materials.

EVERY SECOND

+ **4** New Babies are Born

− **2** People Die

2 NET GAIN
People every Second

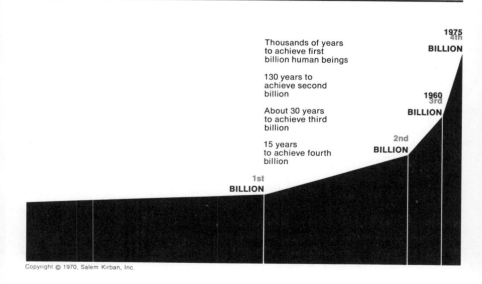

Thousands of years to achieve first billion human beings

130 years to achieve second billion

About 30 years to achieve third billion

15 years to achieve fourth billion

1st **BILLION**

2nd **BILLION**

1960 3rd **BILLION**

1975 4th **BILLION**

| PAST | PRESENT | RAPTURE | FIRST 3 1/2 | LAST 3 1/2 | ARMA- | MIL- | NEW |
| | | | TRIBULATION | | GEDDON | LENNIUM | HEAVENS &EARTH |

17 And he measured the wall thereof, an hundred *and* forty *and* four cubits; *according to* the measure of a man, that is, of the angel.
18 And the building of the wall of it was *of* jasper: and the city *was* pure gold, like unto clear glass.
19 And the foundations of the wall of the city *were* garnished with all manner of precious stones. The first foundation *was* jasper; the second, sapphire; the third, a chalcedony; the fourth, an emerald;
20 The fifth, sardonyx; the sixth, sardius; the seventh, chrysolyte; the eighth, beryl; the ninth, a topaz; the tenth, a chrysoprasus; the eleventh, a jacinth; the twelfth, an amethyst.

Rev. 14:1; 7:4

Commentary

17. The cubit was the distance from the elbow to the tip of the extended fingers of the hand. It is usually approximated at 1 1/2 feet. If the angel speaking to John was about the size of a man, which is the usual Scriptural way in which angels manifest themselves (Gen. 18:2; etc.), then the 1 1/2 foot per cubit may not be far from accurate.

At this rate the wall which surrounds the city would be about 216 feet high. Such a wall size might better fit a pyramid shaped city. Against this, however, is the obvious allusion that this city is a Holy of Holies, and hence cubical.

18-20. Here John tells us of the appearance of the city, with its several foundations glistening as huge gemstones which he names. Oh, the glory that abides here in the city where God and His ransomed people will forever dwell.

Background

How long is ETERNITY?

Eternity is forever. In this world, man must either decide to accept Christ as personal Lord and Saviour...or by sinful indecision, reject Him.

Based on that decision he destines himself either for God's forgiveness and an eternity in Heaven or for God's judgment and an eternity in Hell.

Try to imagine that this earth upon which we dwell is nothing but sand. Now try to imagine that a little bird could fly through space from a faraway planet to ours and carry back with him a tiny grain of sand, and that the round trip would take a thousand years.

Now try to imagine how long it would take for that little bird to carry away this entire earth, a grain of sand each thousand years!

The time required for this would be *but a moment* in comparison to eternity!

Where do you want to spend ETERNITY?

PAST	PRESENT	RAPTURE	FIRST 3 1/2 LAST 3 1/2 TRIBULATION	ARMA-GEDDON	MIL-LENNIUM	NEW HEAVENS & EARTH

Revelation 21

21 And the twelve gates *were* twelve pearls; every several gate was of one pearl: and the street of the city *was* pure gold, as it were transparent glass.

VERSE 21

Psa. 84:10

Rev. 22:2; Zech. 8:4,5

Commentary

21. Many indeed are the folk songs which sing of walking through "those pearly gates" and of walking down "those golden streets!" The redeemed will someday have the privilege of walking upon these streets.

The Greek word for pearl is *margarites,* and hence the names Margaret and Marguerite mean "Pearl." We are informed that each of the twelve city gates will be a pearl. Apparently John saw these gates as large glistening white orbs with probably an archway gate through each.

Sometimes you hear believers disputing over the exact chemical composition of these gates. Let us remember that John here speaks in the *language of appearance*—he saw the gates to be large, white, glistening, and to be round. He is thus proper and accurate to call them "pearls." In fact, what else could he call them? He did not have either the opportunity nor the irreverence to attempt to chemically test the gates so as to ascertain their precise composition. Will they be chemically identical to the pearl formed within the shells of oysters? Perhaps yes—God could certainly duplicate this substance on a large scale; or perhaps no—God may be pleased to make His gates of a compound even superior to that of natural pearl. In any case it is obvious that this city will be in every respect exceedingly wonderful.

The same for the street of gold which glistened "as transparent glass." This is what John saw and this is what these gates and this street will be like. The important thing today is to make sure that you are trusting in Christ as the one who paid the just penalty for your sins. Then when that day comes you will have ample time to think about the pearly gates and the golden street.

"The street of the city."—It appears that here John is calling our attention to the main boulevard through this city.

Background

It is interesting to compare the first Jerusalem that we know on this earth with the Heavenly Jerusalem.

Present JERUSALEM:

Built by man's hands

Built of stones,
            mortar, wood

Home for a few generations
            of people

Embroiled in conflict

Heavenly JERUSALEM:

Built without hands -
            hence built by God

Built of transparent gold,
            precious stones

An everlasting home for
            all in Christ

Peace forevermore

The glory of the Holy City, the new city of Jerusalem, will lie in the fact that it is the city wherein God dwells - with the redeemed. Here ALL THINGS NEW, not all new things. The things that God once made and called good are not now abandoned to never again come into being - light, trees, water, animals...they are rather now made anew, afresh.

PAST	PRESENT	RAPTURE	FIRST 3 1/2 LAST 3 1/2 TRIBULATION		ARMA-GEDDON	MIL-LENNIUM	NEW HEAVENS & EARTH
PAST	PRESENT	RAPTURE	FIRST 3 1/2	LAST 3 1/2	ARMA-GEDDON	MIL-LENNIUM	NEW HEAVENS & EARTH

Revelation 21

22 And I saw no temple therein: for the Lord God Almighty and the Lamb are the temple of it.

VERSE 22

2 Chr. 7

Mal. 3:1

Commentary

22. 2 Chronicles 7 is the chapter which tells of the dedication of the Temple which Solomon built (10th century B.C.). From it, as well as from other places in the Scriptures, we can see that the Temple was a place wherein the Holy God would dwell in a special way in the midst of His people. Because all the inhabitants of the earth were sinners God's holiness demanded some type of isolation from this sin—this the Temple provided. But since God was a merciful God who was willing to forgive His people for their sins when they called upon His name in repentance and prayer, the Temple also provided a localized manifestation of His presence where this could be done.

In the world to come, however, since all sinners will have already been excluded at the Great White Throne judgment and since the New Earth will never have been touched by sin's defilement, there will no more be a need for a Temple building. There will no more be a need for God to be isolated from His people—for they will all be sinless. Thus the ever omnipresent God will fill the New Jerusalem, and in fact the entire New Earth, with His manifest presence. Now the cubical New Jerusalem with all of its hugeness becomes the inner Holy of Holies where the Lord abides, and the entire New Earth becomes the outer Holy Place wherein the Lord also dwells.

PAST	PRESENT	RAPTURE	FIRST 3 1/2 LAST 3 1/2 TRIBULATION		ARMA-GEDDON	MIL-LENNIUM	NEW HEAVENS & EARTH
			FIRST 3 1/2	LAST 3 1/2			

23 And the city had no need of the sun, neither of the moon, to shine in it: for the glory of God did lighten it, and the Lamb *is* the light thereof.

24 And the nations of them which are saved shall walk in the light of it: and the kings of the earth do bring their glory and honour into it.

Isa. 60:1

Isa. 60:3

Zech. 16:19*

* Speaking of the Millennium.

Commentary

23. The Scriptures declare that "God is light;" and Christ referred to Himself as "The light of the world" (1 John 1:5; John 8:12). While these verses speak primarily of spiritual light rather than physical light, nevertheless the Bible frequently tells of manifestations of physical light when God's presence draws nigh.

Thus at the dedication of Solomon's Temple all of Israel could physically see a divine manifestation of light in the Temple when the "glory of the Lord filled the house" (2 Chron. 7:1-3). So too when God's presence suddenly manifested itself at the Mosaic tabernacle in order to give some pronouncement suddenly the people could see the glory of the Lord by the presence of some type of illuminated cloud (Nu. 16:41,42).

This light of God's presence has been called the *Shechinah* Glory. The word "Shechinah" is an Aramaic-Hebrew word, though not found in the Bible, which means "residence [of God]." Thus the entire city of New Jerusalem will be illuminated by this Shechinah Glory of God. Although we do not yet understand the physics of precisely how this light will operate, we can be assured that it will function and come to pass just as here described.

24. *"And the nations...which are saved..."*—The words "which are saved" are not in the ancient Greek manuscripts. All the nations which are in the world to come will, however, be "saved."

From this verse, brief as it is, we get the impression that there will be an organization of the world to come into nations and rulers. Further, if the "kings of the earth do bring their glory...into it" then the city, the New Jerusalem, cannot be equated with the New Earth, and in this city the King especially dwells. This is similar to the case of ancient Israel. Jerusalem was not all of Israel, but the King and the Temple dwelled in Jerusalem in a special way. Here, all the redeemed will have access to the capital New Jerusalem.

PAST	PRESENT	RAPTURE	FIRST 3 1/2 TRIBULATION	LAST 3 1/2	ARMA-GEDDON	MIL-LENNIUM	NEW HEAVENS & EARTH

(1 Corinthians 15:24)

THE KING and the KINGDOM

God promised the Kingdom to David and his seed in the Old Testament (2 Samuel 7:8-17). And this promise is unchanged in the New Testament (Luke 1:31-33).

1. Christ, as King, was born in Bethlehem of a virgin (Matthew 2:1; 1:18-25).

2. John the Baptist, Christ and the Twelve apostles announced that the Kingdom was "at hand" (Matthew 4:17).
   The Jews, however, rejected their King. He was crowned with thorns and crucified.

3. Mysteries of the Kingdom were revealed by Christ prior to His crucifixion. These were to be fulfilled in the interval between His rejection and His return to glory (Matthew 13:1-50).

4. Christ announced His purpose: to build His church (**ekklesia**—*church*, that is, a "congregation" of the King's people; never in the New Testament is it a building. Matthew of 16:18).

5. At the Rapture the mysteries of the kingdom will be brought to an end by the "harvest" (Matthew 13:39-43, 49-50).

6. Dispersed Israel (the Jewish people) will finally be fully regathered upon His return to earth. He will establish His power over all the earth. See Matthew 24:27-30; Acts 15:14-17; Zechariah 12:10.

7. The Kingdom of Heaven will then be established under David's divine Son, Jesus Christ. He will reign 1000 years—the Millennium (Daniel 2:44; 7:13-14; Revelation 20:1-10).

8. When Christ defeats the last enemy, death, He will deliver the kingdom to "God, even the Father" (1 Corinthians 15:24-28).

Christ must be King and reign until He has put all His enemies under His feet (Psalm 110:1).

What a thrilling picture, a photographer's conception of how the table at the Marriage Supper of the Lamb might appear.

25 And the gates of it shall not be shut at all by day: for there shall be no night there.
26 And they shall bring the glory and honour of the nations into it.
27 And there shall in no wise enter into it any thing that defileth, neither *whatsoever* worketh abomination or *maketh* a lie: but they which are written in the Lamb's book of life.

Zech. 14:16-21*

Ezek. 44:9

*Speaking of the Millennium.

Commentary

25-26. My neighbors some years ago in Winona Lake used to keep their door unlocked day and night; we locked ours. Our Lord told us that on this earth "thieves break through and steal" (Matt. 6:19; John 10:1). In the eternal state there will be no more sinners, so the gates of the city will not have to be locked at night as were the entrances to the ancient cities (Josh. 2:5,7).

27. No sinner will ever enter. It is not that they will be upon the New Earth, but not permitted to come into the city. No, rather, they have been destroyed previously at the Great White Throne judgment and they are now forever in the Lake of Fire and thus unable to enter this heavenly originated city.

That the liar is specifically mentioned ought to give pause to any who have fallen into the sin of telling lies.

The Greek of this verse is quite interesting. The construction, "And there shall in no wise enter...but...," is made by the Greek emphatic double negative *ou me* translated "in no wise" and then by an emphatic exception *ei me* translated "but." The force of this might be paraphrased, "And there shall positively-not enter...except-however-only..."

Let it be acknowledged as clear, only the repentant sinners who have been washed by the blood of the Lamb will partake of the life to come; those who die in their sins "shall positively-not enter" the Holy City.

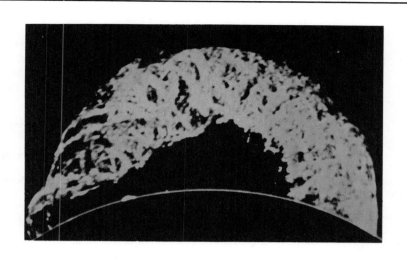

Background

Through God's providence our earth's atmosphere acts as a shield to protect us, at present, from the sun. In June, 1946 the Sun sent out an arch of flame that soared above the Sun over ONE MILLION MILES - which is more than the diameter of the Sun!

The power of the sun? The sun is a fantastically hot cosmic radiation powerhouse similar to the countless stars out in the vast unfathomable distances of space. Its surface temperature is 11,000° F., and its interior temperature is estimated as high as 18,000,000° F. Imagine, if you can, a cake of ice one and one-half miles square and 93 million miles high. It would reach from earth to sun. Scientists tell us that this gigantic cake of ice would be completely melted in 30 *seconds* if the full power of the sun could be focused upon it!

Now, can you see what natural elements now already create a "fervent heat"...a heat, such as this, stands waiting for the moment of God's kindling it.

One day, in God's time, this earth will be purged by fire. This is the day the Earth burns up!

But for the Christian it is a day of new life:

> We, according to His promise, look for new heavens and a new earth.

(2 Peter 3:13)

PAST	PRESENT	RAPTURE	FIRST 3 1/2	LAST 3 1/2	ARMA-GEDDON	MIL-LENNIUM	NEW HEAVENS & EARTH
			TRIBULATION				

CHAPTER 22

1 AND he shewed me a pure river of water of life, clear as crystal, proceeding out of the throne of God and of the Lamb.
2 In the midst of the street of it, and on either side of the river, *was there* the tree of life, which bare twelve *manner of* fruits, *and* yielded her fruit every month: and the leaves of the tree *were* for the healing of the nations.

Ezek. 47:1; Zech. 14:8-9*

Gen. 3:22; Rev. 2:7

Gen. 3:7; Matt. 21:19

*Speaking of the Millennium

Commentary

CHAPTER 22

22:1-5 DESCRIPTION OF THE NEW JERUSALEM CONTINUED
22:6-21 EPILOGUE

1. Out of the throne—from underneath it or actually gushing from its base—proceeds the River "of water of life." Are the contents of this river called "The Water of Life" as a symbolic name to remind all forever that Christ was truly the giver of the water of life (John 4:13-14; 1 Cor. 10:4 and Exod. 17:6)? Or *in addition* do these waters somehow have life giving properties???

2. Here we see in the everlasting kingdom a "Tree of Life." From the description placing it in the midst of the street (the main boulevard of the city) and on both sides of the river, it appears that this is a type of tree rather than merely one single specimen.

This tree also apparently yields a different type of fruit each month in a yearly cycle. This alone should still the anxious hearts of those who have heard someone philosophizing that in the eternal state there shall be no time sequence—all will be one big now. No, here we see a continuing time sequence of twelve-month years.

How will the fruit of this tree be for the healing of the nations? The word translated "healing" is *therapeia.* It means "serving, care, or healing" (Hence, "therapy").

Since there will be no wounds or sickness in the eternal state (21:4) the fruit of this tree would not be for the healing of that which is injured or decayed. Thus the fruit of this tree must be, it would seem, for the "service and care" *(therapeia)* of the nations—that is, for their nutrition and well being.

A sermon by Arthur W. Pink, which I read long ago, still lingers in my mind. It concerned the crucial Biblical trees:

The Tree of the Knowledge of Good and Evil (Gen. 2:17)
The Tree of Life (Gen. 3:22)
The Tree of Calvary (Acts 5:30; Gal. 3:13; 1 Pet. 2:24)
The Tree of Life (Rev. 22:2)

Background

> He the pearly gates will open
> So that I may enter in,
>
> For He purchased my redemption
> And forgave me all my sin!

It is hard for man to fathom the characteristics of this New City, Jerusalem. It is also an eternal city WITHOUT a Temple!

You will recall that there will be a Temple in the Millennial earth. But here in the New City, Jerusalem, there will be no need for a Temple. Christ will be that Temple. The entire city will be that Temple - a vast cubical (Revelation 21:16) Holy of Holies wherein God dwells.

Since our redemption will have been completed and our conversation and thoughts will be holy we will be dwelling with God in that Holy City. Thus behold how God fully saves us from sin:

Past - When we initially believed in Christ - we were saved from the PENALTY OF sin;

Present - When we abide daily in Christ - we are saved from the POLLUTION of sin;

Future - When we shall dwell in our glorified bodies in the New Jerusalem with Christ - we will be saved from the PRESENCE of sin.

PAST	PRESENT	RAPTURE	FIRST 3 1/2 LAST 3 1/2 TRIBULATION	ARMA-GEDDON	MIL-LENNIUM	NEW HEAVENS & EARTH

3 And there shall be no more curse: but the throne of God and of the Lamb shall be in it; and his servants shall serve him: 4 And they shall see his face; and his name *shall be* in their foreheads.

Gen. 3:14-19
Rom. 1:1; 1 Cor. 7:22

Commentary

3. In the new world the awful curse that fell upon man and upon the earth as the penalty for Adam's sin is no more (Gen. 3:14-19). The Apostle Paul spoke of this curse when he said, "For we know that the whole creation groaneth and travaileth in pain together until now" (Rom. 8;22). No, in "that land beyond the river" the ground will no longer be cursed and bear thorns and thistles; nor will man be separated from his God any more because of sin. Truly that will be "The Sweet By and By" so celebrated in the hymn.

4. Now we can hear the hymn, "When I Shall See Him Face To Face—and tell the story Saved by Grace." Words cannot express the joy which will be ours to see the Blessed Redeemer's face. Alas, what an opposite fate awaits the lost who do not wish to have Christ to rule over them (Matt. 7:23).

"His name...in their foreheads."—This is promised to the overcomer in 3:12. In 13:16 the False Prophet was seen placing the Antichrist's name on the foreheads of his faithful. That too was the Satanic imitation of what God would someday do for His own.

Today we can see high school students often proudly displaying their school button or banner. At sports events buttons are everywhere seen. People especially desire to be identified with a winning team. Pilots wear their wings with pride—and, alas, many communists with joy display their emblem of red. All the joy that these for the moment give their wearers pales into nothingness at the supreme joy which the believers will someday own forever at the privilege of bearing the name of their wonderful Saviour upon their brow.

Israeli paratroopers at Western Wall believed Six-Day War would bring them peace. But peace eludes and more trials are ahead. One day there shall be no more curse, but blessing.

PAST	PRESENT	RAPTURE	FIRST 3 1/2 TRIBULATION	LAST 3 1/2	ARMA-GEDDON	MIL-LENNIUM	NEW HEAVENS & EARTH

Revelation 22

5 And there shall be no night there; and they need no candle, neither light of the sun; for the Lord God giveth them light: and they shall reign for ever and ever.

VERSE 5

Exod. 28:36-38

Rev. 18:23

Commentary

5. Again, as in 21:23, we are assured that the light of the Lord's glory will sufficiently illuminate the eternal land. And God must know, for He it was who said, "Let there be light," and "there was light" (Gen. 1:3).

"And they shall reign for ever and ever."—Literally: "Unto the ages of the ages"—hence forever and ever. It was good enough for the Gibeonites, having escaped death at the hands of Israel, to become their hewers of wood and drawers of water (Josh. 9:22-27). It would likewise be more than enough for us, who have been saved from judgment as sinners by Christ, to become bondslaves in the eternal state. And yet what saith the Scripture of the redeemed people?—"They shall reign forever and ever." We shall willingly be His bondslaves (1 Cor. 7:22); but we shall also reign with Him. Oh what grace!

Eternal time has no divisions to mark its passage; there is never a thunderstorm or blare of trumpets to announce the beginning of a new year. Even when a new century begins, it is only we mortals who ring bells and fire off pistols.

Background

Those infidels who haughtily claim that they would not wish to spend eternity "in heaven" because "it would get boring" know neither the wonderful Biblical teaching about "heaven" nor the awful truths about "hell."

PAST	PRESENT	RAPTURE	FIRST 3 1/2 — LAST 3 1/2 TRIBULATION	ARMA-GEDDON	MIL-LENNIUM	NEW HEAVENS & EARTH

REUNION or SEPARATION?

Soldier returns from dead. S/Sgt. James O. Williams is greeted by relatives as he arrives at airport in Detroit, Michigan on a 30-day leave. William's widowed mother had been notified by Army officers that her son had died in Vietnam. A telegram confirmed his death. But the next day Army authorities again called to report the Army had made a mistake.

What a wonderful reunion those who have accepted Christ as personal Saviour will have with their loved ones who have "gone ahead" from this earth. And what tragic sorrow and inexpressible grief awaits those who reject Christ. "And whosoever was not found written in the book of life was cast into the lake of fire" (Revelation 20:15).

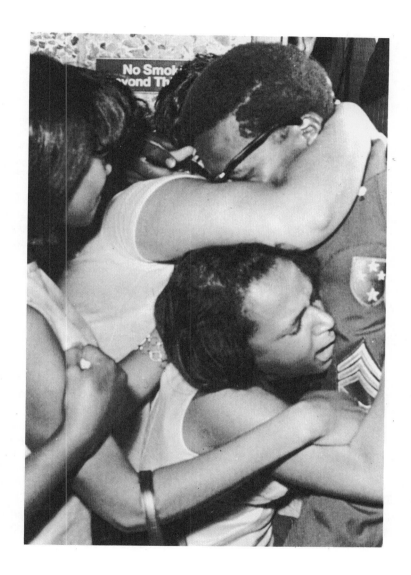

361

6 And he said unto me, These sayings *are* faithful and true: and the Lord God of the holy prophets sent his angel to shew unto his servants the things which must shortly be done.

7 Behold, I come quickly: blessed *is* he that keepeth the sayings of the prophecy of this book.

Rev. 3:14; Isa. 11:5
Rev. 1:1

Rev. 1:7; 22:20; Acts 1:11

Commentary

22:6-21 EPILOGUE (Final Word)

6. Again we are assured that the wondrous things and events recorded in this book are "faithful and true." How much this constant encouragement toward belief is needed can well be judged by the great unbelief, antipathy, and skepticism which everywhere greets this Apocalypse.

This book gives the final chapters in the world's history yet it has a bond with the remotest antiquity, for we read that the ultimate divine author of this book is none other than "the Lord God of the holy prophets."

Compare this first verse of the Epilogue with 1:1, the first verse of the introductory Prologue (1:1-8).

"To shew unto his servants the things which must shortly be done."— These words in the Greek are word for word and letter for letter identical to those of 1:1 which were translated, "To shew unto his servants things which must shortly come to pass." The slight differences in the English are due most likely to a translation committee that inadvertently did not compare the two.

7. *"Behold, I come quickly."*—Here just as in verse 6 in the words, "...the things which must shortly be done," we see time as God sees it. As I write it has been almost 1900 years since the Apostle John wrote. Jesus still has not yet come. This span of almost two millennia, however, is but a moment to God...and now we too, as we look back, can feel the rapidity at which the centuries have passed.

To us the promise still stands that those who keep the prophecy of this book will be blessed. But how do we "keep the sayings of the prophecy of this book"? Do we do this by "keeping" (remembering) them in our minds or do we do this by "keeping" (obeying) the admonitions?

Actually the Greek word translated "keep" *(tereo)* is used in both of these senses: (a) to hold, retain, preserve—John 2:10; and (b) to obey, observe, heed—Mt. 23:3. Thus here in Rev. 22:7 the one who will be blessed is the one who (a) retains and (b) obeys the message of this book.

Background

What will Heaven be like in this New City, JERUSALEM?

There will be no more separation!

All the saints of the ages will be there. No more will friends have to part again. No more will families have to have tearful farewells. What a grand reunion saints in Christ will enjoy forever and forever!

As Dr. Wilbur M. Smith has so wonderfully reminded us...there will be no need to carry photographs of our absent loved ones in order for us to renew our memory of them...for those who have been absent for years...will now be ever present. No more disagreements, or misunderstandings, with our loved ones. Together, the believers will rejoice in everlasting joy and companionship.

PAST	PRESENT	RAPTURE	FIRST 3 1/2 LAST 3 1/2 TRIBULATION	ARMA-GEDDON	MIL-LENNIUM	NEW HEAVENS & EARTH
Verse 6	Verse 7	Verse 7		Verse 7		

Revelation 22

VERSES 8, 9, 10

8 And I John saw these things, and heard *them*. And when I had heard and seen, I fell down to worship before the feet of the angel which shewed me these things.

John 21:24;
1 John 1:1-3

9 Then saith he unto me, See *thou do it not*: for I am thy fellowservant, and of thy brethren the prophets, and of them which keep the sayings of this book: worship God.

Acts 14:11-18

10 And he saith unto me, Seal not the sayings of the prophecy of this book: for the time is at hand.

Dan. 12:4

Rev. 1:3

Commentary

8-9. Peter, in 2 Peter 1:16, assures us that he and the other apostles "have not followed cunningly devised fables...but were eyewitnesses of his majesty." Luke endeavors to do the same when in Luke 1:1-4 at the beginning of his gospel he certifies that his information comes from eyewitnesses.

John follows Peter and Luke and here affirms to us that he personally saw and heard the things recounted in this Apocalypse. The Greek literally reads:"And I John am the one hearing and seeing these things."

As has been mentioned before, here we see the angel absolutely refusing to allow himself to be worshipped. God alone, he says, is to be worshipped. Yet when John falls at the feet of Jesus (1:17)—or when Peter falls at Jesus' feet (Luke 5:8)—we have no record ever of Jesus rebuking them for this. No, Jesus accepted the homage of men which was due only to God. Jesus accepted the worship of the heavenly beings when they reverenced him along with God the Father. Why? Answer: Jesus is God. There is no other acceptable explanation. The Church has held this doctrine through the centuries, and all cultists who deny it are misled heretics.

10. The angel's command in this verse is in direct contrast to Daniel 12:4 wherein that prophet was ordered to "seal the book."

Since Christ's death and resurrection we have been in the "last times" and the spirit of Antichrist (though not yet the *person* of the Antichrist) has been growing in the world. 1 John 2:18 reads, *"Little children, it is the last time: and as ye have heard that Antichrist shall come, even now are there many antichrists; whereby ye know that it is the last time."*

Since the spirit of Antichrist is growing and since Christ's second coming may take place at any time, John is told not to seal up this prophecy. "The time is at hand" must be understood in the same way as "Behold, I come quickly" (22:7).

364

Dome of the Rock on Temple site area in Jerusalem.

Background

The Bible tells us the measurements of the New City, JERUSALEM in Revelation 21:16-21.

Size: About 1500 miles in each direction.

Dr. Wilbur M. Smith, in his book, THE BIBLICAL DOCTRINE OF HEAVEN gives us some insight from an Australian engineer.

The City will give you an area 2,250,000 square miles. This makes it 15,000 times as big as London; 20 times as big as New Zealand; 10 times as big as Germany and 10 times as big as France.

And it is 40 times as big as all England and even much bigger than India!

Taking the number of people to a square mile in the city of London, this Australian engineer, computed that the City Foursquare (the New Jerusalem) could hold 100 thousand MILLIONS - or about 70 times the present population of the globe!

PAST	PRESENT	RAPTURE	FIRST 3 ½ LAST 3 ½ TRIBULATION		ARMA-GEDDON	MIL-LENNIUM	NEW HEAVENS & EARTH

11 He that is unjust, let him be unjust still: and he which is filthy, let him be filthy still: and he that is righteous, let him be righteous still: and he that is holy, let him be holy still.
12 And, behold, I come quickly; and my reward *is* with me, to give every man according as his work shall be.
13 I am Alpha and Omega, the beginning and the end, the first and the last.

1 Cor. 3:12-15; 2 Cor. 5:10; Matt. 25:31-46; 7:21-23; Rev. 19:20 Rev. 1:8,17

Commentary

11. Now and to the end of the book through verse 20 (22:11-20) the Epilogue breaks into the rapturous *finale* with the speaker being Christ Himself. Note,

      1:1-8 PROLOGUE............22:6-21   EPILOGUE
      1:4-8 THE OVERTURE....22:11-20   THE FINALE

Here at the close of the book is a declaration not of "fixity of species," but of "fixity of character." This is the decree of eternity...the redeemed, made righteous by Christ's blood will forever remain righteous; while the unregenerate will retain their iniquitous nature forever.

12. Christ comes and brings His reward. How glorious. When I go away on trips my children wait anxiously for me to return for they know that at my arrival at the airport I will always have some trinket for them as a reward for their being good in my absence. This excitement of children at the return of their Daddy from a far off land can at most be only dimly compared to THE BLESSED HOPE OF THE CHURCH, THE SECOND COMING OF JESUS CHRIST.

"To give every man according as his work shall be."—To the believer at Christ's coming at the rapture this means the Judgment Seat of Christ when we shall be judged not in respect to salvation, but with respect to rewards (2 Cor. 5:10; 1 Cor. 3:12-15). To those alive at the close of the Tribulation Christ shall judge them as to their entrance into the Millennial Kingdom. The saved alone shall enter (Matt. 25:31-46).

Romans 14:10-13 is one of the passages most ignored in practice by Christians. It commands us not to judge our fellow Christians as if we were God. Our judgment is so often inaccurate; and we have beams in our eyes (Matt. 7:1-5). How reassuring it is for us to know that Christ is coming and that when He does come He personally will judge and reward all—both ourselves and others—accurately.

13. Again as in 1:8 and 1:17 we hear Jesus make the claim that He is deity as He claims to be the "Alpha and Omega..." (22:16 shows that Jesus is the speaker here in vs. 13).

NO GUARD
BUT GOD

Background

The Walls, Gates, and Foundations of the New Jerusalem

The Walls, Gates, and Foundations of the New Jerusalem

Wall:	The wall is approximately 216 feet high.
Gates:	It will have 12 gates.

The 12 gates are as 12 pearls in appearance, glistening! There are 3 gates facing in each direction. They are guarded by 12 angels. The names of the 12 tribes of Israel are on these gates.

Foundations: There are 12 foundations to the City, each named for one of the Apostles.

For he looked for a city which hath foundations, whose builder and maker is God.

(Hebrews 11:10 King James Version)

PAST	PRESENT	RAPTURE	FIRST 3 1/2 / LAST 3 1/2 TRIBULATION	ARMA-GEDDON	MIL-LENNIUM	NEW HEAVENS & EARTH

Revelation 22

14 Blessed *are* they that do his commandments, that they may have right to the tree of life, and may enter in through the gates into the city.

15 For without *are* dogs, and sorcerers, and whoremongers, and murderers, and idolaters, and whosoever loveth and maketh a lie.

16 I Jesus have sent mine angel to testify unto you these things in the churches. I am the root and the offspring of David, *and* the bright and morning star.

Rev. 21:24-26
Rev. 21:27

Rev. 1:1

Isa. 9:7; 11:1
2 Pet. 1:19

Commentary

14-15. Here in this pair of contrasting verses we have basically the identical message as in 21:24-27. In 21:24-26 as here in verse 14 we learn that...Blessed are the redeemed, for they will be allowed to enter the Holy City. In 21:27, as here in verse 15 we find that...Cursed are the unrepentant sinners, for they will remain forever outside of the City.

The fate of the righteous and of the unrighteous is oft times contrasted —as in Deut. 28:1ff, "Blessed...," and 28:15ff, "Cursed...." Men who claim to be the intellectuals of this world may becloud the issue, but God here makes both the choices for Him and against Him and the fates that each shall receive as a result crystal clear.

"For without are..."—It should not be thought that they are upon the New Earth immediately outside the walls of the New Jerusalem. No, these were sent away forever into the Lake of Fire (Rev. 20). They are "without" (Greek: *exo),* that is, "outside" of both the New Earth and the New Jerusalem forever. They have been cast into the "outer darkness" (Matt. 8:12; 22:13; 25:30).

16. *"I Jesus have sent mine angel."*—This portion of the Epilogue is similar to 1:1 of the Prologue. "Angel" (Greek, *angelos)* means "messenger." This may refer to John or to the angel that spoke to John—or even to Jesus Himself, for "the Lord" Himself is called "the messenger of the covenant" in Malachi 3:1 (In Mal. 3:1 the first usage of the word "messenger" refers to John the Baptist; the second to Christ).

"I am the root and offspring of David."—Messianic prophecy, as given by Isaiah seven centuries before Christ, showed the coming Messiah to be a shoot (branch, root, offspring) that would grow up out of the cut down stump of the House of Jesse (David's father) and David. Messiah was thus to sit upon "the Throne of David...forever" (Isa. 9:7; 11:1). "Morning star."— Discussed with verse 20.

The beauty of New Jerusalem will surpass all earthly scenes.

Background

The Temple, the Sunlight, and the River in the NEW JERUSALEM

The Temple: And I saw no temple therein: for the Lord God Almighty and the Lamb are the temple of it. The tabernacle of God is with men.

(Revelation 21:22 and 21:3)

The Sunlight: The Glory of God and the Lamb

And the city had no need of the sun, neither of the moon, to shine in it: for the glory of God did lighten it, and the Lamb is the light thereof.

(Revelation 21:23)

The River: A pure river, clear as crystal

This is the river of paradise with its fountain-head being God and the Lamb.

While the streams of earth are polluted, this river of life is pure and clear as crystal.

(Revelation 22:1)

PAST	PRESENT	RAPTURE	FIRST 3½ LAST 3½ TRIBULATION	ARMA– GEDDON	MIL– LENNIUM	NEW HEAVENS & EARTH

Verse 16

Vss. 14-15

17 And the Spirit and the bride say,
Come. And let him that heareth say,
Come. And let him that is athirst come.
And whosoever will, let him take the wa-
ter of life freely.

Rev. 1:3
Isa. 55:1-3
Matt. 5:6; Rev. 3:20

Commentary

17. Our final anthem now swells into four invitations given to the sinner
beseeching and commanding him to come to Christ in order to receive
forgiveness and life. *First,* the Holy Spirit and the Bride (the Church)
give the invitation. The force of the Greek present imperative *erchou*
("Come") is: "Be thou continually coming." It is a coaxing command
saying, "Keep on coming...come until you arrive." It, of course, does
not mean "come repeatedly...again and again."

Secondly, the one hearing these words—John, an angel, or you and I—
is admonished to say, "Come." *Thirdly,* the one who is thirsty for righteousness is invited to come (Matt. 5:6). One need only be a lost sinner
who desires forgiveness and eternal life to meet these qualifications.

Finally, with the beautiful English words, "whosoever will," all are invited. Here the words "whosoever will" mean "whosoever is desiring"
(thelo—to will, wish, desire). We have all heard someone at one time
implore, "Come on take it; if you want it then it is yours for the taking."
This is God's gracious invitation to those who wish to have life. It can be
taken "freely" *(dorean*—as a gift, free, gratis) because Jesus by His
expiatory death at Calvary has paid the infinite price for the sins of all
who will come.

Have you already come to Him for this water by a prayer to Him con-
fessing that you are a sinner, acknowledging that He has died for you,
and asking Him to save your soul?

Background

The City: TRANSPARENT GOLD

This may be hard to imagine now as nothing on earth can presently duplicate a pure gold, clear and transparent like glass.

Yet God showed John in the Revelation a sight of this new city, New Jerusalem, which he could only describe as made of Gold so clear and transparent that it resembled glass *(Revelation 21:18).*

What a marvelous revelation of our new home! and what a marvelous promise:

...the gates of it shall not be shut at all by day: for there shall be no night there....
but nothing and no one
...shall ever enter it...but they which are written in the Lamb's book of life.

(Revelation 21:25,27 King James Version)

No unsaved person will be in Heaven...nothing that would defile this Heavenly Kingdom. How true that old things will have passed away and all things will then be new!

PAST	PRESENT	RAPTURE	FIRST 3 1/2 LAST 3 1/2 TRIBULATION	ARMA–GEDDON	MIL–LENNIUM	NEW HEAVENS & EARTH

18 For I testify unto every man that heareth the words of the prophecy of this book, If any man shall add unto these things, God shall add unto him the plagues that are written in this book:

19 And if any man shall take away from the words of the book of this prophecy, God shall take away his part out of the book of life, and out of the holy city, and *from* the things which are written in this book.

1 Kg. 12:11; Prov. 10:22; 1 Sam. 12:19

Deut. 18:1; Josh. 22: 25,27

Definition:

Unpardonable Sin.—*All sins can be forgiven through Christ—except for one, "the unpardonable sin" (See Matt. 12:22-32). This involves a person so going against the clear call and witness of the Holy Spirit so as to blaspheme the Spirit by attributing His witness and work to Satan and calling it evil. This seems to be a final unchangeable decision of the heart which forever shuts off the Spirit's witness—and thus leaves the person forever lost.*

Commentary

18-19. Certainly these words show that God is concerned that the Biblical message which He has revealed be preserved and transmitted accurately. In 21:5, as well as in other places, He assures us that His "words are true and faithful." In accord with this Christ (the speaker as shown from 22:16 and 1:1) warns all against tampering with the sacred message found in this Book of Revelation. Both adding to and subtracting from God's prophecy are here equally forbidden.

Ample are the admonitions against false prophets and those who alter the message of God (Jer. 23:9-40; Deut. 13:1-5; Matt. 7:15-20; 24:11,24). Here in Revelation 22:18-19 the Lord not only condemns he who would tamper with the contents of this book, but He adds specific promises of judgment. To the one who *adds,* God shall *add* to him the plagues mentioned in this book which are to be the portion of those who are lost. To the one who dares to *subtract* from this book, God shall *subtract* from him that everlasting life which will come to those who trust in the Lord. In other words, one must be irrevocably lost in sin to add unto or take away from those things written in this Apocalypse. It would seem from the language here used that the sin of doing this is a direct blasphemy of the Holy Ghost, the inspirer of Scripture, and as such it constitutes an "unpardonable sin" (Matt. 12:31-32).

Background

No Temptation: NO MORE CURSE

Satan is no longer present...and the curse has been removed as promised:

And there shall be no more curse: but the Throne of God and of the Lamb shall be in it....

(Revelation 22:3 King James Version)

No Night: GOD is the Light

There will be no need for candles, light bulbs or even sunlight for the Lord God will by His very presence illuminate this New Jerusalem *(Revelation 22:5).*

As Dr. J. Dwight Pentecost has so excellently pointed out in his fine book, THINGS TO COME, life in that eternal city of the New Jerusalem will include:

1. A life of fellowship with Him
2. A life of rest
3. A life of full knowledge
4. A life of holiness

5. A life of joy
6. A life of service
7. A life of abundance
8. A life of glory

9. A life of worship

PAST	PRESENT	RAPTURE	FIRST 3 1/2 LAST 3 1/2 TRIBULATION		ARMA– GEDDON	MIL– LENNIUM	NEW HEAVENS & EARTH

20 He which testifieth these things saith, Surely I come quickly. Amen. Even so, come, Lord Jesus.

John 21:24

21 The grace of our Lord Jesus Christ *be* with you all. Amen.

Commentary

20. Jesus, the One who "is testifying" to us in this book of the "things which must shortly come to pass," now certifies again to us that His Second Coming will soon occur.

When you were a child your mother kissed you good night and said, "Shhhh, close your eyes morning will come quickly." Night seemed to be so long to us as little ones, but mother in her wisdom and age knew that it would be over quickly. Soon the night would pass and "the bright and morning star" would arise as a precursor of the dawn. Jesus is that "bright and morning star."

And...just as Venus, when it is in its morning star phase, comes up over the horizon in *brilliant glory* with the sun's rise not far behind...so Jesus at His Second Coming in power and glory will be the morning star that precedes the wonderful Millennial and Eternal Ages (vs. 16; 2 Pet. 1:19).

"The night is far spent, the day is at hand..." (Rom. 13:12). The night has already endured almost 1900 years...from 96 A.D. to the present, since Christ renewed before the Apostle John at Patmos His pledge to return to earth. Surely there are streaks of light in the East...Christ's coming must be near at hand.

21. *"The grace...Amen."*—Paul characteristically closes his epistles with this prayerful benediction addressed to the recipients of his letters. John now follows this practice—perhaps directly as a result of his having read Paul's writings. It is a beautiful sentiment with which to end this book of prophecy. It acknowledges that the man Jesus is the Messiah, the Christ, and that He is the Lord over all. It prays that Christ's freely given salvation and His continued blessing—His grace—be with the reader. What better supplication could be made toward any man?

"Amen." This is taken directly from the Hebrew verb, *amn,* "It is faithful." It hence comes to mean agreement with all that has preceded in a prayer (1 Cor. 14:16). Because reverent scribes have at times added "Amen" at the end of a manuscript—without intending at all to add to the contents—it is often, as here, difficult to be certain whether John originally wrote it or not. If he did not write it, he must have at least orally breathed it after seeing so vast and so blessed a vision from the Saviour and of the Saviour. We can surely say with him, "Amen."

"(They) cast their crowns before the throne..." (Rev. 4:10).

Background

Christ promises that He will come quickly to call for His own, and He thus urges us in the scriptures to be strong in the Last Days, not to give in to false doctrine nor to those who would say, "Where is the promise of His Coming?" But rather, Christ tells His followers:

"...hold that fast which thou hast, that no man take thy crown,"
and Christ promises
"Him that overcometh will I make a pillar in the temple of my God..."
(Revelation 3:11,12 King James Version)

How overjoyed we will be in this New Jerusalem!

> Then we shall be
>   where we would be
> Then we shall be
>   what we should be
> Things that are not now
>   nor could be
> Soon shall be our own!

What joy will be ours, eternally, in the Day that Never Ends!

PAST	PRESENT	RAPTURE	FIRST 3 1/2 LAST 3 1/2 TRIBULATION	ARMA-GEDDON	MIL-LENNIUM	NEW HEAVENS & EARTH

Verse 21   Verse 20

WHAT ARE YOUR PLANS FOR ETERNITY?

Now that you have read GOD'S PROMISES TO THE ARAB, TO THE JEW you should be fully aware that these PROMISES can also be yours!

You should also be aware of the mounting turmoil that embroils our present world. From a human standpoint there is no answer to resolve these problems.

BUT THERE IS AN ANSWER! It is found in God's Word, the Bible. God has given you as an individual a CHOICE.

1. You may determine your own personal opinions about Heaven, or you may believe the opinions of others.

2. Or you may accept God's Word as it is written and accept the Lord Jesus Christ as your personal Saviour and Lord.

This is your choice. Only you can make this decision. And it *must* be made while you are *living*. Otherwise it will be too late. Your lack of decision to accept Christ as Saviour and Lord will leave you to an eternity in Hell...regardless of what your personal opinions may be.

THERE IS AN ANSWER! And that answer is GOD! Before you were born...Christ has told us in the Bible:

> ...Come, ye blessed of my Father (Believers), inherit the King-dom prepared for you from the foundation of the world. . . .
> *(Matthew 25:34 King James Version)*

You do not automatically go to Heaven. And your works, no matter how good they are, will not earn your way into Heaven. For you cannot earn your way into Heaven . . . regardless of how good your intentions are!

Eternal life in Heaven is a *gift* of God:

> ...God commendeth His love toward us, in that, while we were yet sinners, Christ died for us.

> ...as by one man (Adam) sin entered into the world, and death by sin; and so death passed upon all men, for that all have sinned. . . .

> For as in Adam all die, even so in Christ shall all be made alive. . . .

> For the wages of sin is death; but the gift of God is eternal life through Jesus Christ our Lord.
> *(Romans 5:8, 12; I Corinthians 15:22; Romans 6:23)*
> *King James Version*

That gift of eternal life is yours . . . by acceptance of Jesus Christ in your heart as your personal Saviour and Lord. The *wages* you have earned as a sinner is *death;* but the gift which God will give to you if you repent of your sins and turn to Him in faith is *eternal life.*

That is the decision you must make for eternal life. It is the only decision you have to make. Don't fear coming to God, for Jesus has promised, "Him that cometh unto me shall in no wise be cast out" (John 6:37).

If you do not make this decision, your lack of decision automatically leaves you condemned already because of your sins to eternal dam-nation in a real, tormenting Hell.

376

It takes NO DECISION on your part to go to Hell!

It does take a DECISION on your part, however, to go to Heaven!

> He that believeth on Him is not condemned: but he that believeth not is condemned already, because he hath not believed in the name of the only begotten Son of God. *(John 3:18)*.

One of Satan's greatest weapons is found in 5 letters: D E L A Y.

And he has used this word very successfully in telling millions—"Sure, you must accept Christ as personal Saviour and Lord to get to Heaven. But why spoil things now. Enjoy life first, live it up, there's plenty of time!"

> But now is the only time you own!
> Decide now what you will;
> Place not faith in "tomorrow" for
> The clock may then be still!

Let's look at it from a practical standpoint. What will be your inheritance if you choose Hell? And what will be your inheritance if you choose eternal life in Heaven?

CHOOSE YOUR FUTURE INHERITANCE

HELL	HEAVEN
Eternal Torment in the Lake of Fire for your sin	Eternal bliss in Heaven for your acceptance of Christ
No hope ever for escape	Heaven is yours forever
A place of constant conscious torment	A place of conscious joy forever
Anguishing torment by fire that is never quenched	No sickness, no sorrow, no death but eternal abundance of life that never ends
Eternal darkness that brings weeping and grinding of teeth	Eternal light for there is no night there...singing praises to God
Eternal separation from loved ones who are believers in Christ. No hope of communication between you and those living on earth to warn them of the reality of Hell	Eternal reunion with loved ones who are believers in Christ
The torment of a memory that will add to your constant suffering, realizing that a decision of repentance and faith on your part, while living on earth, could have changed your destination	Eternal happiness in a New Heaven and a New Earth with all the former things passed away and remembered no more
Eternal torment of unsatisfied lustful cravings	Complete fulfillment of all of God's Promises

Just as there is one word Satan uses that is 5 letters—DELAY . . . so Christ offers one word that is 5 letters—FAITH.

By delaying your decision you forget that the clock of your life may stop suddenly, and your obstinate clinging to your still unforgiven sin will rob you of your inheritance of Heaven.

And to many in this world, the word FAITH is their biggest stumbling block to acceptance of Christ and an eternity in Heaven.

While they exercise FAITH every day when they cross a bridge, or fly in an airplane, or turn the ignition on of their car . . . they find it impossible to exercise FAITH in the acceptance of Christ as their own personal Saviour and Lord.

And yet,

> . . . without FAITH, it is impossible to please Him: for he that cometh to God must believe that He is, and that He is a rewarder of them that diligently seek Him.
>
> FAITH is the substance of things hoped for, the EVIDENCE of things not seen.
>
> And we desire that every one of you . . . through FAITH . . . inherit the promises. . . .
>
> And for this cause He (Christ) is the mediator of the new testament, that by means of (His) death (on the Cross at Calvary for our sins), they (the believers) which are called might receive the promise of eternal inheritance (Heaven).
>
> *(Hebrews 11:6; 11:1; 6:11,12; 9:15 King James Version)*

Faith in God sees the invisible, believes that which has been historically validated, and receives that which has been promised. The action of FAITH in the most plain language I can convey to you is

F orsaking
A ll
I
T ake
H im

There are thousands of ways of pleasing God, but not one is possible without first having FAITH.

What about your faith today? Will it be placed in this world and its feeble attempts to make this a heaven on earth?

Or will you right now, in prayer to God, humbly place your faith in our Lord Jesus Christ, who at this very moment stands at your heart's door KNOCKING! By FAITH, will you let Him in and inherit something this world can never offer, an eternity with Christ in HEAVEN! Hear His words,

> Behold, I stand at the door, and knock: if any man hear my voice, and open the door, I will come in to him and will sup with him, and he with me.
>
> *(Revelation 3:20 King James Version)*

Hell in constant torment OR Heaven in joy eternally?

What will be your destination when it comes time on this earth for YOUR LAST GOODBYE!

WHAT WILL I DO WITH JESUS?

Will you accept Jesus Christ as your personal Saviour and Lord or will you reject Him?

This you must decide yourself. No one else can decide it for you. The basis of your decision should be made on God's Word—the Bible.

God tells us the following:

". . . him that cometh to me I will in no wise cast out. (37)

Verily, verily (truly) I say unto you, He that believeth on me (Christ) *hath* everlasting life" (47)—(John 6:37, 47).

He also is a righteous God and a God of indignation to those who reject Him. . . .

". . . he that believeth not is condemned already, because he hath not believed in the name of the only begotten Son of God"—

"And whosoever was not found written in the book of life was cast into the lake of fire"—(John 3:18; Revelation 20:15).

YOUR MOST IMPORTANT DECISION IN LIFE

Because sin entered the world in the days of our first parents and because God hates sin, God sent His Son Jesus Christ to die on the cross to pay the price for your sins and mine.

If you place your trust in Him, God will freely forgive you of your sins.

"For by grace are ye saved through faith; and that not of your-selves: it is the gift of God: (8)

Not of works, lest any man should boast" (9)—(Ephesians 2:8,9).

". . . He that heareth my word, and believeth on Him that sent me, *hath* everlasting life, and shall not come into condemnation: but is passed from death unto life"—(John 5:24).

What about you? Have you accepted Christ as your personal Saviour?

Do you realize that right now you can know the reality of this new life in Christ Jesus? Right now you can dispel the doubt that is in your mind concerning your future. Right now you can ask Christ to come into your heart. And right now you can be assured of eternal life in heaven.

All of your riches here on earth—all of your financial security—all of your material wealth, your houses, your land will crumble into nothing-ness in a few years.

And as God has told us:

"As it is appointed unto men once to die, but after this the judg-ment: (27)

So Christ was once offered to bear the sins of many; and unto them that look for Him shall He appear the second time without sin unto salvation" (28)—(Hebrews 9:27,28).

Are you willing to sacrifice an eternity with Christ in Heaven for a few years of questionable material gain that will lead to death and destruction? If you do not accept Christ as your personal Saviour, you have only yourself to blame for the consequences.

Or would you right now, as you are reading these very words of this book, like to know without a shadow of a doubt that you are on the road to Heaven—that death is not the end of life but actually the climactic beginning of the most wonderful existence that will ever be—a life with the Lord Jesus Christ and with your friends, your relatives, and your loved ones who have accepted Christ as their Saviour.

It's not a difficult thing to do. So many religions and so many people have tried to make the simple Gospel message of Christ complex. You can not work your way into heaven—*heaven is the gift of God to those who believe in Jesus Christ.*

No matter how great your works—no matter how kind you are—no matter how philanthropic you are—it means nothing in the sight of God, because in the sight of God, your riches are as filthy rags.

". . . all our righteousnesses are as filthy rags. . ."—(Isaiah 64:6).

Christ expects you to come as you are, a sinner, recognizing your need of a Saviour, the Lord Jesus Christ.

Understanding this, why not bow your head right now and give this simple prayer of faith to the Lord.

Say it in your own words. It does not have to be a beautiful oratorical prayer—simply a prayer of humble contrition.

My Personal Decision for CHRIST

"Lord Jesus, I know that I'm a sinner and that I cannot save myself by good works. I believe that you died for me and that you shed your blood for my sins. I believe that you rose again from the dead. And now I am receiving you as my personal Saviour, my Lord, my only hope of salvation. I know that I'm a sinner and deserve to go to Hell. I know that I cannot save myself. Lord, be merciful to me, a sinner, and save me according to the promise of Your Word. I want Christ to come into my heart now to be my Saviour, Lord and Master."

Signed ....

Date ....